Child Custody in Islamic Law

Premodern Muslim jurists drew a clear distinction between the nurturing and upkeep of children, or "custody," and caring for the child's education, discipline, and property, known as "guardianship." Here, Ahmed Fekry Ibrahim analyzes how these two concepts relate to the welfare of the child, and traces the development of an Islamic child welfare jurisprudence akin to the Euro-American concept of the *best interests of the child* enshrined in the Convention on the Rights of the Child (CRC). Challenging Euro-American exceptionalism, he argues that child welfare played an essential role in agreements designed by early modern Egyptian judges and families, and that Egyptian child custody laws underwent radical transformations in the modern period. Focusing on a variety of themes, including matters of age and gender, the mother's marital status, and the custodian's lifestyle and religious affiliation, Ibrahim shows that there is an exaggerated gap between the modern concept of the *best interests of the child* and premodern Egyptian approaches to child welfare.

Ahmed Fekry Ibrahim is Assistant Professor of Islamic Law at McGill University. He has been writing about the theory and practice of Islamic law in the premodern and modern periods by examining both juristic discourse and court records. His research has been supported by numerous bodies, including the Berlin-Brandenburg Academy of Sciences and Humanities, the Social Sciences and Humanities Research Council of Canada, the Max Planck Institute for Comparative and International Private Law, the American Research Center in Egypt, and the School of Foreign Service at Georgetown University in Qatar.

Cambridge Studies in Islamic Civilization

Other titles in the series are listed at the back of the book.

Child Custody in Islamic Law

Theory and Practice in Egypt since the Sixteenth Century

AHMED FEKRY IBRAHIM
McGill University

CAMBRIDGE
UNIVERSITY PRESS

CAMBRIDGE
UNIVERSITY PRESS

University Printing House, Cambridge CB2 8BS, United Kingdom

One Liberty Plaza, 20th Floor, New York, NY 10006, USA

477 Williamstown Road, Port Melbourne, VIC 3207, Australia

314–321, 3rd Floor, Plot 3, Splendor Forum, Jasola District Centre, New Delhi – 110025, India

79 Anson Road, #06–04/06, Singapore 079906

Cambridge University Press is part of the University of Cambridge.

It furthers the University's mission by disseminating knowledge in the pursuit of education, learning, and research at the highest international levels of excellence.

www.cambridge.org
Information on this title: www.cambridge.org/9781108470568
DOI: 10.1017/9781108648042

First published 2018

Printed and bound in Great Britain by Clays Ltd, Elcograf S.p.A.

A catalogue record for this publication is available from the British Library.

Library of Congress Cataloging-in-Publication Data
Names: Ibrahim, Ahmed Fekry, author.
Title: Child custody in Islamic law : theory and practice in Egypt since the sixteenth century / Ahmed Fekry Ibrahim.
Description: New York : Cambridge University Press, 2018. | Series: Cambridge studies in Islamic civilization | Includes bibliographical references and index.
Identifiers: LCCN 2018006189 | ISBN 9781108470568 (alk. paper)
Subjects: LCSH: Custody of children (Islamic law) | Parent and child (Islamic law) | Custody of Children – Egypt – History. | Custody of Children.
Classification: LCC KBP602.5 .I27 2018 | DDC 346.6201/73–dc23
LC record available at https://lccn.loc.gov/2018006189

ISBN 978-1-108-47056-8 Hardback

To my mother, Nabawiyya Naji
To my children, Alya and Zayn
To their mother, my friend, Sara Nimis

Contents

Acknowledgments

The work on this book took place over several years, during which I sought help from friends, colleagues, and family members. I thank my PhD students Ahmad Munir and Omar Edaibat for their efficient and thorough research help in 2014–2018. I also thank my undergraduate research assistants Ommu-Kulsoom Abdul-Rahman and Meghan van Aardt for helping with the revision stage of the manuscript in 2017–2018. I owe a great debt to my PhD supervisor, Felicitas Opwis, for her continuous support and help, and to my professors Ahmad Dallal, Judith Tucker, and John Voll for all they have taught me.

I am grateful to both the Social Sciences and Humanities Research Council of Canada (SSHRC) and the Fonds de recherche du Québec – Société et Culture (FRQSC) for providing me with generous grants (2014–17) to conduct research in Egypt, Germany, England, Morocco, and Turkey. Without the resources at the Max Planck Institute for Comparative and International Private Law, this work would have lacked important insights. I am grateful to Nadjma Yassari and Lena-Maria Möller from the Max Planck Institute for exposing me to important aspects of child rights that informed my analysis. Over the past four years, I have presented different chapters of this book in workshops and lectures organized by Nadjma Yassari and Lena-Maria Möller as part of the successful and important project led by Nadjma, "Changes in God's Law – An Inner Islamic Comparison of Family and Succession Laws." These workshops and lectures, held in cities as far away as Hamburg and Rabat, were organized by Tess Chemnitzer, who helped make them very productive and efficient.

I also owe a great debt to Gudrun Krämer and Birgit Krawietz from the Institute of Islamic Studies at the Free University of Berlin for providing me with the resources available at the Berlin Graduate School of Muslim Cultures and Societies to conduct my research in the summer of 2014 and 2016. I am grateful to Georges Khalil from the Forum of Transregional Studies and Islam Dayeh from Free University of Berlin for all the great seminars that they organized in 2014–2018, from which I benefited richly in thinking about different aspects of this monograph. I thank David Powers for taking an interest in this project and for helping me with my current project on child adoption.

I am blessed to have wonderful interlocutors in the field of Islamic law such as Ayesha Chaudhry, Anver Emon, Sarah Eltantawi, and Rumee Ahmed. As scholars engaged in the concerns of Islamic law, and more importantly in those of contemporary Muslim women, men, and children, I always left our conversations with new questions and more to think about. I am grateful to my friends Henri Lauzière, Prashant Keshavmurthy, Sarah Albrecht, and Michael Allan for enduring long conversations about child custody in Islamic law.

In the theoretical framing of legal practice, I benefited from exchanges with Talal Asad. At McGill University, I had productive conversations with Helge Dedek from the law faculty and Arash Abizadeh, who pointed me to some important philosophical works related to the early concerns of this monograph. I am grateful to Brinckly Messick and Wael Hallaq for inviting me to present my research at the Sharia Workshop at Columbia University in 2017 and to those in attendance for their useful comments, including Marion Katz, Najam Haider, Omar Farahat, and Aseel Nabeel Najib. I am also grateful to Katharina Ivanyi and Manan Ahmed for inviting me to present part of this monograph at the Institute of Religion, Culture, and Public Life at Columbia University in 2017, and to Felicitas Opwis and Emma Gannagé from Georgetown University for inviting me to speak at the Islamic Studies Lecture Series. I am indebted to Mirjam Künkler for taking interest in this project and for inviting me to present part of this monograph in Hanover in 2017.

I owe a great debt to my copy editor, Emily Pollokoff, who did a great job with the final edits of the book manuscript. I thank the staff at Egypt's National Archives (Dār al-Wathā'iq al-Qawmiyya), Egypt's National Library (Dār al-Kutub), the British Library, the Library of the Free University of Berlin, the Berlin State Library, the Institute of Islamic Studies Library at McGill University, and the library of the Max Planck Institute for Comparative and International Private Law in Hamburg.

Introduction

> In all actions concerning children, whether undertaken by public or private social welfare institutions, courts of law, administrative authorities or legislative bodies, the best interests of the child shall be a primary consideration.
>
> Convention on the Rights of the Child, art. 3, para. 1

The title of this book, *Child Custody in Islamic Law*, generally refers to Islamic law in the Sunni tradition. I focus on Sunni Islamic juristic discourse, especially in early modern Egypt, as well as Ottoman-Egyptian court practice to write a history of the concept of the best interests of the child in early modern Egypt based on a reading of both juristic discourses and court practices. These earlier discourses and practices are juxtaposed with those dominating contemporary Egyptian law as a result of modernity. The contemporary discourses of the child's best interests represent a hybrid of both Islamic and Euro-American modes of lawmaking. This book examines overall themes relating to child custody and guardianship, and concentrates on pivotal points of continuity and change, as well as tensions and incompatibility between premodern Islamic law and the child-centered modern international standard of the best interests of the child as the main principle that drives decisions concerning children in many jurisdictions across the world. One of the main questions this book addresses is whether there was a concept similar to the Euro-American concept of the best interests of the child (henceforth the best interests standard) in early modern Egyptian juristic discourse and practice. This comparative aspect, where scholars try to see how certain historically prevalent religious concepts overlapped or varied from modern legal discourses, has already been done, for instance, in the Jewish tradition but not with regard to Sunni Islam, rendering this investigation groundbreaking in this regard.[1]

In the Euro-American legal historiographical imaginary, there is an inherent teleological vision of progress, the result of the hard labor of Euro-American lawyers, legislators, and feminist organizations, whose combined efforts produced the best-interests-of-the-child standard. The main achievements of this standard were (1) making the determination of custody *child-centered*; (2) bringing into focus the individual needs of each child; and (3) utilizing social science research in determining what is best for each child on a case-by-case basis. The best interests standard, where each child's best interests are determined by the judge, cannot escape being culturally contingent, especially since legislators in many Western jurisdictions offer little guidance to judges on what exactly constitutes the child's best interests, allowing social perceptions to shape such a standard more dynamically.[2] Historical research dealing with countries such as England, France, and the United States, to mention a few, has shown that the maturation of the modern concept of the best interests of the child in Euro-America was the result of a long and nonlinear process of evolution wherein two main approaches persisted. In early modern England, for instance, one approach defined the child's welfare in the negative, wherein judges were only allowed to interfere with the father's absolute common law right to custody when the child's physical or moral health was seriously threatened. Absent gross abuse, judges generally awarded full custody and guardianship rights to fathers.

In the Sunni Islamic legal tradition, the situation was similar among many jurists whose presumptive rules – themselves justified through

[1] More recently, similar comparative work has been done between Jewish and American tort law theories. Yuval Sinai and Benjamin Shmueli, "Calabresi's and Maimonides's Tort Law Theories-A Comparative Analysis and a Preliminary Sketch of a Modern Model of Differential Pluralistic Tort Liability Based on the Two Theories," *Yale Journal of Law & the Humanities* 26: 1 (2015).

[2] On the concept of the best interests of the child and its inherent indeterminacy, see Abdullahi An-Na'im, "Cultural Transformation and Normative Consensus on the Best Interests of the Child," *International Journal of Law, Policy and the Family* 8:1 (1994): 62–81; Philip Alston, *UNICEF, and International Child Development Centre, The Best Interests of the Child: Reconciling Culture and Human Rights* (Oxford; New York: Clarendon Press; Oxford University Press, 1994); Philip Alston, "The Best Interests Principle: Towards a Reconciliation of Culture and Human Rights," *International Journal of Law, Policy and the Family* 8:1 (1994): 1–25; Stephen Parker, "The Best Interests of the Child – Principles and Problems," *International Journal of Law, Policy and the Family* 8:1 (1994): 26–41; John Eekelaar, "The Interests of the Child and the Child's Wishes: The Role of Dynamic Self-Determinism," *International Journal of Law, Policy and the Family* 8:1 (1994): 42–61.

welfare of children discourse as well as paternal rights – were based on a host of calculations such as the child's age and gender, the mother's marital status, and the parents' religious affiliation and lifestyle choices. These presumptive rules were only abandoned when the child was in danger of being subjected to gross abuse or serious harm. We shall call this narrow, negatively defined approach the *basic interests approach* or simply the *child welfare approach*. Both of these terms refer to a general concern for the well-being of children, but they fall short of the technical meaning of the best interests of the child as it is often understood in international law. The *best interests approach* defines the child's welfare positively, in terms of who provides the best care for a given child, without relying on presumptive rules for all children based on the gender and age of the child, and the marital status or religious affiliation of the parent. Without drawing a distinction between these terms, one may fall into the trap of always equating conceptualizations of premodern Islamic juristic discussions of the welfare of the child with modern Euro-American and Muslim nation-state legislation about the best interests of the child. One must caution here that this bifurcation of rules between a concern for the basic interests of the child when there is a conflict with the rights of custodians and a wider, positive focus on the best interests of the child was not the only factor determining rules of custody. The final rules often obtained nuance from a matrix of social practices, hermeneutic commitments,[3] and methodological approaches that go beyond this distinction.

Let us now turn to child custody in Islamic juristic discourse in the premodern period, that is, prior to the early nineteenth century for Middle Eastern jurisdictions. Premodern Muslim jurists drew a clear distinction between the nurturing and upkeep of a child, or "custody" (*ḥaḍāna*), and caring for the child's education, discipline, general acculturation, and managing her or his property, known as "guardianship" (*wilāya*). These two terms are similar to "physical custody" and "legal custody" in some US jurisdictions, where physical custody refers to where and with whom the child resides, and legal custody refers to the person or persons who make decisions about the child's education, healthcare, and religious instruction. In this book, I examine both *ḥaḍāna* and *wilāya* as they relate

3 Based on Iser's premise that the text imposes some logical constraints, a semi-objective view of hermeneutics and reception, one would argue that the textual sources on child custody, which were limited to a few reports, must have placed limited constraints on jurists. On hermeneutics, see further Terry Eagleton, *Literary Theory: An Introduction* (Minneapolis: University of Minnesota Press, 1983).

to the welfare of the child, both in premodern Islamic juristic discourse and Ottoman-Egyptian court practice.

In premodern Islamic legal discourse, jurists used many words to refer to the well-being of the child, but they did not use them consistently as technical terms in all discussions of custody. These terms include "the benefit of the child" (*manfa'at al-walad*), "the welfare of the child" (*maṣlaḥat al-walad*), and "the good fortune of the child" (*ḥaẓẓ al-walad*).[4] These terms were not necessarily used by jurists to denote an overriding principle to be applied by judges in the narrow sense of the best interests of a given child in a particular historical context in the same way that technical legal terms such as "best interests of the child" (*maṣlaḥat al-ṭifl*" or *maṣlaḥat al-maḥḍūn*) are sometimes used in modern state legislation.

In order to locate the logic of child custody lawmaking in premodern Islamic law, I will focus on three main avenues, namely (1) finding explicit discussions of whether custody is a right of the custodian or the child; (2) exploring the rationalizations advanced by jurists to justify different rules; and (3) examining court decisions to theorize child welfare considerations. It is therefore necessary to link the macrodiscussion of whether child custody is a right of the custodian or the ward to discussions of the justifications of different microrules of positive law. Through juristic justifications, we can gauge how much impact considerations of the welfare of the child had on lawmaking.

Jurists assumed that child custody law was designed to promote the welfare of children. According to jurists, wards, custodians, and guardians have interlocking rights and the latter two have duties. When a conflict of rights arises, the child's most *basic interests* (as opposed to her or his *best interests*, such as simply who can provide the best care) are prioritized by all jurists to avoid risking the child's physical health or moral uprightness. Jurists assigned the physical and moral well-being of the child the highest value in times of conflict between the child's right to be cared for and the custodial parent's right to assume custody. This is the minimum threshold of the child's interests supported by all Sunni jurists, regardless of where they stand on the issue of whether custody is a right of the ward or of the custodian.

To give an example, some jurists argued that certain forms of bad morality do not justify taking a child away from his or her mother (more

[4] Muwaffaq al-Dīn Ibn Qudāma al-Maqdisī, *Al-Mughnī*, ed. Rā'id b. Ṣabrī b. Abī 'Alafa (Beirut: Bayt al-Afkār al-Dawliyya, 2004), 2:2007–2008; Ibn Qayyim al-Jawziyya, *Zād Al-Ma'ād Fī Hudā Khayr Al-'Ibād*, ed. Shu'ayb al-Arna'ūṭ and 'Abd al-Qādir al-Arna'ūṭ, 3rd edn. (Beirut: Mu'assasat al-Risāla, 1998), 5:392.

on this in Chapter 2), as long as there was no danger to the child's life or religion. In other words, most jurists would not take away custody from a custodial mother upon the request of the father even if he could provide the best care for a given child. These rules may be seen as violating the best interests of the child in favor of the rights of the custodial parent. Conversely, allowing the child to choose the parent with whom he or she wishes to reside upon reaching the age of discernment (*tamyīz*),[5] as is the case in the Shāfiʿī and Ḥanbalī schools, represents a juristic best interests approach, which transcends the basic needs of children. In this case, the child's decision is presumably driven by a sense of comfort with and attachment to one parent more than the other. One could argue that the child's needs are prioritized over those of the father in this case, for the father may never have any right to custody should the child choose to continue living with his mother until puberty, according to Shāfiʿī law. As we shall see, some of the rules of jurists were based on a basic interests approach (defined negatively as the absence of gross abuse), while others based their rules on a best interests approach (defined positively as the *accrual of benefits*, not only the *avoidance of harm*, such as soliciting the child's preferences), which resembles the modern Euro-American concept of the best interests of the child. Despite the presumed *origins* of these rules as being based on a negative or positive definition of child welfare, once they were established as the law of the different Sunni schools after the dominance of legal conformism (*taqlīd*), they were assumed by most jurists to be universal in their application. They were deemed to represent the *welfare* of all children at all times, rather than looking at the best interests of a particular child at a particular moment. Thus, even though many of the justifications may have originated from a best interests ethos, once they were frozen in the age of *taqlīd* as the school doctrines, they ceased to be compatible with the best interests of the child as they are understood in international law.

Whether child custody is a right of the child or the custodian can be misleading because although jurists who consider custody to be a right of the child are more likely to maximize considerations of the best interests of the child over the rights of the custodian, there is not always a consistent correlation between the jurist's position on who has the right of custody and the positive rules of the various questions of age of custody transfer,

[5] This is also the age at which to start systematic education. On the age of discernment, see further Avner Giladi, *Children of Islam: Concepts of Childhood in Medieval Muslim Society* (New York: St. Martin's Press, 1992), 52–54.

visitations, travel, guardianship, and so on (more on this in Chapter 2). Although conceptualizations of the threshold at which jurists were willing to privilege the child's interests over those of the custodian must have played a role in Islamic positive laws on custody, there are many interlocking factors that were equally, if not more, important. These include the practices of early Muslim communities and/or hermeneutic restrictions such as the existence of famous prophetic traditions denying women custody upon remarriage, and the collective interpretation within the school unit. What complicates this question further is that it is often hard to gauge where a particular jurist stands on the question of who has the right of custody. It is sometimes equally hard to gauge what the predominant school position is and how strong the minority position is. The Mālikī school is a case in point. We see many references to Mālik and some very important Mālikī authorities considering child custody to be a right of the child, all while asserting that the Mālikī dominant position is the exact opposite. It is unlikely that the Mālikī dominant position that custody is a right of the custodian had always been such, given the views of Mālik himself.

This book aims to investigate the logic of both Islamic juristic discourse and Ottoman court practice in the early modern period and the ways in which these discourses and practices offer non-Euro-American "strange parallels" and idiosyncrasies.[6] My contention is that early modern (and medieval) Islamic juristic discourse contains both a narrow and a broad notion of child welfare. Both the narrow and broad notions were cited by jurists in justifications of their various child custody and guardianship rules. With the dominance of legal conformism (*taqlīd*), most jurists treated custody and guardianship norms as presumptive rules that were assumed to dominate adjudication with little discretion left for judges, except in cases of serious harm to the child. In actual court practice in Ottoman Egypt, the situation was different. Judges allowed families to agree on any child custody arrangements that they deemed fit, even when the arrangements violated the discourse of jurists not only in the official Ḥanafī school but also according to the majority of Sunni jurists. Between 1517 and the middle of the seventeenth century, parents were able to enter into private separation deeds, according to which women were able to travel with their children and remarry without losing custody. Some women were even able to have veto power over the father's exclusive guardianship rights (both of person and property). They were also able

[6] Lieberman, *Strange Parallels*, 2:xxi–117.

to preempt the father's prerogative to take the children with him if he relocated to another town. These private separation deeds, which were notarized by Ottoman-Egyptian judges, were binding. There is hardly an Egyptian court register of the sixteenth or first half of the seventeenth century where such agreements did not appear in such a formulaic manner as to suggest that they were happening on a large scale. These agreements were taking place in Mamluk Egypt and continued during the Ottoman period until the second half of the seventeenth century, with the last case I found coming from 1670. After this date, no such agreements appear in a large sample numbering over 17,200 divorce cases, approximately 600 cases of which deal with custody and guardianship issues.

These private separation deeds were binding against the almost unanimous Ḥanafī position, which completely rejected many such agreements as contrary to the welfare of the child based on their presumptive rules of what benefits all children of all times. The Ḥanafīs assumed, for instance, that all boys must not live with their mothers beyond the age of ten, lest they internalize feminine dispositions. Allowing families to agree on any custody arrangement contradicting the rules of author-jurists, as long as the welfare of a given child was not harmed, represented a unique vision of the child's welfare; the Mālikīs, for example, did not justify or perhaps even imagine the types of agreements that were notarized in Ottoman Egypt.[7]

Some of these agreements appear in *shurūṭ* works, where sample separation deeds are presented, such as al-Asyūṭī's (d. 880/1475) *Jawāhir al-ʿUqūd wa-Muʿīn al-Quḍāh wa'l-Muwaqqiʿīn wa'l-Shuhūd* (*The Pearls of Contracts: Manual for Judges, Scribes, and Witnesses*).[8] These contract formula manuals presented contracts in the four Sunni schools, each formula satisfying the specific school's applicable rules, and were followed in Ottoman Egypt, with some of the formulas appearing almost verbatim. By the second half of the seventeenth century, the Ḥanafī position dominated and private separation deeds were no longer binding, while the more problematic agreements completely disappeared from the court registers.

With the Ḥanafization policy of the nineteenth century, the system of child custody became more rigid. This rigidity coexisted with the revival of

[7] Abū al-ʿAbbās Aḥmad b. Yaḥyā al-Wansharīsī, *Al-Manhaj Al-Fāʾiq Wa'l-Manhal Al-Rāʾiq Wa'l-Maʿnā Al-Lāʾiq Bi-Ādāb Al-Muwaththiq Wa-Aḥkām Al-Wathāʾiq*, ed. ʿAbd al-Raḥmān b. Ḥammūd b. ʿAbd al-Raḥmān al-Aṭram (Dubai: Dār al-Buḥūth li'l-Dirāsāt al-Islāmiyya, 2005), 2:565–566.

[8] Shams al-Dīn Muḥammad b. Aḥmad al-Minhājī al-Asyūṭī, *Jawāhir Al-ʿUqūd Wa-Muʿīn Al-Quḍāh Wa'l-Muwaqqiʿīn Wa'l-Shuhūd*, ed. Musʿad ʿAbd al-Ḥamīd Muḥammad Saʿdanī (Beirut: Dār al-Kutub al-ʿIlmiyya, 1996), 2:89–99.

the strand of thought on child custody that defined the welfare of the child more broadly. This approach began to dominate legal thinking on child custody toward the end of the nineteenth century, with the rise of a new hybrid family ideology where mothers were assumed to be the nourishers of children. In 1929, influenced by the domestic ideology and the new emphasis on the nuclear family, Egypt started a process of legislation in a bid to minimize the rigidity of Ḥanafī law. Judges were given greater discretion in child custody arrangements, and the child's age requiring female custody was raised successively over the course of the twentieth and early twenty-first centuries, mirroring Euro-American nineteenth- and early twentieth-century values, as well as international child-welfare conventions.

In my discussions of child custody and guardianship, whether in juristic discourses or court practices, I focus on eight main themes that should give us a good, albeit not an exhaustive idea, of the ways in which custody and guardianship interacted with child welfare. These themes are (1) age and gender; (2) the mother's marital status; (3) the custodian's lifestyle; (4) the custodian's religious affiliation; (5) visitation rights; (6) relocation with the ward; (7) maintenance; and (8) guardianship. Due to the comparative nature of this project, both implicitly and explicitly, it is fitting to start this book with a brief historical overview of the evolution of child custody jurisprudence in a few Western jurisdictions (Chapter 1). Chapter 2 establishes the centrality of the child's welfare in premodern juristic discourse. I then pose the question of whether Ottoman-Egyptian judges were permitted to exercise a level of discretion in their rulings whereby they could assess the child's best interests (Chapters 3 and 4). Chapter 5 covers Egyptian child custody law during the period of 1801–1929, while Chapter 6 discusses the age of codification of Islamic child custody law from 1929 to 2014, which often responded to changes in Euro-American and international law. But before we embark on our journey, it is fitting to investigate a few important threads, the first of which are the political implications of this study, especially in the context of Islamophobia, and questions of cultural imperialism or specificity and exceptionalism.

CULTURAL IMPERIALISM AND THE HEGEMONY OF HUMAN RIGHTS DISCOURSES

The notion of the best interests of the child, the basis of international conventions regulating the welfare of children, which have become an essential standard in many modern Muslim-majority countries, cannot escape being comparative since it has been presented as a Euro-American product exported into other countries through international treaties backed by Western hegemons. One of the objectives of the comparative aspect of this monograph is to free Islamic law from its "historiographic ghetto," to use Victor Lieberman's words in reference to Southeast Asia, as well as challenge European exceptionalism by arguing for comparability and overlaps, rather than reinforce dichotomies between legal cultures that "evolved" organically to accommodate child rights, and others that were mere recipients of legal innovation.[9]

The comparative approach shows that despite the absence of clear cultural or material links between early modern England and the United States on the one hand and early modern Egypt on the other, one finds similar processes of accommodation of child welfare in the courts. This comparative approach can be deeply problematic, as it considers Western conceptualizations of the best interests of the child as the yardstick by which to judge how countries respect children's rights. This is arguably another hegemonic discourse in which Western nations, through their influence on international law standards, set the parameters of the discussion, overlooking cultural specificities and communal approaches to children's welfare that go beyond the interests of each particular child. In a word, it privileges the individual over the collective, and therefore some have rejected it as a Western tool of cultural imperialism. For example, Jād al-Ḥaqq, Egypt's late rector of al-Azhar, had some reservations about certain stipulations of the Convention on the Civil Aspects of International Child Abductions (CCACA), as an attempt to maintain a sense of cultural purity.[10] Others, as we shall see in Chapter 6, have embraced this discourse as part of the modern promise of progress.

While acknowledging that the welfare of the child is the underlying logic behind the entire system of Islamic child custody law, opponents of the best interests standard often assume that this welfare had already been determined by jurists in immutable general rules linked to such factors as gender, age, and lifestyle choices. These cultural purists – not only with respect to child custody but also regarding human rights discourses more broadly – often exaggerate cultural difference. Ironically, they have found allies in scholars forging a postmodernist critique of liberalism,

[9] Victor B. Lieberman, *Strange Parallels: Southeast Asia in Global Context, c 800–1830: Volume 2 Mainland Mirrors: Europe, Japan, China, South Asia, and the Islands* (New York: Cambridge University Press, 2013), 2:xxi, 2.

[10] Dār al-Iftā' al-Miṣriyya, *Al-Fatāwā Al-Islāmiyya Min Dār Al-Iftā' Al-Miṣriyya* (Cairo: Maṭba'at Dār al-Kutub wa'l-Wathā'iq al-Qawmiyya, 2012), 13:221–230.

secularization, and enlightenment discourses, which they cogently argue were often manipulated and instrumentalized in the service of empire and Euro-American neo-imperialism. The association between these discourses and postcolonial authoritarian regimes on the one hand, and between them and Euro-American neocolonialism on the other, especially in the context of post-9/11 warmongering, places the proponents of these discourses in a precarious situation. Nothing is more telling about the tension inherent in engaging in discussions of human rights in an accommodationist mode than the debate that erupted over the Palestinian hip-hop group DAM's song about honor killing when Lila Abu Lughd and Maya Mikdashi charged that the group succumbed to an international machine that blames only tradition for people's problems.[11] In other words, the projects of scholars critical of the way in which minority rights, women's rights, or queer rights were manipulated as tools of neo-imperialism often coalesce with purist approaches to tradition within Islamic law. The second approach, which we may call "modernist," buys into the discourse of modernity and some forms of liberalism and seeks to find sites of compatibility between Islamic law and international conventions. It is in this spirit that I frame this discussion, while being sensitive to the theoretical and political implications of this project, but also of the support it receives in Muslim jurisdictions, as evidenced by the internal critical readings of tradition aimed at accommodating human rights discourses.

Both approaches and their concomitant critiques warrant further interventions, but this is not the objective of this study. My objective is not prescriptive in that it does not claim that the best interests standard *should* be followed by Muslim societies on philosophical grounds or that Muslim nations *should* resist the discursive and international law tyranny of Euro-America, which aims to make the legal systems of these Muslim nations in its own image. It is rather a descriptive study that seeks to understand *how* premodern juristic discourses and practices compare to the best interests standard. Certainly, choosing to study this topic may be itself seen as

[11] On the debate over the hip-hop group's dealing with honor crimes, see Rochelle Terman, "Islamophobia, Feminism and the Politics of Critique," *Theory, Culture & Society Theory, Culture & Society*, 2015. On the charge that secular Arabs became proxies of a secular project, see Saba Mahmood, *Religious Difference in a Secular Age: A Minority Report* (Princeton, NJ: Princeton University Press, 2015), 79. On the Euro-American exportation of gay identity in the Arab world, see Joseph A. Massad, *Desiring Arabs* (Chicago, IL: University of Chicago Press, 2008), 160–190; Rosalind C. Morris and Gayatri Chakravorty Spivak, *Can the Subaltern Speak?: Reflections on the History of an Idea* (New York: Columbia University Press, 2010).

cheerleading Euro-American hegemony. To this potential critique, I would counter that since many Muslim nation-states, women's groups, NGOs, and religious scholars consider the best interests standard a model to be emulated and accommodated, the topic is therefore worthy of study as an indigenized discourse. Further, considering the interests of the children as the ultimate goal of child custody law should not be a prerogative left to one hegemonic discourse to claim. As I show in this study, Islamic juristic discourses and practices challenge the assumption about the uniqueness of the Euro-American experience in this respect. Indeed, there are "strange parallels" in Islamic juristic discourses and practices and sites of convergence with and divergence from the best interests evolution of child custody in some Euro-American jurisdictions.[12]

Despite the largely descriptive mode that I adopt in this book, I argue, however, that if we view Islamic law as a *discursive tradition* that contains both praxial and doctrinal elements,[13] the best interests of the child becomes part of the legacy of Islamic law and can therefore be mobilized as such by those who search for an overlapping consensus with liberal discourses of child rights. The mobilization of the best interests standard as an essential part of the legacy of Islamic law can be achieved if we treat the judicial and scribal practices of Ottoman judges and scribes to be part of the normative structure of premodern Islamic law.[14] As we shall see in our discussion of private separation deeds (Chapter 3), which were in tension or contradiction with the discourses of author-jurists, judicial authorities devised a very formulaic language that was used with little change over centuries in early modern Egyptian courts. The consistent use of these formularies over centuries represents an act of valorization of these socio-legal practices of child custody, making them part and parcel of the legacy of Islamic law both as a legal tradition and a normative system. To both premodern jurists and modern reformers, this view of Islamic legal practice is counterintuitive due to the dominance of *taqlīd* as a legal hegemony in the eleventh through thirteenth centuries and the ensuing shift of authority from judges to author-jurists.[15] In other words, for judicial

12 Lieberman, *Strange Parallels*, 2:xxi–117.

13 Ahmed Fekry Ibrahim, "Islamic Law as a Discursive Tradition," in *Sustainable Diversity in Law: Essays in Memory of H. Patrick Glenn*, ed. Helge Dedek (Oxford: Oxford University Press, forthcoming); Talal Asad, *The Idea of an Anthropology of Islam* (Washington, DC: Center for Contemporary Arab Studies, Georgetown University, 1986).

14 Shahab Ahmed, *What Is Islam?: The Importance of Being Islamic* (Princeton, NJ: Princeton University Press, 2015), 1–175.

15 Ahmed Fekry Ibrahim, "Rethinking the *Taqlīd* Hegemony: An Institutional, *Longue-Durée* Approach," *Journal of the American Oriental Society* 136:4 (2016): 801–816.

practices to have the force of law, they must be valorized by author-jurists rather than judicial authorities. With some aspects of the law, certain practices in contradiction with the law were valorized by author-jurists through subsidiary sources such as "judicial practice" (*ʿamal*) or "custom" (*ʿurf*). Other practices, however, were never normalized by author-jurists. One might think of modern reform as continuing this naturalization of judicial practices in the case of child custody law.[16]

These practices were driven by pragmatic considerations that went beyond the limited options available to judges and scribes in the ideal juristic discourses of Sunni author-jurists. The pragmatic nature of some of the judicial decisions on child custody warrant a broader discussion of pragmatic adjudication and pragmatism from a comparative perspective.

PRAGMATISM

Pragmatism comes in many varieties, and the differences among pragmatists are rife, which makes the task of outlining its main tenets exceedingly complex.[17] In what follows, I discuss some of the central tenets of pragmatism, both in its philosophical and legal varieties. *Philosophical pragmatism* is a movement that originated in the United States during the second half of the nineteenth-century. It represents a critique of foundationalism and a shift to the practical consequences of propositions. In the *Fixation of Belief*, Charles Sanders Peirce, credited by many as the father of pragmatism, rejected Cartesian epistemological foundationalism, opting for a fallibilist view consistent with realism. Other philosophers

16 For examples of the process of valorization of judicial practices introduced by author-jurists in the case of cash *waqf* (endowment) and the valorization of the judicial practice of forum selection, see further Ibrahim, "Islamic Law as a Discursive Tradition"; Miriam Hoexter, "*Qāḍī, Muftī* and Ruler: Their Roles in the Development of Islamic Law," in *Law, Custom, and Statute in the Muslim World*, ed. Ron Shaham (Leiden: Brill, 2006), 67–85; Ahmed Fekry Ibrahim, *Pragmatism in Islamic Law: A Social and Intellectual History*, 2nd edn. (Syracuse: Syracuse University Press, 2017).

17 On different pragmatisms and the difficulty of determining who is a pragmatist, see John P. Murphy, *Pragmatism: From Peirce to Davidson* (Boulder: Westview Press, 1990), 21–79; Ruth Anna Putnam, "Taking Pragmatism Seriously," in *Hilary Putnam: Pragmatism and Realism*, ed. James Contant and Urszula M. Żegleń (London; New York: Routledge, 2002), 7–11; Nicholas Rescher, *Realistic Pragmatism: An Introduction to Pragmatic Philosophy* (Albany, NY: State University of New York Press, 2000), 1–56. On different stages of the development of both "classical" pragmatism and neo-pragmatism, see further Michael Bacon, *Pragmatism: An Introduction* (Cambridge, UK; Malden, MA: Polity, 2012); John R. Shook and Joseph Margolis, *A Companion to Pragmatism* (Malden, MA; Oxford: Blackwell Pub., 2006).

associated with this movement include William James, John Dewey, and Richard Rorty. The so-called pragmatic maxim central to pragmatism assumes that we can only have reflective clarity about propositions when we identify their "practical consequences,"[18] a focus consistent with Peirce's endorsement of fallibilism. According to Peirce, we are constantly approaching the truth, but we may at times veer away from it. In Peirce's optimistic view, society as a whole, rather than the individual, and possibly all sentient beings can ultimately reach the truth through self-correction.[19] According to James, pragmatism does not tell us its view of the good; neither does it stand for specific results. What it offers is a method of inquiry and a theory of truth, both of which were derived from the pragmatists' view of knowledge. To pragmatists, knowledge is neither absolute nor permanent. It is tied to action, rather than contemplation. Truth is what works in shaping our world, which Dewey limited to the empirical.[20]

Legal pragmatism draws on the anti-formalism and anti-foundationalism of philosophical pragmatism, viewing law as a practice that depends on context and instrumentality, rather than secure formal foundations. Legal pragmatism is both a descriptive and a normative legal movement. Pragmatists hold that human thought only arises in a situated context and that it is not in fact possible to view matters a-contextually.[21] The theory of pragmatism, therefore, necessarily has a descriptive element, since legal decisions have historically been informed by contexts that can be unmasked to show the frequent fallacies of claims of formalist determinacy. In its normative version, legal pragmatism calls for an instrumentalist jurisprudence based on empirical data.

According to pragmatists, the foundationalist views of law are illusory, for they do not describe the reality of legal reasoning and the pragmatic approach to law is better suited to bringing about *substantive* justice, that is, doing what is right in a particular case even if that goes against legal rules.

[18] On the essential differences between canonical pragmatists and neo-pragmatists, see further Richard Rorty, "The Banality of Pragmatism and the Poetry of Justice," *Southern California Law Review* 63 (1989–1990): 1813–1814; Christopher Hookway, *The Pragmatic Maxim: Essays on Peirce and Pragmatism* (Oxford: Oxford University Press, 2012), 1–4.

[19] B. Z. Tamanaha, "Pragmatism in U.S. Legal Theory: Its Application to Normative Jurisprudence, Sociolegal Studies, and the Fact-Value Distinction," *American Journal of Jurisprudence* 41: 1 (1996): 325; Hookway, *The Pragmatic Maxim*, 5–10; Richard Rorty, *Consequences of Pragmatism: Essays, 1972–1980* (Minneapolis: University of Minnesota Press, 1982), xiii–xliv, 160–175; Cornel West, *The American Evasion of Philosophy a Genealogy of Pragmatism* (Madison, WI: University of Wisconsin Press, 1989).

[20] Tamanaha, "Pragmatism in U.S. Legal Theory," 321–329.

[21] Tamanaha, 334.

The pragmatic focus on the consequences supports paying greater attention to substantive justice since what matters is the consequences of legal decisions, rather than the slavish following of rules. This does not mean that legal rules should be ignored, but rather that they must be treated as only one of many factors to be considered when deciding a case. This notion of substantive justice is the product of the values of the judge, which may be similar to those of the larger collective in a homogenous society, but not necessarily in a heterogeneous society. In this sense, pragmatism does not promote a particular ideology or legal result; rather, it links legal decisions to societal values.[22] As such, some legal theorists rejected pragmatism (or "practical reason") as subjectivist and visceral, and therefore, pragmatic adjudication, in their view, contradicts the rule of law, that is, certainty, stability, and predictability. Others argue that "unprincipled" decisions could be taken in a morally appalling, unegalitarian direction. However, as Rorty reasons, legal theory does not offer a defense against those types of decisions, while Farber contends that practical reason can indeed provide legal predictability and stability.[23] The critical legal studies movement (also known as "critical pragmatism") is a recent child of the pragmatic movement, although critical legal scholars eventually disagreed with some of the tenets of canonical pragmatism. They also rejected pragmatic acceptance of liberal democratic institutions, themselves the objects of the ire of critical legal scholars.[24]

22 Tamanaha, 335–337; Thomas F. Cotter, "Legal Pragmatism and Intellectual Property Law," in *Intellectual Property and the Common Law*, ed. Shyamkrishna Balganesh (Cambridge University Press, 2013); Thomas F. Cotter, "Legal Pragmatism and the Law and Economics Movement," *Georgetown Law Journal* 84:6 (1996): 2071–2142; Richard A. Posner, "Pragmatic Adjudication," *Cardozo Law Review* 18 (1996–1997): 1–20; Richard A. Posner, *Overcoming Law* (Cambridge, MA: Harvard University Press, 1995); Richard A. Posner, *The Problems of Jurisprudence* (Cambridge, MA: Harvard University Press, 1990), 18–26; Joseph Singer, "Legal Realism Now," *California Law Review* 76:2, no. 2 (1988): 468–470; Duncan Kennedy, "Form and Substance in Private Law Adjudication," *Harvard Law Review* 89:8 (1976): 1685–1778; Helge Dedek, "The Splendour of Form: Scholastic Jurisprudence and 'Irrational Formality'," *Law and Humanities* 5:2 (2011): 349–383.

23 Daniel A. Farber, "The Inevitability of Practical Reason: Statutes, Formalism, and the Rule of Law," *Vanderbilt Law Review* 45 (1992): 533–534; Rorty, "The Banality of Pragmatism and the Poetry of Justice," 1818; Nancy Levit, "Practically Unreasonable – A Critique of Practical Reason: A Review of the Problems of Jurisprudence by Richard A. Posner," *Northwestern University Law Review* 85:2 (1991): 494–518; Ronald Dworkin, *Law's Empire* (Cambridge, MA: Belknap Press, 1986); Tamanaha, "Pragmatism in U.S. Legal Theory," 336–338; Hart argues that any legal system requires some judicial discretion in some cases, despite the importance of predictability in the law. H. L. A Hart, *The Concept of Law* (Oxford: Clarendon Press, 1961), 138–144.

24 Tamanaha, "Pragmatism in U.S. Legal Theory," 337–338, 348; Critical pragmatists such as Singer argue that in order to combat "complacent pragmatism," judgements should focus

To sum up, legal pragmatists emphasize (1) contextualism, (2) anti-foundationalism, and (3) consequentialism. In their view, the a priori and abstract style of legal reasoning, which does not account for context and relies heavily on formalistic rules rather than consequences, does not reflect the reality of legal reasoning. Pragmatists also argue that empirically and scientifically relevant data should have an impact on legal decisions, without a narrow focus on *stare decisis*. They contended that judges should turn their attention to the consequences, context, and contingency of laws, rather than narrowly rely on precedent and analogical reasoning.[25] According to Dewey, the logic of judicial decisions should be "*relative to consequences rather than to antecedents.*"[26]

Viewing precedent and formal rules as less important in actual legal decisions than the judge's own context buttresses the philosophy of legal realism as well. Legal realism and pragmatism are both instrumentalist in their outlook and their incorporation of the social sciences in the legal process.[27] Tamanaha explains that philosophical pragmatism influenced legal theory in two phases: the first through the work of Oliver Wendell Holmes, and the second via the work of legal realists. Holmes was a member of the conversation society named "the Metaphysical Club" in Cambridge, Massachusetts, which included Charles Sanders Peirce and William James. Judge Holmes applied many of the precepts of philosophical pragmatism to law,[28] and famously declared that courts "decide cases first and determine the principle afterwards."[29] Commenting on Holmes's work, Richard Posner, an American judge and one of the main figures associated with pragmatic adjudication, argues that Holmes emphasized

on the underlying power structures and therefore one must wonder not just whether a legal practice works but also for whom. Joseph William Singer, "Property and Coercion in Federal Indian Law: The Conflict between Critical and Complacent Pragmatism," *Southern California Law Review* 63 (1989–1990): 1821–1841; Ruth Anna Putnam, "Justice in Context," *Southern California Law Review* 63 (1989–1990): 1797–1810.

25 Some have defined the essential elements of pragmatism differently. Hilary Putnam, for instance, focused his attention on such traits as: antiskepticism, fallibilism, the rejection of the fact-value distinction (a question on which pragmatists held different positions), and the primacy of practice. Richard Warner, "Pragmatism and Legal Reasoning," in *Hilary Putnam: Pragmatism and Realism*, ed. James Contant and Urszula M. Żegleń (London; New York: Routledge, 2002), 25.

26 John Dewey, "Logical Method and Law," *Philosophical Review* 33:6 (1924): 26 emphasis in the original.

27 Tamanaha, "Pragmatism in U.S. Legal Theory," 315–319.

28 Tamanaha, "Pragmatism in U.S. Legal Theory."

29 Cited in Oliver Wendell Holmes, *The Common Law* (Boston: Little, Brown, and Co., 1881), xviii; Steven Harmon Wilson, *The U.S. Justice System: Law and Constitution in Early America* (ABC-CLIO, 2012), 161.

ethical relativism, turning law "into dominant public opinion in much the same way that Nietzsche turned morality into public opinion."[30] Benjamin Cardozo was another important jurist who advocated pragmatic jurisprudence in *The Nature of the Judicial Process*. Cardozo advocated an instrumental, forward-looking concept of law, a pragmatic approach that makes law subservient to human needs. According to him, the lawmaking choices of judges should be concerned with the goal, which raises the question of where should the judge get the knowledge of what serves social interests. Cardozo's answer points to experience, study, and reflection. In Posner's view, Holmes, Cardozo, and legal realists were also pragmatists, since pragmatism gave legal realism most of its shape.[31] Pragmatism, according to Posner, is not simply the method that should be followed in American courts; it is also the method that has historically been followed in reality despite claims to the contrary. In other words, he makes both positive and normative claims about the place of pragmatic adjudication in American jurisprudence.[32] In *The Banality of Pragmatism and the Poetry of Justice*, Rorty argues that while pragmatism was novel and shocking when it emerged, by his time it had been fully absorbed into American common sense. He cites Thomas Grey as saying that it is indeed the "implicit working theory of most good lawyers."[33] Fish exclaims, "If the pragmatist account of things is right, then everyone has always been a pragmatist anyway."[34]

Three definitions of pragmatic adjudication may illuminate what is at stake in bringing philosophical pragmatism into the realm of law. Dworkin, an unsympathetic opponent of pragmatic adjudication, describes it thusly: "The pragmatist thinks judges should always do the best they can for the

[30] Posner, *The Problems of Jurisprudence*, 240.

[31] Cotter, "Legal Pragmatism and Intellectual Property Law"; Cotter, "Legal Pragmatism and the Law and Economics Movement"; Posner, "Pragmatic Adjudication"; Tamanaha, "Pragmatism in U.S. Legal Theory," 342; Posner, *Overcoming Law*; Posner, *The Problems of Jurisprudence*, 18–26; Singer, "Legal Realism Now."

[32] Posner, *The Problems of Jurisprudence*, 9–33, 462–465; Posner, *Overcoming Law*, 1–29; Cotter, "Legal Pragmatism and the Law and Economics Movement," 2071–2142; Daniel A. Farber, "Legal Pragmatism and the Constitution," *Minnesota Law Review* 72 (1987–1988): 1331–1387; Cotter, "Legal Pragmatism and Intellectual Property Law," 213–217; Posner, "Pragmatic Adjudication," 1–20. Rescher argues that pragmatism is the epistemological counterpart of ethical utilitarianism: Rescher, *Realistic Pragmatism*, 7–8; Benjamin N Cardozo, *The Nature of the Judicial Process* (New Haven, CT: Yale University Press, 1991), 51–97.

[33] Rorty, "The Banality of Pragmatism and the Poetry of Justice," 1811–1813.

[34] Cited in Tamanaha, "Pragmatism in U.S. Legal Theory," 353; Stanley Fish, "Almost Pragmatism: Richard Posner's Jurisprudence," *The University of Chicago Law Review* 57:4 (1990): 1464.

future, in the circumstances, unchecked by any need to respect or secure consistency in principle with what other officials have done or will do." Posner offers his own counter-definition: "Pragmatist judges always try to do the best they can do for the present and the future, unchecked by any felt *duty* to secure consistency in principle with what other officials have done in the past."[35] These definitions of pragmatic adjudication have two principles in common despite being offered by both an opponent and a proponent of pragmatic adjudication, to wit: (1) a focus on consequences, (2) a relativist, contextual anti-foundationalism. It is these two elements of pragmatic adjudication that will inform my use of the term in this book, that is, in the sense that the focus should be on the consequences of actions and the context,[36] rather than immutable formal rules.[37]

In his critique of adherence to old formal rules, Dewey admonishes:

> Here is where the great practical evil of the doctrine of immutable and necessary antecedent rules comes in. It sanctifies the old; adherence to it in practise [sic] constantly widens the gap between current social conditions and the principles used by the courts. The effect is to breed irritation, disrespect for law, together with virtual alliance between the judiciary and entrenched interests that correspond most nearly to the conditions under which the rules of law were previously laid down.[38]

Incidentally, if one replaces "the doctrine of immutable and necessary antecedent" in Dewey's critique of common law formalism with *taqlīd*, we would end up with something similar to a common critique of the formalism of Islamic law under the regime of *taqlīd* in the work of Schacht

[35] Richard A. Posner, *The Problematics of Moral and Legal Theory* (Cambridge, MA: Belknap Press of Harvard University Press, 1999), 241; Dworkin, *Law's Empire*, 161.

[36] Posner was taken to task for neglecting differences between different types of pragmatism by Matthew H. Kramer, "The Philosopher-Judge: Some Friendly Criticisms of Richard Posner's Jurisprudence," *The Modern Law Review* 59:3 (1996): 465–478; Posner, *The Problems of Jurisprudence*, 27; Richard A. Posner, *The Problematics of Moral and Legal Theory* (Cambridge, MA: Belknap Press of Harvard University Press, 1999), 227–228.

[37] Posner has a very narrow definition of pragmatism which is: "looking at problems concretely, experimentally, without illusions, with full awareness of the limitations of human reason, with a sense of the 'localness' of human knowledge, the difficulty of translations between cultures, the unattainability of 'truth,' the consequent importance of keeping diverse paths of inquiry open, the dependence of inquiry on culture and social institutions, and above all the insistence that social thought and action be evaluated as instruments to valued human goals rather than as ends in themselves." Posner, *The Problems of Jurisprudence*, 465.

[38] Dewey, "Logical Method and Law," 26; Also cited in Tamanaha, "Pragmatism in U.S. Legal Theory," 333.

(a contemporary of Dewey) and Coulson, to mention but two.[39] According to this assumption, a gap is created between social conditions and legal principles, leading to a tension between law and society. By contrast, the idea of "practical reason," which is what American pragmatists use to reach their judgments, includes analogy, pattern recognition, intuition, social experience, and tacit knowledge,[40] all of which may be the ingredients of *ra'y*, a form of reasoning that was rejected by early Islamic formalists such as al-Shāfiʿī.[41]

Although the formal rules of author-jurists under the regime of *taqlīd* in Islamic law correspond in many ways to the formalism of the common law, one important difference between the concept of pragmatic adjudication in the American context and my use of the term in the Islamic context has to do with the nature of legal interpretation. Unlike the common law, Muslim judges of the postclassical period were left with far less discretion,[42] which means that their pragmatic adjudication looked distinctly different from that of their common law brethren. This is not to say that postclassical Islamic judges did not make interpretive choices, but rather that these choices were often circumscribed by the legal establishment, which means that most forms of pragmatic adjudication were institutionally driven, that is, they were designed by the judiciary and the state, such as the permission of forum selection by the Egyptian Ottoman judiciary.[43] What is described as *pragmatic* in my discussion of Islamic law does not refer to the justification of judicial decisions, that is to say, it is not a form of practical reasoning offered to justify decisions,[44] but pragmatic choices made both by the

39 Joseph Schacht, *An Introduction to Islamic Law* (Oxford [Oxfordshire]; New York: Clarendon Press, 1964), 69–75; Noel James Coulson, *A History of Islamic Law* (Edinburgh: Edinburgh University Press, 1962), 7, 73, 182–201.

40 Posner, *The Problems of Jurisprudence*, 71–123; Farber, "The Inevitability of Practical Reason," 542.

41 Schacht, *An Introduction to Islamic Law*, 37–48; Coulson, *A History of Islamic Law*, 36–61.

42 Ahmed Fekry Ibrahim, "The Codification Episteme in Islamic Juristic Discourse between Inertia and Change," *Islamic Law and Society* 22:3 (2015): 157–220.

43 Ibrahim, *Pragmatism in Islamic Law*, 2017.

44 Posner defines practical reason as "the methods by which people who are not credulous form beliefs about matters that cannot be verified by logic or exact observation." These methods include, among other things, common sense, experience, intuition, precedent, and custom. On practical reason, see Posner, *The Problems of Jurisprudence*, 71–72; John M. Cooper, *Reason and Human Good in Aristotle* (Cambridge, MA: Harvard University Press, 1975); Levit takes Posner to task for his notion of practical reasoning and his call for its utilization in adjudication. She argues that it runs counter to the scientific method, which teaches simplicity, depth, falsifiability, and openness. According to her, practical reasoning, its reliance on common sense, visceral intuition, and common sense

judiciary and by individual judges to accommodate perceived social goods, against the formal rules of author-jurists.

I have previously used the term "pragmatic eclecticism" to refer to forum shopping and doctrinal shopping to achieve certain sociolegal results. The concern of jurists, or more specifically the Ottoman judiciary, was to find legal solutions to what they perceived to be social problems, and, for that reason, they facilitated forum shopping. In this book, another form of pragmatism emerges in Ottoman-Egyptian courts. It was premised, not on forum selection, but rather on treating the austere parent-centered juristic discourse as default rules, rather than mandatory rules, allowing many private separation deeds to be made in contradiction to the discourse of jurists in order to accommodate a social expectation that parents know what is best for their children on a case-by-case basis. This move, which took the spirit of the law over its letter, is similar to American legal pragmatism in that it was concerned with accommodating dominant social (or judicial) values. In fact, the pragmatism that one finds both through pragmatic eclecticism and the pragmatic adjudication on child custody discussed in this book functioned, as we shall see, alongside a formalist strand in Islamic law, where judges followed the letter of the law in some cases. Thus, I argue in this book that Islamic law used a mix of formalist and pragmatic approaches alongside one another. This reminds me of Posner's insightful observation about American law: "Extreme positions are more fun, but in jurisprudence the true as well as the good is to be found between the formalistic and 'realistic' extremes."[45] Posner's centrist position is borne out by the historical evolution of child custody adjudication in the United States, as we shall see in Chapter 1. Despite divergent approaches to accommodating social values regarding childrearing in both Euro-American and Egyptian societies of the early modern era, both approaches represent clear examples of pragmatic adjudication.

PREMODERN JURISTIC DISCOURSE AND PRACTICE: TIME AND GEOGRAPHY

In this monograph, I make a clear distinction between discourse and practice, even though judicial practice itself is accessed through discourse.

mean that decisions cannot be falsifiable or open. For a critique of Posner's practical reasoning, see further Levit, "Practically Unreasonable – A Critique of Practical Reason: A Review of the Problems of Jurisprudence by Richard A. Posner."

45 Posner, *The Problems of Jurisprudence*, 32.

I use "discourse" here to refer to the legal doctrines and rules articulated by jurists outside of the court. This discourse includes various genres, some of which are closer to the activities of judges than others. Legal responsa (*fatāwā*) collections are arguably far closer to the work of judges, than say a work on positive law (*furūʿ*). By the same token, a work on legal theory (*uṣūl*) is further from the activities of judges, especially after the thirteenth century, than a work on positive law. Since we must access the activities of judges through discourse written by court scribes with practical rather than theoretical legal knowledge, the distinction between discourse and practice is more concerned with the context of lawmaking as opposed to the medium of its communication.

The concept of premodern juristic discourse may be seen as treating all juristic discourses of over a millennium as a monolith. It implies that the juristic discourses on custody were unchanged, suggesting that Muslim societies were static and somehow committed to their textual sources in a way that smacks of orientalism. This was certainly not the case. There were many ways in which Muslim societies changed their legal discourses and practices depending on the area of law under examination and the socioeconomic contexts of the different regions.

Premodern Sunni Muslim jurists often treated existing legal pluralism and its ensuing multiplicity of legal rules as equally normative. These rules existed both within each of the four surviving Sunni schools and across school boundaries, as a result of geographical and hermeneutic differences dating as far back as the formative period of Islamic law. Another reason for the persistence of Sunni legal pluralism is the absence of a central code imposed by early Muslim polities due to the historical relationship between jurists and the state. As early as the eighth and ninth centuries under the Abbasids (750–1258), there was hostility among many scholars to state intervention in matters of law and theology, as evidenced by the jurists' position on the Abbasids' desire to impose a central code during the reign of al-Manṣūr (r. 754–775), as well as the Qur'an Inquisition of 833–848.[46]

This unique politico-legal context gave rise to potentially unlimited legal pluralism and uncertainty. Many jurists perceived extreme legal pluralism as a threat to legal predictability and the efficient administration of justice. It fell to jurists to balance the requirements of justice and legal

[46] Dimitri Gutas, *Greek Thought, Arabic Culture the Graeco-Arabic Translation Movement in Baghdad and Early 'Abbāsid Society (2nd–4th/8th–10th Centuries)* (London; New York: Routledge, 1998), 75–83; Ahmed Fekry Ibrahim, *Pragmatism in Islamic Law: A Social and Intellectual History* (Syracuse: Syracuse University Press, 2015), 35–36.

predictability by managing two competing modes of lawmaking – "personal interpretive freedom" (*ijtihād*) and "interpretive conformism" (*taqlīd*) – within the school unit. They gradually limited interpretive freedom over the course of the eleventh to thirteenth centuries by arguing for the dearth of legal skills.[47] This process reached maturity in the thirteenth century, when jurists sought to sift through legal pluralism to determine the more preponderant views within each school, a process known as *tarjīḥ*.[48] These preponderant (*rājiḥ*) or dominant views were supposed to be applied by judges in their court rulings. Despite the jurists' efforts to rein in doctrinal diversity through the limits they placed on *ijtihād*, Sunni Islamic law retained much of its pluralism in the four extant schools as well as in intra-school doctrine.

The slow dominance of *taqlīd* coincided with a juristic justification of forum and doctrinal selection, known in the primary sources as *tatabbu' al-rukhaṣ/takhayyur*, that is, picking and choosing legal doctrines on the basis of the legal result rather than their hermeneutic weight. When this selection was combined in the same transaction, it was known as *talfīq*. This process of forum and doctrinal selection, which I elsewhere named "pragmatic eclecticism," was utilized in Egyptian Ottoman courts, as we shall see in this monograph, to facilitate various social and economic needs. In the modern period, it became the bread and butter of Islamic legal reform.[49]

To offer a nuanced view of the Islamic law of child custody, one must pay attention to time and geography. The best way to speak to the general trends of Islamic juristic discourse toward child custody is to examine works of juristic discourse that were considered paradigmatic, and indeed the texts of practice in entire regions. By covering most of these famous texts, which were utilized in many regions of the Islamic world, it is hoped that we will have a good sense of the various juristic discourses on child custody. Most of the works consulted here were written by jurists who were either from Egypt, or studied and taught there, or whose works were

47 Ibrahim, "Rethinking the *Taqlīd* Hegemony: An Institutional, *Longue-Durée* Approach."

48 Wael B. Hallaq, *Sharī'a: Theory, Practice, Transformations* (Cambridge, UK; New York: Cambridge University Press, 2009), 73–77; Mohammad Fadel, "The Social Logic of *Taqlīd* and the Rise of the *Mukhtaṣar*," *Islamic Law and Society* 3:2 (1996): 193–233; Sherman A. Jackson, "*Taqlīd*, Legal Scaffolding and the Scope of Legal Injunctions in Post-Formative Theory: *Muṭlaq* and *'Āmm* in the Jurisprudence of Shihāb Al-Dīn Al-Qarāfī," *Islamic Law and Society* 3:2 (1996): 165–192; Ahmed Fekry Ibrahim, "Rethinking the *Taqlīd-Ijtihād* Dichotomy: A Conceptual-Historical Approach," *Journal of the American Oriental Society* 136:2 (2016): 285–303.

49 Ibrahim, *Pragmatism in Islamic Law*, 2017.

widely used in Egypt. For example, Muḥammad b. al-Ḥasan b. Masʿūd al-Bannānī (d. 1194/1780) was born in Fez but studied and taught at al-Azhar, where his commentary on al-Zarqānī was popular. Another example is *al-Fatāwā al-Hindiyya*; though it was not written in Egypt or by an Egyptian jurist, it was highly influential in Egyptian Ḥanafī jurisprudence, as evidenced by its frequent citation by Egyptian jurists.

With regard to time, I will focus on works authored in the early modern period, which for the purposes of this book starts with the Ottoman invasion of Egypt and ends in the nineteenth century, or books that may have been authored before that period but which were considered important texts by early modern jurists. Many of the works authored by early modern Egyptian jurists were commentaries on earlier medieval works. One example is *Minhāj al-Ṭālibīn* of al-Nawawī, which received many commentaries throughout the early modern period. Important variations found in the discourses of major works of jurisprudence will be further explored. This approach, while extremely time-consuming, is hoped to ensure that periodic transformations in child custody arrangements do not go unnoticed. It is important to caution that the absence of clear transformations in juristic discourses does not mean that the Muslim societies of the early modern period were static or that social changes were not reflected in the realm of law. As we shall see in Chapters 3 and 4, the dynamic natures of the Ottoman-Egyptian societies of the sixteenth, seventeenth, and eighteenth centuries was matched in legal practice inside the courtroom but not always in juristic discourses.

In order to make consistent the process of determining the most influential works in the four Sunni schools, my choice of legal manuals of analysis will be informed by the following approach. I will (1) look at biographical dictionaries to see how the school's textual authorities were constructed in the school's communal imaginary; (2) pay attention to works of law cited in court records of Ottoman Egypt; and (3) look for works which received commentaries, suggesting that they were considered important enough to act as a *matn*. In the Shāfiʿī school, for instance, there is hardly disagreement that the works of al-Nawawī and al-Rāfiʿī represent the climax of the school's achievement in the thirteenth century. In later centuries, the works of al-Ramlī and al-Haytamī were specifically mentioned by Shāfiʿī authors as the authoritative works followed in different regions, with al-Ramlī's *Sharḥ al-Minhāj* being mentioned in many court records.[50] The probate courts

[50] "Court of Miṣr Al-Qadīma, Sijill 22 (1092–1681), Archival Code 1006–000160," Dār al-Wathāʾiq al-Qawmiyya, Cairo, doc. 199, 70.

(both the Qisma ʿArabiyya and Qisma ʿAskariyya) contain book titles found both in the private libraries of jurists and those of the literati.[51]

THE COURT RECORDS AND THE QUESTION OF VOICE

Also related to the question of discourse is the issue of voice. How can we know that the words that scribes are using to refer to the interaction between litigants and the judge are the actual words of the legal actors? These legal documents were written in the court in the presence of litigants and later used as legally binding documents, and therefore one should assume that when facts are presented, they are a good reflection of the events. Most court documents were written in full while the litigants were in attendance, and detail was corrected by the litigants in attendance, as evidenced by the corrections of information and crossing out of other information that are found in the court records. One also notices, however, that there are many formulaic expressions that keep appearing where they are supposed to be the words of the different actors in the court. One example is when many litigants ask judges to "do what is required by the sharīʿa" (*fiʿl mā yarāh al-sharʿ*) so frequently and formulaically in the court records.[52] It is unlikely that litigants would make such an obvious request, since they are standing before a judge who is supposed to implement Islamic law. In these cases, one should safely assume that these are part of the scribes' repertoire of expressions that fill in the logical blanks in the case. While the details contained in these documents must have been a faithful reflection of the information provided by subjects of the law, the language used may not always have been the exact words of those individuals. One should also assume that the testimonies were often presented in the vernacular, rather than the formulaic legalese of Ottoman scribes.[53]

[51] For examples of books found in the probate inventories of seventeenth-century personal libraries of jurists, see "Court of Qisma ʿAskariyya, Sijill 26 (1019/1610), Archival Code 1003–000105," Dār al-Wathāʾiq al-Qawmiyya, Cairo, doc. 81, 41; doc. 85, 45.

[52] See, for instance, "Court of Al-Bāb Al-ʿĀlī, Sijill 293 (1190/1776), Archival Code 1001–000656," Dār al-Wathāʾiq al-Qawmiyya, Cairo, doc. 131, 90.

[53] For a discussion of the use of court records as evidence as well as larger historiographical questions about the accuracy of court records, see Dror Ze'evi, "The Use of Ottoman Sharīʿa Court Records as a Source for Middle Eastern Social History: A Reappraisal," *ILS Islamic Law and Society* 5:1 (1998): 35–56; Leslie P. Peirce, *Morality Tales: Law and Gender in the Ottoman Court of Aintab* (Berkeley: University of California Press, 2003), 8–9; Iris Agmon, *Family & Court: Legal Culture and Modernity in Late Ottoman Palestine* (Syracuse, NY: Syracuse University Press, 2006), 41–46; Boğaç A. Ergene, *Local Court,*

For sixteenth- to late nineteenth-century courts, I have examined a total of 17,200 cases drawn from 11 courts (al-Bāb al-ʿĀlī, Bābay al-Saʿāda wa-l-Kharq, Būlāq, al-Gharbiyya, Mudīriyya Asyūṭ, Miṣr al-Sharʿiyya, Miṣr al-Qadīma, Qanāṭir al-Sibāʿ, al-Qisma al-ʿArabiyya, al-Qisma al-ʿAskariyya, and al-Ṣāliḥiyya al-Najmiyya). Approximately 600 cases of this sample had some relation to child custody or guardianship. The earliest register, the first of Miṣr al-Qadīma, was dated 934/1528.[54] The last register of this sample, which I examined at Dār al-Wathāʾiq al-Qawmiyya in six long visits over three years, comes from 1895, the court of Miṣr al-Sharʿiyya.[55] I have also examined hundreds of published sharīʿa court records from the period of 1929–1954, shortly before the integration of the sharīʿa courts into a national court system.

PERIODIZATION

I divide this book into three periods: 1517–1801, 1801–1955, and 1955–2014. My division is informed by legal transformations, rather than the important questions of modernity and Ottoman vis-à-vis Egyptian identity. The first period begins with the Ottoman conquest of Egypt and ends with the Ottoman reconquest of Egypt after the French occupation of 1798. The choice of 1801 was motivated by the new Ottoman policy of Ḥanafization reported by al-Jabartī, which was to increase in tempo throughout the nineteenth century, radically transforming the legal system as well as child custody and guardianship. Beginning in 1801, I will only use Gregorian dates for simplicity. This period ends with another momentous event, namely the abolition of the sharīʿa courts and the incorporation of Islamic family law into a unified judiciary in 1955.

Provincial Society, and Justice in the Ottoman Empire Legal Practice and Dispute Resolution in Çankırı and Kastamonu (1652–1744) (Leiden; Boston, MA: Brill, 2003); Guy Burak, "Evidentiary Truth Claims, Imperial Registers, and the Ottoman Archive: Contending Legal Views of Archival and Record-Keeping Practices in Ottoman Greater Syria (Seventeenth-Nineteenth Centuries)," *Bulletin of the School of Oriental and African Studies*, 2016, 1–22; Baber Johansen, "Signs as Evidence: The Doctrine of Ibn Taymiyya (1263–1328) and Ibn Qayyim Al-Jawziyya (d. 1351) on Proof," *Islamic Law and Society* 9:2 (2002): 168–193; Baber Johansen, "Formes de Langage et Fonctions Publiques: Stéréotypes, Témoins et Offices Dans La Preuve Par l'écrit En Droit Musulman," *Arabica* 44:3 (1997): 333–376; Wael B. Hallaq, "The *Qāḍī*'s *Dīwān* (*Sijill*) Before the Ottomans," *Bulletin of the School of Oriental and African Studies* 61: 3 (1998): 415–436.

54 "Court of Miṣr Al-Qadīma, Sijill 1 (934/1528), Archival Code 1006–000001," Dār al-Wathāʾiq al-Qawmiyya, Cairo.

55 "Court of Miṣr Al-Sharʿiyya, Sijill 61 (1306/1895), Archival Code 1017–000160," Dār al-Wathāʾiq al-Qawmiyya, Cairo, 1017–000160.

Within this judiciary, legislators continuously "reformed" Islamic custody laws in line with evolving conceptions of female domesticity and child welfare. This process continued until Egypt's 2014 constitution.

For the period 1517–1801, I will use the words "Ottoman" (especially to describe a polity) and "Egyptian" (to describe a geography) interchangeably. These terms should not be taken to refer to distinct ethnic groups that stood in tension with one another. In my view, like Toledano, it would be anachronistic to impose such an ethnic distinction. To give an example, no distinction would be made between "Ottoman" judges and "Egyptian" or "Arab" judges since some of the judges sent by Istanbul were ethnically non-Turkic and spoke several Islamicate languages. In addition, when the sources discuss judges and their deputies, they generally do not make a distinction based on ethno-linguistic categories. To be sure, there are some limited exceptions to this, especially immediately following the Ottoman conquest, when the local judiciary and scholars opposed some of the judicial practices of the invaders. Within decades of Ottoman rule, this trend slowly dissipated as Ottoman rule and judicial practices were normalized over time.[56] A more fruitful distinction between different actors is one based on status as a scholar or a member of the military elite or merchants, all of which were linguistically and ethnically diverse.[57]

With respect to Islamic legal development, my periodization scheme consists of (1) the formative period, which starts with the birth of Islam in the seventh century and ends with the rise of schools roughly around the tenth century; (2) the classical period starts with the rise of schools and ends with the institutionalization of *taqlīd* by the end of the twelfth century and beginning of the thirteenth century; (3) the postclassical period extends from the thirteenth century to 1500; and (4) the early modern period extends from the 1500s to 1820s. Many important social and legal changes took place during these different periods of Islamic legal history. Though I focus on the early modern period in this monograph, much of the discourse of child custody law remained largely unchanged throughout these different periods. Although there are gradual breaks that

[56] Ahmed Fekry Ibrahim, "Al-Shaʿrānī's Response to Legal Purism: A Theory of Legal Pluralism," *Islamic Law and Society* 20:1–2 (2013): 118–119.

[57] Ehud R. Toledano, "Review Article: Mehmet Ali Paşa or Muhammad Ali Basha? An Historiographic Appraisal in the Wake of a Recent Book," *Middle Eastern Studies* 21:4 (1985): 141–159; Khaled Fahmy, *All the Pasha's Men: Mehmed Ali, His Army, and the Making of Modern Egypt* (Cairo; New York: American University in Cairo Press, 2002), 1–37.

mark these different periods, these changes are usually limited to legal institutions and legal theory and less to substantive law.[58]

TERMINOLOGY

The word *guardianship* in English refers to two types of childcare, the first restricted to managing the child's estate, while the other refers to physical custody, which in turn includes both nurturing the child and making decisions about his or her education and other major decisions.[59] The terms *ḥaḍāna* and *wilāya* do not always fit exactly the English terms "custody" and "guardianship." Another complication is the word *wiṣāya*, which means "testamentary guardianship," with the caveat that guardianship here refers only to making decisions about the child's education and managing his or her financial assets. To make it easier for English speakers to read this book, I will use the word "custody" to refer to *ḥaḍāna* and "guardianship" to refer to *wilāya*. The English reader should be aware that when I use the word "guardianship" to refer to Islamic law, I am using only part of the semantic space of the English word, namely that of dealing with management of the child's assets and major life decisions such as education and marriage. By the same token, when I use the word "custody" to refer to Islamic law, I am restricting the term to the sense of providing the child with basic nurture and care.

Muslim legal scholars used several technical terms to describe their various activities, including *muftī* ("juris-consult"), *qāḍī* ("judge"), *uṣūlī* ("specialist in legal methodology"), and *faqīh* ("jurist"). The term "jurist" is so general that it captures all of these terms, which is why I use "jurist" and "author-jurist" (*muṣannif*), with the latter emphasizing the juristic function of writing legal manuals, to refer to the activities of writing law books whether dealing with substantive law, procedural law, or legal methodology. Otherwise, I will use the terms *muftī* and *judge* to refer to the juristic activities of giving nonbinding legal opinions and issuing legal rulings, respectively.

58 Ibrahim, *Pragmatism in Islamic Law*, 2015, 21–28.

59 Mary Ann Mason, *From Father's Property to Children's Rights: The History of Child Custody in the United States* (New York: Columbia University Press, 1994), 65–67.

Part I

Child Custody and Guardianship in Comparative Perspective

1

Child Custody in Civil and Common Law Jurisdictions

In what follows, I briefly discuss some of the child custody patterns in the major Western legal traditions, which have had a significant impact on the modern concept of the "best interests of the child," the basis of most international conventions on children. I must caution here that the following account should not be seen as a teleological march toward the ultimate pinnacle of legal progress with regard to children. Despite the seemingly neat progression toward the emergence of the best interests concept, the trajectory was never linear. This is particularly clear in the common law tradition, where many small decisions and interpretations of judges sometimes contributed to a solidification of this concept, but at other times created relapses in such a progression. I first briefly discuss child custody in Jewish law due to its important historical interactions with Islamic law and the development of the former in both European and Middle Eastern contexts. I then discuss the French, English, and American evolutions of child custody and guardianship, as they all contributed to the hegemonic best interests standard.

This comparative aspect is useful in two ways. First, it sheds light on the development of child custody law in Western jurisdictions, which had an impact on the family ideology of nineteenth-century Egypt. This is particularly true in the case of the laws of France, which had a deep influence on Egypt's middle- and upper-class conceptions of the family. Another objective of the comparative aspect of this study is to show how completely different legal systems (such as common law in England and Islamic law in Egypt) dealt with a similar problem, namely the coexistence of rigid rules and evolving social values that did not fit well with those rules.

CHILD CUSTODY AND GUARDIANSHIP IN JEWISH LAW

The basic assumption concerning the legal relationship between parents and their children in the biblical legal system emphasized the parents' legal rights to their children. The welfare of children was not highlighted in these ancient systems of law. The father had absolute authority over his children, while mothers did not receive similar rights; when Abraham was commanded to sacrifice his son, he did not consult his wife. According to biblical scholars, the father's authority over his children extended to questions of life and death. According to some scholars of Jewish law, Reuben, son of Jacob, for instance, said that if he did not succeed in bringing Benjamin back from Egypt, Jacob could kill both his sons. Fathers could sell their children, as evidenced by biblical laws relating to the sale of daughters. Despite this common wisdom, some scholars of Jewish law have argued that unlike Roman law, Jewish law framed the relationship between father and child in terms of responsibility rather than right. Others emphasized the restrictions on the father's arbitrary power, especially that of death, over his children. Such punishments, they contended, were implemented by the Jewish court rather than the father.[1]

According to the *Mishnah*, one of the obligations of the wife toward the husband is nursing her infant child. This obligation does not stand when she has been divorced.[2] According to the *Babylonian Talmud*, the husband cannot compel his divorcee to nurse their infant. This suggests that the obligation emanates from marriage, rather than motherhood. The husband can only compel his divorcee to nurse the infant if the latter

[1] Y. S. Kaplan, "Child Custody in Jewish Law: From Authority of the Father to the Best Interest of the Child," *Journal of Law and Religion* 24:1 (2009): 91–94.

[2] Incidentally, this is the same position of many Mālikī jurists who excepted only married women of high birth from the obligation to nurse children. In fact, according to the seventeenth-century Egyptian Mālikī jurist, al-Zarqānī, it was the practice of Muslims over many generations for married women to nurse their children. A divorced woman, however, was under no such obligation unless the child did not accept other women's milk. Most Shāfiʿīs, however, did not require the mother to nurse her children regardless of whether or not she was still married to the father, unless of course the child's health was in danger if not nursed by the mother. ʿAbd al-Bāqī b. Yūsuf al-Zarqānī, *Sharḥ Al-Zarqānī ʿalā Mukhtaṣar Sayyidī Khalīl Wa-Maʿahu Al-Fatḥ Al-Rabbānī Fīmā Dhahala ʿanhu Al-Zarqānī*, ed. ʿAbd al-Salām Muḥammad Amīn (Beirut: Dār al-Kutub al-ʿIlmiyya, 2002), 4:468; ʿAbd al-Ḥamīd al-Shirwānī, Aḥmad b. Qāsim al-ʿIbādī, and Ibn Ḥajar al-Haytamī, *Ḥawāshī Tuḥfat Al-Muḥtāj Bi-Sharḥ Al-Minhāj*, n.d., 8:350; Shams al-Dīn Muḥammad b. al-Khaṭīb al-Shirbīnī, *Mughnī Al-Muḥtāj Ilā Maʿrifat Maʿānī Alfāẓ Al-Minhāj*, ed. Muḥammad Khalīl ʿAytānī, 1st edn. (Beirut: Dār al-Maʿārif, 1997), 3:588; Avner Giladi, *Infants, Parents and Wet Nurses: Medieval Islamic Views on Breastfeeding and Their Social Implications* (Leiden; Boston: Brill, 1999), 101–106.

refuses to nurse from another woman, to save the infant from serious harm. Compelling the mother to nurse an infant who does not accept the milk of other women was grounded in the welfare of the child. Boys were assumed to have a special bond with their fathers, and girls with their mothers, an assumption that must have influenced child custody decisions at that time. In the *Mishnah*, the mother is preferred in custody of daughters. Other rules of Jewish law imply a concern for the child's welfare, such as the rule that children of tender age (under the age of six) should be in the custody of their mother.[3] These assumptions about the child's welfare were often restricted to protecting his or her life, rather than a broader conception of welfare in which the rights of the father are subsidiary to the general interests of the child.

It was in the medieval, post-Talmudic sources that the welfare of the child emerges as an explicit consideration of child custody determinations. It was in the period between the Geonic era, which began in the fifth century AD, and the *Rishonim* period, ending in the sixteenth century, when Jewish law of the Franco-German (Ashkenazi) and Spanish–North African (Sephardi) populations was codified, that the rules of child custody were developed. Jewish legal scholars preferred mothers when the child was in need of their nurture, with an explicit articulation of the child's welfare as the guiding principle.[4] Grandmothers were sometimes preferred over parents who had remarried based on the *Babylonian Talmud* rule that it is not in the child's interests to live with his or her stepmother.[5] Mothers were always assumed to be the better custodians for girls. According to the rabbinic leadership of the Geonic era, if the mother remarried, the preferred custodians of daughters were relatives of the mother such as her mother or sister. If this arrangement was not feasible, the mother would retain custody despite her remarriage. As for sons, the mother was assumed to be better suited to nurture boys of tender age. Fathers were better suited to take care of sons after the age of six.[6]

Medieval Jewish legal scholars stated explicitly that the welfare of the children should be evaluated on a case-by-case basis. The thirteenth-century Spanish scholar Rabbi Meir Halevi Abulafia, for instance, stated that the mother is presumed to be the better custodian for a child of tender age and that the welfare of the child was the main principle that courts should follow in determining child custody. Thus a father's designation of a testamentary guardian does not forgo the court's oversight over the

[3] Kaplan, "Child Custody in Jewish Law," 93–99. [4] Ibid., 99–101. [5] Ibid., 99–101.
[6] Ibid., 102–104.

guardian to guarantee that he functions in the interests of the child. Another thirteenth-century Sephardic scholar, Rabbi Solomon Ben Aderet, agreed that the mother is the best guardian of her daughters, but he also believed that the court should investigate each case individually to determine which parent better served the interests of the child, since the court was "the father of orphans." By the end of the medieval period, the child's wishes were considered a reflection of her or his interests.[7] The Jewish laws of custody in the early modern period, starting in the sixteenth century, went further in reinforcing the interests of the child. Medieval presumptive rules giving preference to the father or mother became much less important than the direct examination of the best interests of the child on a case-by-case basis. This new emphasis gave rise to concepts such as shared custody.[8]

CHILD CUSTODY AND GUARDIANSHIP IN FRANCE

Before we discuss child custody in France, we should take a short excursus into child custody in both Roman and Germanic laws, both of which influenced French law. According to the ancient Roman principle of *patria potestas* (power over one's children), fathers had absolute authority over their offspring in the same way they had absolute control over their wives. This absolute power included the right to sell the child. Over the course of the Roman Empire, the power of *patria potestas* was gradually reduced to the power of correction, rather than absolute power over the person of the child. Organized religion played a significant role in reducing the power of the father over children. The *Twelve Tables* contained provisions penalizing the head of the family for abusing his power over his sons, such as limiting the sale of sons to no more than three times.[9] Under the Roman

[7] Ibid., 111–113.

[8] In the twentieth century, rabbinical courts in Israel emphasized the welfare of the child as an explicit principle in determining child custody. In one telling case, Chief Rabbis Hertzog and Uziel, and Rabbi Shabtai, of the High Rabbinical Court of Appeals, ruled that the father should resume custody of his two daughters, arguing that the presumption that mothers are better suited to assume custody of their daughters refers only to what is usually the case. According to them, there are situations in which it is better for daughters to live with their father. Rabbi Eliezer Yehudah Waldenberg argued that the rules of Jewish law preferring mothers' custody of girls and of both genders until the age of six should only be implemented rigidly when there is no material difference between the two parents regarding the best interests of the child. Kaplan, "Child Custody in Jewish Law," 114–117.

[9] Christopher Blakesley, "Child Custody and Parental Authority in France, Louisiana and Other States of the United States: A Comparative Analysis," *Boston College International*

Empire, the absolute power of the father slowly diminished. Under Trajan, fathers who mistreated their children had to emancipate them, while Hadrian deported fathers who killed their children. Some emperors allowed only newborns to be sold or permitted the sale of children only in cases of extreme poverty, slowly diminishing the father's absolute right.[10]

Germanic customary law, which prevailed in Scandinavia, Germany, Central France, England, and Northern Italy, included paternal obligations as well as rights. In contrast to the Roman extended family, which was under the power of the patriarch, or *paterfamilias*, the Germanic model was based on informal kinship groupings, with several nuclear families having equal powers inside the group. Each nuclear family was headed by a patriarch, but there was a collective obligation to safeguard against the abuse of power by any of the nuclear family patriarchs.[11] Despite its patriarchy, the Germanic system of child custody included some obligations imposed on the father in addition to his rights. The patriarch could be punished for abusing his power, which could include forfeiture of paternal authority. In some places, paternal authority could be withdrawn due to unworthiness.[12]

Custody laws in France were influenced by both Germanic and Roman laws,[13] but Roman law had a greater impact on France, especially from the thirteenth century onwards. The authority of the father over both the person and property of his children increased from the sixteenth century

and Comparative Law Review 4:2 (1981): 286–287, http://lawdigitalcommons.bc.edu/iclr/vol4/iss2/3; Peter Stein, "Interpretation and Legal Reasoning in Roman Law," *Chicago-Kent Law Review* 70:4 (June 1, 1995): 1541.

[10] Blakesley, "Child Custody and Parental Authority," 288; Stein, "Interpretation and Legal Reasoning in Roman Law," 1541.

[11] Blakesley, "Child Custody and Parental Authority," 288.

[12] Blakesley, "Child Custody and Parental Authority," 288–290.

[13] Customary law (*droit coutumier*), which developed in the Middle Ages and the early modern period in Northern France, was influenced by the Germanic model, whereas Southern France (*pays de droit écrit*) followed Roman law. The Loire River generally separated the two legal systems. In French customary law, paternal authority belonged to both father and mother. This authority was restricted to the child's person but not to her or his patrimony. The *droit coutumier* contained the important notion that paternal authority was based on protecting the child. This concept was later incorporated into the Civil Code, which abandoned the Roman view of parental authority as an absolute right of the father. Blakesley, "Child Custody and Parental Authority," 88–290.

due to the monarchy's support of the authority of fathers, and the revival and vogue of Roman law.[14]

In early modern France and across European cities, the father continued to have almost absolute custody rights. Infants were often given out to be wet-nursed due to a host of social and economic reasons, including women's increased employment in industries and a social attitude privileging the husband's access to his wife over childrearing. There was also a cultural reason that contributed to the increasing rate of wet-nursing, namely that it was assumed to be in line with Hellenistic medicine that having sexual relations with a nursing mother harms the child. Due to the cultural privileging of the man's conjugal rights over maternal breastfeeding, the rate of wet-nursing was so high that by 1789 in Paris, over 90 percent of babies were being wet-nursed.[15] The situation was similar across European cities in England, France, Spain, and Germany. By the second half of the eighteenth century, Enlightenment opinion was against wet-nursing and for maternal nursing, partly due to an increased interest in "maternal love." Many elite and middle-class women campaigned for maternal breastfeeding. One of the earliest proponents of maternal breastfeeding was Marie-Angélique Le Robours (1731–1821), who published a treatise against wet-nursing in 1767. She was converted to maternal nursing after losing several infants who had died with wet-nurses. Some historians have speculated that Le Robours must have had an impact on her friend Jean-Jacques Rousseau. The campaign succeeded slowly in decreasing the percentage of wet-nursed babies among elite classes.[16] In the late eighteenth and early nineteenth centuries, the Enlightenment focus on the nuclear family as the building block of society led to a growing aversion to the employment of household servants and nannies.

[14] Jean-Louis Flandrin, *Families in Former Times: Kinship, Household, and Sexuality in Early Modern France* (Cambridge; New York, NY: Cambridge University Press, 1979), 130.

[15] One reason for the proliferation of wet-nursing in early modern France was the assumption that sexual relations spoil the milk of a nursing mother, leading mothers in early modern France to choose between the husband's sexual access and nursing. Women were advised by the church to privilege their husband's conjugal due by putting their children out to nurse. The concomitant high rate of wet-nursing was accompanied by a high rate of fertility and infant mortality. Flandrin, *Families in Former Times,* 203–212; 235–238; Margaret Hunt, *Women in Eighteenth Century Europe* (Abingdon: Routledge, 2014), 140–145.

[16] Flandrin, *Families in Former Times*, 203–212; 235–238; Hunt, *Women in Eighteenth Century Europe*, 140–145.

The nuclear family ideal was associated with two other interconnected notions that reached maturity by the nineteenth century: the ideology that the women's role should be restricted to managing the affairs of the home ("the cult of womanhood" or the "domesticity doctrine"), and the "cult of motherhood," that is, the notion that mothers had a special bond with their children.[17]

These changes in the French family took place prior to and during the French Revolution. Before the promulgation of the French Civil Code in 1804, family relations were regulated in both Roman and French customary laws in such a way as to give wide powers to the head of the family. This authoritarian system mirrored the authoritarianism of the political realm, with the family being a miniature of the larger society. The revolutionaries presented a less despotic paternal authority, with the Code Civil offering certain protections to children. The term "benefit of the child" (*avantage des enfants*) was utilized by the drafters of the code to refer to the standard that was to be used to resolve custody disputes. Commentators on the Civil Code, such as Demolombe, argued that paternal power was not established in the interests of the father, as was the case in the law of Southern France (*le droit romain*), nor in the interests of the children as in prior laws of Northern France (*le droit coutumier*); it was in the interests of everyone, including father, mother, and state, with a priority given to children due to their weakness. This new conceptualization bears striking resemblance to premodern Islamic juristic discourse on child custody and guardianship, as we shall see in Chapter 2. A late nineteenth-century manual of civil law stated that the history of paternal authority resembled the history of the royalty – it had been tempered after having been despotic. Despite the consistent utilization of this standard, the right of the father often prevailed in order to protect the cohesiveness of the family, a concept that was itself considered to be in the interests of children. Throughout the nineteenth and twentieth centuries, the father's authority was taken over by the state, which decided whether children could work or study and at what age they could do so.[18]

17 Patricia Mainardi, *Husbands, Wives, and Lovers: Marriage and Its Discontents in Nineteenth-Century France* (New Haven, CT: Yale University Press, 2003), 104–106; Patrick Kay Bidelman, *Pariahs Stand Up!: The Founding of the Liberal Feminist Movement in France, 1858–1889* (Westport, CT: Greenwood Press, 1982), 21–30; On the cult of motherhood in the American context, see Mason, *From Father's Property to Children's Rights*, 51–53; For the Russian importation of the cult of motherhood, see further Barbara Alpern Engel, *Breaking the Ties That Bound: The Politics of Marital Strife in Late Imperial Russia* (Ithaca, NY: Cornell University Press, 2011), 233–251.

18 Blakesley, "Child Custody and Parental Authority," 315–316; Jacqueline Rubellin-Devichi, "The Best Interests Principle in French Law and Practice," *International Journal*

The Civil Code's clear paternal preference was challenged throughout the nineteenth century through jurisprudence. In judicial interpretation of the law, a maternal preference in matters of custody emerged. This was taking place in jurisprudence despite Art. 302, which required judges to award custody to the spouse who was not at fault during the divorce. The article also allowed the judge to grant custody to a third party or to the spouse at fault if that served the welfare of the child. With the rise in the importance of the cult of motherhood in the nineteenth century, maternal custody was presumptively considered to be in the interests of children based on the common assumption that children were better cared for by their mothers during their tender years. It was therefore not surprising that judges granted custody to mothers in most cases. This maternal preference continued throughout the twentieth century.[19]

Art. 290 of the Civil Code, the result of the reforms of the 1970s, provides the judge with some guidance on what to consider as part of the best interests of the child (*le plus grand bien*), including agreements made by the spouses (see Chapters 3 and 4 for similar conceptions of such agreements in Ottoman Egypt), information obtained through social investigations, and the preferences of the child. The law does not, however, obligate the judge to follow the recommendations of the social investigator or the child's preferences. Although French legislators recognized the private separation agreements of parents regulating their custody to represent part of the best interests of the child, they gave the judge the right to refuse to

of Law, Policy and the Family 8:2 (August 1, 1994): 261; Olivier Faron, "Father–Child Relations in France: Changes in Paternal Authority in the Nineteenth and Twentieth Centuries," *The History of the Family* 6:3 (2001): 365–370.

19 In the first half of the twentieth century, the notion of the child's welfare or the best interests of the child was in tension with the concept of paternal power. Courts argued that paternal power was a function rather than an absolute right, since it could only be exercised in the best interests of the child. Two court decisions emphasized this trend and were later cited extensively by legal commentators and judges. The first is the decision of the *Cour de Paris* of April 30, 1959, which gave visitation rights to the godparents of a child, despite the objections of the parents. According to the judge, the parents took a narrow conception of parental authority and that the child's welfare acted as a limit on parental power. In the second case, adjudicated by the *Tribunal de Versailles* on September 24, 1962, the court did not allow the parents to force their child to follow the Protestant church, affirming that paternal power was not absolute, but rather had to conform with the best interests of the child. The court decided that in the case of conflict, the judge is the ultimate authority with the power to decide what is in the best interests of the child. Blakesley, "Child Custody and Parental Authority," 315–316; Rubellin-Devichi, "The Best Interests Principle in French Law and Practice," 260–262.

approve agreements that did not sufficiently protect the interests of the child or of one of the parents. Legislators explained their decision to include the agreements of the parents as a guiding principle of the best interests of the child by saying that we must de-dramatize divorce procedure and try to reduce conflict. According to them, the amicable agreements of parents represented the interest of the child (*l'intérêt de l'enfant*).[20]

The law of June 4, 1970, changed "paternal" authority to "parental" authority, emphasizing the equality of the spouses in matters of guardianship.[21] Prior to the reforms of 1970 and under the old system of paternal power, only the father had authority with respect to decisions regarding the child's education and religious indoctrination. In theory, a mother could have physical custody but the father would have exclusive power to make major decisions in the child's life. Both parents now had to consult each other regarding such decisions. Again, the reforms of 1970 were able to bring the code in line with jurisprudence, which accorded the mother not only physical custody but also the power to make decisions regarding the child's education. The situation prior to the reforms is similar to many Muslim jurisdictions today, where mothers have extensive custody rights while fathers have almost exclusive parental authority or guardianship. Art. 288 of the Code Civil, amended in 1975, grants the noncustodial parent the right to participate in rearing the child and to contribute to her or his maintenance and moral, social, and formal education.[22] The law of July 22, 1987, established joint custody and guardianship, while Law 4 of March 2002 systematized the joint exercise of parental authority and eliminated the traditional distinction between "legitimate child," and "natural child."[23]

CHILD CUSTODY AND GUARDIANSHIP IN ENGLAND

In Anglo-Saxon England, as in Germanic customary law more generally, the power of the patriarch was controlled and tempered, compared to

[20] Hugues Fulchiron, *Autorité parentale et parents désunis* (Paris: Editions du Centre national de la recherche scientifique, 1985), 27–72, 121–129; Blakesley, "Child Custody and Parental Authority," 318–320.

[21] Fulchiron, *Autorité parentale et parents désunis*, 27–72; Blakesley, "Child Custody and Parental Authority," 295–300.

[22] Blakesley, "Child Custody and Parental Authority," 307–311; Fulchiron, *Autorité parentale et parents désunis*, 31–72.

[23] Hugues Fulchiron, "Custody and Separated Families: The Example of French Law," *Family Law Quarterly* 39:2 (2005): 303–308.

Roman law. Under the combined powers of the feudal system and the church,[24] the father had natural rights of association and benefit from his children's services and absolute custody rights, which continued until the famous *Shelley* v. *Westbrooke* case of 1817, where Shelley lost custody of his children due to his immoral and atheistic lifestyle.[25] Changes in family structures from the seventeenth century onward had an enduring impact on the concept of childhood. Around the middle of the eighteenth century, there was a growing concern for children's emotional happiness. Jean-Jacques Rousseau's educational tract *Emile* (1762) had an impact on the development of the concept of the welfare of the child on both sides of the Channel. By the middle of the eighteenth century, there was a growing consensus that mothers were by nature nurturing and attentive to children's needs, and there was a subsiding of the practice of wet-nursing among the middle classes in England, as was the case in France. The increasing reliance on maternal breastfeeding among the middle class reinforced and was reinforced by the belief that women are the most suitable custodians of young children, especially girls but also including boys up to the age of seven. The hallmarks of the more egalitarian eighteenth-century "companionate" nuclear family included affective bonds between husband and wife, as well as between parents and children.[26] By the end of the eighteenth century, there was an unprecedented literary interest in children.[27] In a case before the King's Bench in 1804, the mother's lawyers argued (albeit unsuccessfully) that the court had a duty to protect the children from seizure by the father, as they needed their mother's care: "of such a tender age, that they cannot without grave danger be separated from the mother."[28]

In early modern England, there were two ways in which disputes of child custody were resolved, either in common law through a writ of habeas corpus brought by the person with the right to custody (usually

[24] The Church reinforced patriarchy, where wives, children, and slaves were to obey their patriarch in the same way they were required to obey God. The authority of the head of the family legitimized the authority of God and vice versa. People who rejected such hierarchies were sometimes dubbed as heretics. On the Church's role in the solidification of family patriarchy, see further Flandrin, *Families in Former Times*, 118–129.

[25] Blakesley, "Child Custody and Parental Authority," 291–292; Mark L. Goldstein, *Handbook of Child Custody* (Springer, 2015), 179–180.

[26] Lawrence Stone, *Road to Divorce: England 1530–1987* (Oxford; New York, NY: Oxford University Press, 1990), 170–172; Susan Maidment, *Child Custody and Divorce: The Law in Social Context* (London: Croom Helm, 1985), 89–93.

[27] Maidment, *Child Custody and Divorce*, 89–93.

[28] Stone, *Road to Divorce*, 170–172.

the father) before the Court of King's Bench, or through the Court of Chancery (the Equity Courts). The Court of King's Bench would enforce the common law principle that gives the father *almost* absolute rights over the custody of his child, regardless of the father's fitness or the child's age. Even when the father was convicted of a crime and was serving a prison sentence, he was able to keep custody and guardianship of his children. In theory, the common law displayed some concern for the child's welfare, but this concern was only relevant when the father's behavior posed a serious risk to the welfare of the child (the basic interests approach). Equity was a system of justice dispensed in the Court of Chancery on behalf of the monarch in his capacity as the *parens patriae*. The original intention was that the Court of Chancery would protect the property of infants, but by 1745, it had started to move beyond the child's property to include the child's general welfare.[29]

Due to the dominance of the father's rights, women were rarely interested in divorce unless their interests were protected in a private separation deed. Without such a separation deed protecting their rights, a separated wife had no legal capacity. All income from her real estate was controlled by her husband, as well as her future earnings and her children.[30] Private deeds of separation often included clauses allocating custody to the mother, as long as the mother had not committed adultery.[31] These separation deeds showed a different side of the patriarchal absolutist rigidity of the common law. Negotiations between spouses, retained in some extant correspondences, show that some fathers were influenced by the rising sentiment about maternal love and the assumption that mothers were best suited to care for their children. In addition, not all fathers were interested in childrearing, especially when they intended to cohabit with a mistress. Private agreements served these conflicting needs and realities. Negotiations included trade-offs such as concessions on the financial obligations of the husband toward the wife in exchange for concessions over child custody and access. Private separation deeds also addressed a general rigidity of the common law, which was considered cruel and unjust, as it contradicted the prevailing social assumptions about maternal love.[32]

[29] For a different account of the development of the English law of child custody emphasizing the *1660 Tenures Abolition Act* at the expense of the role played by the Court of Chancery, see Maidment, *Child Custody and Divorce*, 93–95; Sarah Abramowicz, "English Child Custody Law, 1660–1839: The Origins of Judicial Intervention in Paternal Custody," *Columbia Law Review* 99:5 (1999): 1344–1391; Stone, *Road to Divorce*, 171–172.

[30] Stone, *Road to Divorce*, 4–5. [31] Ibid., 171–172. [32] Ibid., 175–177.

Despite the increasing emphasis on the child's welfare in the late eighteenth and nineteenth centuries, the power of private separation agreements over child custody was reversed in a court decision issued in 1820. Lord Westmeath had signed a separation deed granting custody to his daughter's mother only to later seize his daughter by force while she was visiting him. A writ of habeas corpus to produce the child was issued, but the judge, Lord Eldon, ruled that the inherent power of the father over his children could not be abrogated by a private agreement. This ruling was confirmed in the 1850s considering the father's right to custody of his children a matter of public policy.[33]

The assumption of maternal love was reinforced in the nineteenth century by the separation of the two world spheres, namely the internal domestic sphere under the wife's control and the external worldly sphere under the control of the husband.[34] The dual power of the women's domesticity ideology and concern for the child's welfare slowly chipped away at the father's common law right of custody and guardianship over his children.[35] But this was a slow and uneven process, with many judges continuing to support the father's absolute right to custody of his children in the nineteenth century. The inherent injustice of this system was not lost on some, such as Lord Chancellor Gottenham, who remarked, "A wife is precluded from seeking redress against her husband by the terror of that power which the law gives him of taking her children from her. The torture of the mother will make the wife submit to any injury rather than be parted from her children."[36] In *Wellesley* v. *Duke of Beaufort* (1827), the father lost custody due to his immoral conduct, with the court explaining, "The court has authority to control the legal rights of the father, if the welfare of the infant renders its interference necessary."[37]

The evolving social attitudes and the moral assumption, especially among the educated elite, of the injustice of the common law on child custody finally resulted in legislative action in 1839. The main catalysts for

[33] Ibid., 171–172; Lawrence Stone, *Broken Lives: Separation and Divorce in England, 1660–1857* (Oxford; New York, NY: Oxford University Press, 1993). See further Stone, *Broken Lives*, note 93.

[34] Stone, *Road to Divorce*, 170–172.

[35] The eighteenth-century consideration of the welfare of the child was translated into statutes in the nineteenth century regulating child labor (e.g., the 1819 Cotton Mills and Factories Act), making children's education a right (e.g., the 1870 Education Act), or preventing cruelty to children (e.g., the 1889 Children's Charter). Maidment, *Child Custody and Divorce*, 89–93; 101–102.

[36] Stone, *Road to Divorce*, 173–174.

[37] Maidment, *Child Custody and Divorce*, 93–95.

this change, in addition to the evolving social context, which was ripe for new legislation, were the pleadings of Caroline Norton, a well-born woman whose husband had accused her of adultery and taken possession of their three children. Despite her acquittal of the charge of adultery, the husband refused to return the three children to her. In 1838, Sergeant Talfourd introduced a child custody bill, which was rejected by the Lords. It was then reintroduced in 1839 and finally passed as the Custody of Infants Act. This act brought the law in conformity with the moral attitudes of the educated upper class, stripping the father of his unlimited patriarchal authority.[38] Recall that the main source of female custody, the private deed of separation, was overruled by judges who viewed the father's absolute custody right as a matter of public policy in 1820; this judicial development made later legislative reform necessary if the law was to address the social values of English society, especially those of the upper and middle classes.

The Custody of Infants Act of 1839 enabled the Court of Chancery to transfer legal custody of children under the age of seven to the mother on the grounds that she was best suited to care for her children of such a tender age. The father could claim his right to custody only after children had attained the age of seven. The act also allowed the noncustodial parent visitation rights at all times, on the grounds that children should be brought up with love for both parents. Women, but not men, who were proven to have committed adultery were excluded from the benefits of the act, maintaining a double standard of morality between husband and wife.[39] The law still gave the judge discretion to decide whether the woman was worthy of custody or not, an assessment that was partly based on her character. In the law's first failed attempt in 1838, Mr. Leader made an impassioned speech supporting the bill in the House of Commons. He made the case for unadulterous women to have custody of their "children of tender age."[40] Mr. Leader's arguments fused the moral responsibility to protect women's rights with the welfare of the child thus: "fair protection should be afforded by the stronger sex, who make the laws, to the weaker sex, for whom the law is made, who have no voice whatever in making the law."[41] And in language emphasizing the welfare of the child, he added,

[38] Stone, *Road to Divorce*, 178–180, 363. [39] Ibid., 178–180.
[40] John Henry Barrow, *The Mirror of Parliament* (Longman, Brown, Green & Longmans, 1838), 737–743.
[41] Ibid., 740.

It may be admitted that the wife is the fitter person to have the care of the early education of her children, to form their habits, to minister to their childish wants, to soothe them in trouble, and to tend them in sickness. All this may be admitted; but the law sternly refuses to listen to the pleadings of natural sympathies and affections, gives to the husband the charge and possession of the children, and denies even the sight of them to the beloved and loving mother.[42]

With respect to women's rights, the bill, according to Mr. Talfourd, still fell short of what "natural justice requires." It was merely a "slender palliative." As for the welfare of the child, he argued that a child in some situations needs to be "rescued from the curse of his father's example," and that "nothing can afford him the blessing of a mother's care."[43]

One of the main themes common among those who opposed the bill was that allowing women this right to custody and access to their children would encourage them to seek divorce, which would lead to the disintegration of British families. One of the opponents of the bill, Sir Edward Sugden, argued:

We must consider whether, if this Bill were passed into a law, it would not remove the strongest tie that binds husband and wife together; for if there be any one thing which prevents the separation of husband and wife more than another, it is the birth of children. Take away that motive, and tell the wife that although separated from husband, she may continue to enjoy the society of her children, and you take away that vital principle which God himself has implanted in the breast of woman, and which the law makes use of only to prevent the groundless and wanton separation of parties in the married state.[44]

The welfare of the child became increasingly central to child custody adjudication after the promulgation of the law. In *Re Fynn* (1848), the welfare of the child was clearly stated as the reason for interfering with the father's common law right. The standards for removing a child from the care of his father were strict, for it had to be shown that the father's custody harmed the child, "either physically, intellectually or morally." Only extreme behavior would lead to the father's loss of custody of his children. Judges had a narrow definition of what constituted the welfare of the child. It was a negative test of no harm, rather than a positive best interests test. Yet the threshold would be relaxed later. By 1848 the established view was that the court should grant custody and access in a way that guarantees that the children continue to love both parents regardless of who was to blame for the separation. A private separation

[42] Ibid., 740. [43] Ibid., 737–738. [44] Ibid., 740.

agreement continued to be not worth the "parchment on which it is engrossed," in the eyes of the court.[45]

The Custody of Infants Act of 1873 made important changes to the Custody of Infants Act of 1839, including increasing the age at which a mother would be granted custody from seven to sixteen, removing the mother's adultery as a bar to custody, and treating separation deeds granting the mother custody as unenforceable unless they were "for the benefit of the infant." The welfare of the child, relative as it may be, was treated as a matter of public policy. Despite these statutory changes, there remained cases in which the father's common law right, as well as prejudice against adulterous mothers, persisted in British courts. In some cases, judges considered an adulterous wife to be unfit to be a custodian, despite the Custody of Infants Act of 1873.[46]

In 1881, the Divorce Court was empowered to grant custody as it saw fit, balancing notions of justice and the welfare of the child.[47] The Guardianship of Infants Act of 1886 gave mothers the right to guardianship after the father's death, either alone or jointly with the testamentary guardian appointed by the father or the court. The mother could also apply for custody or access, regardless of the child's age, but the final decision belonged to the court in accordance with the welfare of the infant. Though not abolishing the father's superior rights, the act further diminished them.[48] In *Re McGrath* (1893), the child's welfare was defined more broadly than it had been before. Disrupting the child's living arrangement in a good foster home to return her to the mother was considered inimical to the interests of the child even though the mother's character was irreproachable.[49] One court explained the welfare of the child thusly:

> The dominant matter for the consideration of the court is the welfare of the child. But the welfare of the child is not to be measured by money only, nor by physical comfort only. The word welfare must be taken in its widest sense. The moral and religious welfare of the child must be considered as well as its physical well-being, nor can the ties of affection be disregarded.[50]

The principal factors of child custody shifted from the absolute right of the father, which dominated until the early nineteenth century, to nurturing the right of both child and mother, and finally absolute priority was given

[45] Stone, *Road to Divorce*, 173–174.
[46] Maidment, *Child Custody and Divorce*, 120–122.
[47] Stone, *Road to Divorce*, 179–180.
[48] Maidment, *Child Custody and Divorce*, 98–101, 129–130.
[49] Maidment, *Child Custody and Divorce*, 98–101. [50] Maidment, 100.

to the welfare of the child, rather than the right of either parent.[51] This approach treats both spouses as equally competent to raise the children depending on their character and circumstances.[52] In 1925, another act stipulated that the welfare of the child should be the paramount consideration in child custody decisions. It also imposed a rule of neutrality between fathers and mothers.[53] Finally, the Guardianship Act of 1973 made the rights of a mother equal to those of a father.[54] Case law shows that some considerations such as the maternal preference, preference for the status quo, and keeping the siblings together have played an important role in defining the child's welfare, as evidenced by judicial decisions in the second half of the twentieth century.[55]

CHILD CUSTODY AND GUARDIANSHIP IN THE UNITED STATES

Although colonial family law in the American colonies traversed the ocean virtually unchanged, some custodial arrangements born of America's unique experience with slavery were unknown to English common law.[56] During the colonial era, fathers, in line with English common law, had absolute authority of custody and control over their natural, "legitimate" children. Fathers had full rights to the labor of their legitimate children and their wages if they worked for others.[57] This relationship was similar to a master–servant relationship.[58] Judges in the new American republic relied mostly on English precedents in settling custody disputes. Some precedents emphasized the interests of the child, while others upheld the absolute right of the father. Two contradictory cases from England, separated by a mere quarter century, can be cited in this respect: *Blissert's Case* (1774) and *Rex v. DeManneville* (1804). In the first case, Lord Mansfield permitted a mother to keep her six-year-old child due to the mistreatment of the father, arguing, "The public right to superintend the education of its citizens necessitated doing what appeared best for the child, notwithstanding the father's natural right." According to Mary Ann Mason, Mansfield "planted the germ of what was to become the best interest standard in the New World."[59] This

[51] Stone, *Road to Divorce*, 179–180. [52] Ibid., 170–172.
[53] Maidment, *Child Custody and Divorce*, 139–141. [54] Ibid., 141–143.
[55] Ibid., 177–230. [56] Mason, *From Father's Property to Children's Rights*, 3.
[57] Ibid., 6–7.
[58] For other forms of custody such as indentured servitude and adoption, see Mason, *From Father's Property to Children's Rights*, 73–78.
[59] Ibid., 59; Michael Grossberg, *Governing the Hearth: Law and the Family in Nineteenth-Century America* (Chapel Hill, NC: University of North Carolina Press, 1985), 237.

precedent would later be invoked by judges to challenge the father's common law right,[60] but this was a slow and nonlinear process. Other judges subsequently produced contradictory precedents solidifying the father's patriarchal custody right.

In the second case (*Rex* v. *DeManneville*, 1804), which established a contradictory precedent in America, the mother had run away with her daughter from an allegedly brutal father. Lord Ellenborough of the King's Bench decided that she must return the child to the father, whose right to his children was paramount. With enough discretion on their hands, American judges varied in their choice of doctrine on this matter. Some judges opted for the father's right approach, with one judge justifying his decision by arguing that the father was placed at the head of the family in order to promote, "the peace and happiness of families and to the best interests of society." Even those judges who privileged fathers would give custody to the mother if the welfare of the child were at risk, but only in the context of gross abuse.[61]

"Guardianship" was used in the nineteenth century to refer either to control over the child's person or estate. Guardianship over the person overlapped with custody since it included not only the education of the child and making life decisions but also his or her care and nurture. In the event of the death of the father, the mother was the "natural" guardian and custodian, unless the father had appointed a testamentary guardian in his will, which the courts had to respect. The male guardian appointed by the father was in charge of the child's estate until a boy reached majority, which was 21 years of age, and until a girl married. By the end of the nineteenth century, legal practice curtailed the father's right to appoint guardians after his death, in favor of more rights of guardianship for the mother.[62]

[60] As Mansfield argues, "In cases of writs of habeas corpus, directed to private persons, to bring up infants, the Court is bound ex debito justitiæ, to set the infant free from an improper restraint; but they are not bound to deliver them over to any body, nor to give them any privilege. This must be left to their discretion, according to the circumstances that shall appear before them." Hugh Davey Evans, *Maryland Common Law Practice: A Treatise on the Course of Proceeding in the Common Law Courts of the State of Maryland* (Baltimore, MD: J. Robinson, 1839), 398.

[61] Mason, *From Father's Property to Children's Rights*, 59; Grossberg, *Governing the Hearth*, 237.

[62] Mothers and their new husbands were generally able to keep custody of orphaned children with estates, while mothers of children without estates often saw their children handed over to another family because they could not support them. The court records of the colonial period are full of cases of widows and officials indenturing estate-less orphans whose mothers were unable to support them. Indenture contracts usually bound boys until

In the nineteenth century, despite the reluctance of the legislatures in most US jurisdictions to grant women equal custody rights, courts were ahead of the curve in reinterpreting common law rules in order to grant women custody more frequently. Their decisions were based, not on women's rights arguments, but rather on the grounds of the nascent concept of the child's welfare and, like in France and England, an increasing emphasis on "the cult of motherhood." Additionally, society witnessed an increasing reliance on fathers going outside the home to find work in urban settings and the waning of home industry, as well as a declining birth rate. The values of motherhood, with their urban roots, spread through a united mass culture emerging under the united American republic, with magazines extolling motherhood. This led to the consistent rise of child welfare sentiments and subsequent laws. Judges slowly prioritized the mother's nurturing role over the man's common law legal right. Contrary to this emerging sentiment of children as emotional beings who were more than mere economic assets, the women's movement, especially in the second half of the nineteenth century, largely viewed custody rights as part of their larger struggle for property rights. As such, the women's movement, in Mary Ann Mason's estimation, perpetuated the common law view of children as economic assets – a view that, as noted, was challenged by the emerging cult of motherhood. The child-welfare, cult-of-motherhood approach had more influence over the judiciary, whereas the women's rights approach had a greater impact on US state legislatures.[63]

American judges relied on the English Chancery courts to side with the welfare of minors against grossly immoral fathers, but they took this trend

21 and girls until 18 years. Mothers could visit their children, but they had no right to regain custody. Unlike the father, the mother could not appoint a testamentary guardian until late in the nineteenth century. Mason, *From Father's Property to Children's Rights*, 17–19, 20–23, 65–67.

[63] The evolving values of Americans about both the interests of the child and motherly love had changed to such an extent that by 1865, a mother who had indentured her daughter until the age of eighteen was able to reverse the indenture contract and regain custody on the grounds that as the judge put it: "because of all the affection she must feel for her offspring." He added, "The laws of nature have given her an attachment for her infant offspring which no relative will be likely to possess in equal degree." It was the interests of the child, not the rights of the master that were given precedence. Mason, *From Father's Property to Children's Rights*, 49–54; On the cult of motherhood and domesticity, see further Nancy F. Cott, *The Bonds of Womanhood: "Woman's Sphere" in New England, 1780–1835* (New Haven, CT: Yale University Press, 1997), 63–100; Michael Gordon, *The American Family in Social-Historical Perspective* (New York, NY: St. Martin's Press, 1973); Maxine L. Margolis, *Mothers and Such: Views of American Women and Why They Changed* (Berkeley, CA: University of California Press, 1984).

further by considering the interests of children even when there was no gross abuse by the father.[64] In other words, American judges broadened their definition of what constituted the welfare of the child, from the narrow context of gross abuse to a much broader consideration of the child's best interests. This diachronic change can be contrasted with the Islamic tradition, where the basic interests approach coexisted with the best interests approach in juristic discourse and practice as we shall see in Chapters 2, 3, and 4.

The changing status of women, including their acquisition of greater property rights, was a critical factor in the transformation of custody law away from patriarchal absolutism.[65] *Prather* v. *Prather* of 1809 was the first published decision in the new republic in which the court challenged the father's monopoly over custody. William Prather lived in open adultery with his mistress, and so the South Carolina court challenged the common law to deny him custody of his five-year-old daughter and confer it to her mother. In 1813, Joseph Lee of Pennsylvania sued for custody of his seven- and ten-year-old daughters from his adulterous wife. Chief Justice William Tilghman, while expressing his dismay at the mother's conduct, argued that despite her sexual misconduct, her care of the two girls was faultless. He explained that his main concern was the children, adding "It appears to us, that considering their tender years, they stand in need of the kind of assistance which can be afforded by none so well as a mother." Three years later, the court returned them to the father on the grounds that they were no longer in need of their mother's nurture.[66]

Judicial decisions throughout the remainder of the nineteenth century suggest that a broad best interests concept was slowly – albeit nonlinearly – becoming the pivotal principle driving child custody adjudication. This was done by judges who pragmatically accommodated their social values against the common law's paternal right. In 1842, a New York court made a natural law argument to challenge the common law, stating "by the law of nature, the father has no paramount right to the custody of his child."[67] Two years later, the New York Supreme Court

[64] Michael Grossberg, *Governing the Hearth: Law and the Family in Nineteenth-Century America* (Chapel Hill: University of North Carolina Press, 1985), 234–237. On other forms of custody such as indentured servitude in England and America, see ibid., 76–78.

[65] Mason, *From Father's Property to Children's Rights*, xiii.

[66] Grossberg, *Governing the Hearth*, 238–240.

[67] Mason, *From Father's Property to Children's Rights*, 60; Grossberg, *Governing the Hearth*, 237–238.

struck down the previous decision, granting custody to the father instead of the mother. The court argued that the father's right as the head of the household should prevail. Interestingly, one of the judges on the New York Supreme Court was aware that the common law's patriarchal custody laws had not kept up with contemporary social values, but he affirmed that "human laws cannot be very far out of the way when they are in accordance with the law of God," even though he was fully aware that the lower court's decision was indeed consistent with the "progress of civilization."[68]

Throughout the nineteenth century, the best interests of the child, especially for girls and young boys, was assumed to lie with the mother. This trend, known as the "tender years doctrine,"[69] established a presumptive rule that judges used to give custody to mothers, unless they were unfit. Women were, however, treated more harshly when they strayed from the nineteenth-century standards of behavior. They often lost their child custody due to adultery or leaving their husbands without "just cause." Fathers who committed adultery were likely to be treated less harshly. In *Lindsay* v. *Lindsay*, referring to the difference between the husband's adultery and the wife's adultery, the court stated that although there is no difference between the chastity of fathers and those of mothers, society thinks otherwise. The mother's adultery is more stigmatized than that of the father and would negatively impact the children raised by an adulterous mother who associates with the "vulgar, the vile and the depraved." Some courts even denied adulterous wives, but not fathers, any visitation rights. A New York court argued that even an adulterous father is entitled to custody, "as long as the child does not come in contact with the adulteress."[70]

Another important assumption of English common law, namely that the mother's remarriage forfeits her right to custody, also witnessed transformation in case law. Nineteenth-century judges started questioning the assumption that the remarried mother's deference and affection she

[68] Mason, *From Father's Property to Children's Rights*, 49–83.

[69] In addition to the tender years doctrine, courts tended to grant custody of older children to a parent of the same gender, even if that led to the separation of siblings. An Alabama court considered a boy of five to have reached the end of the tender years in which he needed his mother. A New Jersey court similarly treated the age of five as the end of the tender years. The court divided the siblings, giving one-year-old Elizabeth and two-year-old Robert to the mother, and five-year-old Charles to the father. Reaching the age of five (or even four sometimes) was considered the time when children had passed the age of nurture. Ibid., 61–62; 72–73.

[70] Ibid., 63–64.

owed her new husband would interfere with her innate maternal instincts. In 1852, the Virginia Court of Appeals upheld the custody petition of a recently remarried mother against her former father-in-law. In addition to case law,[71] some states passed statutes removing the remarriage impediment.[72]

In the late nineteenth century, the second wave of feminism shifted its attention from child custody as a woman's right and focused instead on children's rights.[73] New organizations, staffed with volunteers and dedicated to the protection of children, sprang up, the first of which was the 1874 New York Society for the Prevention of Cruelty to Children. By the turn of the century, most of these organizations were staffed with paid social workers. Once abuse or neglect was identified by these organizations, the matter would be investigated by the organization, sometimes in collaboration with the police, and referred to a court.[74]

Following the Progressive Era (1890–1920), and by the end of the 1920s, women's sexual conduct had become less relevant to child custody determinations. The cult of motherhood and the special relationship between mother and child, especially during the tender years, was considered to be far more important than the mother's sexual behavior. An Arkansas 1922 court gave custody to the mother despite the mother's attempt to murder her husband, the father of the children, by cutting his throat with a razor blade and stabbing him in the back. The court's reasoning was that despite the mother's fit of anger, the record indicates that she loved her children and cared for them properly. This approach was not uniformly followed by judges, who had much discretion in punishing the mother for sexual or violent behavior by denying her custody of her children. What later legislation achieved was that it created uniformity between the context-inspired, pragmatic adjudication of judges and the letter of the law. By 1936, 42 state legislatures gave mothers equal child custody rights. Forty-seven states gave women guardianship rights upon the death of the father. These legislative actions represented a codification

[71] Ibid., 66–67; Grossberg, *Governing the Hearth*, 243.

[72] With the greater rights of custody that women achieved in the nineteenth century, there was a process of decoupling of custody and child support. In the nineteenth century, there was no precedent in the common law to a father paying support without receiving custody, but new case law in the nineteenth century started separating child support from custody. Fathers, who were denied child custody were still required to support their children. This new approach accelerated in the twentieth century, giving rise to new legislation criminalizing nonsupport. Judges were willing to throw fathers who failed to support their children in jail. Mason, *From Father's Property to Children's Rights*, 85–87; 112; 114–115.

[73] Ibid., 83, 89–90. [74] Ibid., 101–104.

of judicial reality, since fathers had by then already lost much of their absolute right to custody and guardianship in nineteenth-century American case law.[75]

The earlier new judicial trend preferring mothers over fathers (due to the tender years doctrine) was reversed in the 1970s, when most US states adopted laws granting equal status of custodial rights to both parents. An important late evolution in the development of child custody law was the entrance of social and behavioral sciences into custody disputes toward the end of the twentieth century, with judges enlisting the help of behavioral scientists through expert testimonies to determine what constituted the best interests of the child.[76] According to legal historian Mary Ann Mason, the move from a colonial household economy to an urban economy elevated the mother to the role of primary child-raiser. In the late twentieth century, the abolition of the maternal preference coincided with women's move from the home and into the labor market, which coincided with second-wave feminism.[77]

Mason writes that the Progressive Era was the "historical nadir for fathers, who were disfavored in custody disputes and vulnerable to criminal prosecution if they fail[ed] to support their children." This situation would change in the period of 1960–1990, when courts and state legislatures removed the maternal preference embedded in the tender years doctrine, leaving the best interests standard as the only yardstick for child custody determinations. With the removal of the tender years doctrine and the emerging assumption of equality of genders, judges and legislators enlisted the help of psychologists to determine what was best for each child on a case-by-case basis. In other words, throughout this thirty-year period, notions such as the tender years doctrine, which was grounded in conceptions of natural law, had to contend with the empirical data of the social sciences.[78] Social science theories were routinely cited by judges and legislators. In the 1970s with the rise of "father studies" that focused on father–child interactions, there emerged the notion that a father can be as good as a mother as a primary caretaker. New gender-neutral arrangements became common such as joint custody and primary caretaker. By 1988, 36 states had introduced a preference for joint custody.[79]

The best interests of the child standard is culturally contingent and influenced by social science theories, the individual discretion of the

[75] Ibid., 112–115. [76] Ibid., xiv, 83. [77] Ibid., xv. [78] Ibid., 164–165.

[79] Ibid., 121–124; 130, 167–174; Lenore J. Weitzman, *The Divorce Revolution: The Unexpected Social and Economic Consequences for Women and Children in America* (New York, NY; London: Free Press ; Collier Macmillan, 1985), 226–227.

judge, and dominant social values, especially of the upper and middle classes. Due to the lack of consensus over the best model for childcare – whether designating joint custody or a primary caretaker – judges often have to make pragmatic choices that suit their values. In this sense, the best interests standard is always relative, even when guidelines are provided by legislators.[80] Driven by growing research that shows that mediation rather than adversarial child custody arrangements better serve the interests of the child and as a way to deal with the relativism inherent in any assessment of what serves the child's best interests, many US jurisdictions have made mediation obligatory at the time of separation to encourage parents to reach amicable out of court agreements. Once these agreements are signed, they are often considered part of the best interests of the child, since the wishes of the parents are treated presumptively as in the interests of children. Consider the following: the National Conference of Commissioners on Uniform State Law put forth the Uniform Marriage and Divorce Act (UMDA), which has been partly enacted in some states, with the objective of making marriage and divorce laws uniform across the United States. According to the UMDA, the best interests of the child are determined by a combination of the following factors: "the wishes of the parents; the wishes of the child; the interaction between the child and its parents, siblings or other person who might significantly affect its best interests; the child's adjustment to its home, school, and community; and, the mental and physical health of all individuals involved."[81] Mediation is consistent with this definition of what constitutes the best interests of the child, with studies unsurprisingly showing that the noncustodial parent's relationship with children and the frequency of his or her contact with the children after divorce is superior in amicable agreements compared with adversarial divorce proceedings.[82] This recent situation, as we shall see in

80 John E. Coons and Robert H. Mnookin, "Toward a Theory of Children's Rights," in *The Child and the Courts*, ed. Ian F. G. Baxter and Mary Eberts (Toronto: Carswell Co., 1978), 394–396.

81 Uniform Law Commission, "Marriage and Divorce Act, Model Summary," accessed February 9, 2015, www.uniformlaws.org/ActSummary.aspx?title=Marriage%20and%20Divorce%20Act,%20Model.

82 Robert E. Oliphant and Nancy Ver Steegh, *Family Law* (New York: Aspen Publishers Online, 2007), 427; Robert E. Emery, *Renegotiating Family Relationships: Divorce, Child Custody, and Mediation* (New York: Guilford Press, 2012), 197–222; Trans-Atlantic Divorce Mediation Conference, Vermont Law School, and Dispute Resolution Project, eds., *The Role of Mediation in Divorce Proceedings: A Comparative Perspective (United States, Canada and Great Britain)* (South Royalton, VT: Vermont Law School, 1987), 219–266.

Chapters 3 and 4, resembles in some ways the private separation deeds that existed in Mamluk and Ottoman Egypt.

CONCLUSION

We have seen thus far that Germanic, Roman, and Jewish laws were patriarchal but they varied in how they checked the power of the patriarch. Germanic laws placed more limits on paternal power than Roman law, and Roman law of the later period more than earlier forms of Roman law. Jewish law, especially in the codification stage of the medieval period, had more checks against the power of the patriarch. In Jewish law of the medieval period, the child welfare discourse emerged as an important principle driving child custody and guardianship rules, but these rules were presumptive categorical rules that were based on the tender age or gender assumptions. It was in the early modern period (the sixteenth through nineteenth centuries) that Jewish law inched closer to making custody arrangements on a case-by-case basis, sometimes overlooking presumptive rules. Similarly, early modern Christianity provided a check against the absolute power of the father.

It was in the early modern period that changes were gradually made in different European jurisdictions leading to increasing focus on children and children's rights. In early modern France, paternal authority was reinforced through the vogue of Roman law and stronger monarchical rule, which sought to solidify paternal authority. A host of social and cultural reasons led to the spread of wet-nursing, especially in the middle and upper classes, in early modern France. This phenomenon made it hard for mothers to bond with their children. By the eighteenth century, a new doctrine emerged that emphasized maternal love and the special bond tying mother to child. This notion was accompanied by a concern for children's welfare and a romanticization of mother–child love. But it was not until the early nineteenth century that this ideology was represented in legislation.

The Code Civil offered some limited checks on the power of the father and used the term "interest of the child." The doctrine of maternal love, also known as the "cult of motherhood," was accompanied by nineteenth-century conceptions of the nuclear family, built on companionate marriage and love between father and mother, as well as parents and children. The nineteenth-century division of the private and public spheres, where a woman's role was restricted to the house and rearing of children (the cult of womanhood), reinforced the cult of motherhood and the tender years doctrine. These changes in the French family slowly shifted the focus in custody and guardianship jurisprudence from father to mother and from parents to children through the nineteenth and twentieth centuries, but legislation was lagging behind these social changes. In the 1970s, various amendments to the French Code Civil granted women equal custody and guardianship rights, while the law of July 22, 1987, established joint custody and guardianship into law. Law 4 (March 2002) made the joint exercise of parental authority more systematic.[83]

Similar to France of the early modern period, English common law gave the father an absolute right of custody. By the seventeenth century, there was a growing concern about children's emotional happiness, a trend reinforced in the eighteenth century by a literary interest in children's emotional happiness. Jean Jacques Rousseau's educational tract *Emile* (1762) was a manifestation of this trend. The cult of motherhood dominated the English middle and upper classes as it did in France by the middle of the eighteenth century. Seventeenth- and eighteenth-century private separation deeds enabled women to have custodial and guardianship rights despite the rigidity of the common law paternal right, which only denied the father paternal authority in extreme cases of gross abuse (the basic interests approach). By the eighteenth century, the court of chancery's jurisdiction moved beyond the child's property and into her or his general welfare, offering a limited reprieve from the absolute paternal power of the common law. These limited curbs on the father's common law right through private separation deeds and the court of chancery did not allow the law to keep abreast of the new family ideology that developed through the eighteenth and nineteenth centuries, placing mothers at the center of child care.

A setback to private separation deeds took place in 1820, when Lord Eldon ruled that the inherent power of the father over his children could not be abrogated by a private agreement. By taking away that element of flexibility in the law, the gap between social values about maternal love and the common law's absolute paternal preference were at odds, prompting a legislative reform 19 years later. The Custody of Infants Act of 1839 enabled the Court of Chancery to transfer legal custody of children under the age of seven to their mother as long as she had not committed adultery. The debates over the bill show that the welfare of the child (coupled with an overlapping women's rights discourse) had by then become a dominant

[83] Fulchiron, "Custody and Separated Families," 303–308.

discourse that was set to chip away at paternal authority. Throughout the remainder of the nineteenth century, case law broadened the definition of what constitutes the child's welfare. Successive acts in the nineteenth and twentieth centuries emphasized the child's welfare, as well as granting women greater rights of custody and guardianship because it was assumed that the fate of mother and child were intertwined. During the course of the twentieth century, the child's best interests became the principal consideration in child custody and guardianship decisions and a rule of neutrality between parents was introduced.

American laws on child custody did not depart significantly from the common law until the end of the colonial period. Throughout the nineteenth century, the common law absolute right was challenged by American case law, which placed greater emphasis on the child's welfare and women's rights, both of which overlapped due to the cult of motherhood. The nineteenth-century tender years doctrine influenced judges, who granted custody to women of young children sometimes making natural law arguments to support their decisions against the father's common law right. The tender years doctrine had become so dominant that mothers were granted custody even when they were violent or adulterous. The doctrine was reversed slowly in the twentieth century when several states established gender neutrality. The entrance of the social sciences into the courtroom since around the 1960s has had an immeasurable impact on child custody by introducing a preference for joint custody and obligatory mediation before divorce in many US states.

One common thread that ties together the laws of France, England, and the United States is that the concept of the best interests of the child developed from a narrow concept only operationalized in situations of gross abuse when the child's life was in danger to a broader concept in which the best environment is chosen for the child's upbringing without assigning presumptive rights to either parent at least in theory. This development was exported and promoted in international conventions, confirming the prediction of Swedish reformer Allen Key, who in 1900 described the twentieth century as the "century of the child." The twentieth century also witnessed what some historians have called the "globalization of childhood," which refers to the promotion of Euro-American ideas about childhood across the world through international conventions.[84] The most

[84] Tatjana Thelen and Haldis Haukanes, *Parenting after the Century of the Child: Travelling Ideals, Institutional Negotiations and Individual Responses* (Farnham, Surrey; Burlington, VT: Ashgate, 2010), 1–4.

important of these is the Convention on the Rights of the Child (CRC), which states in Art. 2, "In all actions concerning the child, whether undertaken by public or private social welfare institutions, courts of law, administrative authorities or legislative bodies, the best interests of the child shall be a primary consideration." And now, this monograph turns to the history of the development of the concept of the best interests of the child in early modern and modern Egypt.

2

The Best Interests of the Child in Islamic Juristic Discourse

Muslim jurists almost exclusively confined themselves to child custody after the dissolution of marriage. It was assumed that if the couple was still married, they would be living together, and, therefore, there would be no need for the discussion of custody. Some jurists, however, envisioned situations in which a married couple would live in different places and have disagreements over custody. Al-Kāsānī (d. 587/1191) argued that a husband had no right to take his minor child on his travel if the child was still within the mother's custodial years under Ḥanafī law.[1] Other than this or similar contexts, jurists assumed that discussions of custody were relevant only to dissolved marriages.

In order to understand whether the best interests approach represented the main source of lawmaking with regard to child custody, one has to use two approaches. The first is to engage the discussion of whether custody is a right of the custodian or the ward, since this debate had a bearing on some of the positive rules of custody in the early development of Islamic legal thinking on child custody. Nevertheless, one cannot predict custody arrangements within a school based on its position of who has this right, simply because, as mentioned in the Introduction, there were other considerations that played an equally, if not more important, role in the evolution of custody laws in the early schools of jurisprudence. The second approach is to look at the justifications of the positive laws on custody to determine the underlying rationale for these laws. To be

1 ʿAlāʾ al-Dīn al-Kāsānī, *Badāʾiʿ Al-Ṣanāʾiʿ Fī Tartīb Al-Sharāʾiʿ*, ed. ʿAlī Muḥammad Muʿawwaḍ and ʿĀdil Aḥmad ʿAbd al-Mawjūd, 2nd edn. (Beirut: Dār al-Kutub al-ʿIlmiyya, 2003), 5:217.

sure, this may raise the old question of whether such justifications were actual reasons for these laws or post-facto rationalizations. Without arguing for either side, I will use rationalizations more generally to point to general trends. After all, it is possible that a rationalization started as a justification after the fact and that there was no direct link between the reason given and the selected law at a particular historical moment. What then do we say about that rationalization continuing to be invoked after the law has already been established for centuries? In this case, what used to be a "disingenuous" after-the-fact rationalization becomes a "genuine" reason for later generations of jurists and legal practitioners. In this sense, justifications offered to explain and valorize social practice themselves become creative of social values and practices. Put differently, when jurists choose one social norm and offer juristic justifications to support it after the fact, the new law creates pressure for adherence, leading to habit formation. Habits then create custom and become a cultural attribute.[2] It is with this caveat in mind that one should approach the reasons given for a particular legal rule.

As we saw in Chapter 1, fathers often had a proprietary right to their children, as was the case in the Roman tradition. Although the Islamic laws of custody do not at all fit this Roman model, we see a competing model that resembles the Roman paternal right. In Islamic juristic discourse, a father killing or stealing money from his child was not punished as severely as he would have been if the victim had not been his child, since the father's proprietary rights to his child and the child's property constitutes doubt (*shubha*), which rules out the more austere punishments for murder and stealing. According to one report, the Prophet said, "A father shall not be killed for his offspring." Most jurists preclude the death penalty as a punishment for the father's intentional murder of his child, except for the Mālikī school, which prescribes the death penalty if it is very clear that the murder was deliberate.[3] This doctrine holds a middle position between giving the father absolute power over the person of the child

[2] Shestack argues, for instance, that the enactment of civil rights laws in the American South brought about changes in Southern culture in a short period of time through this process. Jerome J. Shestack, "The Philosophic Foundations of Human Rights," *Human Rights Quarterly* 20:2 (1998): 233.

[3] Abū al-Barakāt Aḥmad b. al-Dardīr and Aḥmad b. Muḥammad al-Ṣāwī, *Al-Sharḥ Al-Saghīr ʿalā Aqrab Al-Masālik Ilā Madhhab Al-Imām Mālik*, ed. Muṣṭafā Kamāl Waṣfī (Cairo: Muṣṭafā Kamāl, 1986), 4:373–374; Muḥammad b. Idrīs al-Shāfiʿ ī, *Al-Umm*, ed. Rifʿat Fawzī ʿAbd al-Muṭṭalib (Manṣūra: Dār al-Wafāʾ, 2001), 7:85–88; Muḥammad Amīr b. ʿUmar Ibn ʿĀbidīn and Muḥammad b. ʿAlī b. Muḥammad al-Ḥiṣnī al-Ḥaṣkafī, *Radd Al-Muḥtār ʿalā Al-Durr Al-Mukhtār Sharḥ Tanwīr Al-Abṣār*, ed. ʿĀdil Aḥmad ʿAbd al-Mawjūd,

and completely denying any such power. According to a sound tradition, a Bedouin man told the Prophet that he had some money that his father wanted to take. The Prophet said, "You and your money belong to your father. Your children are the best of your earnings, so eat what your children have earned."[4] This model may suggest that pre-Islamic Arabia might have had a tempered position on the father's patriarchal right to the life and property of his children, as compared with Roman law. Given this position, what was the early Islamic position on paternal authority over child custody and guardianship rights? Before we embark on the discussion of the positive laws relating to child custody and guardianship, it is important to first examine the debate about whether custody was considered a right of the custodian or the child.

IS *ḤAḌĀNA* A RIGHT OR A RESPONSIBILITY?

The tensions between the rights of the custodian and the rights of the child become clear in the dominant assumption of Sunni jurists that child custody is a collective obligation (*farḍ kifāya*) of close relatives of the child, but it becomes an individual obligation (*farḍ ʿayn*) of the last remaining relative. In other words, no specific relative is required to assume custody of the child as long as there is another relative – even if far more distant – willing to take that responsibility. This assumes that the right to custody belongs to the parent who can "drop" it rather than to the child.[5] But the relative's right is not absolute. It has to be weighed against

ʿAlī Muḥammad Muʿawwaḍ, and Muḥammad Bakr Ismāʿīl (Riyadh, Saudi Arabia: Dār ʿĀlam al-Kutub, 2003), 10:175; Ibn Qudāma al-Maqdisī, *Al-Mughnī*, 2:2031–2032.

4 Abū Dāwūd Sulaymān b. al-Ashʿath al-Sijistānī, *Sunan Abī Dāwūd*, ed. Shuʿayb al-Arnaʾūṭ and Muḥammad Kāmil Qurabellī (Damascus: Dār al-Risāla al-ʿĀlamiyya, 2009), 5:390; Abū Bakr Aḥmad b. al-Ḥusayn b. ʿAlī Bayhaqī, *Al-Sunan Al-Kubrā*, ed. Muḥammad ʿAbd al-Qādir ʿAṭā, 3rd edn. (Dār al-Kutub al-ʿIlmiyya, 2003), 7:789.

5 On different aspects of the discussion of whether custody is a right of the ward or custodian, see Mahdi Zahraa and Normi A. Malek, "The Concept of Custody in Islamic Law," *Arab Law Quarterly* 13: 2 (1998): 155–177, at 158–159; Abū ʿUmar Yūsuf Ibn ʿAbd al-Barr, *Al-Kāfī Fī Fiqh Ahl Al-Madīna Al-Mālikī*, 2nd edn. (Beirut: Dār al-Kutub al-ʿIlmiyya, 1992), 296; al-Dardīr and al-Ṣāwī, *Al-Sharḥ Al-Ṣaghīr ʿalā Aqrab Al-Masālik Ilā Madhhab Al-Imām Mālik*, 2:763; Ibrāhīm b. Muḥammad b. Ibrāhīm al-Ḥalabī, ʿAbd al-Raḥmān b. Muḥammad b. Sulaymān al-Kalībūlī Dāmād Afandī, and Muḥammad b. ʿAlī b. Muḥammad al-Ḥiṣnī al-Ḥaṣkafī, *Multaqā Al-Abḥur; Majmaʿ Al-Anhur: Al-Durr Al-Muntaqā Fī Sharḥ Al-Multaqā* (Beirut: Dār al-Kutub al-ʿIlmiyya, 1998), 2:166; Ibn Nujaym Zayn al-Dīn al-Miṣrī, Abū al-Barakāt ʿAbd Allāh Ḥāfiẓ al-Dīn al-Nasafī, and Muḥammad Amīn Ibn ʿĀbidīn, *Al-Baḥr Al-Rāʾiq Sharḥ Kanz Al-Daqāʾiq Wa-Maʿahu Al-Ḥawāshī Al-Musammāh Minḥat Al-Khāliq ʿalā Al-Baḥr Al-Rāʾiq*, ed. Zakariyyā ʿUmayrāt (Beirut: Dār al-Kutub al-ʿIlmiyya, 1997), 4:280–283.

the child's welfare in the narrow, negative sense of avoiding serious harm to the child. Thus, child custody can only become an individual obligation when a parent is the only person available before the state has to intervene, or when the physical well-being of the child depends on a specific person, such as the mother if the child does not accept the milk of women other than her in the first two years, the age at which children are supposed to be weaned.[6] Preferring relatives taking care of children to the state, jurists considered the intervention of the state as a last resort because, as one early modern Egyptian Shāfiʿī jurist explained,[7] relatives are more kind and have more time than the sultan (*ashfaq wa-akthar farāghan min al-sulṭān*).[8]

The question of whether custody is a right of the custodian or of the ward is somewhat misleading, then, because no jurist saw custody in absolute terms as either a right of the custodian or the ward. Despite the prevalence of discussions of *ḥaḍāna* as a right of the custodian, which is the "well-known" (*mashhūr*) position of the Mālikīs for instance,[9] all jurists privileged the basic interests of the child over those of the custodian, regardless of whether they considered the act of child custody to be a right of the ward or the custodian. What makes this discussion more complex is that the dominant position of the Sunni schools was supposedly that in times of conflict the custodian's right took precedence (absent serious harm), but according to the minority position, custody was a right of the ward.[10]

Despite the jurists' claim that the first position dominated, we find that rules related to custody were sometimes based on the majority position, but at other times they were based on the minority position. Consider

[6] Al-Miṣrī, al-Nasafī, and Ibn ʿĀbidīn, *Al-Baḥr Al-Rāʾiq Sharḥ Kanz Al-Daqāʾiq Wa-Maʿahu Al-Ḥawāshī Al-Musammāh Minḥat Al-Khāliq ʿalā Al-Baḥr Al-Rāʾiq*, 4:280–283.

[7] Al-Miṣrī, al-Nasafī, and Ibn ʿĀbidīn, 4:280–283.

[8] Al-Shirbīnī, *Mughnī Al-Muḥtāj Ilā Maʿrifat Maʿānī Alfāẓ Al-Minhāj*, 3:597.

[9] There is a debate over what *mashhūr* means among the Mālikīs. One position, which is more dominant, links it to the number of jurists who uphold a certain position. Others link it to the view with stronger evidence. But either way, jurists on both sides of the debate juxtapose the *mashhūr* with "judicial practice" (*ʿamal*), as they acknowledge that sometimes the dominant position of the school jurists is not what is applied in courts by judges. Badr al-Dīn Muḥammad b. Yaḥyā al-Qarāfī, "*Taḥqīq Al-Ibāna Fī Ṣiḥḥat Isqāṭ Mā Lam Yajib Min Al-Ḥaḍāna*," in *Min Khizānat Al-Madhhab Al-Mālikī*, ed. Jalāl ʿAlī al-Qadhdhāfī (Beirut: Dār Ibn Ḥazm, 2006), 426–427.

[10] According to Ibn ʿĀbidīn, this was the dominant position of the school (*wa-ʿalayhi al-fatwā*) Muḥammad b. ʿAlī b. Muḥammad al-Ḥiṣnī al-Ḥaṣkafī and Muḥammad b. ʿAbd Allāh b. Aḥmad al-Ghazzī al-Timurtāshī, *Al-Durr Al-Mukhtār Sharḥ Tanwīr Al-Abṣār Wa-Jāmiʿ Al-Biḥār*, ed. ʿAbd al-Munʿim Khalīl Ibrāhīm (Beirut: Dār al-Kutub, 2002), 255; al-Miṣrī, al-Nasafī, and Ibn ʿĀbidīn, *Al-Baḥr Al-Rāʾiq Sharḥ Kanz Al-Daqāʾiq Wa-Maʿahu Al-Ḥawāshī Al-Musammāh Minḥat Al-Khāliq ʿalā Al-Baḥr Al-Rāʾiq*, 4:280.

the Mālikī school: the dominant position is that custody is a right of the custodian, and the minority position is that it is a right of the ward. However, as al-Zarqānī (d. 1122/1710) perceptively noted, some of the rules of his school were based on the minority position that privileged the rights of the child, while others were based on the dominant position.[11] In the Ḥanafī school, similarly, a dominant position treated an agreement made by the mother to give up her right to custody as nonbinding since the right of custody belonged to the child and the mother had no right to give up her responsibility. Yet mothers were not forced to assume custody unless there was no one else to take care of the child, suggesting that absent serious danger to the child, they could drop their right at will. These two positions, which had contradictory justifications (the right of the custodian versus the right of the ward), coexisted as two dominant doctrines within the Ḥanafī school in the early modern period,[12] which suggests that jurists were pragmatic in that they were *sometimes* more concerned about substantive law than they were about the consistency of their justifications.[13] It is, therefore, hard to establish a clear and transparent link between the substantive laws of custody (and guardianship by extension) and the more theoretical discussion of to whom this right belongs.

Custody and guardianship can therefore more accurately be seen as a matrix of rights and responsibilities consisting of (1) the right of the ward; (2) the right of the custodian; (3) the right of the guardian. The emphasis on one side shifts not only depending on the specifics of the situation at hand but also with regard to the individual jurist, social context, school affiliation, hermeneutic methodology, and the restrictions

[11] Al-Zarqānī, *Sharḥ Al-Zarqānī ʿalā Mukhtaṣar Sayyidī Khalīl Wa-Maʿahu Al-Fatḥ Al-Rabbānī Fīmā Dhahala ʿanhu Al-Zarqānī*, 4:486; al-Wansharīsī, *Al-Manhaj Al-Fāʾiq Wa'l-Manhal Al-Rāʾiq Wa'l-Maʿnā Al-Lāʾiq Bi-Ādāb Al-Muwaththiq Wa-Aḥkām Al-Wathāʾiq*, 2:604–606.

[12] ʿAlāʾ al-Dīn Abū al-Ḥasan ʿAlī b. Sulaymān al-Mardāwī, *Al-Inṣāf Fī Maʿrifat Al-Rājiḥ Min Al-Khilāf*, ed. Rāʾid b. Ṣabrī Ibn Abī ʿAlfa (Beirut: Bayt al-Afkār al-Dawliyya, 2004), 2:1647; Muḥammad b. Maḥmūd b. al-Ḥusayn Astarūshinī, *Aḥkām Al-Ṣighār*, ed. Muṣṭafā Ṣumayda (Beirut: Dār al-Kutub al-ʿIlmiyya, 1997), 103; al-Miṣrī, al-Nasafī, and Ibn ʿĀbidīn, *Al-Baḥr Al-Rāʾiq Sharḥ Kanz Al-Daqāʾiq Wa-Maʿahu Al-Ḥawāshī Al-Musammāh Minḥat Al-Khāliq ʿalā Al-Baḥr Al-Rāʾiq*, 4:280, 342. According to the majority of Sunni jurists, in the absence of a threat to the child's well-being, the judge is not permitted to force the parents to assume custody. One can speculate that jurists must have assumed that forcing an unwilling relative to assume custody if there was no desire to do so would not serve the interests of the child and that a better caregiver would be one who voluntarily wished to take care of the child. There is no discussion in the primary sources of the psychological effects of the judge coercing a relative to take care of the child.

[13] On the juristic shift from legal methodology to positive law or law-as-process to law-as-content, see further Ibrahim, "The Codification Episteme."

of the available textual sources. The view that custody was a right of the child, however, lent itself more readily to privileging the child's best interests (in a broad sense, such as who can provide the best care), as opposed to focusing only on basic interests (avoiding serious harm) in times of conflict with the rights of the custodian. The Mālikī Ibn ʿAbd al-Barr (d. 463/1071) was fully aware that privileging the welfare of children in times of conflict implies that custody is a right of the child, rather than the custodian. According to him, this was also the view of Mālik and some of his disciples. This explains, as Ibn ʿAbd al-Barr reasoned, their position that a sinner cannot be a custodian, since that would pose harm to the child.[14] Similarly, the Ḥanbalī Ibn Qudāma al-Maqdisī (d. 620/1223) argued that the reason Ḥanbalī jurists granted the choice among the two parents to boys once they attain the age of seven was due to the assumption that decisions about priority of custodianship were based on the "right of the child" (*li-ḥaqq al-walad*), and, therefore, priority should be given to the custodian who is more kind (*ashfaq*) to the child.[15] Ibn Qudāma's comments suggest that the child's welfare was defined broadly, in a way similar to the best interests standard. Similarly, Ibn Nujaym al-Miṣrī (d. 970/1563) argued that custody was a right of the child and that the reason women were preferred during the tender years over men was due to their kindness.[16]

The main function of this discussion of whether custody is a right of the custodian or of the ward is its bearing on the threshold at which certain dangers to the interests of the child are deemed sufficient for the transfer of custody from the presumptive custodian. All jurists, whether they considered custody to be a right of the child or of the custodian, would agree that custody is designed for the welfare of the child and therefore they would not permit custody arrangements to lead to the destruction of the ward or his religion (*halākih wa-halāki dīnih*).[17] They considered the avoidance of gross physical and moral abuse, rather than the accrual of benefit to the child, to be the minimalist approach to defining these interests.

In theory, jurists who considered custody to be a right of the custodian were less likely to make rules forfeiting the custodian's right unless

[14] Ibn ʿAbd al-Barr, *Al-Kāfī Fī Fiqh Ahl Al-Madīna Al-Mālikī*, 296.
[15] Ibn Qudāma al-Maqdisī, *Al-Mughnī*, 2:2008.
[16] Al-Miṣrī, al-Nasafī, and Ibn ʿĀbidīn, *Al-Baḥr Al-Rāʾiq Sharḥ Kanz Al-Daqāʾiq Wa-Maʿahu Al-Ḥawāshī Al-Musammāh Minḥat Al-Khāliq ʿalā Al-Baḥr Al-Rāʾiq*, 4:280. Ibn ʿĀbidīn's commentary is published along with al-Nasafī's *Kanz al-Daqāʾiq* and Ibn Nujaym's *al-Baḥr al-Rāʾiq*.
[17] Ibn Qudāma al-Maqdisī, *Al-Mughnī*, 2:2007–2008.

a serious moral or physical damage was likely to affect the child were he or she to be cared for by the given custodian (basic interests). In other words, they defined the interests discourse narrowly and negatively, that is, based on the danger of harm. Jurists who considered custody as a right of the child were more likely to define "interests" more broadly, leading to decisions such as denying custody to someone who may not provide the best custody, albeit without posing serious physical or moral harm to the child. Ibn ʿAbd al-Barr, for instance, supported this view, attributed to Mālik and a group of his companions, explaining that a custodian who could not provide the requisite safety (*maʾmūn*) would forfeit her or his right to custody.[18] This is not necessarily a reference to a life-threatening situation, but simply a matter of who can better take care of the child and teach her or him "good deeds" (*al-khayr*). Ibn ʿAbd al-Barr's approach privileges the child's best interests, broadly defined, over the rights of a particular custodian, based on age or gender configurations for instance. The threshold for changing custody based on the safety of the child in this case is much lower than the "gross abuse" threshold established by other jurists.[19]

To sum up, the difference between jurists who considered child custody to be a right of the child and those who considered it a right of the custodian was one of emphasis. Although all jurists agreed that the child's interests are the ultimate objective of the law, the debate over custody as a right of one side over the other informed the establishment of the threshold of what constitutes those interests. Nevertheless, jurists accepted that some of the dominant rules of their schools relied on the right belonging both to the parent and the child.

Sunni jurists agreed over a number of requirements that all custodians and guardians must possess in order to qualify to care for a child: custody and guardianship cannot be given, for instance, to someone who is mentally ill. Attaining the age of majority (*bulūgh*) is another precondition for someone to assume custody and guardianship, as well as the ability to perform the necessary functions of custody, which means that the custodian cannot be too old or too sick to take care of the child. This condition excludes people with different types of disabilities.[20] These widely

[18] Ibn ʿAbd al-Barr, *Al-Kāfī Fī Fiqh Ahl Al-Madīna Al-Mālikī*, 296.

[19] Ibn ʿAbd al-Barr, 296.

[20] The question of the mother's job constituting a hurdle to custody has arisen in the modern period. Some jurists argued that a full-time job is incompatible with the requirements of maintaining a healthy child and, therefore, full-time workers should be disqualified from custody. In modern Egypt, it was the practice in Egyptian courts that mothers who worked full

accepted rules were explained by jurists as guarantees for the upkeep and care of children. There are other areas over which Sunni jurists have disagreements, which are caused, at least partly, by different approaches to the threshold for what constitutes harm to the child's best interests.

It is important to caution, before our discussion of custody rules, that there are many disagreements, not only among the four Sunni schools, but also within each school about the order of custodial priority and other aspects of custody. The dominant positions of the various schools changed over time under the influence of evolving social values. There are also situations in which there is either no agreement within a given school over what constitutes the dominant doctrine or in which there are geographical variations. With these caveats in mind, this discussion represents dominant trends in the four Sunni schools over a long period of time, and opinions should not be considered immutable, especially in actual court practice, where judges, due to disagreements and their own assessments of the child's best interests, accepted custody arrangements were contradictory to a simple reading of the normative legal juristic discourse. In what follows, I discuss the eight main themes of age and gender, the mother's marital status, the custodian's lifestyle, the custodian's religion, visitation rights, relocation of the custodian with the ward, child maintenance, and guardianship.

JURISTIC DISCOURSE ON CHILD CUSTODY AND GUARDIANSHIP

The postclassical (after the thirteenth century AD/seventh century AH) juristic discourse on child custody was based on reports and practices that can be found in the jurisprudence of the formative period of Islamic law. An examination of early legal texts such as Mālik's *Muwaṭṭa'*, al-Shaybānī's *Aṣl*, and al-Shāfiʿī's *al-Umm*, shows that the reports about women's rights to child custody during the tender age, their forfeiture of custody through marriage, the ineligibility of non-Muslims or people with bad morals, and the restrictions on the guardian's travel with the ward resemble postclassical formulations of custody. It is clear therefore that most of the laws of custody developed quite early on. This is not surprising given the centrality of custody laws to the cultivation of Muslim identity amid largely

time as teachers and doctors were still able to assume custody of their children, as long as the mother arranged for caregivers, whether they were relatives or paid help. The same approach was followed in Syrian legislation. On this discussion, see further Wahba al-Zuḥaylī, *al-Fiqh al-Islāmī wa-Adillatuhu*, 2nd edn. (Damascus: Dār al-Fikr, 1985), 7:726.

non-Muslim demographics, whether in Umayyad Syria or Abbasid Baghdad and Cairo. The tenacity of early practices suggests that the laws of custody were perhaps ultimately influenced by pre-Islamic customary laws, but this does not exclude the possibility that some of the practices of child custody may have originated in the new religion.[21]

As I mentioned in the Introduction, the child welfare discourse may be located in two ways. The first is through explicit references to who has the right of custody, as discussed previously. In what follows, I discuss the second approach, that is, examining the justifications of different rules of custody to gauge whether they were based on the welfare of the child or other considerations. Most of the rules of child custody, such as those relating to age and gender, were justified on welfare grounds, but these principles were often assumed to be stable and ahistorical, categorical in their scope and immutable in their permanence.[22] In the age of *taqlīd*, these were presumptive rules that could not be overruled by judges, according to the majority of jurists, except in limited cases of serious harm or gross abuse.

Age and Gender

The Sunni approach to the early years of the child's life somewhat evokes the tender years doctrine of nineteenth-century England.[23] During this early period, whose duration varies among jurists and so is represented generically here as the "tender years," custody devolves on the mother or maternal female relatives, and may devolve on the father or other male relatives only in limited circumstances such as in default or unwillingness of a long list of female relatives to assume custody. The basic logic that unifies the four Sunni schools is that children need their mother or other female relatives (usually on the mother's side) in their tender years, but once they reach a certain age, they need their father or a close male relative in his absence, and are no longer in need of their female relatives.[24] Most

[21] Muḥammad b. al-Ḥasan al-Shaybānī, *Al-Aṣl*, ed. Mehmet Boynukalın (Beirut: Dār Ibn Ḥazm, 2012), 4:544–549, 6:396–398, 10:348–354; al-Shāfiʿ ī, *Al-Umm*, 6:238–342.

[22] If the child, who has reached the age of discernment (*tamyīz*), gets sick, the mother has the right (*aḥaqq*) to take the child to her house for treatment, the justification being that sickness renders the child a minor (*ṣaghīr*) because he or she becomes weak like a child of tender age. Ibn Qudāma al-Maqdisī, *Al-Mughnī*, 2:2009.

[23] See further John Wroath, *Until They Are Seven: The Origins of Women's Legal Rights* (Winchester: Waterside Press, 2006), 61–118.

[24] Al-Miṣrī, al-Nasafī, and Ibn ʿĀbidīn, *Al-Baḥr Al-Rāʾiq Sharḥ Kanz Al-Daqāʾiq Wa-Maʿahu Al-Ḥawāshī Al-Musammāh Minḥat Al-Khāliq ʿalā Al-Baḥr Al-Rāʾiq*, 4:280–284; al-Shirbīnī, *Mughnī Al-Muḥtāj Ilā Maʿrifat Maʿānī Alfāẓ Al-Minhāj*, 3:592; Shams al-Dīn Muḥammad

jurists assumed that there is an essential difference between the genders,[25] and that children in the tender years are weak and in need of female care. The mother, the logic goes, has more mercy (*shafaqa*) toward her children. Premodern Muslim jurists attributed their privileging of females in the early years of the child's life to some essential qualities, such as tenderness, patience, and kindness, which they assumed enabled women to provide better care for children in their most vulnerable years.

The logic underlying the rules for who should be given priority of custody during the child's tender years was based on three general principles: (1) women take priority over men; (2) closer relatives take priority over more distant relatives; and (3) the mother's side of relatives often takes precedence over the father's side (especially in the Ḥanafī and Mālikī schools). Jurists permitted male custodians such as the father to assume custody only after a number of female relatives forwent their right to custody or were deemed unfit. Even when custody was assumed by the father (or a male relative in his absence) during the tender years, there was an underlying assumption among jurists that a member of the father's family such as his wife, mother, sister, or someone he hired such as a domestic would care for the child.

The Ḥanafīs and Mālikīs converge on many points of law, forming a cluster of rules, while the Shāfiʿīs and Ḥanbalīs form an opposing cluster. Neither the Ḥanafīs nor the Mālikīs permitted the child to choose a parent at the end of the tender years.[26] The Ḥanafīs argued that children do not know what is best for them (*lā yaʿrifu ḥaẓẓahu*) at the end of their tender years. Their decisions, they reasoned, would most likely be motivated by frivolity and would end up harming them. Ḥanafī and Mālikī jurists disagreed over the age at which the tender years end, and since it was they who determined the ages at which children's needs change, their decisions limited both the choices of children and the discretion of judges in the determination of the child's welfare. The Mālikīs assumed that boys were in need of their mothers (or female relatives) until puberty and girls until marriage. Ibn Taymiyya explained that Mālik's position entails that the mother has custody of the girl beyond her attainment of physical maturity.

Ibn Mufliḥ al-Maqdisī, *Kitāb Al-Furūʿ*, ed. ʿAbd Allāh b. ʿAbd al-Muḥsin Turkī (Riyadh: Muʾassassat al-Risāla, 2003), 9:336–347.

[25] See further, Ibn Qayyim al-Jawziyya, *Zād Al-Maʿād Fī Hudā Khayr Al-ʿIbād*, 5:392–393.

[26] The point about the similarities between the Ḥanafī and Mālikī schools on the one hand and the Shāfiʿī and Ḥanbalī schools on the other was also observed by Yvon Linant De Bellefonds, "Ḥaḍāna," ed. P. Bearman et al., *EI2* (Leiden: Brill, 2005); Bahrām al-Damīrī, *Al-Shāmil Fī Fiqh Al-Imām Mālik*, ed. Aḥmad b. ʿAbd al-Karīm Najīb (Cairo: Markaz Najībwayh li'l-Makhṭūṭāt wa-Khidmat al-Turāth, 2008), 2:506–507.

An adult woman, according to Mālik, stays with the mother even if she is 40 years old.[27]

According to the Ḥanafīs, though, the boy no longer needs the care of his mother at seven years of age, at which point he is transferred to the male agnatic line (*ʿaṣaba*). Early Ḥanafī jurists held that if the custodian is the mother or grandmother, a girl may stay with either of them until she reaches physical maturity, which is marked by menstruation or pregnancy, but if the custodian is another female relative, then custody ends at seven years just like a boy, or at the age of carnal awareness (*ḥadd al-shahwa*), estimated at nine years, according to other Ḥanafī jurists such as Abū Ḥanīfa's disciple Muḥammad al-Shaybānī.[28] Reducing the age from physical maturity (*bulūgh*) to carnal awareness was meant to guarantee the girl's moral uprightness,[29] since it was assumed that patrilineal relatives

[27] Ibn ʿAbd al-Barr, *Al-Kāfī Fī Fiqh Ahl Al-Madīna Al-Mālikī*, 297; al-Damīrī, *Al-Shāmil Fī Fiqh Al-Imām Mālik*, 2:506–507; al-Wansharīsī, *Al-Manhaj Al-Fāʾiq Wa'l-Manhal Al-Rāʾiq Wa'l-Maʿnā Al-Lāʾiq Bi-Ādāb Al-Muwaththiq Wa-Aḥkām Al-Wathāʾiq*, 2:558; Taqī al-Dīn Ibn Taymiyya, *Majmūʿ Fatāwā Shaykh Al-Islām Aḥmad Ibn Taymiyya*, ed. ʿAbd al-Raḥmān b. Muḥammad Ibn Qāsim and Muḥammad b. ʿAbd al-Raḥmān b. Muḥammad Ibn Qāsim (Riyadh: Wizārat al-Shuʾūn al-Islāmiyya wa'l-Awqāf wa'l-Daʿwa wa'l-Irshād, 2004), 34:115; Yvon Linant de Bellefonds, *Traité de Droit Musulman Comparé* (Paris, LaHaye: Mouton et Cie, 1965).

[28] This position attributed to al-Shaybānī does not appear in *al-Aṣl*. It is only attributed to him in the *nawādir*, which are the views attributed to the early authorities of the Ḥanafī school, especially Abū Ḥanīfa, Abū Yūsuf, al-Shaybānī, Zufar b. al-Hudhayl, and al-Ḥasan b. Ziyād in secondary books of jurisprudence that were often written by later Ḥanafī jurists. It is perhaps safe to assume that this development in Ḥanafī law came after the generation of Abū Ḥanīfa's disciples. On the different levels of juristic authority in the Ḥanafī school, see further the introduction to the excellent recently published edition of *al-Aṣl*, al-Shaybānī, *Al-Aṣl*, 1:38–40; Shams al-Dīn al-Sarakhsī *Al-Mabsūṭ* (Beirut: Dār al-Maʿrifa, 1993), 5:207–208; al-Shaybānī, *Al-Aṣl*, 10:348–354; al-Kāsānī, *Badāʾiʿ Al-Ṣanāʾiʿ Fī Tartīb Al-Sharāʾiʿ*, 5:202–222; Sarakhsī Ibn ʿĀbidīn and al-Ḥaṣkafī, *Radd Al-Muḥtār ʿalā Al-Durr Al-Mukhtār Sharḥ Tanwīr Al-Abṣār*, 5:267–268; Niẓām al-Dīn Balkhī, *Al-Fatāwā Al-Hindiyya*, 2nd edn. (Cairo: Al-Maṭbaʿa al-Kubrā al-Amīriyya, 1893), 1:541–543; al-Miṣrī, al-Nasafī, and Ibn ʿĀbidīn, *Al-Baḥr Al-Rāʾiq Sharḥ Kanz Al-Daqāʾiq Wa-Maʿahu Al-Ḥawāshī Al-Musammāh Minḥat Al-Khāliq ʿalā Al-Baḥr Al-Rāʾiq*, 4: 283–293.

[29] The Sunni schools agreed that majority (*bulūgh*) is determined when specific physical changes occur in children. For girls, it is menstruation or pregnancy; for boys it is having wet dreams or causing pregnancy. What the Sunni schools disagreed on is, in the absence of these physical signs, which are often hard to determine, what are the ages at which boys and girls can be presumptively determined to have reached majority? In the absence of physical signs, the presumptive age of majority was presumed to be 15 for the Ḥanafīs, Shafiʿīs, and Ḥanbalīs, and 18 years according to the Mālikīs. According to Abū Yūsuf and Muḥammad al-Shaybānī, both girls and boys reach puberty at 15 years if no signs exist. These different possibilities and permutations, must have allowed judges a level of discretion that shifted according to the values of their societies. For more on majority, see Astarūshinī, *Aḥkām Al-Ṣighār*, 101; Giladi, "Ṣaghīr," *Encyclopaedia of Islam* (Leiden:

were more invested in the girl's sexual chastity and, therefore, more likely to better protect it.[30] By the Ottoman period, according to one of the most important works of Ottoman Ḥanafism, *Multaqā al-Abḥur* of Ibrāhīm al-Ḥalabī (d. 956/1549), the "preferred opinion" (*fatwā*) within the school in his time was to follow the lower age of nine due to the "corruption of the time" (*fasād al-zamān*). During the time of Dāmād Afandī (d. 1078/1667) and al-Ḥaṣkafī (d. 1088/1677), the dominant doctrine continued to be that of al-Shaybānī.[31]

Al-Ḥaṣkafī added that once a boy had reached puberty, he could choose whether to live with his mother, with his father, or on his own. A prepubescent boy who had reached the age of discernment (*ghulām*) could also live on his own. His father, al-Ḥaṣkafī reasoned, had no right to force a boy into his custody unless the child was not to be trusted with his own safety and chastity (*lam yakun ma'mūnan 'alā nafsih*). The father would have no obligation toward such an independent child. Ibn 'Ābidīn (d. 1252/1836) understood al-Ḥaṣkafī's use of *ghulām* as referring to a pubescent boy. By Ibn 'Ābidīn's time, it was perhaps not likely or acceptable for a prepubescent boy to live on his own, a possibility that had seemed imaginable centuries earlier. A postpubescent girl, however, had to live with the father if she was a virgin, unless she had grown older (*dakhalat fī al-sinn*), in which case she could choose where to live as long as there was no fear about her safety and chastity. If she was not a virgin, then the guardian had no right to force her to live with him unless he did not trust that she could maintain her own safety and chastity.[32]

Neither Ḥanafī nor Mālikī jurists gave male relatives the right of custody unless a long list of female relatives either gave up their rights or were disqualified. In the Ḥanafī school, the mother was followed by her maternal female ascendants, paternal female ascendants, sisters of the child, the sisters' daughters, and the child's aunts. All of these relatives had priority

Brill, 2013); P. Bearman et al., eds., "Bāligh," *Encyclopaedia of Islam* (Leiden: Brill, 2013); al-Sarakhsī, *Al-Mabsūṭ*, 5:208.

30 Ibn 'Ābidīn and al-Ḥaṣkafī, *Radd Al-Muḥtār 'alā Al-Durr Al-Mukhtār Sharḥ Tanwīr Al-Abṣār*, 5:267–268; Ibn Qayyim al-Jawziyya, *Zād Al-Ma'ād Fī Hudā Khayr Al-'Ibād*, 5:423–424.

31 Al-Ḥaṣkafī and al-Timurtāshī, *Al-Durr Al-Mukhtār Sharḥ Tanwīr Al-Abṣār Wa-Jāmi' Al-Biḥār*, 256; al-Ḥalabī, Dāmād Afandī, and al-Ḥaṣkafī, *Multaqā Al-Abḥur; Majma' Al-Anhur: Al-Durr Al-Muntaqā Fī Sharḥ Al-Multaqā*, 2:169; Balkhī, *Al-Fatāwā Al-Hindiyya*, 1:541–543; Yvon Linant de Bellefonds, *Traité de Droit Musulman Comparé*.

32 Ibn 'Ābidīn and al-Ḥaṣkafī, *Radd Al-Muḥtār 'alā Al-Durr Al-Mukhtār Sharḥ Tanwīr Al-Abṣār*, 5:270–271.

over the father and other male relatives. There were, however, disagreements over certain relatives on the list. The Ḥanafīs, for example, disagreed over whether the child's full sister has priority over the father's mother. Disagreements aside, female relatives on the mother's side were given priority over female relatives on the father's side, and female relatives were prioritized over male relatives during the tender years. In the Mālikī school, the mother comes first, followed by her ascendants, sisters of the child, and the child's aunts. In default or unwillingness of all relatives on this list, care of the child is entrusted to the father's mother, followed by her ascendants.[33] After the list of female relatives is exhausted, custody in the tender years shifts to men. At the top of this secondary Mālikī list comes the father, followed by his ascendants, the child's brothers, nephews, uncles, and so on.[34] Once the tender years end, triggering a transfer of custody to males, male agnates assume custody, with the child's father taking priority, followed by his ascendants, the child's brothers, nephews, uncles, and so on.[35]

In default of female relatives or when the child reaches the so-called age of male custody, jurists were careful not to grant custody to an agnatic relative of the opposite sex who was not a *maḥram* by blood (as opposed to *maḥram* by marriage), that is, they would not assign custody to a male relative who was not within the "prohibited degrees of marriage." In fact, most jurists did not allow a male cousin to take custody of a female child who had reached the age of carnal awareness, since there is no obstacle to the marriage of full cousins in Islamic law.[36] If the child had only male cousin relatives, however, some jurists made the decision a prerogative of

33 Ibn ʿĀbidīn and al-Ḥaṣkafī, Radd al-Muḥtār ʿalā Al-Durr Al-Mukhtār Sharḥ Tanwīr Al-Abṣār, 5:262–266; al-Zuḥaylī, *Al-Fiqh Al-Islāmī Wa-Adillatuhu*, 7:728; al-Miṣrī, al-Nasafī, and Ibn ʿĀbidīn, *Al-Baḥr Al-Rāʾiq Sharḥ Kanz Al-Daqāʾiq Wa-Maʿahu Al-Ḥawāshī Al-Musammāh Minḥat Al-Khāliq ʿalā Al-Baḥr Al-Rāʾiq*, 4:283–293.

34 Al-Sarakhsī, *Al-Mabsūṭ*, 5:210–213; al-Zarqānī, *Sharḥ Al-Zarqānī ʿalā Mukhtaṣar Sayyidī Khalīl Wa-Maʿahu Al-Fatḥ Al-Rabbānī Fīmā Dhahala ʿanhu Al-Zarqānī*, 4:473–474; Radd al-Muḥtār ʿalā Al-Durr Al-Mukhtār Sharḥ Tanwīr Al-Abṣār, al-Nasafī, and Ibn ʿĀbidīn, *Al-Baḥr Al-Rāʾiq Sharḥ Kanz Al-Daqāʾiq Wa-Maʿahu Al-Ḥawāshī Al-Musammāh Minḥat Al-Khāliq ʿalā Al-Baḥr Al-Rāʾiq*, 4:183–184.

35 Al-Zarqānī, *Sharḥ Al-Zarqānī ʿalā Mukhtaṣar Sayyidī Khalīl Wa-Maʿahu Al-Fatḥ Al-Rabbānī Fīmā Dhahala ʿanhu Al-Zarqānī*, 4:473–474; al-Miṣrī, al-Nasafī, and Ibn ʿĀbidīn, *Al-Baḥr Al-Rāʾiq Sharḥ Kanz Al-Daqāʾiq Wa-Maʿahu Al-Ḥawāshī Al-Musammāh Minḥat Al-Khāliq ʿalā Al-Baḥr Al-Rāʾiq*, 4:183–184.

36 See al-Dardīr and al-Ṣāwī, *Al-Sharḥ Al-Ṣaghīr ʿalā Aqrab Al-Masālik Ilā Madhhab Al-Imām Mālik*, 2:759; Shams al-Dīn Muḥammad b. ʿArafa al-Dasūqī, *Ḥāshiyat Al-Dasūqī ʿalā Al-Sharḥ Al-Kabīr* (Cairo: Dār Iḥyāʾ al-Kutub al-ʿArabiyya, 1984), 2:528; al-Miṣrī, al-Nasafī, and Ibn ʿĀbidīn, *Al-Baḥr Al-Rāʾiq Sharḥ Kanz Al-Daqāʾiq Wa-Maʿahu Al-Ḥawāshī Al-Musammāh Minḥat Al-Khāliq ʿalā Al-Baḥr Al-Rāʾiq*, 4:183–184; Ibn ʿĀbidīn and al-Ḥaṣkafī,

the judge, who could elect to place her with an unrelated female or with the cousin.[37] In default of any relatives, jurists required that the judge find a Muslim custodian on the public purse.[38]

Both the Shāfiʿī and Ḥanbalī schools granted women custody in the tender years. Unlike the Mālikīs and Ḥanafīs, the Shāfiʿīs allowed both boys and girls to choose a custodian once they reached the age of discernment (often estimated at seven or eight years old).[39] The Shāfiʿīs did not give the judge much discretion even when the child made no choice between the parents; in this case, the judge would draw lots.[40] The Ḥanbalīs allowed the boy, once he reached the age of seven, to choose a parent or, in their default, whoever would replace them. Granting the choice to children was framed in the child welfare discourse, though, and Shāfiʿī and Ḥanbalī jurists were sure to emphasize that if the judge sensed that the children's choices were not based on a genuine preference, he had the prerogative to ignore their wishes to avoid harmful choices (*iḍāʿat al-walad*). According to the Ḥanbalī school, a boy could change his mind any number of times, as often as he changes his mind about food and beverages.[41] As for girls, the Ḥanbalīs insisted that they must be transferred to the father (or male line) once they reached the age of seven (or nine according to some Ḥanbalīs) because male agnates were more capable of protecting a girl's honor and chastity. After all, as Ibn Qudāma al-Maqdisī argued, the whole point of custody is to protect the child. In the case of girls, this protection, he explained, could only be guaranteed by the father or another male.[42]

The Ḥanbalī distinction between boys and girls in which only boys were allowed to choose their custodian amounts to considering only the boy's

Radd Al-Muḥtār ʿalā Al-Durr Al-Mukhtār Sharḥ Tanwīr Al-Abṣār, 2:265. The commentary of al-Ṣāwī is printed below the text of al-Dardīr.

37 See further, Astarūshinī, *Aḥkām Al-Ṣighār*, 101.

38 Ibn Qudāma al-Maqdisī, *Al-Mughnī*, 2:2008.

39 Abū Ḥasan ʿAlī al-Māwardī, *Al-Ḥāwī Al-Kabīr*, ed. Maḥmūd Maṭrajī, et al. (Beirut: Dār al-Fikr, 1994), 15:100–101.

40 Al-Shirwānī, al-ʿIbādī, and al-Haytamī, *Ḥawāshī Tuḥfat Al-Muḥtāj Bi-Sharḥ Al-Minhāj*, 8:363.

41 Ibn Qudāma al-Maqdisī, *Al-Mughnī*, 2:2008; Ibn Mufliḥ al-Maqdisī, *Kitāb Al-Furūʿ*, 9: 336–347.

42 There was a debate in the Ḥanbalī school over whether the maternal sisters and aunts were to be privileged over their paternal counterparts. Some important jurists, including the illustrious Ibn Qudāma (d. 620/1223), Ibn Taymiyya (d. 728/1328), and al-Mardāwī (d. 885/1480), supported prioritizing some females on the paternal side. See al-Mardāwī, *Al-Inṣāf Fī Maʿrifat Al-Rājiḥ Min Al-Khilāf*, 2:1647; Muwaffaq al-Dīn Ibn Qudāma al-Maqdisī, *ʿUmdat Al-Fiqh Fiʾl-Madhhab Al-Ḥanbalī*, ed. Aḥmad Muḥammad ʿAzzūz (Beirut: Al-Maktaba al-ʿAṣriyya, 2003), 112; Ibn Qudāma al-Maqdisī, *Al-Mughnī*, 2:2008; al-Jawziyya, *Zād Al-Maʿād Fī Hudā Khayr Al-ʿIbād*, 5:417.

best interests to be contextual. Conversely, a girl's best interests were immutable, frozen in established configurations of age-transfer rules made by author-jurists, with no choice granted to the child and little discretion to the judge. In the case of a boy, there are two potential levels of decisionmaking in the courtroom, the first being the child's and the second the judge's power to overrule the child's decision if he was convinced that it was harmful to the child. In the case of a girl, the norm would be a transfer of custody once requested, as long as there was no serious risk posed to the moral and physical well-being of the child by the new custodian's residence and lifestyle.

Both the Shāfiʿī and Ḥanbalī schools placed the father higher than the Ḥanafī and Mālikī schools on the list of custodians in the tender years. In the Shāfiʿī school, the father is preceded only by the mother and her female ascendants, and is *followed* by his mother and her female ascendants. In default of these four categories (mother, her female ascendants, father, his female ascendants), the Shāfiʿīs determined custody based on the gender and proximity of relatives to the child, with women and closer relatives getting priority over men and more distant relatives.[43] In the Ḥanbalī school, the father is similarly preceded only by the mother and her ascendants and is followed by his mother and her female ascendants.[44] Despite the dominance of this order among the Ḥanbalīs, Aḥmad b. Ḥanbal (d. 241/855) was reported to have held a position allowing the father to take custody of the child immediately after the mother and before the maternal grandmother during the tender years.[45] Another position attributed to Ibn Ḥanbal is that he placed the father's mother right after the mother and ahead of the mother's mother, which also means the transfer of custody directly from the mother's side to the father's side. Presumably, when the father receives custody, as already noted, the children would be raised by the female relatives in the family, as indicated by the discourse of jurists and the prevailing values of Muslim societies at the time of Ibn Ḥanbal and Ibn

[43] See further, al-Shirbīnī, *Mughnī Al-Muḥtāj Ilā Maʿrifat Maʿānī Alfāẓ Al-Minhāj*, 3: 592–595.

[44] There was a debate within the Ḥanbalī school over whether the maternal sisters and aunts were to be privileged over their paternal counterparts. Some important jurists, including the illustrious Ibn Taymiyya, Ibn Qudāma (d. 620/1223) and al-Mardāwī, supported prioritizing some females on the paternal side. Al-Mardāwī, *Al-Inṣāf Fī Maʿrifat Al-Rājiḥ Min Al-Khilāf*, 2:1647; Ibn Qudāma al-Maqdisī, *ʿUmdat Al-Fiqh Fiʾl-Madhhab Al-Ḥanbalī*, 112; Ibn Mufliḥ al-Maqdisī, *Kitāb Al-Furūʿ*, 9:336–347.

[45] Zahraa and Malek, "The Concept of Custody in Islamic Law," 161; Ibn Qudāma al-Maqdisī, *Al-Mughnī*, 2011.

Qudāma.[46] Ibn Ḥanbal's was reported by al-Mardāwī (d. 885/1480) as a minority position,[47] the dominant view being that the mother's mother takes priority over the father and his mother.[48]

Remarriage of the Mother or Marriage of Female Relatives

According to the dominant positions of the four Sunni schools, remarriage of the mother to a "stranger" (*ajnabī*), a man who is not a close relative of the child, forfeits her right to custody even when the child is within the tender years. Jurists framed this position in the language of the welfare of the child, since it was assumed that there was an essentially hostile relationship between the new husband and the children of the first marriage. Another explanation was that the new marriage creates a conflict of responsibilities between the new household and the needs of previous children. These reasons combined led jurists to conclude that it is in the interests of children to be with a female relative other than the mother.[49]

The dominant position in the Mālikī, Shāfiʿī, and Ḥanbalī schools is that marriage to an agnatic relative of the child, even if a non-*ma ḥram* such as a cousin, does not disqualify the female custodian. It is also a position of the Mālikīs that the female custodian's marriage to a non-agnatic relative, such as a maternal uncle, does not disqualify his custodial new wife. The Shāfiʿīs and Ḥanbalīs set some conditions, such as the requirement that the husband be a close enough relative that he himself would be on the school's list of custodians. The Shāfiʿīs also made it a condition that the new husband consent to this custody arrangement. Ḥanafī jurists, on the other hand, maintain the disqualification of the remarried female custodian, even if her new spouse is a relative but not a *maḥram* to the child. Therefore, when the female custodian marries a cousin of the child, she is still

[46] Ibn Qudāma al-Maqdisī, *Al-Mughnī*, 2:2010.

[47] See al-Mardāwī, *Al-Inṣāf Fī Maʿrifat Al-Rājiḥ Min Al-Khilāf*, 2:1647.

[48] Incidentally, this minority position is the dominant position in the Shīʿī Jaʿfarī school, where the father follows the mother as a custodian. Abū al-Qāsim Najm al-Dīn Jaʿfar b. al-Ḥusayn al-Muḥaqqiq al-Ḥillī, *Sharāʾiʿ Al-Islām Fī Masāʾil Al-Ḥalāl Wa'l-Ḥarām*, ed. Āyat Allāh al-Sayyid Ṣādiq al-Shīrāzī, 10th edn. (Beirut: Markaz al-Rasūl al-Aʿẓam li'l-Taḥqīq wa'l-Nashr, 1998), 1:584.

[49] Al-Sarakhsī, *Al-Mabsūṭ*, 5:210; al-Shirbīnī, *Mughnī Al-Muḥtāj Ilā Maʿrifat Maʿānī Alfāẓ Al-Minhāj*, 3:596; al-Miṣrī, al-Nasafī, and Ibn ʿĀbidīn, *Al-Baḥr Al-Rāʾiq Sharḥ Kanz Al-Daqāʾiq Wa-Maʿahu Al-Ḥawāshī Al-Musammāh Minḥat Al-Khāliq ʿalā Al-Baḥr Al-Rāʾiq*, 4:285.

disqualified from custody despite the relationship between the child and the female custodian's new husband.[50]

In line with the position that custody is a right of the custodian, most Mālikī jurists allowed a female custodian to retain custody of a child, despite remarriage to someone who is not a close relative of the child, if the child's biological father does not sue for custody for a year or longer from the time of being informed of his former wife's remarriage.[51] The implication behind this position is that the father's lack of judicial recourse is an implicit consent to give away his *right* to custody. Had custody been a right of the child, the father would not have been able to practically waive it with his lack of action. Another underlying assumption that can be deduced from this rule is that it is treated as a default, rather than a mandatory rule, since its application was left to the discretion of the parties (more on this in the next section). Mālikī jurists mention another situation in which marriage to a non-relative does not disqualify the female custodian, namely when the child refuses to "accept" custodians other than the remarried female custodian. In this scenario, the custodian maintains custody on grounds of necessity (*ḍarūra*). What is the nature of this sort of refusal on the part of the child? Is it a life-threatening situation in which the child refuses to nurse and so removal of the mother's custody may lead to damage to the child's health (basic interests approach)? Some jurists restricted this dispensation to an unweaned child, assuming that the necessity could only be obtained in this case because the infant's refusal to nurse could pose a serious health risk. For other jurists, however, no such age limit was required, suggesting that the child's refusal to accept another custodian was not life-threatening but could have emotional grounds (best interests approach).[52] This is a particularly telling example in the Mālikī school, which grants women custody until a boy reaches puberty and until a girl is married. In this case, the lack of an age limit on how young the child should be for his refusal to be taken into account suggests that Mālikī jurists did not think it was strictly a matter of a life-threatening situation inspiring the child's refusal of an alternate custodian, for it is hard to

[50] Al-Astarūshinī, *Aḥkām Al-Ṣighār*, 100; al-Dardīr and al-Ṣāwī, *Al-Sharḥ Al-Ṣaghīr ʿalā Aqrab Al-Masālik Ilā Madhhab Al-Imām Mālik*, 2:760; al-Shirwānī, al-ʿIbādī, and al-Haytamī, *Ḥawāshī Tuḥfat Al-Muḥtāj Bi-Sharḥ Al-Minhāj*, 8:351–365.

[51] See al-Dardīr and al-Ṣāwī, *Al-Sharḥ Al-Ṣaghīr ʿalā Aqrab Al-Masālik Ilā Madhhab Al-Imām Mālik*, 2:764.

[52] See al-Zarqānī, *Sharḥ Al-Zarqānī ʿalā Mukhtaṣar Sayyidī Khalīl Wa-Maʿahu Al-Fatḥ Al-Rabbānī Fīmā Dhahala ʿanhu Al-Zarqānī*, 4:479–481; al-Dardīr and al-Ṣāwī, *Al-Sharḥ Al-Ṣaghīr ʿalā Aqrab Al-Masālik Ilā Madhhab Al-Imām Mālik*, 2:760; al-Dasūqī, *Ḥāshiyat Al-Dasūqī ʿalā Al-Sharḥ Al-Kabīr*, 2:529.

imagine that the life of, say a 14-year-old, was likely to be in danger due to a custody transfer.[53]

Despite the general agreement among jurists that the marriage of the female custodian is a cause of forfeiture of custody rights, there is a minority position attributed to al-Ḥasan al-Baṣrī (d. 110/728) and Ibn Ḥazm (d. 456/1064) that the mother's custody right is not forfeited by remarriage. Another challenge to the mainstream position is to be found in a view attributed to Aḥmad b. Ḥanbal that allows the mother to retain a female ward despite remarriage. This legal opinion was based on a report that there was a custody dispute over the daughter of Ḥamza b. ʿAbd al-Muṭṭalib. The Prophet's decision to grant custody to the girl's maternal aunt, after her mother's death, despite the aunt's married status, was cited in support of this position.[54] Ibn Qudāma rejected Ibn Ḥanbal's position, explaining that remarriage preoccupies the wife with responsibilities toward her husband, which makes her more like a "slave."[55] Returning to the child's interests, Ibn Qudāma reasoned that the husband's rights over the wife would make it hard for her to provide the necessary care to the child.[56] He also argued that the reason the child's maternal aunt was granted custody despite her remarriage is that the husband was the child's cousin, and he pointed to another report in which the Prophet told a woman that she had the right to custody of her child unless she remarried.[57]

Lifestyle

In premodern juristic discourse, a parent's lifestyle choices, such as whether or not he or she performs religious rituals, could have an impact on the granting or denial of custody. Women's work outside the home was rarely discussed in the context of child custody in the precolonial period; it

[53] Also when choosing between a trustworthy mother who is married, an untrustworthy relative who is not married, and a stranger appointed by the judge in the absence of any eligible relatives, some Mālikī and Ḥanbalī jurists utilizing the best-interests discourse chose the married mother, whom they deemed the best option. See al-Dardīr and al-Ṣāwī, *Al-Sharḥ Al-Ṣaghīr ʿalā Aqrab Al-Masālik Ilā Madhhab Al-Imām Mālik*, 2:761; al-Jawziyya, *Zād Al-Maʿād Fī Hudā Khayr Al-ʿIbād*, 5:413.

[54] Ibn Qudāma al-Maqdisī, *Al-Mughnī*, 2:2009–2010; al-Jawziyya, *Zād Al-Maʿād Fī Hudā Khayr Al-ʿIbād*, 5:406.

[55] Ibn Qudāma al-Maqdisī, *Al-Mughnī*, 2:2010. On comparisons between marriage and slavery, see Kecia Ali, *Marriage and Slavery in Early Islam* (Cambridge, MA: Harvard University Press, 2010).

[56] Ibn Qudāma al-Maqdisī, *Al-Mughnī*, 2:2012.

[57] Ibn Qudāma al-Maqdisī, 2:2010.

only received more attention in the nineteenth and twentieth centuries, but the availability of the mother did play into custody rulings. I have only been able to locate discussions of women's work in juristic discourses of the precolonial period as part of discussions of spousal support. Early modern Egyptian jurists such as the Shāfiʿī al-Shirbīnī (d. 977/1569–1570) also made references to an exceptional class of women known as *mukhaddara* ("kept at home"),[58] most likely a reference to secluded upper-class women. These women did not work or go to the market or the farm, because they had servants and slaves who performed these tasks.[59] In contrast to women kept at home, Ibn Nujaym al-Miṣrī, describing women's work in sixteenth-century Egypt, argued that it was common in his time (*wāqiʿa fī zamāninā*) that women who worked outside of the home full time (*muḥtarifāt*) and spent their entire day at work (*kārkhāne*) were not entitled to maintenance since they did not make themselves available to their husbands during the day.[60] He also argued that husbands could prevent their wives from working outside of the home since they were responsible for their maintenance.[61] Contrapositively, al-Shirbīnī argued that if a husband does not pay his wife her due maintenance, he has no right to prevent her from leaving the house during the day to work to support herself.[62]

One of the sentences that recurs frequently in discussions of custody is "there is no custody for a woman who leaves so frequently that the girl [or child] is lost" (*wa-lā ḥaḍāna li-man takhruj kulla waqt wa-tatruk al-bint* [or "*al-walad*"] *ḍāʾiʿa* [or "*ḍāʾiʿ*"]).[63] This sentence refers to women who frequently left their children unattended for long periods of time and were negligent in their maternal duties. Leaving the child unattended was grounds for taking away custody, suggesting that if the mother works and arranges for childcare, she does not lose custody; leaving a child to be cared for by a relative or domestic did not constitute negligence. Although

58 Al-Shirbīnī, *Mughnī Al-Muḥtāj Ilā Maʿrifat Maʿānī Alfāẓ Al-Minhāj*, 3:599.

59 On *mukhaddarāt*, see further Kenneth M. Cuno, *Modernizing Marriage: Family, Ideology, and Law in Nineteenth and Early Twentieth Century Egypt* (Syracuse: Syracuse University Press, 2015), 91; Judith E. Tucker, *Women, Family, and Gender in Islamic Law*, (Cambridge; New York, NY: Cambridge University Press, 2008), 183–195.

60 Al-Miṣrī, al-Nasafī, and Ibn ʿĀbidīn, *Al-Baḥr Al-Rāʾiq Sharḥ Kanz Al-Daqāʾiq Wa-Maʿahu Al-Ḥawāshī Al-Musammāh Minḥat Al-Khāliq ʿalā Al-Baḥr Al-Rāʾiq*, 4:305.

61 Al-Miṣrī, al-Nasafī, and Ibn ʿĀbidīn, 4:332.

62 Al-Shirbīnī, *Mughnī Al-Muḥtāj Ilā Maʿrifat Maʿānī Alfāẓ Al-Minhāj*, 3:582.

63 Al-Miṣrī, al-Nasafī, and Ibn ʿĀbidīn, *Al-Baḥr Al-Rāʾiq Sharḥ Kanz Al-Daqāʾiq Wa-Maʿahu Al-Ḥawāshī Al-Musammāh Minḥat Al-Khāliq ʿalā Al-Baḥr Al-Rāʾiq*, 4:283; Balkhī, *Al-Fatāwā Al-Hindiyya*, 1:542; al-Wansharīsī, *Al-Manhaj Al-Fāʾiq Wa'l-Manhal Al-Rāʾiq Wa'l-Maʿnā Al-Lāʾiq Bi-Ādāb Al-Muwaththiq Wa-Aḥkām Al-Wathāʾiq*, 2:605.

leaving an infant in a cradle unattended in the house was not by itself considered negligent, if a child was shown to be suffering, negligence could be proven.[64] Consider that according to al-Asyūṭī's model petitions in his fifteenth-century court manual, a father could petition for custody on the grounds that the mother is negligent in caring for the child, as she "frequently leaves him at home unattended with the door closed and the child screaming."[65] The reason for her leaving the house, whether it is to work or simply to visit her neighbors as in this case, is irrelevant. When women working as street vendors brought their children with them to the market, this did not by itself constitute negligence.

The previous sentence about women's frequent outings did not carry an inherent aversion to women's work, especially since many women of the lower classes worked outside of the home in the early modern period. This sentence obtained a new meaning, however, in the nineteenth and twentieth centuries, as we shall see in Chapters 5 and 6, where some jurists understood it to refer to women's work in itself, rather than negligence. Influenced by the colonial European domestic ideology, many nineteenth-century judges assumed, contrary to premodern juristic discourse, that the very fact of working full time constituted grounds for the denial of child custody. By the twentieth century, this presumption was no longer operative, and women were considered fit to assume custody if they were able to make childcare arrangements while working, as we shall see in Chapter 6.

In terms of other lifestyle factors, it is the predominant doctrine in all four Sunni schools that the custodian must not be of bad morals (*fāsiq*). A person who had been convicted of murder, robbery, fornication, or alcohol consumption would be disqualified from custody. The Ḥanafī school developed two views, the standard mainstream one being that a woman who is morally reproachable should not be allowed to assume custody. This is the dominant position that was followed in fatwas. Fornication, stealing, failure to perform prayers, and even professional singing, or wailing (*niyāḥa*), could disqualify a mother from custody. The standards for women's moral uprightness were extremely high, and fathers were not subjected to the same standards. The causes for disqualification were often popular practices associated with women and considered reproachable, such as singing and wailing.[66]

[64] Al-Miṣrī, al-Nasafī, and Ibn ʿĀbidīn, *Al-Baḥr Al-Rāʾiq Sharḥ Kanz Al-Daqāʾiq Wa-Maʿahu Al-Ḥawāshī Al-Musammāh Minḥat Al-Khāliq ʿalā Al-Baḥr Al-Rāʾiq*, 4:290.

[65] Al-Asyūṭī, *Jawāhir Al-ʿUqūd Wa-Muʿīn Al-Quḍāh Wa'l-Muwaqqiʿīna Wa'l-Shuhūd*, 2:192.

[66] See al-Shirwānī, al-ʿIbādī, and al-Haytamī, *Ḥawāshī Tuḥfat Al-Muḥtāj Bi-Sharḥ Al-Minhāj*, 8:351–365; al-Ḥaṣkafī and al-Timurtāshī, *Al-Durr Al-Mukhtār Sharḥ Tanwīr Al-Abṣār Wa-Jāmiʿ Al-Biḥār*, 254–255; Ibn ʿĀbidīn and al-Ḥaṣkafī, *Radd Al-Muḥtār ʿalā Al-Durr*

Another view within the Ḥanafī school was that what mattered was the mother's impact on the child. This view can be found in Ibn Nujaym al-Miṣrī's influential work *al-Baḥr al-Rā'iq*, Dāmād Afandī's *Majma' al-Anhur*, and the early nineteenth-century work of Ibn 'Ābidīn. They were not interested in punishing the mother for her behavior. Rather they were interested in making sure that the child's welfare was maintained, without allowing the child to be collateral damage in the male-dominated society's desire to discipline women through child custody. These jurists allowed mothers exhibiting signs of bad morality to assume custody. Some of them reasoned that if non-Muslims were allowed to have custody (more on this to come), a Muslim mother who did not observe the ritual prayers or fasting should not be denied custody. After all, they reasoned, nonobservance of rituals does not negatively affect the mother's ability to care for the child. Some Ḥanafīs even argued that only certain types of ill-repute should disqualify the mother, such as a sexual behavior that keeps the mother from looking after her child. Others went as far as to grant custody to an adulterous mother, as long as her adultery did not lead to neglect of the child and as long as the child was not old enough to be influenced by her behavior. According to Ibn 'Ābidīn, what matters is whether or not the child would be harmed by the mother's behavior.[67] It would follow that the person to decide whether or not the mother's behavior would harm the child is the judge. Under this model, the welfare of the child trumps author-juristic determinations, giving more power to the judge to decide what is best for a particular child in a given historical context.[68] Using that logic, these jurists even allowed the judge to take a child away from a mother who was so pious that she spent too much of her time praying to properly care for the child.[69]

Al-Mukhtār Sharḥ Tanwīr Al-Abṣār, 5:253–255; al-Zarqānī, *Sharḥ Al-Zarqānī 'alā Mukhtaṣar Sayyidī Khalīl Wa-Ma'ahu Al-Fatḥ Al-Rabbānī Fīmā Dhahala 'anhu Al-Zarqānī*, 4:475–476. The prohibition against wailing covers both professional and nonprofessional wailing.

67 Al-Ḥaṣkafī and al-Timurtāshī, *Al-Durr Al-Mukhtār Sharḥ Tanwīr Al-Abṣār Wa-Jāmi' Al-Biḥār*, 254–255; al-Miṣrī, al-Nasafī, and Ibn 'Ābidīn, *Al-Baḥr Al-Rā'iq Sharḥ Kanz Al-Daqā'iq Wa-Ma'ahu Al-Ḥawāshī Al-Musammāh Minḥat Al-Khāliq 'alā Al-Baḥr Al-Rā'iq*, 4:181–182; al-Ḥalabī, Dāmād Afandī, and al-Ḥaṣkafī, *Multaqā Al-Abḥur; Majma' Al-Anhur: Al-Durr Al-Muntaqā Fī Sharḥ Al-Multaqā*, 2:166; Ibn 'Ābidīn and al-Ḥaṣkafī, *Radd Al-Muḥtār 'alā Al-Durr Al-Mukhtār Sharḥ Tanwīr Al-Abṣār*, 5:253–255.

68 Ibn 'Ābidīn and al-Ḥaṣkafī, *Radd Al-Muḥtār 'alā Al-Durr Al-Mukhtār Sharḥ Tanwīr Al-Abṣār*, 5:253–255.

69 Al-Ḥaṣkafī and al-Timurtāshī, *Al-Durr Al-Mukhtār Sharḥ Tanwīr Al-Abṣār Wa-Jāmi' Al-Biḥār*, 254–255; al-Miṣrī, al-Nasafī, and Ibn 'Ābidīn, *Al-Baḥr Al-Rā'iq Sharḥ Kanz Al-Daqā'iq Wa-Ma'ahu Al-Ḥawāshī Al-Musammāh Minḥat Al-Khāliq 'alā Al-Baḥr Al-Rā'iq*, 4:181–182; al-Ḥalabī, Dāmād Afandī, and al-Ḥaṣkafī, *Multaqā Al-Abḥur; Majma' Al-Anhur: Al-Durr Al-*

Similarly, Ibn Qayyim al-Jawziyya (d. 751/1350) disagreed with the dominant position in the four Sunni schools, which denies parents of bad morals custody of their children. Reasoning on pragmatic sociological grounds, he argued that had bad morals been a cause of forfeiture of custody, children would have been lost because, in his estimation, the majority of parents in his time belonged to this category. He added that empirically one sees that even people with bad morals (*fussāq*) do their best to protect their children. According to Ibn Qayyim, it was never the practice of the Prophet or his Companions to stop a parent from raising his child because he drank alcohol or had sex outside of wedlock.[70] Ibn Qayyim al-Jawziyya's reasoning sounds remarkably similar to that of a Georgia court in 1907, which noted that "even a sinning and erring woman still clings to the child of her shame, and though bartering her own honor, will rarely fail to fight for that of her daughter."[71] Ibn Qayyim al-Jawziyya's reasoning represents a strand of thought similar to the approach that developed in nineteenth-century England and in the new American republic. His approach coexisted parallel to the other more dominant position that denied women custody, at least *in theory*, for immoral behavior.

As we saw previously, English and American case law on child custody did not develop in a linear and teleological way toward a progressive, child-centered notion of the best interests of the child. In the eighteenth and early nineteenth centuries, the old father-centered approach coexisted with the emerging child-centered approach, leading in the end to the modern concept of the best interests of the child. One cannot help but notice a similar phenomenon in Islamic juristic discourse, where (at least) two strands of thought (one child-centered and the other parent-centered) coexisted throughout most of Islamic history. As we shall see, practice in

Muntaqā Fī Sharḥ Al-Multaqā, 2:166; Ibn ʿĀbidīn and al-Ḥaṣkafī, *Radd Al-Muḥtār ʿalā Al-Durr Al-Mukhtār Sharḥ Tanwīr Al-Abṣār*, 5:253–255.

70 There are disagreements within the four Sunni schools over what constitutes unacceptable lifestyle choices that may make the child's parents and other relatives ineligible as custodians. Jurists agreed that there was no need to investigate the moral uprightness of a custodian and resorted to the presumption of uprightness unless there is evidence to the contrary. A person who is not known to be either upright or not is assumed to be a qualified custodian unless there appears proof to the contrary. Al-Zarqānī, *Sharḥ Al-Zarqānī ʿalā Mukhtaṣar Sayyidī Khalīl Wa-Maʿahu Al-Fatḥ Al-Rabbānī Fīmā Dhahala ʿanhu Al-Zarqānī*, 4:475–476; Ibn Qudāma al-Maqdisī, *ʿUmdat Al-Fiqh Fi'l-Madhhab Al-Ḥanbalī*, 112; al-Jawziyya, *Zād Al-Maʿād Fī Hudā Khayr Al-ʿIbād*, 5:411–412.

71 Mason, *From Father's Property to Children's Rights*, 85.

some ways followed a mix of Ibn Qayyim's approach fused with a notion of family autonomy.

Religion

It is a requirement of the majority of Shāfiʿī and Ḥanbalī jurists, and a minority position in the Mālikī school, that the custodian be a Muslim whether male or female.[72] The reasoning presented by jurists for disqualifying non-Muslim custodians was often framed in the potential moral harm (*ḍarar*) that would befall children should they be raised by a non-Muslim parent.[73] The issue of non-Muslim custodians often arose from the ability of men to marry non-Muslim women. Some Ḥanbalīs resorted to an analogy to sinfulness (*fisq*), already a cause of forfeiture for most Ḥanbalīs, arguing that the potential moral harm inflicted on a child from a disbeliever is graver than that of a sinful Muslim.[74] According to most Mālikī jurists, a custodian can be non-Muslim, and a non-Muslim mother can assume custody of the child until her normal right to custody expires (puberty for boys and marriage for girls).[75] However, if there is concern that the non-Muslim parent may feed the child pork or alcohol, the child must be transferred to the father, according to one position. Another position was that the mother should maintain custody, with the judge charging Muslim neighbors with supervising the mother's raising of the child.[76]

The majority of Ḥanafīs allowed non-Muslim women to assume custody, but they did not extend the same dispensation to non-Muslim male relatives. This permission only holds until the child reaches the age of discernment (often estimated at seven), which is normally within the time of female custodianship for the Ḥanafīs with respect to boys. Ḥanafī jurists argued that once children reach an age at which they may be influenced by the non-Muslim parent's behavior, it is not in their interests to be cared for by the non-Muslim parent. The non-Muslim mother could also lose her

[72] If either parent is Muslim, most jurists assumed that the child is considered Muslim since the child follows the "better religion." See al-Astarūshinī, *Aḥkām Al-Ṣighār*, 137.

[73] Ibn Qudāma al-Maqdisī, *Al-Mughnī*, 2:2007.

[74] Al-Shirwānī, al-ʿIbādī, and al-Haytamī, *Ḥawāshī Tuḥfat Al-Muḥtāj Bi-Sharḥ Al-Minhāj*, 8: 351–365; Ibn Qudāma al-Maqdisī, *Al-Mughnī*, 2:2007.

[75] Ibn ʿAbd al-Barr, *Al-Kāfī Fī Fiqh Ahl Al-Madīna Al-Mālikī*, 297; al-Dasūqī, *Ḥāshiyat Al-Dasūqī ʿalā Al-Sharḥ Al-Kabīr*, 2:529; al-Zarqānī, *Sharḥ Al-Zarqānī ʿalā Mukhtaṣar Sayyidī Khalīl Wa-Maʿahu Al-Fatḥ Al-Rabbānī Fīmā Dhahala ʿanhu Al-Zarqānī*, 4:478.

[76] Ibn ʿAbd al-Barr, *Al-Kāfī Fī Fiqh Ahl Al-Madīna Al-Mālikī*, 297; al-Dasūqī, *Ḥāshiyat Al-Dasūqī ʿalā Al-Sharḥ Al-Kabīr*, 2:529.

custody rights earlier than the age of discernment if it becomes clear to the judge, in his capacity as the *parens patriae* of children, that she is teaching the child her own religion.[77] The evidence mobilized by Ḥanafīs to support this interpretation was a Prophetic tradition, in which Rāfiʿ b. Sinān was reported to have converted to Islam but his wife refused to convert with him. The couple brought their custody dispute to the Prophet, who asked them to stand on different sides. When the girl came in, she leaned more toward her mother. The Prophet then prayed that God would guide her aright, at which point she leaned toward her father. The Ḥanafīs argued that had it been unacceptable for a non-Muslim to take custody of a child, the Prophet would not have given any choice to the child. By contrast, Ḥanbalī jurists, for instance, argued that perhaps the Prophet knew that the child would end up choosing the father, which is why he let her choose in the first place. Other Ḥanbalīs challenged the very validity of the report, pointing out that there were different versions of it or that it had a weak chain of transmission.[78]

According to the dominant position of the four Sunni schools, conversion forfeits the mother's right to custody.[79] Save for the Ḥanafīs, premodern jurists understandably paid less attention to this question, owing to the fact that under Islamic juristic discourse, albeit rarely implemented in reality, converts from Islam were condemned to death, making the point of them having custody rights moot. There is, however, one exception in the Ḥanafī school: to wit, female converts were to be imprisoned until they recanted their conversion. Interestingly, many Ḥanafī jurists explained the different approaches they adopted toward converts as opposed to non-Muslims by birth by saying that a mother is unlikely to provide the child with the necessary care while she is in jail as a punishment for apostasy.[80] This explanation, coupled with the fact that the Ḥanafīs enabled non-Muslim women to assume custody of Muslim children can point to the fact that for many Ḥanafī jurists, there is nothing *essentially* wrong with non-Muslim women (including apostates) being custodians of Muslim children, as long as they do not teach the children their own faith and as long as they are indeed capable of carrying out the duties of custody.

[77] This Ḥanafī approach was adopted by Egyptian legislators in the modern period. See al-Zuḥaylī, *Al-Fiqh Al-Islāmī Wa-Adillatuhu*, 7:727–728.

[78] Ibn Qudāma al-Maqdisī, *Al-Mughnī*, 2:2007.

[79] Al-Astarūshinī, *Aḥkām Al-Ṣighār*, 100; al-Sarakhsī, *Al-Mabsūṭ*, 6:171.

[80] Al-Miṣrī, al-Nasafī, and Ibn ʿĀbidīn, *Al-Baḥr Al-Rāʾiq Sharḥ Kanz Al-Daqāʾiq Wa-Maʿahu Al-Ḥawāshī Al-Musammāh Minḥat Al-Khāliq ʿalā Al-Baḥr Al-Rāʾiq*, 4:282.

Visitation Rights and Joint Custody

Provided that visitation does not pose a danger to the child, jurists explicitly stated that custodians are not allowed to prevent children from visiting their noncustodial parents. However, most jurists in the four schools assumed that visitation could happen whenever either the child or the parent wished it, no matter how frequently it happened. In the Ḥanafī school, neither parent has the right to stop the other from seeing her or his children, but children were assumed to sleep in the house of the custodial parent. Likewise, custodians were not to "stop a child" from visiting her or his noncustodial parent.[81] In times of disputes, the judge must have had some discretion in assessing the child's wishes, as well as both the rights of the noncustodial parent and local custom.[82] However, some jurists limited visitations to once every few days if the mother visited the child at the father's house.[83] Though inspired by analogy to the wife's visits with her relatives, the right to visiting one's children was more frequent. Typically, jurists obligated the husband to allow his wife to see her parents once a week and once a year for more distant relatives such as uncles and aunts.[84]

The child welfare discourse can also be found in situations that resemble joint custody. Jurists did not dogmatically oppose atypical custody arrangements. As I mentioned previously, the Ḥanbalīs, who allowed a boy to choose his custodian at the age of seven, gave the boy the full choice to change his mind as often as he wished. Ibn Qudāma went as far as to insist on the validity of frequent changes (for boys) that may seem frivolous by saying that a boy could change his mind about with whom he wanted to live as frequently as he may change his mind about food and beverage preferences. He may choose to stay with the

[81] Al-Shirwānī, al-ʿIbādī, and al-Haytamī, *Ḥawāshī Tuḥfat Al-Muḥtāj Bi-Sharḥ Al-Minhāj*, 8361–8362; al-Astarūshinī, *Aḥkām Al-Ṣighār*, 103; Balkhī, *Al-Fatāwā Al-Hindiyya*, 1:543; Ibn Qudāma al-Maqdisī, *Al-Mughnī*, 2:2009.

[82] Visitation was gender-coded. In the Ḥanbalī school, for instance, if the mother does not have custody of a boy, visits should be made by the boy to the mother's house; if the child is a girl, the mother would be the one to visit the girl. The logic behind this differentiation is based on the jurists' interest in gender segregation and minimizing women's public presence. In the case that the choice is between the mother leaving her house to visit the daughter or vice versa, the mother is required to make the visit because she is older and, therefore, according to jurists, less vulnerable than her daughter. Ibn Qudāma al-Maqdisī, *Al-Mughnī*, 2:2009.

[83] Al-Shirwānī, al-ʿIbādī, and al-Haytamī, *Ḥawāshī Tuḥfat Al-Muḥtāj Bi-Sharḥ Al-Minhāj*, 8: 361–362.

[84] Al-Miṣrī, al-Nasafī, and Ibn ʿĀbidīn, *Al-Baḥr Al-Rāʾiq Sharḥ Kanz Al-Daqāʾiq Wa-Maʿahu Al-Ḥawāshī Al-Musammāh Minḥat Al-Khāliq ʿalā Al-Baḥr Al-Rāʾiq*, 4:330.

mother at certain times and with the father at other times (*ʿinda aḥadihimā fī waqt wa-ʿinda al-ākhar fī waqt*). Ibn Qudāma continued: "But they cannot both [the parents] assume custody simultaneously" (*lā yumkin ijtimāʿuhumā*).[85] Does his last statement contradict his prior insistence on the child's right to choose different times to be with different parents? What Ibn Qudāma meant is that the two parents may not assume custody of the child at the exact same times, that is, the same days or evenings, which would make sense in the context of gender segregation. This suggests that joint custody, in which the child divides the week's evenings or days between the two parents, is possible on the grounds of this Ḥanbalī discussion.

What confirms my reading of Ibn Qudāma is the following. There are juristic positions that by necessity assumed that custody might be split into some days for one custodian and other days for another. In his discussion of a person who is partly a slave and partly free, a situation that could take place if the slave was able to partially purchase him or herself from the master, Ibn Qudāma attributed a view to Aḥmad b. Ḥanbal that permitted the partial slave to assume partial custody. Ultimately, the question was about whether this partial slave, who was not in control of some of her or his days, could have custody on the days she or he owned. According to Ibn Ḥanbal's view, the partial slave could receive custody during the days of freedom from obligations toward the master.[86] This view assumed that on the other days, another custodian took care of the child.

Another place where a form of joint custody can be gleaned from juristic discourse is when jurists described the responsibilities of the parents toward a male child. Since the father has guardianship over his children at all times, regardless of which parent has custody, jurists often spoke of the responsibilities of guardianship, such as teaching the boy a trade, or taking him to a school, while he resides with his mother. In order for the father to be able to perform his guardianship duties, the boy must stay with his father during the day and with the mother at night. A girl, however, had to stay with her custodian at all times, since the skills a girl needed, such as cooking and weaving, did not require her to leave the house. The transfer of custody based on the child's wishes, as well as the rule that the boy stays with his father during the day and his mother at night is justified in welfare of the child (*ḥaẓẓ al-walad*) discourse.

[85] Ibn Qudāma al-Maqdisī, *Al-Mughnī*, 2:2008. [86] Ibid., 2:2007.

Relocation with the Ward

There was a perception among Sunni jurists that travel was especially dangerous for children, and therefore if the trip posed a threat to the child's life, jurists privileged the residing parent over the traveling parent.[87] The discussion of whether or not a parent could travel with the child to a place other than the child's habitual residence dealt mostly with the tender years period since, according to jurists, this was the time when the child needed both the care of his or her mother and the guardianship of the father. Once a child reaches the end of the tender age, the father (or male agnates) became both custodian and guardian and, therefore, the father could travel with the ward at will without the mother's consent since the father was, *in theory*, the only parent responsible for the child. Sunni jurists distinguished between relocation and temporary travel. If travel was temporary, most jurists privileged the relative who was staying in the place of habitual residence over the traveling parent.[88] Mālikī jurists, however, allowed the mother to travel with the ward if she had custody of the child, as long as her travel was temporary.[89] If the mother's intended new place of residence was close enough to the guardian that the child could see him every day, then the mother could remove the child from the original habitual place of residence. When there was a conflict between the guardian's right to look after the child's education and the custodian's right to provide basic nurture, such as nursing, non-Ḥanafī jurists almost always prioritized the guardian. The reasoning for favoring the father over the mother again invoked the child welfare parlance, rather than claiming that the father's right is inherently superior to that of the mother.[90]

When travel was (1) safe, (2) permanent, and (3) long distance, Sunni jurists generally privileged the legal guardian, often a male, over the custodian, often a female, regardless of which parent was the traveler.

87 Al-Zarqānī, *Sharḥ Al-Zarqānī ʿalā Mukhtaṣar Sayyidī Khalīl Wa-Maʿahu Al-Fatḥ Al-Rabbānī Fīmā Dhahala ʿanhu Al-Zarqānī*, 4:482–483; al-Sarakhsī, *Al-Mabsūṭ*, 6:169–170; al-Ḥaṣkafī and al-Timurtāshī, *Al-Durr Al-Mukhtār Sharḥ Tanwīr Al-Abṣār Wa-Jāmiʿ Al-Biḥār*, 257; al-Kāsānī, *Badāʾiʿ Al-Ṣanāʾiʿ Fī Tartīb Al-Sharāʾiʿ*, 5:217; al-Ḥalabī, Dāmād Afandī, and al-Ḥaṣkafī, *Multaqā Al-Abḥur; Majmaʿ Al-Anhur: Al-Durr Al-Muntaqā Fī Sharḥ Al-Multaqā*, 2:171; Balkhī, *Al-Fatāwā Al-Hindiyya*, 1:543–544.

88 Ibn ʿAbd al-Barr, *Al-Kāfī Fī Fiqh Ahl Al-Madīna Al-Mālikī*, 297; Ibn Qudāma al-Maqdisī, *Al-Mughnī*, 1:2009.

89 Al-Dasūqī, *Ḥāshiyat Al-Dasūqī ʿalā Al-Sharḥ Al-Kabīr*, 2:531–532.

90 Al-Zarqānī, *Sharḥ Al-Zarqānī ʿalā Mukhtaṣar Sayyidī Khalīl Wa-Maʿahu Al-Fatḥ Al-Rabbānī Fīmā Dhahala ʿanhu Al-Zarqānī*, 4:482–483; al-Miṣrī, al-Nasafī, and Ibn ʿĀbidīn, *Al-Baḥr Al-Rāʾiq Sharḥ Kanz Al-Daqāʾiq Wa-Maʿahu Al-Ḥawāshī Al-Musammāh Minḥat Al-Khāliq ʿalā Al-Baḥr Al-Rāʾiq*, 4:283–293; Ibn Qudāma al-Maqdisī, *Al-Mughnī*, 2:2009.

What qualifies as long-distance relocation (*safar*) from the place of habitual residence of the child was estimated either according to the distance at which prayers could lawfully be abridged (*masāfat al-qaṣr*), or by the distance at which the father could not see the child and return to his home on the same day. If the distance was less than *masāfat al-qaṣr* or if the father could see the child and return on the same day, jurists treated the short-distance traveler as a resident.[91] The only school that restricted the guardian's absolute power over the child in case of the father's relocation was the Ḥanafī school. It did not allow the father to take the child away until the mother's custody period had ended. As soon as the child reached the end of the tender years, though, the father could relocate to a distant locality without seeking the mother's consent.[92] There was disagreement in the Ḥanafī school over whether a woman had the right to take her child away from the place of habitual residence, i.e., where she was divorced. The dominant position allowed the mother to take the child back only to her hometown if the marriage took place there, but they did not grant her mother the same license.[93] This was an important license for women since they often returned to live with their extended families following divorce or the death of the husband.

According to Mālikī jurists, if the guardian wished to settle permanently at a long distance (more than approximately six *buruds*, or 72 miles) from the place of habitual residence, he always got priority to take the child with him even if the mother was entitled to custody. In other words, the father's decision to move six *buruds* from the place of the child's habitual residence triggered a custody transfer at the request of the father, regardless of the age of the child. The only way the mother could retain custody in this case was if she was willing to travel to the same place.[94] Jurists were aware of

[91] Al-Shirwānī, al-ʿIbādī, and al-Haytamī, *Ḥawāshī Tuḥfat Al-Muḥtāj Bi-Sharḥ Al-Minhāj*, 8: 363–364; Ibn Qudāma al-Maqdisī, *Al-Mughnī*, 2:2009; al-Wansharīsī, *Al-Manhaj Al-Fā'iq Wa'l-Manhal Al-Rā'iq Wa'l-Ma'nā Al-Lā'iq Bi-Ādāb Al-Muwaththiq Wa-Aḥkām Al-Wathā'iq*, 2:589–596. There is much disagreement among jurists over this distance. Many jurists consider it to be the distance that one walks for three days, estimated at 48 miles.

[92] Al-Zarqānī, *Sharḥ Al-Zarqānī ʿalā Mukhtaṣar Sayyidī Khalīl Wa-Maʿahu Al-Fatḥ Al-Rabbānī Fīmā Dhahala ʿanhu Al-Zarqānī*, 4:482–483; al-Sarakhsī, *Al-Mabsūṭ*, 6:169–170; al-Ḥaṣkafī and al-Timurtāshī, *Al-Durr Al-Mukhtār Sharḥ Tanwīr Al-Abṣār Wa-Jāmiʿ Al-Biḥār*, 257; al-Kāsānī, *Badā'iʿ Al-Ṣanā'iʿ Fī Tartīb Al-Sharā'iʿ*, 5:217; al-Ḥalabī, Dāmād Afandī, and al-Ḥaṣkafī, *Multaqā Al-Abḥur; Majmaʿ Al-Anhur: Al-Durr Al-Muntaqā Fī Sharḥ Al-Multaqā*, 2:171; Balkhī, *Al-Fatāwā Al-Hindiyya*, 1:543–544.

[93] Al-Astarūshinī, *Aḥkām Al-Ṣighār*, 102–105; al-Asyūṭī, *Jawāhir Al-ʿUqūd Wa-Muʿīn Al-Quḍāh Wa'l-Muwaqqiʿīna Wa'l-Shuhūd*, 2:198–199.

[94] Al-Zuḥaylī, *Al-Fiqh Al-Islāmī Wa-Adillatuhu*, 7:730, 39; Ibn ʿAbd al-Barr, *Al-Kāfī Fī Fiqh Ahl Al-Madīna Al-Mālikī*, 297.

the ways in which their rules could be undermined by recalcitrant fathers wishing to spite their divorcees. In this scenario, a father traveling for business could claim to be moving permanently in order to gain custody of his child. Alternatively, he could choose to travel the necessary distance not out of necessity but so that he could gain custody. Aware of these abusive practices, jurists gave judges the discretionary power to determine the intent of the guardian. According to them, if it became clear to the judge that the guardian's move was designed specifically to gain custody, he could rule against him. Other jurists made it a condition that the judge verify that the father was indeed planning to leave the place of habitual residence, relying on such indications as the father's sale of his property. Others required the father to swear an oath that he indeed intended to relocate and that his residence in the new town was for no less than six months, the period of permanent residence (*istīṭān*).[95] Ibn Qayyim al-Jawziyya challenged this widely held view, arguing that fathers have no right to take children during the custodianship of mothers even if they decide to relocate permanently.[96] His position was contrary to what amounted to a consensus among the four schools. The wide relocation rights granted by jurists to fathers and the lack of similar dispensations for mothers was partially remedied through private separation deeds, as we shall see in Chapters 3 and 4. Many mothers were able to secure the right to permanently relocate from the place of habitual residence and retain custody. Such agreements were considered binding only in the Mālikī school.

*Child Maintenance (*nafaqa*)*

The rules of child maintenance and guardianship were justified on the basis of the welfare of the child. If the child had financial assets, her or his money was used to pay for maintenance. Absent any assets, it was the child's father who was responsible for the maintenance. There are four obligatory types of child maintenance. The first is for the upkeep of the child,

[95] Al-Jawziyya, *Zād Al-Maʿād Fī Hudā Khayr Al-ʿIbād*, 5:413–414; Manṣūr b. Yūnus b. Idrīs al-Buhūtī, *Sharḥ Muntahā Al-Irādāt Daqāʾiq Ūlā Al-Nahy Li-Sharḥ Al-Muntahā*, ed. ʿAbd Allāh b. ʿAbd al-Muḥsin al-Turkī (Beirut: Muʾassasat al-Risāla, 2000), 5:697; al-Wansharīsī, *Al-Manhaj Al-Fāʾiq Wa'l-Manhal Al-Rāʾiq Wa'l-Maʿnā Al-Lāʾiq Bi-Ādāb Al-Muwaththiq Wa-Aḥkām Al-Wathāʾiq*, 2:594–595.

[96] Ibn Qayyim al-Jawziyya, *Iʿlām Al-Muwaqqiʿīn ʿan Rabb Al-ʿĀlamīn*, ed. Abū ʿUbayda Mashhūr b. Ḥasan Āl Salmān and Abū ʿUmar Aḥmad ʿAbd Allāh Aḥmad (Riyadh: Dār Ibn al-Jawzī, 2002), 5:253–256.

including the cost of food, clothing, bedding, and so on (*nafaqat al-walad*). The second and third types are the cost of nursing (*ujrat al-riḍā'*), and the cost of dedicating the time and energy to the care of the child (*ujrat al-ḥaḍāna*). According to most Ḥanafī (*al-mukhtār*) and Mālikī jurists (*bihi al-fatwā*), the father is also responsible for paying for the housing of the custodian and the ward (*maskan al-ḥaḍāna*) if the custodian had no place to live.[97] As we shall see, a housing allowance was rare in the courts because women almost always had a family member or a new husband with whom they and their children lived. Jurists were divided over whether the female custodian is entitled to custody wages (*ujrat al-ḥaḍāna*). Unlike the Ḥanafīs, most Mālikīs, Shāfi'īs, and Ḥanbalīs did not require the guardian to provide a custody wage to the female custodian. The logic of non-Ḥanafī jurists in denying female custodians a wage for custody is that their support is already the responsibility of their husbands if they are married, or their fathers or other male relatives if they are not married.[98] Despite education being an additional cost associated with both children and young adults, most jurists did not make it compulsory, and we rarely see early modern judges obligating fathers to pay for a child's education.[99] If the father was unable to pay his child support, it became a debt that had to be repaid when he became solvent.[100]

These rules with respect to custody wages and nursing fees applied if no one stepped forward to offer her services for free. If a relative of the child offered her nursing or custodial services for free, most Sunni jurists gave the mother two options: to either provide the same services for free or transfer custody to the volunteering relative. Yet many jurists restricted the mother's options in this manner only when the father was insolvent or when the child had assets. The logic here was to protect the child's money if she or he had some, but if she or he did not, then it was a way to find a solution to the father's insolvency. If the volunteer was not related to the child, some jurists argued that the mother should be allowed to keep the child while being entitled to custody or nursing payments. According to

97 Ibn 'Ābidīn and al-Ḥaṣkafī, *Radd Al-Muḥtār 'alā Al-Durr Al-Mukhtār Sharḥ Tanwīr Al-Abṣār*, 5:260–262; al-Dasūqī, *Ḥāshiyat Al-Dasūqī 'alā Al-Sharḥ Al-Kabīr*, 2:533.

98 Ibn Ḥajar al-Haytamī, *Al-Fatāwā Al-Kubrā Al-Fiqhiyya*, 4 vols. (Cairo: 'Abd al-Ḥamīd Aḥmad Ḥanafī, n.d.), 4:216; al-Zuḥaylī, *Al-Fiqh Al-Islāmī Wa-Adillatuhu*, 7:734–735; al-Ḥalabī, Dāmād Afandī, and al-Ḥaṣkafī, *Multaqā Al-Abḥur; Majma' Al-Anhur: Al-Durr Al-Muntaqā Fī Sharḥ Al-Multaqā*, 191–205.

99 Al-Zuḥaylī, *Al-Fiqh Al-Islāmī Wa-Adillatuhu*, 7:735–736; Ibn 'Ābidīn and al-Ḥaṣkafī, *Radd Al-Muḥtār 'alā Al-Durr Al-Mukhtār Sharḥ Tanwīr Al-Abṣār*, 5:261–262.

100 Al-Zuḥaylī, *Al-Fiqh Al-Islāmī Wa-Adillatuhu*, 7:735–736; Ibn 'Ābidīn and al-Ḥaṣkafī, *Radd Al-Muḥtār 'alā Al-Durr Al-Mukhtār Sharḥ Tanwīr Al-Abṣār*, 5:261–262.

Ibn Nujaym, many fathers brought nonrelatives to the courts of his time who volunteered to provide their services for free. He valorized the practice of giving the mother the options of maintaining custody for free or handing over the child to a relative, but did not extend the same rule to the unrelated volunteer.[101] The logic was that an unrelated volunteer does not have kindness toward the child, and therefore the financial gain accrued to the child or the father from the volunteer would be outweighed by a lack of kindness, compared to that of a relative.

In the case of the father's indigence, according to the Ḥanafīs, the maintenance arrears would not become a debt on the father unless there was a judicial ruling establishing maintenance (often allowing the mother to take debts that the father has to repay) or an agreement between the parents. Absent such an agreement, the Ḥanafīs did not require the father to repay maintenance arrears, unlike the Shāfiʿīs, Mālikīs, and Ḥanbalīs.[102] Ibn Nujaym al-Miṣrī pointed to the practice in his time of judges accepting women's petitions against their absent husbands to establish maintenance and allowing them to take loans that became the father's debt. This strategy was meant to ascertain that any arrears are the responsibility of the father in the case of child maintenance, or the husband in the case of spousal maintenance once he returns. Allowing the judge to accept women's petitions against absent fathers was a minority position in the Ḥanafī school, attributed to Zufar, which was practiced in Ottoman-Egyptian courts as we shall see. In Ibn Nujaym's estimation, this was permitted because it was more lenient (*arfaq bi-l-nās*), or more specifically, toward mothers and their children.[103]

101 Al-Shirwānī, al-ʿIbādī, and al-Haytamī, *Ḥawāshī Tuḥfat Al-Muḥtāj Bi-Sharḥ Al-Minhāj*, 8: 351–352; al-Miṣrī, al-Nasafī, and Ibn ʿĀbidīn, *Al-Baḥr Al-Rāʾiq Sharḥ Kanz Al-Daqāʾiq Wa-Maʿahu Al-Ḥawāshī Al-Musammāh Minḥat Al-Khāliq ʿalā Al-Baḥr Al-Rāʾiq*, 4:346; al-Ḥaṣkafī and al-Timurtāshī, *Al-Durr Al-Mukhtār Sharḥ Tanwīr Al-Abṣār Wa-Jāmiʿ Al-Biḥār*, 255, 264; al-Ḥalabī, Dāmād Afandī, and al-Ḥaṣkafī, *Multaqā Al-Abḥur; Majmaʿ Al-Anhur: Al-Durr Al-Muntaqā Fī Sharḥ Al-Multaqā*, 2:191–205; Ibn ʿĀbidīn and al-Ḥaṣkafī, *Radd Al-Muḥtār ʿalā Al-Durr Al-Mukhtār Sharḥ Tanwīr Al-Abṣār*, 5:262; al-Haytamī, *Al-Fatāwā Al-Kubrā*, 4:216; al-Shirbīnī, *Mughnī Al-Muḥtāj Ilā Maʿrifat Maʿānī Alfāẓ Al-Minhāj*, 3:590; al-Wansharīsī, *Al-Manhaj Al-Fāʾiq Wa'l-Manhal Al-Rāʾiq Wa'l-Maʿnā Al-Lāʾiq Bi-Ādāb Al-Muwaththiq Wa-Aḥkām Al-Wathāʾiq*, 2:647–650.

102 Abū ʿAbd Allāh Muḥammad al-Maghribī Al-Ḥaṭṭāb al-Ruʿaynī, *Mawāhib Al-Jalīl Li-Sharḥ Mukhtaṣar Khalīl*, ed. Zakariyyā ʿUmayrāt (Beirut: Dār al-Kutub al-ʿIlmiyya, 1995), 4: 601–602; al-Dardīr and al-Ṣāwī, *Al-Sharḥ Al-Ṣaghīr ʿalā Aqrab Al-Masālik Ilā Madhhab Al-Imām Mālik*, 2:747–748; Sharaf al-Dīn Mūsā b. Sālim Abū al-Najā al-Ḥajjāwī, *Al-Iqnāʿ Li-Ṭālib Al-Intifāʿ*, ed. ʿAbd Allāh b. ʿAbd al-Muḥsin al-Turk, 3rd edn. (Riyadh: Darat al-Malik ʿAbd al-ʿAzīz, 2002), 4:61.

103 Al-Miṣrī, al-Nasafī, and Ibn ʿĀbidīn, *Al-Baḥr Al-Rāʾiq Sharḥ Kanz Al-Daqāʾiq Wa-Maʿahu Al-Ḥawāshī Al-Musammāh Minḥat Al-Khāliq ʿalā Al-Baḥr Al-Rāʾiq*, 4:334–335; al-Shirbīnī, *Mughnī Al-Muḥtāj Ilā Maʿrifat Maʿānī Alfāẓ Al-Minhāj*, 3:578.

As we shall see in Chapters 3 and 4, early modern Egyptian women often made sure that their private separation deeds included a clause for maintenance and a permission from the judge that they could borrow money that the father would repay upon becoming solvent.[104]

Guardianship

As was mentioned previously, guardianship (*wilāya*) is the responsibility to care for an incapacitated person or a minor child in two ways: (1) guardianship of person (*wilāya ʿalā al-nafs*); and (2) guardianship of property (*wilāya ʿalā al-māl*). Guardianship of person refers to taking care of the ward's personal affairs, such as education, discipline, and marriage, whereas guardianship of property refers to the administration of the ward's financial affairs.[105] Just in the same way as *ḥaḍāna* was considered a female-dominated task, guardianship was considered a male-dominated category of care for the child's welfare. The child's welfare was also invoked to justify the various rules of guardianship, as was the case with custody. There are two types of guardians: guardians by natural right and guardians by designation. The latter type is subdivided into testamentary guardians and judicially appointed guardians. There was consensus among the four Sunni schools that non-Muslims cannot be the guardians of Muslim children.[106]

The Natural Guardian

I borrow the term "natural guardian" from the common law tradition to refer to a presumptive guardian (*walī*), as we saw previously in the case of

[104] Al-Miṣrī, al-Nasafī, and Ibn ʿĀbidīn, *Al-Baḥr Al-Rāʾiq Sharḥ Kanz Al-Daqāʾiq Wa-Maʿahu Al-Ḥawāshī Al-Musammāh Minḥat Al-Khāliq ʿalā Al-Baḥr Al-Rāʾiq*, 4:316–318, 366–368; al-Astarūshinī, *Aḥkām Al-Ṣighār*, 82; al-Ḥaṣkafī and al-Timurtāshī, *Al-Durr Al-Mukhtār Sharḥ Tanwīr Al-Abṣār Wa-Jāmiʿ Al-Biḥār*, 261; Balkhī, *Al-Fatāwā Al-Hindiyya*, 1:560–564.

[105] Zahraa and Malek, "The Concept of Custody in Islamic Law," 155–177, at 157; al-Zarqānī, *Sharḥ Al-Zarqānī ʿalā Mukhtaṣar Sayyidī Khalīl Wa-Maʿahu Al-Fatḥ Al-Rabbānī Fīmā Dhahala ʿanhu Al-Zarqānī*, 4:471.

[106] The Ḥanafīs, Ḥanbalīs, Shāfiʿīs, and Mālikīs do not allow a non-Muslim to be a guardian over a Muslim. Al-Ḥajjāwī, *Al-Iqnāʿ Li-Ṭālib Al-Intifāʿ*, 3:173–174; al-Shirbīnī, *Mughnī Al-Muḥtāj Ilā Maʿrifat Maʿānī Alfāẓ Al-Minhāj*, 3:97; al-Dardīr and al-Ṣāwī, *Al-Sharḥ Al-Ṣaghīr ʿalā Aqrab Al-Masālik Ilā Madhhab Al-Imām Mālik*, 4:604–605; Muḥammad b. Ḥussain b. ʿAlī al-Ṭūrī al-Qādirī, *Takmilat Al-Baḥr Al-Rāʾiq Sharḥ Kanz Al-Daqāʾiq*, ed. Zakariyyā ʿUmayrāt (Beirut: Dār al-Kutub al-ʿIlmiyya, 1997), 9:310.

the United States. This term is useful since it is similar to the way a father is treated as a presumptive guardian in Islamic law. By contrast, a mother can only be appointed by a male (e.g., the father or the judge) to be a "guardian by designation." This presumption of male–female power and responsibility is well captured by using "natural guardian" to distinguish between *walī* on the one hand, and *waṣī* (testamentary designation) and *qayyim* (judicial designation) on the other, even though premodern jurists never used "natural guardian" to refer to the father or the male agnatic relatives. Male agnates (the child's father; the father's ascendants; and the child's brothers, nephews, and uncles) dominated natural guardianship in juristic discourse.[107] The distinction between the three categories is very clear in juristic discourse as early as al-Shaybānī's *al-Aṣl*, where he referred to three categories: the father, the father's designee (*waṣī*), and the judicial designee (*qayyim*).[108] These types of guardians have varying powers, with the natural guardian being at the top of the guardianship hierarchy and the other two categories having far fewer powers. Unlike the natural guardian, the *qayyim*, for instance, cannot conduct financial transactions without the judge's approval. Unless there is a reason to specify the category, I will use the term "guardian" to refer to all three categories since, according to the court records, they all acted as such despite their divergent powers.

One indication that the welfare of the child is the foundational logic behind guardianship jurisprudence is that the judge has the right to reverse financial transactions made by the child's guardian, including his father or grandfather, if he sees that the financial transaction is not in the interests of the minor (*maṣlaḥa li-l-ṣaghīr*).[109] The judge is also not allowed to be the beneficiary of financial transactions made on behalf of the child, such as by selling the child's property to himself.[110] If a judge buys the orphan's property, a new judge has to decide if it is in the best interests of the child or not, and he has the power to either approve the sale or annul it.[111] Similarly, Ḥanafī jurists did not allow the judge to marry an orphan girl under his guardianship due to the same conflict of interest.[112] The Mālikīs also made the judge the ultimate authority who has the power to make the final decisions regarding guardianship issues. For

[107] Al-Zarqānī, *Sharḥ Al-Zarqānī ʿalā Mukhtaṣar Sayyidī Khalīl Wa-Maʿahu Al-Fatḥ Al-Rabbānī Fīmā Dhahala ʿanhu Al-Zarqānī*, 4:473–474; al-Miṣrī, al-Nasafī, and Ibn ʿĀbidīn, *Al-Baḥr Al-Rāʾiq Sharḥ Kanz Al-Daqāʾiq Wa-Maʿahu Al-Ḥawāshī Al-Musammāh Minḥat Al-Khāliq ʿalā Al-Baḥr Al-Rāʾiq*, 4:183–184; al-Shaybānī, *Al-Aṣl*, 9:305–306.

[108] Al-Shaybānī, *Al-Aṣl*, 9:305–306. [109] Al-Astarūshinī, *Aḥkām Al-Ṣighār*, 187.

[110] Ibid., 188. [111] Ibid., 189. [112] Ibid., 189.

instance, in the event that two appointed guardians disagree over the management of the child's financial affairs, the judge makes the final decision. The judge also determines whether the guardian, including the father, has misappropriated or mismanaged the child's money.[113] According to the Ḥanafīs, the judge can lend some of the money of the child, but the father cannot.[114] The judge is also required to take over the guardianship of the child from the father if it turns out that the father is not trustworthy.[115]

Guardianship by Designation

There are two types of guardianship by designation. One is a "testamentary guardian," often designated by the father known as *waṣī mukhtār* (a term used in the courts),[116] and the other is designated by the judge (often known as *qayyim*).[117] The Ḥanafī al-Sarakhsī reasoned that when a mother is appointed as a testamentary guardian, she acts not out of any right to guardianship as a mother but rather by the power of appointment.[118] The Mālikīs permitted female testamentary guardianship, but they did not allow them to conclude marriages on behalf of minors.[119] The dominant position of the Shāfiʿī school (*ʿalā al-madhhab*) does not allow the mother an automatic guardianship without appointment by agnates or judges.[120] Yet the majority of Shāfiʿī jurists held that the mother should take priority over agnatic male relatives after the father's death if she was equally capable of running the children's financial affairs because of her greater kindness toward her children, compared to the other relatives.[121]

113 Al-Dardīr and al-Ṣāwī, *Al-Sharḥ Al-Ṣaghīr ʿalā Aqrab Al-Masālik Ilā Madhhab Al-Imām Mālik*, 4:606, 8.

114 al-Astarūshinī, *Aḥkām Al-Ṣighār*, 191. 115 Ibid., 293.

116 "Court of Qisma ʿArabiyya, Sijill 1 (968–969/1561), Archival Code 1004–000001," Dār al-Wathāʾiq al-Qawmiyya, Cairo, doc. 355, 161.

117 Jurists agree that the father takes priority of guardianship, but there were some disagreements over the order of priority. Some jurists placed the person designated by the father as a testamentary guardian to take priority over the paternal grandfather, followed by other agnatic male relatives in order of their proximity to the child. See al-Astarūshinī, *Aḥkām Al-Ṣighār*, 226–227, 342–346.

118 Al-Sarakhsī, *Al-Mabsūṭ*, 6:171.

119 Ibn ʿAbd al-Barr, *Al-Kāfī Fī Fiqh Ahl Al-Madīna Al-Mālikī*, 548–549; al-Damīrī, *Al-Shāmil Fī Fiqh Al-Imām Mālik*, 986–987.

120 Al-Shirbīnī, *Mughnī Al-Muḥtāj Ilā Maʿrifat Maʿānī Alfāẓ Al-Minhāj*, 3:99.

121 Muḥyī al-Dīn Abū Zakariyyā al-Nawawī, *Rawḍat Al-Ṭālibīn*, ed. Zuhayr al-Shāwīsh (Beirut: Maktab al-Islāmī, 1991), 5:273; al-Shirbīnī, *Mughnī Al-Muḥtāj Ilā Maʿrifat Maʿānī Alfāẓ Al-Minhāj*, 3:98.

The practice of testamentary appointment, allowing many mothers to assume guardianship of their children, was so commonplace that the early modern Egyptian jurist al-Khaṭīb al-Shirbīnī encouraged his readers to make wills indicating who should take care of their children, especially if their paternal grandfather had passed away.[122] As we shall see, this principle was operationalized in Ottoman courts on a large scale, with mothers often receiving custody over agnatic male relatives. Jurists did not view women as essentially inferior to men on matters of guardianship, but rather as socially less capable of caring for the financial and disciplinary needs of the child. Appointment, whether in the form of a bequest by the father or judicial appointment, was assumed to provide a check by patriarchs to guarantee that the woman in question was capable of assuming guardianship.

In agreement with the other schools, the Mālikīs ruled that guardians of Muslim children must be Muslim.[123] According to the *Mudawwana*, if the father appoints someone as a testamentary guardian, the designated guardian has the right to marry off the children. The same holds true for whomever the testamentary guardian appoints. There is disagreement over whether a mother has the right to designate a guardian for her children. If the father was still alive, most jurists, including Mālik, considered her testament (*waṣiyya*) null and void, but if the father was dead, there was disagreement among jurists. For Mālik, she could appoint a guardian over her own money that she would pass on to the children, but not other property. Others did not allow the mother this power at all, arguing that women should be allowed to appoint someone only through testamentary guardianship if the object of the guardianship is negligible, such as a small amount of money. Otherwise, it is the sultan, that is, the judge as the sultan's representative, who has that power. Interestingly, the Mālikīs, despite being divided over the testament of a mother, grant mothers more rights than they do both the child's grandfather and brother. The grandfather and brother, according to Mālik's position, are not allowed to issue such testaments, the reason being that the mother has more rights to the child than the brother.[124]

122 Al-Shirbīnī, *Mughnī Al-Muḥtāj Ilā Maʿrifat Maʿānī Alfāẓ Al-Minhāj*, 3:97.

123 Al-Dardīr and al-Ṣāwī, *Al-Sharḥ Al-Ṣaghīr ʿalā Aqrab Al-Masālik Ilā Madhhab Al-Imām Mālik*, 4:604–605.

124 Saḥnūn b. Saʿīd al-Tanūkhī, *Al-Mudawwana Al-Kubrā* (Beirut: Dār al-Kutub al-ʿIlmiyya, 1994), 4:331–334.

PRIVATE SEPARATION DEEDS

Premodern Muslim jurists never explicitly discussed whether their rules were mandatory (*règles impératives*) or default rules (*règles supplétives*), but it is clear that the majority of jurists treated most of the rules made by author-jurists (such as the age at which custody is transferred from mother to father) as mandatory, since many of them rejected certain custody arrangements concluded by the parents in violation of these rules. The assumption that these rules are mandatory was motivated by the belief that their violation would entail harming children. Save for litigation, however, there were no judicial enforcement mechanisms or penalties for violating these rules, and therefore they served mostly to resolve custody and guardianship disputes in the courtroom. Nevertheless, their ethical–social weight must have also played a role in out-of-court custody arrangements.

Some jurists, such as many Mālikīs, allowed several departures from author-jurists' rules, permitting the judge to notarize agreements contradicting the presumptive rules as long as the agreement would not allow harm (*ḍarar*) to befall a given child.[125] Describing actual court practice, as we shall see, the early modern Egyptian jurist al-Zarqānī argued that an agreement in which the mother receives the father's consent to move far away from the place of habitual residence could include in exchange a stipulation that the mother would be responsible for the child's maintenance.[126] By endorsing such agreements, judges essentially treated the rules of author-jurists as default rules (despite the assumption common among most Sunni jurists that the rules are mandatory), and the child's welfare as a contextual question to be handled on a case-by-case basis. One discussion, in which we see that a minority of author-jurists in the four Sunni schools recognized that some child custody configurations were default rules (*règles supplétives*), relates to the no-fault, "for-compensation" divorce known as *khulʿ*.[127] Some jurists relaxed their own rules, often based on noncontextual conceptions of the welfare of

[125] Al-Wansharīsī, *Al-Manhaj Al-Fāʾiq Waʾl-Manhal Al-Rāʾiq Waʾl-Maʿnā Al-Lāʾiq Bi-Ādāb Al-Muwaththiq Wa-Aḥkām Al-Wathāʾiq*, 2:544.

[126] Al-Zarqānī, *Sharḥ Al-Zarqānī ʿalā Mukhtaṣar Sayyidī Khalīl Wa-Maʿahu Al-Fatḥ Al-Rabbānī Fīmā Dhahala ʿanhu Al-Zarqānī*, 4:483.

[127] This type of separation was often requested by the wife or her legal representative and entailed the wife giving up her dower and other financial obligations in exchange for an irrevocable termination of the marriage. However, the divorce's irrevocability was disputed by some jurists, while others considered this separation to be an annulment (*faskh*). On *khulʿ*, see further Ibrahim, "The Codification Episteme," 174.

all children at all times, once parents reached an amicable custody agreement at the time of separation.

Some Shāfiʿī and Ḥanbalī jurists accepted a *khulʿ* arrangement in which a mother commits herself to the care and maintenance of a child for ten years. Al-Shīrāzī accepted such an agreement, but other Shāfiʿīs were more reluctant. The Ḥanbalīs debated the same question and allowed the mother to pay for the child's maintenance for ten years while she assumed custody.[128] As we have seen so far, Ḥanafī jurists stated that custody of boys ends at seven and of girls until nine, according to one view, or puberty, according to another. Ḥanafī jurists assumed that these ages were designed for the welfare of boys and girls, whose needs vary according to gender. Despite their blanket assumptions about the needs of boys and girls, many Ḥanafīs permitted a *khulʿ* settlement to include a commitment on the part of the mother to support her children and to have custody of them until ten years of age. For boys, this is an increase to the "ideal" age at which boys need the discipline of their father or agnatic relatives, estimated at seven. In this case, determination of the welfare of the boy affected by this arrangement was left to the discretion of the judge, who had the power to allow or block custody arrangements made in *khulʿ* agreements. Jurists permitted this dispensation only until the child is ten years old.[129]

Can a mother have custody of children until puberty as part of a separation agreement? The Ḥanafīs, some of whom already held a view allowing women to have custody of girls until puberty, did not object to a *khulʿ* arrangement to that effect for girls, but they refused to allow the same for boys. They argued that a boy needs to learn the manners and "dispositions of men" (*ādāb al-rijāl*). In this case, the rule is mandatory. If a boy stays too long with women, they reasoned, he would internalize female dispositions. Ḥanafī jurists did not allow judges and parents this discretion, and instead forbade a *khulʿ* arrangement allowing the woman to have custody of a boy until puberty. Certainly, enforcement of this prohibition could only take place when one parent files a petition against the other parent. They also forbade the contracting of a *khulʿ* arrangement in which the mother retains custody of a child despite remarriage to a person who is not a close relative of the child. Similarly, the majority of Ḥanafīs considered a mother's decision to give up her right to custody of a child in a *khulʿ* arrangement to be null and void because they presumed

[128] Ibn Qudāma al-Maqdisī, *Al-Mughnī*, 2:1754; Abū Isḥāq al-Shīrāzī, *Al-Muhadhdhab Fī Fiqh Al-Imām Al-Shāfiʿī*, ed. Muḥammad al-Zuḥaylī (Damascus: Dār al-Qalam, 1996), 4:261–262.

[129] Balkhī, *Al-Fatāwā Al-Hindiyya*, 1:490–491; al-Sarakhsī, *Al-Mabsūṭ*, 6:169–170.

that this would be detrimental to the child, with children being treated again in a categorical manner.[130] From the perspective of these jurists, although the separation itself is valid, these stipulations were not worth the ink with which they were written. According to the Ḥanafī al-Sarakhsī, Islamic law grants custody to women because they are more gentle and kind than men, with the objective being the welfare of the child (*manfaʿat al-walad*).[131] In his view, custody is a right of the child (*ḥaqq al-walad*) and, therefore, mothers were not allowed to give up custody as part of a *khulʿ* agreement.[132]

In a similar vein, the nineteenth-century Ibn ʿĀbidīn claimed that he read one opinion written by a number of jurists including Abū-l-Suʿūd (d. 982/1574) that declared that the mother had the right, but not the obligation, to assume custody despite any prior agreement to forgo her custody, because the child has the stronger right. The mother, Ibn ʿĀbidīn reasoned, cannot drop the child's right.[133] In other words, while a mother can drop her right to custody, she can always change her mind and reclaim that right. Unlike the Mālikī school, her prior forgoing of custody does not constitute a permanent obligation in Ḥanafī law. If Ḥanafī jurists were to allow such agreements to be binding, as the argument goes, that would place children (and by extension their mothers) at a disadvantage. Again, this rule applied to all children, leaving the judge with little discretion.[134] Even when women agreed to enter into separation agreements in exchange for bearing the child's nursing fees or maintenance, this condition was only valid if a period of time was stipulated. In addition, Ḥanafī jurists held that if the mother becomes indigent, the father was still responsible for the child's maintenance despite the separation agreement.[135] As we shall see in our discussion of court practice, Ḥanafī judges operating in Ottoman Cairo overlooked these rules in favor of more discretion to the family of the child, treating almost all custody laws as default rules as long as, in their

[130] Al-Miṣrī, al-Nasafī, and Ibn ʿĀbidīn, *Al-Baḥr Al-Rāʾiq Sharḥ Kanz Al-Daqāʾiq Wa-Maʿahu Al-Ḥawāshī Al-Musammāh Minḥat Al-Khāliq ʿalā Al-Baḥr Al-Rāʾiq*, 4:134, 150–151; Balkhī, *Al-Fatāwā Al-Hindiyya*, 1:490–491; al-Sarakhsī, *Al-Mabsūṭ*, 6:169–170; al-Ḥalabī, Dāmād Afandī, and al-Ḥaṣkafī, *Multaqā Al-Abḥur; Majmaʿ Al-Anhur: Al-Durr Al-Muntaqā Fī Sharḥ Al-Multaqā*, 2:110; al-Ḥaṣkafī and al-Timurtāshī, *Al-Durr Al-Mukhtār Sharḥ Tanwīr Al-Abṣār Wa-Jāmiʿ Al-Biḥār*, 236–237.

[131] al-Sarakhsī, *Al-Mabsūṭ*, 5:207, 6:169. [132] Ibid., 6:169; 5:207.

[133] Ibn ʿĀbidīn and al-Ḥaṣkafī, *Radd Al-Muḥtār ʿalā Al-Durr Al-Mukhtār Sharḥ Tanwīr Al-Abṣār*, 5:258.

[134] Balkhī, *Al-Fatāwā Al-Hindiyya*, 1:490–491; al-Sarakhsī, *Al-Mabsūṭ*, 6:169–170.

[135] Al-Ḥalabī, Dāmād Afandī, and al-Ḥaṣkafī, *Multaqā Al-Abḥur; Majmaʿ Al-Anhur: Al-Durr Al-Muntaqā Fī Sharḥ Al-Multaqā*, 2:110.

estimation, such agreements did not seriously harm the particular child in question.

Even if jurists blocked certain agreements as contrary to the welfare of the child, many parents (or more precisely families) made all sorts of child custody arrangements out of court even when they contradicted juristic rules. The state was not interested in establishing any mechanisms to oversee the private lives of children. Other families wished to have binding private separation deeds with the backing of the state judiciary for enforcement instead of informal out of court agreements. And jurists obliged. Contrary to Ḥanafīs, the Mālikīs, the majority of whom considered custody to be a right of the custodian,[136] allowed mothers to give up their right to custody in a *khulʿ* arrangement as long as the decision was not detrimental to the child.[137] There was, however, a minority Mālikī position based on the assumption that custody is a right of the child, rather than the custodian, which treated the mother's giving up of her custody as nonbinding.[138] Women were able to secure these private separation deeds granting them child custody despite remarriage, for instance, in exchange for paying for the child's maintenance,[139] but sometimes they did not pay anything in exchange because it was assumed that this arrangement would be better for the given child and family.

Despite the general acceptance of a wide range of stipulations in separation deeds among the Mālikīs, they rejected some conditions, such as the mother's agreement with the father to send the child to eat at the father's house instead of the father paying maintenance, a stipulation that they contended would harm the child, who would not be able to eat as regularly as she or he needed.[140] The binding nature of these agreements, according to the Mālikīs, was effective as long as the person's giving up of her or his right happened "without a valid reason" (*bi-ghayri ʿudhr*), such as falling

[136] Al-Dasūqī, *Ḥāshiyat Al-Dasūqī ʿalā Al-Sharḥ Al-Kabīr*, 2:532.

[137] Al-Dardīr and al-Ṣāwī, *Al-Sharḥ Al-Ṣaghīr ʿalā Aqrab Al-Masālik Ilā Madhhab Al-Imām Mālik*, 2:522; al-Dasūqī, *Ḥāshiyat Al-Dasūqī ʿalā Al-Sharḥ Al-Kabīr*, 2:527; al-Zarqānī, *Sharḥ Al-Zarqānī ʿalā Mukhtaṣar Sayyidī Khalīl Wa-Maʿahu Al-Fatḥ Al-Rabbānī Fīmā Dhahala ʿanhu Al-Zarqānī*, 4:117–118.

[138] Al-Zarqānī, *Sharḥ Al-Zarqānī ʿalā Mukhtaṣar Sayyidī Khalīl Wa-Maʿahu Al-Fatḥ Al-Rabbānī Fīmā Dhahala ʿanhu Al-Zarqānī*, 4:470–471; Jamāl al-Dīn b. ʿUmar Ibn al-Ḥājib, *Jāmiʿ Al-Ummahāt*, ed. Abū ʿAbd al-Raḥmān al-Akhḍar al-Akhḍarī (Damascus: Al-Yamāma, 1998), 290.

[139] Ibn al-Ḥājib, *Jāmiʿ Al-Ummahāt*, 290; al-Zarqānī, *Sharḥ Al-Zarqānī ʿalā Mukhtaṣar Sayyidī Khalīl Wa-Maʿahu Al-Fatḥ Al-Rabbānī Fīmā Dhahala ʿanhu Al-Zarqānī*, 4: 117–118.

[140] Al-Zarqānī, *Sharḥ Al-Zarqānī ʿalā Mukhtaṣar Sayyidī Khalīl Wa-Maʿahu Al-Fatḥ Al-Rabbānī Fīmā Dhahala ʿanhu Al-Zarqānī*, 4:485–486.

sick or performing the pilgrimage; that is, without such a "valid reason" to have given up custody, a person could not change her or his mind and request custody again.[141]

Allowing parents to sign separation deeds violating the rigid rules of most jurists and considering these agreements as binding as the Mālikīs do, *except where the judge deemed the arrangement to violate the welfare of the child,* created a complex system of child custody that could accommodate the varying needs of children and families while violating the indiscriminate rules of author-jurists. This position of the Mālikīs was followed in the Mamluk period, as al-Asyūṭī (d. 880/1475) clearly tells us about the types of contracts used in Egypt in his time. In one contract, he gives a standard contract formula, which was based on the rules of the Mālikī school. His example is a formula of a private separation deed that violates the ideal conditions established by most Sunni jurists, wherein the mother has custody of the child for a certain period of time "whether she is single or married, having moved away [from the child's place of residence] or is still resident, and whether he [the father] has moved away or is still a resident" (*ʿazban kānat aw mutazawwija muqīma kānat aw musāfira musāfiran huwa kāna aw muqīman*). The entire formulaic text of one full printed page continued to be used verbatim in Ottoman Egypt, as we shall see in Chapters 3 and 4.[142] This Mālikī contract would be widely used in Ottoman Egypt but with more controversial stipulations that were not envisioned by the Mālikīs themselves. Looking further west to the Maghrib, al-Wansharīsī's (d. 914/1509) manual of court documentation discussed such private separation deeds, but, unlike al-Asyūṭī, he did not give concrete examples of these contracts.[143]

When a mother dropped her right to custody in a *khulʿ* separation during the Mālikī tender years (until puberty for boys or marriage for girls), Mālikī jurists were divided over whether the next in line (say her mother or sister) should assume custody or the father. According to ʿAbd al-Bāqī al-Zarqānī (d. 1099/1687) – not to be confused with Abū ʿAbd Allāh Muḥammad b. ʿAbd al-Bāqī al-Zarqānī, (d. 1122/1710) – there were two positions in the Mālikī school. The early well-known opinion was that

141 Al-Zarqānī, 4:484; al-Wansharīsī, *Al-Manhaj Al-Fāʾiq Wa'l-Manhal Al-Rāʾiq Wa'l-Maʿnā Al-Lāʾiq Bi-Ādāb Al-Muwaththiq Wa-Aḥkām Al-Wathāʾiq*, 2:608; Ibn Taymiyya, *Majmūʿ Fatāwā Shaykh Al-Islām Aḥmad Ibn Taymiyya*, 34:110.

142 Al-Asyūṭī, *Jawāhir Al-ʿUqūd Wa-Muʿīn Al-Quḍāh Wa'l-Muwaqqiʿīna Wa'l-Shuhūd*, 2: 192–193.

143 Al-Wansharīsī, *Al-Manhaj Al-Fāʾiq Wa'l-Manhal Al-Rāʾiq Wa'l-Maʿnā Al-Lāʾiq Bi-Ādāb Al-Muwaththiq Wa-Aḥkām Al-Wathāʾiq*, 2:536–600.

the parents could agree on a direct transfer to the father, yet the minority position gives custody to the next in the school's line of female custodians. Muḥammad b. al-Ḥasan b. Masʿūd al-Bannānī (d. 1194/1780), while acknowledging that the first position was the well-known view of the Mālikī school according to the *Mudawanna* of Saḥnūn (d. 240/854), he explained that it was the practice of courts of his time (in Egypt) to transfer the right to the next in line.[144] This was also the practice of the fifteenth-century and early sixteenth-century Maghrib according to al-Wansharīsī (d. 914/1509).[145]

Al-Wansharīsī was aware of the same practice of private separation deeds taking place in Egypt, as he cites a case from *al-Qāhira al-maḥrūs*" (*Cairo the Protected*), where a late Mamluk Cairene woman was concerned that her husband would take away custody of her child if she decided to remarry. The child's parents agreed that the mother would pay the father a sum of money that he could keep if she remarried in exchange for not petitioning for custody of his son. If he did petition for custody, he would repay her that sum of money. As it happens, the mother remarried and the father never petitioned for custody, per their agreement. Yet upon the mother's remarriage, the maternal grandmother took custody of the child. The mother wanted to get the money back from the husband, arguing that she paid the money in exchange for having custody of the child, and since she no longer had custody of the child, she was entitled to her money. Some Mālikī jurists from the East (Mashriq) reasoned that she had no right to the money. Al-Wansharīsī countered this dominant position with a hypothetical: "one may argue" (*wa-li-qāʾil an yaqūl*) that this agreement is null and void since the father sold a contingent right, that is, a right that he had not yet possessed. This hypothetical counter-argument is precisely the reasoning of the majority of Sunnis, including the Ḥanafīs. In a word, the mother was the custodian and she had not yet remarried. Therefore, the father had no custody right to exchange for money. This hypothetical was a window into al-Wansharīsī's awareness of the weakness of the dominant Mālikī doctrine and practice, which allowed such agreements where certain contingent (that is *potential*) rather than real rights were exchanged for money and even

144 See al-Dasūqī, *Ḥāshiyat Al-Dasūqī ʿalā Al-Sharḥ Al-Kabīr*, 2:532–533; al-Zarqānī, *Sharḥ Al-Zarqānī ʿalā Mukhtaṣar Sayyidī Khalīl Wa-Maʿahu Al-Fatḥ Al-Rabbānī Fīmā Dhahala ʿanhu Al-Zarqānī*, 4:117–118, 484.

145 Al-Wansharīsī, *Al-Manhaj Al-Fāʾiq Wa'l-Manhal Al-Rāʾiq Wa'l-Maʿnā Al-Lāʾiq Bi-Ādāb Al-Muwaththiq Wa-Aḥkām Al-Wathāʾiq*, 2:538–539.

made them binding (*pace* the Ḥanafī critiques).[146] I say weakness because in other areas of the law the Mālikīs had accepted the principle that one could not sell or give up a right one had not yet acquired, creating internal inconsistency in Mālikī law.[147]

This internal tension over the question of whether private separation deeds were binding would flare up among sixteenth-century Cairene Mālikīs. Sherman Jackson discusses a response to the debate written in 975/1567 by the Mālikī jurist and judge Badr al-Dīn al-Qarāfī (*circa* 939–1008/1533–1599). What happens when a father reneges on his agreement to give up his future right to custody should his divorcee remarry? According to al-Qarāfī, who was a judge in the Ottoman judiciary and notarized such agreements himself, he received many questions about men petitioning for custody despite prior custody arrangements made with the mother. This was a very controversial issue among Mālikīs in Cairo, who were divided into two camps: one arguing that the agreements are binding and the other supporting the fathers' reneging on their prior commitments by petitioning for custody. The camp supporting the unenforceability of these private separation deeds held that the father's petition to assume custody would trigger a removal of the child from the mother's custodianship upon her remarriage despite having signed a separation deed.[148] The child would then be transferred to the next in the normal line of custodians, which would often be the mother's mother or sister. It may seem odd to the modern reader that the father would petition the court to transfer the child from the mother's house to that of the maternal grandmother or aunt, if they are willing and fit for custody. Yet this would make sense given that, as the court records suggest, some men considered the fact of the child living with the mother's new husband in the same household to be inherently detrimental to the child's welfare. Mālikī jurists even mentioned a situation in which fathers bequest substantial amounts of money to the mothers of their children on the condition that they do not remarry.[149]

What made the issue more controversial is that many important near-contemporary Mālikī authorities claimed a *mashhūr* ("well-known/dominant") status to the view that one cannot forfeit a contingent right, and

[146] Al-Wansharīsī, 2:564. [147] Al-Wansharīsī, 2:538–539.

[148] Sherman A. Jackson, "Kramer versus Kramer in a Tenth/Sixteenth Century Egyptian Court: Post-Formative Jurisprudence between Exigency and Law," *Islamic Law and Society* 8:1 (2001): 27–51; Badr al-Dīn Muḥammad b. Yaḥyā al-Qarāfī, "*Taḥqīq al-Ibāna fī Ṣiḥḥat Isqāṭ Mā Lam Yajib Min al-Ḥaḍāna*," in *Min Khizānat Al-Madhhab Al-Mālikī*, ed. Jalāl ʿAlī al-Qadhdhāfī (Beirut: Dār Ibn Ḥazm, 2006), 349–428.

[149] Al-Qarāfī, "*Taḥqīq Al-Ibāna Fī Ṣiḥḥat Isqāṭ Mā Lam Yajib Min Al-Ḥaḍāna*," 414–415.

therefore a husband's forfeiture of his contingent right of custody was null and void. Proponents of this view included important Mālikī authorities such as Jamāl al-Dīn al-Aqfaṣī (d. 823/1420), Abū Bakr al-Damāmīnī (d. 827/1425), Muḥammad al-Tatāʾī (d. 942/1535), and Muḥammad al-Ḥaṭṭāb (d. 953/1547).[150] Given this wide opposition to private separation deeds among Mālikīs, notwithstanding their wide practice in both Mamluk and Ottoman-Egyptian courts, al-Qarāfī's hurdle to overcome the *mashhūr* status and defend court practice seemed insurmountable. In his defense of court practice, al-Qarāfī argued that there were 30 exceptions to the general rule that prohibits the forfeiture of a contingent right, adding that even this list was in dispute among Mālikīs. Though unrelated to child custody, he cited that some of these exceptions gained support among important Mālikī authorities such as Mālik (d. 179/795), Ibn al-Qāsim (d. 191/806), Ibn ʿArafa (d. 803/1401), and Nāṣir al-Dīn al-Laqqānī (d. 958/1551). By offering these exceptions, al-Qarāfī sought to challenge the general applicability of the prohibition of the forfeiture of a contingent right in order to argue that the rule does not apply to private separation deeds.[151]

Given the difficulty of challenging the *mashhūr* status of the position he wished to counter, al-Qarāfī's final move was to invoke "judicial practice" (*ʿamal*) itself to settle the dispute. According to him, people in his day practiced these private separation deeds before the accrual of the right of custody, allowing women to retain custody should they remarry or travel from the place of habitual residence. Al-Qarāfī then concludes, "Even if we assume the existence of the 'well-known' (*mashhūr*) status [that the agreements are not binding] side by side with judicial practice [that the agreements are binding], we would follow judicial practice. The 'late' (*mutaʾakhkhirīn*) North Africans (*maghribīs*) prioritized judicial practice over the *mashhūr*." In other words, there is an acknowledged gap between what jurists assume is the rule and what judges actually apply in the court. This gap was motivated by "public welfare" (*maṣlaḥa*) and "custom" (*ʿurf*).[152]

150 See Jackson, "Kramer versus Kramer in a Tenth/Sixteenth Century Egyptian Court," 50–51, n72, n73.

151 Jackson, "Kramer versus Kramer in a Tenth/Sixteenth Century Egyptian Court," 27–51; Yaḥyā al-Qarāfī, "*Taḥqīq al-Ibāna fī Ṣiḥḥat Isqāṭ Mā Lam Yajib Min al-Ḥaḍāna*," 349–428.

152 The term "late" (*mutaʾakhkhirīn*) is different from "postclassical," since the latter is used by modern scholars in the Western academy to refer to the period after around the beginning of the twelfth or thirteenth centuries. See al-Qarāfī, "*Taḥqīq Al-Ibāna Fī Ṣiḥḥat Isqāṭ Mā Lam Yajib Min Al-Ḥaḍāna*," 408–428, quote at 425. In the Western academy see, for instance, Gideon Libson, *Jewish and Islamic Law: A Comparative Study*

The motivations of the camp against whom al-Qarāfī wrote his treatise are hard to determine, but it is fair to assume that they were either interested in creating methodological consistency within the Mālikī school or they supported the fathers. By contrast, al-Qarāfī's treatise sought to realign juristic discourse with judicial practice, but his appeal seems to have fallen on deaf ears among his colleagues and later Mālikīs. Many Mālikīs after al-Qarāfī's time continued to oppose the bindingness of these separation deeds, including such important jurists such as Aḥmad al-Dardīr (d. 1201/1786) and Muḥammad al-Dasūqī (d. 1230/1815).[153] His treatise was copied in early modern North Africa with a *maghribī* script. The copy at Egypt's National Library was made in 1146/1733, which suggests that the debate continued to be relevant long after al-Qarāfī's death.[154]

Faced with the reality of private separation deeds and failing to offer a logical justification for them, Mālikī jurists could either treat these private separation deeds as nonbinding, as the other Sunni schools did, in order to create consistency between child custody law and the logic of the law of obligations, or they could allow private separation deeds to stand in contradiction with other rules in the Mālikī school, owing to the awkward exceptions made to the general prohibition of forfeiting contingent rights. Judging by Ottoman court practice until 1670, they chose the latter. As we shall see in Chapter 3, the reason for their choice was the wide utilization of these separation deeds in early modern Egypt, as well as in North Africa according to al-Wansharīsī. Al-Qarāfī, himself a judge in the Ottoman courts that widely notarized these agreements considered both public welfare and custom to be legitimate justifications for permitting them.

If this was the practice of courts in early modern Egypt (and the Mālikī stronghold of the Maghrib where such binding agreements were taking place according to al-Wansharīsī),[155] let us return to the question of why fathers negotiated custody in a *khulʿ* agreement, if custody was transferred to the mother's mother? A question raised by many early modern Egyptian Mālikīs should offer some insight. They discussed the following

of Custom during the Geonic Period (Cambridge, MA; London: Harvard University Press, 2003), 250–251, at n. 12.

[153] See Jackson, "Kramer versus Kramer in a Tenth/Sixteenth Century Egyptian Court," 50–51, n72, n73.

[154] Al-Qarāfī, "*Taḥqīq Al-Ibāna Fī Ṣiḥḥat Isqāṭ Mā Lam Yajib Min Al-Ḥaḍāna,*" 360–361.

[155] Al-Wansharīsī, *Al-Manhaj Al-Fāʾiq Waʾl-Manhal Al-Rāʾiq Waʾl-Maʿnā Al-Lāʾiq Bi-Ādāb Al-Muwaththiq Wa-Aḥkām Al-Wathāʾiq*, 2:563.

scenario: what happens when, before the mother gives up her right to custody as part of a *khulʿ* arrangement, the mother's mother and aunt give up their right to custody as well? Mālikī jurists held that this ceding (*isqāṭ*) of the right to custody on the part of the relatives succeeding the mother is invalid because, at the time of giving up the right, they had not yet acquired a right that they could then forfeit. According to al-Zarqānī and al-Dasūqī, their forfeiture becomes valid only if performed after the mother has already done the same, which would signal the transfer of right to them.[156] Further west, al-Wansharīsī had argued that when drawing up separation deeds, the conjunction *thumma* ("then") signifying sequence, rather than *wa* ("and") signifying simultaneity, should be used when discussing the mother and her mother ceding their rights to custody. The point is to ascertain that the grandmother's forfeiture happened after acquiring the right to custody, which could only take effect *after* the mother's forfeiture. According to him, this is the dominant view that is practiced by muftis and judges.[157]

Does this concern about the order of ceding the right to custody relate to actual cases? As we shall see in in Chapters 3 and 4, the next two chapters, child custody was an important bargaining chip in the hands of the mother and her immediate female relatives, who collectively took advantage of the rules of custody privileging maternal female relatives during the tender years to help the mother obtain a *khulʿ* separation. These were extended family affairs in which many relatives attended court proceedings and entire quarters were aware of the outcome.

Some jurists went further than granting licenses allowing families to sign private separation deeds that contradicted the categorical rules of child custody. These jurists assumed that child custody should not be based on rigid rules but rather tied to the best interests of each child on a case-by-case basis, with default rules as a baseline. Two jurists argued especially strongly for this perspective: Ibn Taymiyya (d. 728/1328) and his student Ibn Qayyim al-Jawziyya (d. 751/1350). Ibn Taymiyya privileged a broader than usual definition of the child's welfare by arguing that a parent is prioritized over another if her or his custodianship brought about benefit to the child or averted them harm. He mentioned the example of a stepmother who either harmed the child or did not strive

[156] See al-Dasūqī, *Ḥāshiyat Al-Dasūqī ʿalā Al-Sharḥ Al-Kabīr*, 2:532–533; al-Zarqānī, *Sharḥ Al-Zarqānī ʿalā Mukhtaṣar Sayyidī Khalīl Wa-Maʿahu Al-Fatḥ Al-Rabbānī Fīmā Dhahala ʿanhu Al-Zarqānī*, 4:117–118, 484.

[157] Al-Wansharīsī, *Al-Manhaj Al-Fāʾiq Wa'l-Manhal Al-Rāʾiq Wa'l-Maʿnā Al-Lāʾiq Bi-Ādāb Al-Muwaththiq Wa-Aḥkām Al-Wathāʾiq*, 2:538–539.

for the child's best interests. According to him, custody in this case should be given to the mother, who would be a better custodian even if she has remarried.[158] This broader, positive definition of the child's welfare would be taken even further by Ibn Qayyim,[159] who in his magnus opus *I'lām al-Muwaqqi'īn 'an Rabb al-'Ālamīn* presents five prophetic reports as all the evidence there is on child custody. In the first report, the Prophet gave custody to the maternal aunt of a girl even though the aunt was remarried. In the second, third, and fourth reports, the Prophet asked the child to choose between the parents. According to the fifth report, the Prophet told the mother that she had the right of custody as long as she did not remarry. Tellingly, Ibn Qayyim reasoned that the rules of custody should be based on these five cases,[160] suggesting that Sunni jurists overlegislated child custody law when they went beyond this limited textual corpus.

Ibn Qayyim was aware of the abusive practice whereby fathers claimed that they are relocating to assume custody of their children. Recall that the Mālikī, Ḥanbalī, and Shāfi'ī schools gave the father absolute right of custody even during the mother's custodial period if the father decides to relocate to a new town. Ibn Qayyim explained that the Prophet said that whoever separates a mother from her child, God will separate him from his beloved ones in the hereafter. He concluded that neither the textual sources, analogy, nor welfare (*maṣlaḥa*) justify the view that the father has the right to take the child if he travels from the child's habitual place of residence.[161]

With such minimal textual sources and an assumption that jurists came up with rules (such as the traveling rule) without any textual, analogical, or welfare justification, one would expect him to use the welfare discourse as an alternative methodology for the construction of custody laws. This is precisely what he did in his *Zād al-Ma'ād*. He gave the judge full discretion

158 Taqī al-Dīn Ibn Taymiyya, *Risāla Fī Taslīm Al-Bint Ilā Al-Abb Aw Al-Umm*, ed. Sa'd al-Dīn b. Muḥammad al-Kibbī (Riyadh: Maktabat al-Ma'ārif li'l-Nashr wa'l-Tawzī', 2010), 64–67.

159 Another example of Ibn Taymiyya's pragmatic jurisprudence is his position on circumstantial evidence. Being aware of the inroads that political power (*siyāsa*) was making upon sharī'a under the Mamluks, he relaxed some of the rules of evidence to reconcile the law with the practices of political power. On Ibn Taymiyya's position on the use of circumstantial evidence, see further Johansen, "Signs as Evidence"; Yossef Rapoport, "Royal Justice and Religious Law: Siyāsah and Shari'ah under the Mamluks," *Mamluk Studies Review* 16 (2012): 71–102; Kristen Stilt, *Islamic Law in Action: Authority, Discretion, and Everyday Experiences in Mamluk Egypt* (Oxford: Oxford University Press, 2011).

160 Al-Jawziyya, *I'lām Al-Muwaqqi'īn 'an Rabb Al-'Ālamīn*, 6:482–484.

161 Ibid., 5:253–256.

in contravening the rules of author-jurists, arguing that there are no conclusive proofs supporting these rigid rules and that the divine law did not intend to privilege one parent over another in an absolute way (*muṭlaqan*). He proposed that the best way to determine custody arrangements is by looking at the best interests of the child (*al-aṣlaḥ*) on a case-by-case basis.[162] Since these rules are not obligatory in Ibn Qayyim's view, it would follow that the family of the child or the judge can make decisions or agreements that they deemed to be in the best interests of the child even if they contradict the rules of author-jurists.[163] Ibn Qayyim's position was motivated by a broader concern for children's welfare, as evidenced by his treatise on childrearing in which he shows deep and unusual concern for the child's psychological well-being.[164]

Contrary to Ibn Qayyim's position, the majoritarian approach of premodern jurists often privileged author-juristic categorical determinations of the welfare of all children at all times in most of their rules (with some exceptions such as allowing the child to choose the custodian upon attaining the age of discernment). This majoritarian approach did not allow the judge, except in limited circumstances, much discretionary power in making custody arrangements on a case-by-case basis, as is the case in the modern concept of the best interests of the child, the modus operandi of international conventions on children. By contrast, Ibn Qayyim al-Jawziyya's views entail de-sanctifying child custody law as developed by jurists, an approach which lends itself readily to giving the judge and the family (through private separation deeds) greater discretion in assessing the child's best interests individually. Although the Mālikī view on private separation deeds and Ibn Qayyim al-Jawziyya's view on the relativity of child custody law represented fringe positions in premodern juristic discourse, they formed the basis of child custody adjudication in Mamluk and Ottoman courts in Egypt albeit without referencing Ibn Qayyim or the Mālikī position.

As an example of a broader conception of the child's welfare being utilized to change default custody and guardianship arrangements,

162 Ibn Qayyim al-Jawziyya, *Zād Al-Ma'ād Fī Hudā Khayr Al-'Ibād*, 5:414–415, 425.

163 Ibid., 5:414–415.

164 In his treatise on childrearing, he told parents, for instance, that they should avoid exposing the child to scary sounds and images that may have a long-term traumatic impact. Such traumas, he argued, could lead to problems in adulthood. He allowed parents to agree on shortening or lengthening the period of breastfeeding or on giving the child out to be wet-nursed as long as such decisions did not harm the child or the mother. Ibn Qayyim al-Jawziyya, *Tuḥfat Al-Mawdūd Bi-Aḥkām Al-Mawlūd*, ed. 'Uthmān b. Jum'a Ḍumayriyya (Jedda: Dār 'Ālam al-Fawā'id, 2010), 338–356; Giladi, *Children of Islam*, 22–34.

consider that al-Haytamī (d. 974/1566–67) cited Ibn al-Ṣalāḥ al-Shahrazūrī (d. 643/1245) as arguing that if a custodial mother lives in a village and the father lives in a town and the child's welfare was negatively impacted by his life in a village with his mother – say because there were no educational opportunities – the father could take the child from the mother because the harm to the mother can be overlooked here in favor of the child's welfare. In this example, the threshold for harm is broader than the "gross harm" approach of many other jurists. The child's welfare was defined broadly as it was by, say, Ibn ʿAbd al-Barr, as seen previously, or Ibn Qayyim al-Jawziyya.[165] The strand of thought that privileged a case-by-case and broader approach to child welfare would be adopted by the early nineteenth-century Ḥanafī jurist Ibn ʿĀbidīn. He challenged, for instance, the dominant view that remarriage to someone who is not a close relative of the child is a cause for forfeiture of custody. Using an argument strikingly similar to Ibn Qayyim's, albeit without citing him, Ibn ʿĀbidīn argued that since the *ratio legis* behind the remarriage juristic rule is to protect the child, the mufti should investigate the particular situation to determine what is best for the child (*aṣlaḥ*). He reasoned that there are situations in which the stepfather is kinder to the child than his relative and that the father may have a wife who harms the child more than the stepfather does.[166]

PRAGMATIC ADJUDICATION AND JURISPRUDENCE

How can we characterize these positions of Ibn Qayyim in light of what we know about his legal methodology? Ibn Qayyim's approach is in a way less formalistic than his peers, who insisted on abiding by the laws of jurists within a *taqlīd*-based system. It represents a critique of jurists who were seen by his teacher Ibn Taymiyya, in Rapoport's estimation, as focusing "on the formalities of the law rather than its intent."[167] In this instance of child custody law, Ibn Qayyim's approach resembles that of the Mamluk authorities who developed a secular legal system (*siyāsa*), which competed

[165] See al-Shirwānī, al-ʿIbādī, and al-Haytamī, *Ḥawāshī Tuḥfat Al-Muḥtāj Bi-Sharḥ Al-Minhāj*, 8361–8362; Ibn Qudāma al-Maqdisī, *Al-Mughnī*, 2:2009; al-Shirbīnī, *Mughnī Al-Muḥtāj Ilā Maʿrifat Maʿānī Alfāẓ Al-Minhāj*, 3:599–600.

[166] Ibn ʿĀbidīn and al-Ḥaṣkafī, *Radd Al-Muḥtār ʿalā Al-Durr Al-Mukhtār Sharḥ Tanwīr Al-Abṣār*, 5:266; al-Miṣrī, al-Nasafī, and Ibn ʿĀbidīn, *Al-Baḥr Al-Rāʾiq Sharḥ Kanz Al-Daqāʾiq*, 4: 181–182.

[167] Rapoport, "Royal Justice and Religious Law: *Siyāsah* and Shariʿah under the Mamluks," 92.

with sharīʿa jurisdiction. The objective of this parallel system of justice was to modify some of the rigidities that resulted from juristic formalism.

The policies of the Mamluks found much opposition from both types of jurists on the formalism-pragmatism spectrum. While being fully aware that most jurists were not always on one side of this spectrum, we may still describe Tāj al-Dīn al-Subkī (d. 771/1370) as a formalist. Compared to Ibn Taymiyya and Ibn Qayyim's approach to child custody and guardianship, al-Subkī was more concerned with applying legal rules as they were articulated by jurists rather than conceptualizing new modes of legal thought based on contextual notions of justice. His formalist tendencies were on full display when he rejected some of the practices of Mamluk police chiefs who departed from the rules established by jurists, such as by making a man who deflowers or impregnates a woman marry the mother so that the child is not without lineage. According to al-Subkī, this is contrary to the "religion of God" (*dīn Allāh*).[168] Al-Subkī was aware that the Mamluk secular authorities saw the juristic rules with respect to children born outside of wedlock to be contrary to the interests of children. He did not challenge the Mamluk practice on grounds of its benefit to the child or the mother but rather on the grounds that it did not abide by the divine law, that is, the formalist rules of jurists.

It would be inaccurate to assume that Ibn Qayyim's approach always ignored the rules of author-jurists or that al-Subkī's approach was always beholden to legal rules. What can be said though about these two approaches is that Ibn al-Qayyim's opposition to clerical authority and his commitment to *ijtihād* on a wider number of issues must have played a role in his treatment of child custody law as an area of the law that was not backed up unequivocally by textual sources for the various rules developed by jurists. One could also add a general tendency in the thought of Ibn Qayyim, partly due to the influence of his teacher Ibn Taymiyya, to criticize legal formalism both in substantive and procedural law.[169] The critique of formalism must be viewed within the anti-clerical attitude that faults jurists for entrenching formal rules as unchangeable sharīʿa determinations, when they were in fact, as the argument goes, based on the whims of jurists.

[168] Tāj al-Dīn al-Subkī, *Muʿīd Al-Niʿam Wa-Mubīd Al-Niqam*, ed. Muḥammad ʿAlī al-Najjār, Abū Zayd Shalabī, and Muḥammad Abū al-ʿUyūn, 1st edn. (Cairo: Maktabat al-Khānjī, 1948), 45.

[169] On Ibn Taymiyya's critique of formalism, see further Ovamir Anjum, *Politics, Law and Community in Islamic Thought: The Taymiyyan Moment* (New York: Cambridge University Press, 2012), 232–235; Johansen, "Signs as Evidence."

One could argue that the tension between the rigid rules of jurists on child custody and the best interests of the child as determined by judges on a case-by-case basis resembles the tension inherent in the creation of the English equity courts which coexisted with the King's Bench, with much jurisdictional overlap and with the objective of overcoming the rigidities of the common law, as we saw in Chapter 1. The letter of the common law failed in certain historical periods to uphold English society's conceptions of justice,[170] giving rise to alternative solutions such as the equity courts' focus on substantive justice in a way similar to the Mamluk Complaint Jurisdiction (*maẓālim*).[171]

Another approach through which the Mamluk and Ottoman judiciaries dealt with the rigidities of child custody law was to pursue private separation deeds. This solution was in tension with the views of most Sunni jurists who did not allow someone to cede a right that she or he had not yet acquired as would be the case with a husband ceding his right to custody should the mother remarry in the future. To the majority of Sunnis, such agreements were not worth the ink with which they were written, as already discussed. The Mālikīs were aware of this technical problem, which caused a heated debate within the school. Despite being a weak, non-*mashhūr* position, the Mālikī view dominated Mamluk and Ottoman court practice until around 1670 CE, as we shall see in the next chapter. Al-Qarāfī's treatise in defense of the practice was a form of *pragmatic jurisprudence* whereby jurists overlooked logical consistency in favor of the benefits to children and families accrued from separation deeds. Some Mālikīs considered this approach superior to the other Sunni approach of giving priority to the child's wishes. Like the Ḥanafīs, the Mālikīs considered children to be incapable of choosing what is beneficial to them. Children's welfare could be achieved through family agreements, which often gave custody to mothers neutralizing many restrictions author-jurists placed on women's remarriage and relocation out of the father's town. As we shall see in Chapters 3 and 4, the same pragmatism would continue in Ottoman courts. It is the spirit of the law, rather than its letter, that the judicial, juristic, and political authorities

[170] On the history of English equity courts, see further Dennis R. Klinck, *Conscience, Equity and the Court of Chancery in Early Modern England* (Surrey: Ashgate, 2010).

[171] The functional equivalent in Islamic history to the English equity courts is the Complaint Jurisdiction (*maẓālim*), which in addition to dealing with the transgressions of government authorities, it had at times expanded jurisdictions that overlapped and competed with the qadi's jurisdiction, acting as a corrective to the rigidities of formalist jurisprudence. On the Complaint Jurisdiction, see further Rapoport, "Royal Justice and Religious Law: *Siyāsah* and Shariʿah under the Mamluks."

tried to accommodate in the evolving conceptions of justice in Mamluk and Ottoman societies.[172]

CONCLUSION

Before we turn to practice, let us summarize the approach of premodern Muslim author-jurists with regard to the binding nature of their rules on custody. We have thus far seen how the mainstream juristic discourse presented author-juristic rules as mandatory (*règles impératives*) over which there was little party autonomy. Jurists presumed, for instance, that if Muslim children are raised beyond a certain age by a non-Muslim mother or if they reside with a stepfather who is not a close relative, their interests would be compromised. Nevertheless, some jurists, especially in the Mālikī school, made limited exceptions allowing parents some party autonomy by treating some rules as "default rules" (*règles supplétives*), that is, permitting parents to agree on custody arrangements that do not correspond to the dominant views of their respective schools. We have seen such exceptions in the context of custody arrangements made in no-fault, for-compensation divorce agreements. Notably, it was only some jurists in the Mālikī school who treated such agreements as binding.

On the most basic level, all jurists assumed that the welfare of the child is the ultimate goal of child custody. In order to reach this ultimate goal, there were three centers of decisionmaking emphasized by the different Sunni schools, namely (1) the categorical rules of author-jurists, (2) family agreements, and (3) the child's wishes. All jurists accepted the categorical rules of jurists as the presumptive rules of custody, but some of them were less willing to allow families to modify these rules (Ḥanafīs), while others gave greater discretion to families to modify them (Mālikīs). The Shāfiʿīs and Ḥanbalīs had a different answer. They gave more discretion to the child herself, rather than the families. These represented different visions of the child's welfare, which were in tension at times. Even within the Mālikī school itself where private separation deeds violating the school's own view of the child's presumptive welfare rules were considered binding, there were tensions over the validity of such agreements as well as an awareness of the logical inconsistency inherent in their acceptance.

[172] For examples of the Mamluk political authorities' substantive justice, see Rapoport, "Royal Justice and Religious Law: *Siyāsah* and Shariʿah under the Mamluks."

Another very important assumption of the juristic discourse on child custody is that although jurists reasoned that a mother was a better caregiver than say a wet-nurse or an aunt due to her kindness, they did not emphasize a unique psychological bond between mother and child, as the nineteenth-century Euro-American cult of motherhood suggests (more on this in Chapters 5 and 6). Thus, when the father had custody of a child of tender age, jurists assumed that he had a wife, a relative, a wet-nurse, a female slave, or a domestic who could take care of the child. Not being in the custodianship of the mother did not by itself constitute harm to the child. A mother could also give up her right to custody of an infant, regardless of her or his age, suggesting that the child's welfare was not presumptively negatively impacted by being cared for by females other than their mothers. When jurists had to choose between saving the child's money by taking her or him away from the mother if she charged a nursing or a custody fee if there was a free option and leaving the child with her or his mother, most of them chose the former, again suggesting a lower benefit accrued to the child from being with her or his mother than the nineteenth-century ideology of the cult of motherhood assumes. In Part II, I discuss Ottoman court practice focusing on private separation deeds in Chapter 3, and custody and guardianship more broadly in Chapter 4 to gain a better understanding of how the rules of author-jurists were operationalized in the courts.

Part II

Ottoman-Egyptian Practice, 1517–1801

3

Private Separation Deeds in Action

WOMEN'S SOCIAL CONTEXT IN LATE MAMLUK AND OTTOMAN EGYPT

Private separation deeds were, as we saw previously, practiced in Mamluk Egypt and in the Mālikī Maghrib prior to the Ottoman conquests of the eastern Mediterranean. The formulaic language reported by the Mamluk jurist al-Asyūṭī continued to be utilized verbatim by Ottoman scribes until the second half of the seventeenth century, offering another area of continuity between the Mamluk and Ottoman administrations.[1] These private

[1] Other examples of this continuity include the Mamluk land registers, which were handed over to the Ottomans allowing the new rulers to extract taxes efficiently. One would expect that the Ottomans and large swathes of the religious elite had a vested interest in taking possession of Mamluk court records in order to guarantee the notarial rights of citizens. Indeed, it is a matter of public order. Although we have clear evidence of the transfer of land registers from the Mamluks to the Ottomans, no such evidence exists for the court records. One could also safely assume that many of the scholars involved in the judiciary under the Mamluks were largely kept in the judicial bureaucracy. In other words, in the same way the Ottomans continued to rely on the Mamluks to administer land taxes under the supervision of the Ottoman governor of Egypt, the Mamluk judiciary was allowed to continue with some adjustments under the oversight of the chief judge of Egypt. This assumption tallies well with the Ottoman approach to bureaucratic and legal control of the Arab provinces. Perhaps the most obvious examples are the Ottomans' decision to accommodate legal pluralism in Arab lands, especially pragmatic eclecticism and the Ottomans' reliance on existing Mamluk authorities to control Egypt's resources and administration. On continuities and discontinuities of Mamluk administrative practices, see further Kumakura Wakako, "Who Handed over Mamluk Land Registers to the Ottomans? A Study on the Administrators of Land Records in the Late Mamluk Period," *Mamluk Studies Review* XVIII (2014–2015): 279–298; Stanford J. Shaw, *The Financial and Administrative Organization and Development of Ottoman Egypt, 1517–1798.* (Princeton, NJ: Princeton University Press, 1962); Stanford J. Shaw, "The Land Law of

separation deeds were meant to serve the interests of women, especially those of elite backgrounds, as well as the welfare of children, since the latter's welfare was verified by the judge before such agreements were notarized. Other methods and procedures such as pragmatic eclecticism were utilized by jurists in the Mamluk period to allow elite women greater access to divorce rights and to grant them the freedom, for instance, to stipulate in their marriage contracts that their husbands cannot move them from their hometown against their will.[2]

The women of Mamluk and Ottoman Egypt had almost full legal capacity. They were able to buy, sell, and inherit from relatives. Mamluk women earned wages from their work, giving them a degree of independence. In Rapoport's estimation, this independence explains the frequent occurrence of divorce. Women were active in both large-scale and petty trade. They had different crafts, including weaving or working as midwives and expert witnesses in the court, while others toiled the land. Some women also had the means to establish endowments, and they were frequently appointed by judges as endowment overseers. Ottoman women also had many of the benefits of their Mamluk counterparts. Like men, some merchant women from 1049/1640 earned the title of "master" (*muʿallima*). Women controlled considerable wealth, as evidenced by the large number of trusts registered by women in seventeenth- and eighteenth-century Egypt.[3] Class did play a factor though, as early modern women of high social and economic status had different expectations from women of more humble backgrounds; the former had more freedoms

Ottoman Egypt (960/1553): A Contribution to the Study of Landholding in the Early Years of Ottoman Rule in Egypt," *Der Islam* 38:1 (1963): 106–137; Ibrahim, *Pragmatism in Islamic Law*; Konrad Hirschler, "From Archive to Archival Practices: Rethinking the Preservation of Mamluk Administrative Documents," *Journal of the American Oriental Society* 136:1 (2016): 1–28; Burak, "Evidentiary Truth Claims, Imperial Registers, and the Ottoman Archive: Contending Legal Views of Archival and Record-Keeping Practices in Ottoman Greater Syria (Seventeenth-Nineteenth Centuries)"; Wael B. Hallaq, "The *Qāḍī*'s *Dīwān* (*Sijill*) before the Ottomans."

2 On the accommodations made by Mamluk jurists to women through pragmatic eclecticism, see further Ibrahim, *Pragmatism in Islamic Law*, 2017, 42–49.

3 Yossef Rapoport, *Marriage, Money and Divorce in Medieval Islamic Society* (Cambridge: Cambridge University Press, 2005), 31–50; Afaf Lutfi Sayyid-Marsot, *Women and Men in Late Eighteenth-Century Egypt* (Austin, TX: University of Texas Press, 1995), 8, 33–68, 90–98; ʿAbd al-Rāziq ʿĪsā, *Al-Marʾa Al-Miṣriyya Qabl Al-Ḥadātha Mukhtārāt Min Wathāʾiq Al-ʿAṣr Al-ʿUthmānī* (Cairo: Dār al-Kutub wa'l-Wathāʾiq al-Qawmiyya, 2012), 61–80; For a discussion of women's legal capacity in the context of Aintab, see Peirce, *Morality Tales Law and Gender in the Ottoman Court of Aintab*, 151–154; Daniel Crecelius, "Incidences of *Waqf* Cases in Three Cairo Courts: 1640–1802," *Journal of the Economic and Social History of the Orient* 29:2 (1986): 186.

in what they could wear, who they visited, and where they lived.[4] Some women, for instance, could make sure that their husbands did not take a second wife or that their husbands would not beat them.[5]

Women were able to work even against their husband's will with no consequence beyond the loss of financial support. This contrasts sharply with the situation in the modern period, where the state became much more invasive in the private lives of people.[6] In the court of al-Bāb al-ʿĀlī in 1190/1776, a husband brought a lawsuit against his wife for disobedience. Muḥammad had told his wife, Khaḍra, to stop working at the local bathhouse (*ḥammām*), but she refused. The judge did nothing but inform her that by not obeying her husband, she was legally disobedient (*nāshiz*) and, as a consequence, she had no right to maintenance or clothing allowance from her husband.[7] The act of disobedience was not treated as a crime but rather as leading to financial, rather than criminal, consequences. No wife in the Ottoman court records that I have examined was subjected to judicial discretionary punishment for disobedience.

According to Nelly Hanna, women in early seventeenth-century Cairo not only wrote stipulations in their marriage contracts that gave them freedom to visit their friends, but they also restricted their husband's right to sleep outside the house. One woman bound her future husband from sleeping outside of the house for more than two consecutive nights without permission from her, her mother, or her brother. Another marriage contract stipulated that the husband could not prevent his Muslim

[4] Jane Hathaway, *The Politics of Households in Ottoman Egypt: The Rise of the Qazdağlis* (New York, NY: Cambridge University Press, 1997), 109–110; Sayyid-Marsot, *Women and Men*, 7–8, 33–36, 53; Halil İnalcık and Donald Quataert, *An Economic and Social History of the Ottoman Empire, 1300–1914* (Cambridge: Cambridge University Press, 1994), 2:596, 674–676.

[5] "Court of Al-Bāb Al-ʿĀlī, Sijill 3 (939/1533), Archival Code 1001–000003," Dār al-Wathāʾiq al-Qawmiyya, Cairo, doc. 72, 16; "Court of Miṣr Al-Qadīma, Sijill 15 (1018/1609), Archival Code 1006–000153," Dār al-Wathāʾiq al-Qawmiyya, Cairo, doc. 43, 14; Cuno makes a similar observation about women of high status, but much later, in nineteenth-century Egypt. Their husbands were expected to abstain from taking a second wife or a concubine. In some cases, marriage contracts gave women the power of divorce in the event that the husband did not respect this assumption. Cuno, *Modernizing Marriage*, 29–30.

[6] On the state's new role, see further Hussein Ali Agrama, *Questioning Secularism: Islam, Sovereignty, and the Rule of Law in Modern Egypt* (Chicago, IL: University of Chicago Press, 2012).

[7] "Court of Al-Bāb Al-ʿĀlī, Sijill 293 (1190/1776), Archival Code 1001–000656," doc. 189, 133.

wife from working as a vendor,[8] and a Jewish woman was able to have a similar stipulation in her marriage contract, as it was written up in an Islamic court.[9] Others were given the power of divorce if physically abused by their husbands.[10] Some even controlled their husband's place of residence. One type of court case granted the wife the power of divorce if the husband left the city for ten days or more without her consent.[11]

Many women were able to look after their own interests and needs. One early modern Egyptian woman stipulated in her marriage contract that if the husband stopped her from visiting her cousin, her mother, or her sister within what was normal (*al-ziyāra al-muʿtāda*) or prevented her from staying with them, she would be entitled to a divorce as soon as she relieved him of her deferred dower.[12] The way this condition worked was that if she could prove that he had prevented her from visiting her family or staying with them, she could conduct a unilateral separation upon pledging to relieve him of his duty to pay the deferred dower. Women were also able to get a separation known as annulment (*faskh*) if a husband was excessively absent, which causes harm to the woman by denying her access to sex.[13] Women's access to this type of divorce assumes a certain level of female control over their social lives and mobility. Not only was women's need for sex discussed publicly (that is, in the court, which was a very public space), but some women were able to acknowledge sexual misconduct publicly and repent in the court without being punished. In one instance, this public repentance preceded a marriage to a member of the community who seemed not to have been the person with whom she had had a relationship outside of wedlock.[14]

[8] Nelly Hanna, "Marriage Among Merchant Families in Seventeenth-Century Cairo," in *Women, the Family, and Divorce Laws in Islamic History*, ed. Amira El Azhary Sonbol (Syracuse, NY: Syracuse University Press, 1996), 143–145.

[9] "Court of Ṣāliḥiyya Al-Najmiyya, Sijill 3 (951/1544), Archival Code 1012–000003," Dār al-Wathāʾiq al-Qawmiyya, Cairo, doc. 167, 52.

[10] The court records are full of agreements in which the wife inserted a stipulation that if the husband were to beat her, she would be divorced without his consent as soon as she relieved him of his deferred dower. See for example, "Court of Miṣr Al-Qadīma, Sijill 15 (1018/1609), Archival Code 1006–000153," doc. 43, 14.

[11] See for example, "Court of Miṣr Al-Qadīma, Sijill 15 (1018/1609), Archival Code 1006–000153," doc. 42, 14.

[12] See for example, "Court of Miṣr Al-Qadīma, Sijill 15 (1018/1609), Archival Code 1006–000153," doc. 103, 29.

[13] "Court of Ṣāliḥiyya Al-Najmiyya, Sijill 3 (951/1544), Archival Code 1012–000003," doc. 31, 11; doc. 41, 15.

[14] "Court of Miṣr Al-Qadīma, Sijill 21 (1081/1670), Archival Code 1006–000159," Dār al-Wathāʾiq al-Qawmiyya, Cairo, doc. 1, 1.

Despite the patriarchal checks against women's sexual conduct and the power of husbands to force mothers to choose between child custody and remarriage, women had some areas of maneuverability that were generally accepted by society. In one case from the Cairo court of al-Ṣāliḥiyya al-Najmiyya in 951/1544, a woman inserted two conditions into her marriage contract. The first was that the husband had no right to move her out of Cairo without her consent, and that he would be responsible for the maintenance of her son, Muḥammad, who was her child from a previous marriage.[15] It is most likely that she had also concluded an agreement with Muḥammad's father that allowed her to remarry in exchange for relieving him of the financial obligation of child maintenance, a duty that she transferred onto the new husband since she did not have the means herself to shoulder this responsibility.

PRIVATE SEPARATION DEEDS

Before we discuss private separation deeds, a word about the structure of the Sharīʿa court system is in order. Early modern Ottoman-Egyptian court records were organized by date, and the transactions brought to the court on a given day were registered chronologically. These transactions include all areas of law, from a case of murder to the notarization of a divorce. Most of the business of early modern Egyptian Sharīʿa courts was related to the notarization of contracts, particularly family law and commercial transactions. An estimated 15 percent of my sample dealt with family law cases, less than 2 percent of which were cases of separation. Certainly, not all separation deeds were recorded in the court. Reliance on the Sharīʿa court records involves an urban bias owing to the fact that some early modern rural communities did not have easy to access to courts. However, given Egypt's geography – most of the population lives around the narrow strip of the Nile Valley – one could assume that access to the courts was neither excessively hard nor expensive for most dwellers of the Nile Valley and the Delta. Judging by the courts that I have examined, such notarizations were done by both elite and non-elite groups. Many regular Egyptians with limited means notarized their separation deeds as a precaution against future litigation. The proliferation of notarization of contracts of small value suggests that notarization was inexpensive and that it was a superior form of documentation compared to contracts signed

[15] "Court of Ṣāliḥiyya Al-Najmiyya, Sijill 3 (951/1544), Archival Code 1012–000003," doc. 125, 39.

out of court. The court records are replete with cases in which a litigant requests a court-true copy of a marriage separation deed that is a decade old or longer. The care with which the Ottoman judicial authorities kept these records must have been another reason why many people notarized separation deeds of low value, for instance, ones containing the basic maintenance of a child for a couple of years.[16] Ottoman archival practices enabled subjects of the law to obtain notarization records that have the power of law even after the death of the witnesses, something that is not possible in informal, out-of-court contracts.

The Ottoman judiciary in Egypt was a mix of local and central judicial authorities. The chief judge of Egypt was sent from Istanbul and was often educated in the imperial educational system set up by the Ottoman ruling elite. While the chief judge usually served for only one year, most of the deputies were local jurists who had close connections and knowledge of Egyptian social and judicial practices. Soon after the Ottoman conquest of Egypt in 1517, tensions between the local and Ottoman juridical authorities arose, but within decades, the tensions subsided. One could argue that the metropole-periphery dialectic in Egypt's judiciary led to a judicial hybrid characterized more by continuity than with rupture, as the story of child custody law shows us.[17]

There were two main types of private separation deeds: one corresponding to mainstream juristic rules and another modifying them substantially.

Agreements Conforming to Categorical Juristic Rules

The first type of agreement, which continued throughout the Ottoman period and was in full conformity with the majority jurisprudence of the Sunni schools, will not concern us further here since it did not challenge the categorical rules of author-jurists. In these agreements, neither party would give up her or his right to custody. It was simply an agreement on the

[16] On Ottoman record-keeping practices, see further Burak, "Evidentiary Truth Claims, Imperial Registers, and the Ottoman Archive: Contending Legal Views of Archival and Record-Keeping Practices in Ottoman Greater Syria (Seventeenth-Nineteenth Centuries)."

[17] On the tensions between the local Egyptian and Ottoman juridical authorities and on the role of scholars in the Ottoman Empire, see further Ibrahim, "Al-Shaʿrānī's Response to Legal Purism"; Guy Burak, *The Second Formation of Islamic Law: The Hanafi School in the Early Modern Ottoman Empire* (Cambridge: Cambridge University Press, 2015); Abdurrahman Atçıl, *Scholars and Sultans in the Early Modern Ottoman Empire* (Cambridge: Cambridge University Press, 2016).

amount of maintenance, nursing fees, establishment of paternity, and acknowledging who would be in physical custody of the child (henceforth, a "simple separation agreement").

Agreements Modifying Categorical Juristic Rules

The second type is the one that we will focus on, since it was problematic for many jurists. Developed by Mālikī jurists, this approach was designed to solve a problem with the rigidity of the juristic laws of custody. It therefore produced agreements in tension with both the majoritarian discourse of Sunni jurists (non-Mālikīs) and the categorical rules of jurists more broadly, whose views were assumed to serve the interests of children with a one-rule-fits-all approach to their care. The Mālikīs opened a new avenue through which they justified departures from these rigid rules, treating them as default, or presumptive, rather than mandatory rules. These separation deeds, which began to appear at least during the Mamluk period, continued from the very beginning of the Ottoman conquest of Egypt. They can be found in the earliest registers held at Egypt's National Archives, from the Cairo Court of Miṣr al-Qadīma in 934/1528, 11 years after the Ottoman conquest.[18] However, by the second half of the seventeenth century, these private separation deeds ceased to be binding and subsequently disappeared from the court records.

These agreements modifying categorical juristic rules were considered binding, in line with Mālikī law in Ottoman courts, even though most of them were brought before non-Mālikī judges. These agreements became so common in the first century of Ottoman rule that they replaced the Shāfiʿī and Ḥanbalī deferral to the child's wishes, a procedure that was completely absent from our sample. Family agreements were treated as a superior arrangement from the perspective of the welfare of the child. The child custody rules of author-jurists were therefore considered simply default rules. For instance, the categorical *rule* that a child should not live with her or his stepfather was modified in court practice, and in line with the Mālikī school, these agreements were considered binding.

These separation deeds often involved one parent giving up a right that she or he did not have at the time of the agreement, such as the typical agreement obliging the father not to sue for custody in the event

[18] "Court of Miṣr Al-Qadīma, Sijill 1 (934/1528), Archival Code 1006–000001," doc. 169, 39.

that the mother remarried or moved, or if the father moved (we may call this subcategory the "remarriage and travel agreement" type). The giving away of a hypothetical future right was rejected by the majority of Sunni jurists and caused some tensions even among the Mālikīs. One example of the tension inherent in this type of agreement is that when a man gives up his custody of a boy above the age of ten, Ḥanafīs assumed this would harm the boy, who would internalize female dispositions. This rule was not contextual and applied to all boys. For the Mālikīs, in this case and in the case of the mother's remarriage for instance, the families were given the freedom to modify juristic rules in accordance with their circumstances and what they deemed fit for the benefit of everyone including the child.

Standard discourse-defying agreements sometimes even included granting the woman joint guardianship with the father over all matters, including the child's marriage. The more egalitarian view of parents inherent in this agreement and other such stipulations were not supported by juristic discourse, since even Mālikī jurists did not discuss these potential guardianship-granting agreements in their discourse to the best of my knowledge. It is important here to emphasize that these separation deeds were never justified in the court records themselves by reference to any schools or jurists. One example from other areas of family law highlights this absence. In Ḥanbalī law, a *khul*ʿ does not count as an instance of repudiation (*ṭalāq*), thus allowing couples an unlimited number of such separations without the need for an intervening marriage by a *muḥallil* – a person who marries the divorced woman and divorces her – before reconciliation between a husband who uttered three instances of repudiation and his wife is possible. In one instance, a *khul*ʿ notarized by a Ḥanafī judge mentions clearly that the separation deed was based on the Ḥanbalī view that *khul*ʿ does not count as an instance of *ṭalāq*.[19] The same judge did not offer any justification by reference to Mālikī law for a stipulation in the same document that the father would lose his right to custody regardless of

[19] It was much more common for judges to refer cases to other judges, rather than cross-school boundaries themselves. Such crossing of school boundaries by judges was generally prohibited by jurists. although some instances can be found in the Ottoman period especially in the early sixteenth century. Later on in the sixteenth century, we find that Ḥanbalī judges increasingly presided over such cases, following juristic discourse more closely. See, for instance, "Court of Miṣr Al-Qadīma, Sijill 10 (978/1570), Archival Code 1006–000010," Dār al-Wathāʾiq al-Qawmiyya, Cairo; "Court of Miṣr Al-Qadīma, Sijill 10 (978/1570), Archival Code 1006–000010," doc. 158, 26; doc. 179, 29; doc. 227, 38; doc. 234, 39; Ibrahim, *Pragmatism in Islamic Law*, 2017; Ibrahim, "Rethinking the *Taqlīd* Hegemony: An Institutional, *Longue-Durée* Approach."

the mother's marital status or where she lived.[20] This perhaps suggests that this practice (stripping fathers of their right to custody because of an agreement) was so normalized – despite the almost universal objection to these agreements in Ḥanafī juristic discourse – that Ḥanafī judges, for instance, did not feel the need to reference Mālikī law as the source of their forum selection.

To get a more refined sense of the radical approach to custody that these separation deeds made possible, consider the following example. On April 7, 1548, only 31 years after the Ottoman conquest of Egypt, a non-elite woman from the neighborhood of Miṣr al-Qadīma in Old Cairo by the name of Hayfā came to the court with both her then-husband and her ex-husband to make a formal agreement and have it notarized by the Mālikī judge. The terms of the agreement were that Hayfā and her new husband, Najā, would pay for all the cost of maintaining Jamīla, Hayfā's minor daughter from the previous marriage. The three parties agreed that in exchange for not asking the father for any child support, Jamīla's mother and her stepfather would keep custody of her until she married, at which point her maintenance would devolve on her husband. Under Mālikī law, as we saw previously, a woman would normally have custody of a minor female until marriage.[21] This fact may explain the choice of the Mālikī judge in this case in an otherwise dominant Ḥanafī context, where most transactions were brought before Ḥanafī judges.[22] It is often the case in Ottoman court records that relevant information (and

20 Couples sometimes conducted their *khulʿ* agreements under Ḥanbalī, rather than Ḥanafī law, explaining that such a choice was designed to make sure that such a separation does not count toward the maximum three instances after which reconciliation is no longer an option, unless there was an intervening marriage to a new person. At other times, the presiding judge was Ḥanafī, but it was clearly stated that the case at hand was indeed in accordance with Ḥanbalī, rather than Ḥanafī law. See "Court of Miṣr Al-Qadīma, Sijill 8 (971/1564), Archival Code 1006–000008," Dār al-Wathāʾiq al-Qawmiyya, Cairo, doc. 26, 5; "Court of Miṣr Al-Qadīma, Sijill 3 (950/1544), Archival Code 1006–000003," Dār al-Wathāʾiq al-Qawmiyya, Cairo, doc. 37, 6.

21 "Court of Miṣr Al-Qadīma, Sijill 4 (955/1548), Archival Code 1006–000004," Dār al-Wathāʾiq al-Qawmiyya, Cairo, doc. 273, 37.

22 In the early decades of the Ottoman conquest of Egypt, there was a drive among the Ottomans to Ḥanafize the Egyptian legal system, but this drive faded in the second half of the sixteenth century. There were cases in that period in which Ḥanafī judges used non-Ḥanafī laws to accommodate some transactions, but this practice which was frowned upon by jurists receded by the end of the sixteenth century. Normal legal procedure in the seventeenth and eighteenth centuries was that judges would refer cases to other judges from other schools rather than cross school boundaries themselves. On the practice of seventeenth- and eighteenth-century Egypt, see further Ibrahim, *Pragmatism in Islamic Law*, 2017.

sometimes even seemingly irrelevant information) about the relationships of different parties would be mentioned in the court records. Had the stepfather been related to the minor child, the court scribes would have naturally emphasized this point, as it has a direct impact on the case at hand. There is no mention of the stepfather being related to this child.[23]

The agreement protects the mother in two ways. First, it stipulates clearly that the mother's right to custody, once this agreement is notarized, should be valid regardless of whether she is single or married, whether she leaves the habitual residence of the child (Cairo) or not, and whether the father stays in Cairo or not. In no situation, the document continues, can the father take the child away from the mother or request that she move away from Cairo with him "whether she is single or married, having moved away [from Cairo] or is still resident, and whether he has moved away or is still a resident" (*ʿazban kānat aw mutazawwija muqīma kānat aw musāfira musāfiran huwa kāna aw muqīman*).[24] (Recall that this is the exact wording of Mamluk separation deeds from a century earlier). And second, it requires the father to share guardianship of the child with the mother, a prospect that not even Mālikī jurists who were more permissive of such separation deeds envisioned based on the lack of discussion of this stipulation in juristic discourse. According to the document, the father cannot make decisions related to the child without both the mother's presence and consent. In other words, the father, who would normally according to juristic discourse have the power as a guardian to marry the child off or make important decisions about her education and so on, agreed to grant the mother a veto over any decisions related to Jamīla.[25] In exchange for the child's maintenance, the father was willing to both give up (*isqāṭ*) his right to custody and share guardianship with the mother.

To sum up the case, the judge notarized the document, even though the agreement clearly contradicts the ideal doctrines of child custody law in legal discourse in broad Sunni terms. As we saw previously, there was an assumption among jurists that a husband who is not related to the child is inherently hostile to that child and therefore the best interests of the child were determined by most jurists to consist of not permitting the mother to maintain custody in this case. This dominant rule was made by author-jurists, leaving very little discretion on this particular issue to judges. But

[23] "Court of Miṣr Al-Qadīma, Sijill 4 (955/1548), Archival Code 1006–000004," doc. 273, 37.
[24] Ibid.
[25] "Court of Miṣr Al-Qadīma, Sijill 4 (955/1548), Archival Code 1006–000004," doc. 273, 37.

under this private separation deed, where one of the two parents to later decide to move away from Cairo, the mother would keep custody of Jamīla. This outcome violates the generalized judgment of author-jurists that it is in the best interests of children to stay with their fathers, because in the event of a conflict between guardianship and custody, guardianship was prioritized. The last general rule that was made by author-jurists in legal manuals but ignored in this private agreement is that guardianship is the prerogative of the father. Here the father's freedom in managing the affairs of the child was curtailed by the mother's stipulation that her consent would have to be solicited. As already noted in Chapter 2, Mālikī jurists sought to normalize this practice by permitting such separation deeds despite the inconsistency they caused to the broader law of obligations in the Mālikī school and the majority position of Sunnis.

More important, this case is no exception in Ottoman-Egyptian courts of the sixteenth and seventeenth centuries. In fact, not only is the agreement found in so many registers of the Ottoman period (until 1670), but the wording of the essential elements of the agreement was also formulaic and fully standardized by Mamluk and Ottoman scribes and judges. The formula stipulating that the mother has the right to maintain custody regardless of her marital status and even if she left town can be found in many Ottoman court registers. These agreements were often part of a *khul*ʿ arrangement in which the two families often bargained maintenance, child custody, and child support in the final separation. For instance, in the same court register, a case of *khul*ʿ appears in which the father would provide child support, while the mother would maintain custody regardless of her marital status and whether she stays in the place of habitual residence of the child or not. In this situation, the mother did not relieve the husband of his financial obligations toward the child in exchange for signing this agreement.[26]

Another example of private separation deeds comes from the Court of al-Bāb al-ʿĀlī, where a woman agreed with her husband in 937/1530 to have custody of her daughter and that the husband "has no right to take her away unless the mother concedes custody to him voluntarily" (*lā yanzaʿhā minhā wa-lā yaʾkhudhhā illā in dafaʿathā lahu bi-riḍā minhā*). Since the presiding judge was Ḥanafī, the girl's custody would be transferred to the father at the age of nine according to the dominant Ḥanafī view in early modern Egypt, but the father had no such right

[26] "Court of Miṣr Al-Qadīma, Sijill 4 (955/1548), Archival Code 1006–000004," doc. 367, 49.

under this agreement.[27] In the first *sijill* (court record) of al-Bāb al-ʿĀlī, one finds another separation deed that gave custody of three children to the mother and emphasized that the father had no right to petition for custody in the future, regardless of the mother's marital status, whether she continued to live in Cairo or moved out of the city, and whether the father stayed in Cairo or moved.[28]

Another example of such separation deeds comes from 1057/1647 Cairo, where a woman asked her husband for a share in the revenue of their baking business. When she requested her share of the revenues for her work in the bakery, her husband verbally and physically abused her. The document suggests that their family dispute was not kept to the confines of their home. The situation escalated, and both sides were making claims against one another (*takhāṣum wa-l-tanāzuʿ wa-l-tadāʿī*). The issue ended up in court before the Ḥanafī judge, where they agreed to a *khulʿ* separation, according to which she would have custody of their infant daughter regardless of the mother's marital status, place of residence, or the father's domicile – whether it was in Cairo or outside of Cairo.[29] It is likely that the entire quarter in Miṣr al-Qadīma knew about this family dispute and about the outcome. The court was a public space where men and women were often in attendance, as evidenced by the many people who are sometimes mentioned in the court procedures. These people often include dignitaries with no judicial function, such as Azhar scholars, as well as people from the neighborhood who are not themselves party to any court transactions. The court therefore was a public space wherein the entire community was knowledgeable about both the law and its functioning. I have not found any judicial decree prohibiting public attendance of court proceedings. Incidentally, what complements this picture of the court as a space of a communal negotiation of the law is the fact that judges smoked inside the court, perhaps along with these important figures in the community. This practice riled the judicial authorities, who issued decrees prohibiting smoking inside the court. In fact, one sometimes finds burn marks on the court records that must hark back to these practices.[30]

[27] "Court of Al-Bāb Al-ʿĀlī, Sijill 1 (937/1530), Archival Code 1001–000001," Dār al-Wathāʾiq al-Qawmiyya, Cairo, doc. 69, 17.

[28] "Court of Al-Bāb Al-ʿĀlī, Sijill 1 (937/1530), Archival Code 1001–000001," doc. 104, 26.

[29] In the first 200 cases of this register, for example, there were six cases of *Future Forfeiture* Agreements and three cases of noncontroversial separation deeds, where the amount of maintenance is established without either party giving up his or her right to custody. "Court of Miṣr Al-Qadīma, Sijill 18 (1057/1647), Archival Code 1006–000156," Dār al-Wathāʾiq al-Qawmiyya, Cairo, doc. 42, 16.

[30] "Court of Miṣr Al-Qadīma, Sijill 22 (1092–1681), Archival Code 1006–000160," doc. 140, 51.

In some cases, the father did not agree to grant the mother these wide powers of movement and remarriage without losing custody and instead they agreed to a payment were the father to change his mind and petition for custody after the mother's remarriage. Consider the example of Badriyya, who in 961/1554 agreed with her husband, Shihāb al-Dīn, to a separation settlement in which the mother would keep custody of their daughter, Sukkar, for two years.[31] Were the father to take Sukkar from the mother, the document continues, he would pay ten gold dinars: a hefty sum that would surely deter him from petitioning for custody. Recall that this is similar to the case reported by al-Wansharīsī about Mamluk Egypt. This type of agreement was not restricted to Muslims. Indeed, some Christian couples signed such agreements in Ottoman-Egyptian courts. In the court of al-Bāb al-ʿĀlī in 1009/1601, a Christian woman by the name of Maryam signed a *khulʿ* agreement with her husband Gabriel, according to which Maryam would keep custody of their two children, regardless of her marital status or where she lived.[32] This couple must have resorted to the Islamic court to conclude a no-fault *khulʿ* divorce, which would not have been possible under Coptic Christian Law, where the grounds for divorce were very limited.

Private separation deeds were nullified in line with juristic discourse in all the four Sunni schools if the judge determined that such an agreement posed harm to the child. In 1666, Salīm, a regular resident of seventeenth-century Miṣr al-Qadīma who lived next to the ʿAmr b. al-ʿĀṣ Mosque, went before the Shāfiʿī judge to sue his ex-wife, Khaḍrā, for custody of their son, ʿAlī (henceforth *The Case of the Abused Child*). The document says that ʿAlī had already been weaned, which suggests that he must have been at least two years old. The father had previously given up his right to custody to the mother who had remarried. The father claimed that the stepfather had been beating ʿAlī and constantly reviling him for the food that he ate in his house. The stepfather, the mother, the father, and the child's paternal and maternal grandmothers were all present during the court proceedings. The father requested that the child's custody be transferred to the paternal grandmother, who had offered to assume both custody and maintenance of the child. Khaḍrā denied the claim made by the father. The child does not seem to have been present at the proceedings, or at least he was not given a voice in this case. Be that as it may, the

31 "Court of Qanāṭir Al-Sibāʿ, Sijill 3 (961/1554), Archival Code 1007–000003," Dār al-Wathāʾiq al-Qawmiyya, Cairo, doc. 159, 40.

32 ʿĪsā, *Al-Marʾa Al-Miṣriyya Qabl Al-Ḥadātha Mukhtārāt Min Wathāʾiq Al-ʿAṣr Al-ʿUthmānī*, 174.

judge did not follow regular procedure to establish the truthfulness of the claimant. Normally, the judge would have asked the father to produce evidence for his claim. Failing that, the mother would have sworn that no beating or constant rebuke over food took place. Instead, the judge transferred custody to the paternal grandmother, erring on the side of caution.[33] In other words, the judge was not willing to take the risk of the father's claim being truthful because that would constitute harm to the child. In this case, the judge did not use formal justice, which would have required abiding by legal procedure. He instead focused on substantive justice in the individual case of the abused child, which to him amounted to taking no risks.

Other fathers were not comfortable with their children being raised in the home of another man. Take, for example, the case of Shaykh ʿAmr, who in 1053/1643 agreed to a *khul*ʿ separation with his wife and gave her custody in exchange for her not asking him for their unweaned infant's maintenance, nursing, or custody wages, as long as she did not remarry.[34] Other fathers did indeed sue for custody when the mother remarried and were granted custody.[35]

Private separation deeds modifying the ideal doctrines of jurists continued throughout the Ottoman period, even though they were no longer considered binding by the last quarter of the seventeenth century. Consider the case of Āmina Khātūn whose 1202/1787 separation deed included a stipulation that the father would give up his right to have custody of his teenage son (*murāhiq*), even though many Ḥanafīs assumed that it is not in the interest of a child to stay with his mother after the age of ten. Unfortunately, we do not know the school affiliation of this judge, but there is no indication that the judge was Mālikī, the only school that would allow a boy to stay with his mother without asking the child's opinion. There is also no mention of the child having been asked to decide which parent he wanted to reside with, in line with Shāfiʿī and Ḥanbalī doctrines. The judge established that the mother had custody of the boy and the amount of maintenance the father had to pay. With this document, the judge could enforce nonpayment and liability for future negligence.[36]

[33] "Court of Miṣr Al-Qadīma, Sijill 20 (1076/1666), Archival Code 1006–000158," Dār al-Wathāʾiq al-Qawmiyya, Cairo, doc. 119, 53.

[34] "Court of Miṣr Al-Qadīma, Sijill 17 (1053/1643), Archival Code 1006–000155," Dār al-Wathāʾiq al-Qawmiyya, Cairo, doc. 143, 57.

[35] See, for instance, "Court of Miṣr Al-Qadīma, Sijill 21 (1081/1670), Archival Code 1006–000159," doc. 3, 2.

[36] "Court of Al-Bāb Al-ʿĀlī, Sijill 311 (1202/1787–8), Archival Code 1001–000702," Dār al-Wathāʾiq al-Qawmiyya, Cairo, doc. 82, 59–60.

What is clear here is that the parents were allowed to write this agreement giving the mother custody of the child, presumably until puberty or beyond. These types of cases continued until the early nineteenth century, but any resulting agreements in which a parent gave up his or her right did not include a stipulation foreclosing a change of mind or emphasizing its binding nature.

By the last quarter of the seventeenth century, language suggesting that private separation deeds were binding disappeared from our sample, so did the remarriage and travel agreement type, suggesting that the Ottoman judiciary treated the categorical rules of jurists as mandatory by that time. In another private separation deed from 1081/1670, the couple agreed that the mother would care for an unweaned, blind (*al-baṣīr bi-qalbih*) infant, while the father would assume custody of a six-year-old son and a three-year-old daughter. One could assume that perhaps part of the reason that the parents agreed that the father would take care of the two children of tender age is so that the mother would have the time to care for their blind brother. The agreement did not contain any stipulation that the father had no future right to ask for child custody if he wished.[37]

Being no longer binding, many agreements were nullified by judges upon the request of the parent who had given up her or his right. Another case that highlights this change comes from the highest court in Egypt under the Ottomans, al-Bāb al-ʿĀlī. In 1190/1776, Muḥammad brought a lawsuit against his ex-wife, ʿĀʾisha, before the Ḥanafī judge over the custody of their son, Ḥasan, whose age is not mentioned. According to the father, the parents had made an agreement in which the mother was to keep the custody of their daughter, ʿAfīfa, who was unweaned (most likely less than two years of age) in exchange for maintenance and nursing fees. The agreement also included a ceding (*isqāṭ*) of the mother's right to custody of Ḥasan who was able to walk (*dārij*), usually used for the period immediately after weaning at around two years and before the age of discernment (*tamyīz*), which was estimated to be at around age seven. The father indicated that the agreement took place at the Jīza court a year earlier, giving the exact date so that the judge could request to examine a true copy of it if the mother were to contest any of the details that he provided.[38] According to the father, the mother had kept Ḥasan in contradiction to their agreement. The mother acknowledged that they

[37] "Court of Miṣr Al-Qadīma, Sijill 21 (1081/1670), Archival Code 1006–000159," doc. 17, 7.

[38] "Court of Al-Bāb Al-ʿĀlī, Sijill 293 (1190/1776), Archival Code 1001–000656," doc. 208, 145–146.

had made an agreement, but she added that he had not provided sufficient money for ʿAfīfa and so she had changed her mind about ceding (*isqāṭ*) her right to care for her son. To the husband's chagrin, the judge allowed the wife to retract her decision to give up her right to custody of her son and ordered the husband to deliver the boy to her.

This decision was not justified by reference to Ḥanafī doctrine, which does not treat such agreements as binding. Neither have I found the Mālikī doctrine being invoked to offer the opposite view. As we saw previously, Ḥanafī judges prior to the second half of the seventeenth century notarized such agreements even though they contradicted their own schools. This judge's decision not to respect the agreement explains the declining popularity of these agreements by the second half of the seventeenth century and the complete disappearance of the remarriage and travel type of agreements by that time. If judges had continued to consistently enforce these agreements, we would have expected informal agreements to this effect to have been notarized in the courts on a large scale and the remarriage and travel agreements to continue appearing in the courts throughout the seventeenth and eighteenth centuries, as was the case in the sixteenth and first half of the seventeenth century. One may wonder: why do we still see examples of such agreements (but not of the remarriage and travel type) being notarized at all if they are unenforceable? These agreements were usually part of larger simple agreements, where it was important to establish who has physical custody of the child and the maintenance arrangements. In this case, for instance, after allowing the mother to change her mind, the judge determined the two children's maintenance, nursing fee, and clothing allowances. He added a clause that any money the mother had to borrow due to the father's failure to meet his financial obligations would be the personal debt of the father.[39] Even nonbinding stipulations made it into these agreements in order to establish who would have physical custody of the child. Once the parent changes her or his mind, such stipulations were unenforceable in the eyes of Ottoman-Egyptian judges of the last quarter of the seventeenth century onward.

39 Some jurists, such as the majority of Ḥanafīs, did not consider the money spent by the mother on her children prior to an agreement to be a debt in the default of the father, and therefore this clause was meant to guarantee that the mother could borrow money from a third party on the assumption that it was a debt of the father. "Court of Al-Bāb Al-ʿĀlī, Sijill 293 (1190/1776), Archival Code 1001–000656," doc. 208, 145–146.

GUARDIANSHIP ARRANGEMENTS

In addition to the custody arrangements made in private separation deeds, there was a process of verification that judges often conducted to ascertain that both the mother and agnatic relatives were in agreement over the person appointed by the judge as guardian of the child. The many references made to the mother's agreement (or the agreement of the agnatic relatives in the case that the mother is appointed as guardian) in the judge's appointment of a guardian suggest that such agreements played an important role in the judge's decision. I will mention a few of these examples to give an idea about the functioning of family autonomy in the courts. Party autonomy functioned in similar ways in matters relating to guardianship as it did in determinations of custody. In 968/1561, the Ḥanafī judge of the Qisma ʿArabiyya probate court appointed a mother as a guardian (*waṣiyya*) over her two children whose father had died. One of the children, Muḥammad, was described as a minor (*qāṣir*), suggesting that he was not an infant and most likely above the age of discernment; and the other is ʿAlī, who is unweaned. The father's full brother was in attendance and he consented to the designation of the mother as guardian.[40] According to juristic discourse, the paternal uncle would have priority of guardianship but due to his non-objection to the mother's assumption of guardianship, the judge had no qualms about granting the mother both custody and guardianship. In this instance, the private arrangements made outside of the normal order of guardianship became operative.

The consent of non-agnatic relatives who are not entitled to custody was also sometimes sought in some court appointments of guardians. In one case, the mother's consent was sought when the paternal uncle was appointed as a guardian,[41] suggesting that her say carried weight. In another instance, the document appointing an agnatic uncle who should naturally receive custody, according to the formalist rules of author-jurists, explicitly references the consent of the mother of four male minors, as well as the consent of their paternal grandmother,[42] or the consent of the mother and the brother, according to another document.[43] Juristic

[40] "Court of Qisma ʿArabiyya, Sijill 1 (968–969/1561), Archival Code 1004–000001," doc. 201, 85.

[41] "Court of Qisma ʿArabiyya, Sijill 1 (968–969/1561), Archival Code 1004–000001," doc. 344, 157.

[42] "Court of Qisma ʿArabiyya, Sijill 1 (968–969/1561), Archival Code 1004–000001," doc. 231, 108; doc. 244, 114.

[43] "Court of Qisma ʿArabiyya, Sijill 2 (970–971/1562–1563), Archival Code 1004–000002," Dār al-Wathāʾiq al-Qawmiyya, Cairo, doc. 30, 19.

discourse does *not* make the guardianship rights of agnatic relatives contingent upon the mother's consent. The mother had custody of these four minor boys (*qāṣirūn*). She was also likely in charge of their education and most of their guardianship-related responsibilities since she was in physical control over them, reducing the guardianship of the uncle to financial matters.

In these instances, judges wanted to ensure that the agnatic relative was to be trusted with the children's property and that there is consensus over the person within the family. One cannot help but think that familial harmony, which is promoted by such non-adversarial agreements, whether in the case of custody or guardianship, was an important objective of the pragmatic adjudicative work of jurists, operating in dialogue with the formalism of juristic discourse. Certainly, these judges were themselves jurists and sometimes, albeit less frequently in the Ottoman period, the ones who developed the juristic discourse in their capacity as author-jurists outside of the court. Yet in their work as judges, they followed a different set of values and approaches from their authorship of juristic manuals. This system of private mediation is similar to the dominant approach in many US jurisdictions today, where families are encouraged, and sometimes required by law depending on the jurisdiction, to mediate before resorting to an adversarial litigation, as we saw in Chapter 1.[44]

DISAPPEARANCE OF THE REMARRIAGE AND TRAVEL SEPARATION DEED

The disappearance of the remarriage and travel type of separation deeds in the last quarter of the seventeenth century and the increasing reliance on the Ḥānafī position that such agreements are not binding seem sudden and clear-cut. Why did this agreement type disappear completely, given the large sample? Was there a social backlash against women being granted such licenses in separation deeds? Was it an assertion of Ḥanafī rules in child custody and guardianship laws? Why did the Ḥanafī-dominated judiciary suddenly consider child custody to be a question of public policy, allowing for little party autonomy on the matter? Was this shift driven by evolving social attitudes, or was it the opposition of some Ḥanafī jurists to the remarriage and travel agreements that impacted social attitudes toward the practice?

44 On mediation in US jurisdictions, see Mason, *From Father's Property to Children's Rights*, 178–185.

In the absence of any discussion, to the best of my knowledge, of child custody law in Ottoman-Egyptian early modern chronicles, the only source of social history for the period would be the court records themselves. We already see signs of tension in the court records, where some fathers inserted a stipulation in their separation deeds that they would give up their right to custody as long as the mother did *not* remarry or move.[45] In other cases, male agnatic relatives gave mothers financial incentive to not remarry by volunteering to donate money toward the child's maintenance as long as the mother remained single.[46] Other fathers and male agnates seemed to have no problems with the mother's maintaining child custody while being married to a "stranger." Take, for example, *sijill* 4 of the Court of Miṣr al-Qadīma dated 955/1548. Out of the first 400 cases, there were eight private separation deeds. Six of them were of the remarriage and travel type.[47] One of the remaining two discussed financial details and established that the mother had custody without discussing the mother's remarriage or where she lived,[48] and the other gave the mother custody as long as she did not remarry or move away from Miṣr al-Qadīma.[49] In one case of the remarriage and travel type, the agreement was entered into by the widowed mother and the deceased father's brother, giving the mother custody regardless of her marital status or place of residence and explicitly stating that the brother also consented to her being appointed as guardian.[50] One could speculate that the social attitude against letting children live with the stepfather must have become the dominant position by the last quarter of the seventeenth century, causing a change in court practice. Once social attitudes changed, there was no longer a demand to allow such separation deeds that were already in tension with Sunni jurisprudence.

The Ottoman state, as represented by both its local representative, the chief judge of Egypt, and its highest legal authority, the Shaykh al-Islām, did not object to these Mamluk Egyptian practices in the courts in the first

45 See, for example, "Court of Miṣr Al-Qadīma, Sijill 18 (1057/1647), Archival Code 1006–000156," doc. 7, 3–4.

46 "Court of Qisma ʿArabiyya, Sijill 2 (970–971/1562–1563), Archival Code 1004–000002," doc. 86, 57.

47 "Court of Miṣr Al-Qadīma, Sijill 4 (955/1548), Archival Code 1006–000004," doc. 37, 7; doc. 70, 12; doc. 151, 22; doc. 273, 37; doc. 367, 49; doc. 296, 52.

48 "Court of Miṣr Al-Qadīma, Sijill 4 (955/1548), Archival Code 1006–000004," doc. 268, 36.

49 "Court of Miṣr Al-Qadīma, Sijill 4 (955/1548), Archival Code 1006–000004," doc. 27, 5.

50 "Court of Qisma ʿArabiyya, Sijill 2 (970–971/1562–1563), Archival Code 1004–000002," doc. 95, 61.

century and a half of Ottoman rule, even though Abū-l-Suʿūd was said to have issued a fatwa that such agreements were not binding according to the Ḥanafī school. Despite his fatwa, Mamluk legal practice continued unchallenged during Abū-l-Suʿūd's life and long after his death. What is striking is that there is no evidence that any judicial authority issued decrees against the practice. The court records contain many official decrees that are repeated verbatim in court registers over many years instructing judges on the types of cases they are allowed or not allowed to hear. It was common for the chief judge to issue judicial decrees prohibiting certain legal transactions, and such decrees were usually written multiple times and copied verbatim in many different court registers for wide publication.[51] After examining over a hundred court registers from different periods, I have not been able to locate a single decree prohibiting the practice, even though the remarriage and travel agreements completely disappeared from the sample after 1670.

So is it possible that jurists were behind this social transformation or even that they engineered it through their religious activities and preaching? It is hard to determine the exact nature of this social transformation and the main socioeconomic or intellectual catalysts for such a change simply due to the absence of a debate over these important agreements in both the court records and chronicles. Without clear debates about the social implications of this law, the social and intellectual historian is left to the throes of speculation. Was there pressure on the judiciary and proselytization among social actors by "purist" preachers in early modern Egypt that perhaps contributed to the end of these practices?[52] Might it be that

[51] James E. Baldwin, *Islamic Law and Empire in Ottoman Cairo* (Edinburgh: Edinburgh University Press, 2017); James Baldwin, "*Islamic Law in an Ottoman Context: Resolving Disputes in Late 17th/Early 18th-Century Cairo*" (New York, NY: New York University Press, 2010), 157–160.

[52] As early as sixteenth-century Cairo, al-Shaʿrānī speaks of a group of people who were opposed to pragmatic eclecticism. These "purists" would continue to operate both in the Ottoman center and in the Arab provinces and gain some support among both the ruling elite and the populace throughout the seventeenth century. Might these purists have influenced the laity's view of what was acceptable or unacceptable in terms of child custody arrangements? We know that the laity had so much legal knowledge as evidenced by their sophisticated legal maneuvers, as we will see in Chapter 4, for instance, with regard to the question of finding free custody options, or their navigation of legal pluralism. Due to the absence of explicit discussions of these separation deeds, the question of whether these purist tendencies which we know existed in Ottoman-Egyptian society might have influenced social attitudes may never have a conclusive answer. On some of these purist tendencies, see further James Muhammad Dawud Currie, "Kadizadeli Ottoman Scholarship, Muḥammad Ibn ʿAbd Al-Wahhāb, and the Rise of the Saudi State," *Journal of Islamic Studies* 26:3 (2015): 265–288;

the purist Ottoman Kadızadelis, named after Qadizade Mehmed Efendi (d. 1045/1635–1636), who became highly influential among the Ḥanafī ʿulamāʾ during the mid- to late seventeenth century, played a role in encouraging adherence to the Ḥanafī position that prohibits agreements that allow mothers to retain custody despite remarriage and relocation? After all, the Kadızadelis gained adherents among the Ottoman elite, who sought to reform provincial administration across the empire, as well as to impose a uniform legal orthodoxy in Egypt. The Kadızadelis recruited supporters from the ranks of the upper echelons of the Ottoman governing elite, including several members of the Köprülü family of grand viziers in Istanbul. The Köprülü family's reform program was extended to Egypt in 1670, when Grand Vizier Köprülü, Fazıl Ahmed Pasha, sent Kara Ibrahim to be the governor of Egypt. Although Ibrahim's reform program concentrated on financial administration, it is possible that some legal changes were also introduced under pressure from Turkish-speaking Ḥanafī elements of the Cairo Kadızadelis on such an intimate matter as the custody of children.[53]

We know that many Ḥanafī jurists were opposed to the binding nature of such contracts according to Mālikī practice. We also know that there were indeed tensions between the local brand of Islam and the Kadızadeli brand that led, for instance, to the Cairo riots of 1711, wherein it was clear, based on the events as told by al-Jabartī, that these purists had a large following in Egypt, especially among Ḥanafī Turkish speakers.[54] In addition to Ḥanafī juristic opposition to the binding remarriage and

Samer Akkach, *Abd Al-Ghani Al-Nabulusi: Islam and the Enlightenment* (Oxford: Oneworld Publications, 2014); Ibrahim, "Al-Shaʿrānī's Response to Legal Purism"; Rudolph Peters, "The Battered Dervishes of Bab Zuwayla: A Religious Riot in Eighteenth-Century Cairo," in *Eighteenth Century Renewal and Reform in Islam*, ed. Nehemia Levtzion and John Voll (Syracuse, NY: Syracuse University Press, 1987).

53 Jane Hathaway, *The Arab Lands under Ottoman Rule, 1516–1800* (Harlow; New York, NY: Pearson Longman, 2008), 76–78; Baldwin, "Islamic Law in an Ottoman Context: Resolving Disputes in Late 17th/Early 18th-Century Cairo," 54–60, 162; Peters, "The Battered Dervishes of Bab Zuwayla: A Religious Riot in Eighteenth-Century Cairo," 93–115; l.

54 Hathaway, *The Arab Lands under Ottoman Rule, 1516–1800*, 76–78; Baldwin, "Islamic Law in an Ottoman Context: Resolving Disputes in Late 17th/Early 18th-Century Cairo," 54–60, 162; Peters, "The Battered Dervishes of Bab Zuwayla: A Religious Riot in Eighteenth-Century Cairo," 93–115; Zilfi, *The Politics of Piety*, 129–181; On Kadızadelis, see further *Ottoman Puritanism and Its Discontents: Ahmad Al-Aqhisari and the Qadizadelis* (Oxford; New York, NY: Oxford University Press, 2017); Katharina Anna Ivanyi, "Virtue, Piety and the Law: A Study of Birgivi Mehmed Efendi's Al-Tariqa Al-Muhammadiyya," 2012, http://dataspace.princeton.edu/jspui/handle/88435/dsp015d86p0259.

travel separation deeds, there were many separation deeds that explicitly rejected these two elements and wherein male agnates did their utmost to dissuade mothers from remarrying. To them, there may have been a cultural taboo against their children residing with stepfathers. It must have been the coalescence of these factors that led to the decision of the state, through its judiciary, to treat child custody as a matter of public policy. Thus, a parent who dropped her or his right to custody could always reclaim it. This is reminiscent of the shift in English common law in 1820 to treating the father's absolute custody right as a matter of public policy, as we saw in Chapter 1. We have focused in this chapter narrowly on understanding private separation deeds without having a detailed discussion of the main themes that form the backbone of this study, namely, age and gender, remarriage of the mother, lifestyle, religion, visitations and joint custody, travel with the ward, maintenance, and guardianship. In Chapter 4, we pay closer attention to these eight themes, despite some overlap with this chapter, in order to present a fuller picture of the practice of child custody in Ottoman-Egyptian courts.

CONCLUSION

Based on our sample, private separation deeds modifying the categorical rules of jurists ceased to be binding by the last quarter of the seventeenth century. The Ḥanafī legal establishment knew full well that they could not stop people from agreeing on informal custody arrangements violating the rules of jurists, but they treated them as nonbinding as soon as one parent challenged them in court. The remarriage and travel separation agreements, which started at least as early as the Mamluk period, continued in the earliest court records of Ottoman Egypt. This type of agreement appeared in the first records of the Court of Miṣr al-Qadīma in 934/1528.[55] It also appeared in the first record of the highest court 937/1530,[56] and the latest case I was able to find came from 1081/1670.[57] These cases were consistently notarized throughout the sixteenth and first three-quarters of the seventeenth century.[58] They were not restricted to one court, but appeared

55 "Court of Miṣr Al-Qadīma, Sijill 1 (934/1528), Archival Code 1006–000001," doc. 169, 39.

56 "Court of Al-Bāb Al-ʿĀlī, Sijill 1 (937/1530), Archival Code 1001–000001," doc. 69, 17.

57 "Court of Miṣr Al-Qadīma, Sijill 21 (1081/1670), Archival Code 1006–000159," doc. 126, 63; doc. 206, 89.

58 "Court of Miṣr Al-Qadīma, Sijill 20 (1076/1665–1666), Archival Code 1006–000158," doc. 119, 53; doc. 123, 54; doc. 150, 67; doc. 480, 192.

in all the court registers I examined, including for example in *sijill* 3 of the Court of Qanāṭir al-Sibāʿ, where in the first 200 cases, I found four such separation deeds in tension with juristic discourse;[59] the Cairo Court of Bābay al-Saʿāda wa-l'Kharq;[60] and the Court of Būlāq.[61] Take, for example, *sijill* 16 of the Court of Miṣr al-Qadīma. Out of a total of 200 court cases in 1616, there were only 20 cases of separation. Four of these 20 contained stipulations allowing the mother to retain custody regardless of her marital status or her place of residence.[62]

The sudden disappearance of the remarriage and travel separation deeds from the sample by the last quarter of the seventeenth century is striking. It may have been the result of the preaching of purist jurists and preachers associated with the Kadızadelis or Egyptian Ḥanafīs more broadly. The court records retain some tension between two social visions of child custody, one permitting mothers to retain custody despite remarriage and another insisting on the opposite position. It is clear that the judiciary changed sides on which social vision to endorse by the last quarter of the seventeenth century.

[59] "Court of Qanāṭir Al-Sibāʿ, Sijill 3 (961/1554), Archival Code 1007–000003," doc. 53, 11; doc. 130, 31; doc. 137, 32; doc. 151, 37.

[60] "Court of Babay Al-Saʿāda Wa'l-Kharq, Sijill 1 (1050/1640), Archival Code 1011–000101," Dār al-Wathāʾiq al-Qawmiyya, Cairo, doc. 123, 65.

[61] In this register, there were three cases of Agreement Type I in the first 200 cases. See "Court of Būlāq, Sijill 26 (1016/1607), Archival Code 1005–000101," Dār al-Wathāʾiq al-Qawmiyya, Cairo, doc. 27, 6; doc. 100 p. 21; doc. 118, 25.

[62] "Court of Miṣr Al-Qadīma, Sijill 16 (1025/1616), Archival Code 1006–000154," Dār al-Wathāʾiq al-Qawmiyya, Cairo, docs 5, 12, 14, 17, 19, 21, 25, 41, 42, 64, 66, 75, 98, 134, 147, 156, 162, 165, 168, 193, pps. 1, 2, 3, 4, 7, 11, 12, 16, 16, 18, 21, 28, 40, 44, 47, 48, 49, 50, 58.

4

Ottoman Juristic Discourse in Action, 1517–1801

In the previous chapter, we discussed binding private separation deeds, an option that was available to couples from at least the late Mamluk period to 1670, which enabled them to accommodate their evolving conceptions of what served the interests of both children and families. In what follows, I present a snapshot of some of the practices of child custody in Ottoman courts prior to the nineteenth century divided by the eight themes forming the basis of our examination of the best interests of the child. These themes are (1) age and gender, (2) remarriage of the mother, (3) lifestyle, (4) religion, (5) visitations and joint custody, (6) travel with the ward, (7) maintenance, and (8) guardianship. This chapter illuminates each theme with examples from court records that demonstrate how jurists combined a variety of methodological approaches to issue rulings corresponding to their social values and needs. This chapter's focus on the eight themes already discussed in the context of France, England, and the United States (Chapter 1) will also afford us further comparative insight into the ways in which Egyptian judges dealt with similar problems that Euro-American judges encountered around the same time.

I conclude that a mix of adherence to the formalist rules of jurists and pragmatic adjudication created a middle position between the two extremes that is similar to the one advocated by the contemporary American judge Richard Posner, as we saw in the Introduction. The general approach to preserving a child's welfare, as reflected in the practices of child custody in Ottoman Egypt, was so complex and multivarious that judges and families were able to tailor the rules to their specific needs through such techniques as pragmatic eclecticism, judicial discretion, and private separation deeds. Age and gender, as outlined by the categorical rules of author-jurists, were not the principal factors defining the welfare of the child. Neither were all children whose mothers had remarried deprived of her care. Interestingly, despite the jurists' concern with modes of behavior, especially that of women, as we saw in Chapter 2, there was no indication that the judiciary used child custody to discipline women for acting in certain (unorthodox) ways. Through a mix of adherence to the formalist rules and pragmatic adjudication, custody and guardianship were designed to protect those whom jurists considered weaker – namely, mother and child.

AGE AND GENDER

As we saw in Chapters 2 and 3, there were three main approaches to dealing with child custody and guardianship, namely (1) the categorical rules of author-jurists in the Ḥanafī and Mālikī schools, where the child's wishes are not solicited; (2) soliciting the child's wishes after the tender age in the Shāfiʿī and Ḥanbalī schools; and (3) family agreements. There is not a single instance in our sample of Ottoman-Egyptian judges asking children about their wishes; therefore, court practice was a mix of the other two approaches. We can surmise from the absence of solicitation of the child's wishes that the values of Ottoman-Egyptian society had changed enough to render the rules of custody contained in the Ḥanbalī and Shāfiʿī schools irrelevant, despite the latter's large following in Egypt. In fact, none of the Sunni schools' formal rules was by itself sufficient for dealing with the contingencies and values of Ottoman-Egyptians, which explains the popularity of private separation deeds. What is striking to note is that all sorts of private agreements were drawn in the Ottoman courts, with judges assuming that these agreements served the interests of children, since they were, by law, the *parens patriae* of Egyptian children and were empowered to block agreements harming children. Due to the diversity of these agreements, there was no clear and consistent age at which girls and boys were transferred from mothers to fathers. Despite the diversity of possible agreements, one can sense the trend that mothers and their mothers maintained custody of children at least until the age of discernment (around seven) but often beyond that age.

One case reveals a common type of agreement in which the mother had custody of an infant, and the father of a child over the age of ten, without there being any concern about separating the siblings. A divorced couple brought their agreement for notarization to the Mālikī judge in the court of

Miṣr al-Qadīma in 950/1544 after mediation by their two extended families. They had two children: an infant who was still unweaned and a ten-year-old daughter. The agreement between the couple was that the mother would have custody of the baby for two years from the date of the agreement. The father would pay for the maintenance of the baby boy for those two years and he would make no claim to custody of the child regardless of the mother's marital status or place of residence, or the father's place of residence. In exchange for that lack of interference, the mother gave up custody of her ten-year-old daughter to the father.[1] In Mālikī law, normally the mother would keep custody of the child until marriage. In this sense, she was "ceding" her right according to the Mālikī judge.

There are other cases in which the age of custody transfer or termination did not correspond to the legal school represented by the presiding judge, but did conform to the perspective of another school. It was common in Ottoman courts for mothers to maintain custody of girls until they got married.[2] Take, for instance, the case of the unweaned infant, Muḥsina, whose parents agreed in 1081/1670 before the Ḥanafī judge that the mother would pay for the child's maintenance and nursing fee, and have custody of her daughter until she is wedded (*ilā ḥīni zifāfihā*). Here, a Ḥanafī judge is allowing the mother to retain custody of her daughter according to the Mālikī age limit (recall that in Ḥanafī law, age nine would be the age of custody transfer).[3] Earlier in 1057/1647, again before the Ḥanafī judge, the parents of Dalāl – an unmarried, physically mature girl, likely of at least 12 or 13 years of age – agreed to place her under the custody of the mother. The document allowed the mother to maintain custody regardless of her own marital status, and expressed no reservation as to the possibility of the mother remarrying a man who was a stranger to the girl.[4]

Absent such agreements, judges generally abided by the age determinations outlined in the Sunni schools, but some parents utilized pragmatic

[1] "Court of Miṣr Al-Qadīma, Sijill 3 (950/1544), Archival Code 1006–000003," doc. 403, 59.

[2] "Court of Miṣr Al-Qadīma, Sijill 18 (1057/1647), Archival Code 1006–000156," doc. 159, 59; "Court of Miṣr Al-Qadīma, Sijill 20 (1076/1665–1666), Archival Code 1006–000158," doc. 123, 54; "Court of Miṣr Al-Qadīma, Sijill 20 (1076/1665–1666), Archival Code 1006–000158," doc. 150, 67.

[3] "Court of Miṣr Al-Qadīma, Sijill 21 (1081/1670), Archival Code 1006–000159," doc. 54, 20; doc. 57, 21.

[4] "Court of Miṣr Al-Qadīma, Sijill 18 (1057/1647), Archival Code 1006–000156," doc. 159, 59.

eclecticism to gain custody. One father brought his petition for custody of his ten-year-old daughter, Zabīda, before a Ḥanbalī judge, who ordered that the girl be transferred to the father.[5] This was a successful maneuver on the part of the father, since he knew that the Ḥanbalī school was in fact the only school that would definitely grant custody to the father. Had he brought his petition, as we saw previously, to the Shāfiʿī school, *in theory* the girl would have been asked about her preference. I say "in theory" because although juristic discourse stipulates such solicitation of the child's wishes, I have not found any evidence that this was indeed practiced in Ottoman-Egyptian courts. Had he brought his petition before a Mālikī judge, the mother would have retained custody until marriage, which is the dominant position of the Mālikī school. The Ḥanafī school has two main positions: either puberty or the age of nine as we saw previously. He chose the safest option for his purpose, the Ḥanbalī school.

One case contains an agreement in which the mother volunteers to pay for the maintenance of her three-year-old son and keep the child's custody until he turned six, regardless of her marital status or place of residence.[6] Sometimes we see children being described as "weaned" (*faṭīma*), which indicates that they were just above two years of age. At other times, they were described as "minor" (*qāṣir*). It is hard to know the exact ages of these girls, but scribes must have referred to a girl perhaps between the age of discernment of seven and physical maturity (*bulūgh*) as a "minor." Below the age of seven, they used either "weaned" for between two and seven or "unweaned," which is below two years.[7] There were short-term agreements for two or three years, but at other times there was no time-frame stipulated, which implies that the mother would keep custody of the child until she or he reached physical maturity or a new agreement was reached at a later date.[8]

In another divorce settlement notarized by a Ḥanafī judge, the parents agreed that the mother would be responsible for the maintenance of her unweaned daughter, Fāṭima, from the date of the divorce until the

[5] "Court of Al-Bāb Al-ʿĀlī, Sijill 55 (1000/1592), Archival Code 1001–000104," Dār al-Wathāʾiq al-Qawmiyya, Cairo, doc. 18, 6.

[6] "Court of Miṣr Al-Qadīma, Sijill 4 (955/1548), Archival Code 1006–000004," doc. 1210, 180.

[7] "Court of Miṣr Al-Qadīma, Sijill 10 (978/1570), Archival Code 1006–000010," doc. 292, 48; "Court of Miṣr Al-Qadīma, Sijill 13 (991/1583), Archival Code 1006–000151," Dār al-Wathāʾiq al-Qawmiyya, Cairo, doc. 13, 5; "Court of Miṣr Al-Qadīma, Sijill 13 (991/1583), Archival Code 1006–000151," doc. 23, 8.

[8] "Court of Miṣr Al-Qadīma, Sijill 18 (1057/1647), Archival Code 1006–000156," doc. 7, 3–4; doc. 27, 11; doc. 42, 16.

daughter married.[9] In another case, there is no time limit placed on the agreement, suggesting that an unweaned boy would stay with his mother until he reaches physical maturity or another agreement is concluded. The father would pay for the child's maintenance for as long as the boy remained under his mother's custodianship. The only restriction placed on this agreement was that the mother's custodianship would continue provided that she remain unmarried. If she were to remarry, the father would petition for custody of the child.[10] In one agreement, the parents decided that the mother would keep custody of the infant daughter to stay with her mother for three years, with no recourse for the father to request custody regardless of the mother's marital status, and regardless of whether the mother stays in the place of habitual residence of the child or not.[11]

Another separation deed (*khul'*) has the parents agreeing that the mother would get a divorce in exchange for her maintenance and clothing allowance. The agreement also included a payment of one silver piece (*niṣf*) every day in maintenance for their three-year-old son, Muḥammad, and that he would remain in the custody of his mother for five years. The Mālikī judge's decision to appoint her as a custodian over the three-year-old was to be effective again regardless of her marital status or her residence.[12] Presumably, the child's custody would be revisited after the five years, when the child would be eight years old.

It was often the case that Egyptian litigants and the Ottoman judicial authorities considered the boy's best interests to be with the mother until he reached the age of discernment, but girls often stayed with their mother longer. For instance, in 955/1548 in the court of Miṣr al-Qadīma, a pregnant woman appeared before the Ḥanafī judge to notarize a *khul'* divorce. The separation agreement was that she would give up her right to maintenance until she delivered the baby. The husband, according to the agreement, was responsible for the maintenance of their weaned daughter, Zaynab, and that she would be under the mother's custodianship for ten years. Considering the fact that the child was already weaned, most likely at least two-year-old, that would place the girl under her mother's custody until she was at least 12-year-old. The mother also agreed to be responsible

[9] "Court of Miṣr Al-Qadīma, Sijill 18 (1057/1647), Archival Code 1006–000156," doc. 190, 70.

[10] "Court of Miṣr Al-Qadīma, Sijill 20 (1076/1665–1666), Archival Code 1006–000158," doc. 75, 29.

[11] "Court of Miṣr Al-Qadīma, Sijill 3 (950/1544), Archival Code 1006–000003," doc. 481, 70.

[12] "Court of Miṣr Al-Qadīma, Sijill 4 (955/1548), Archival Code 1006–000004," doc. 151, 22.

for the maintenance of the unborn child and to keep custody of her or him for the same ten years.[13] There was no concern about the sex of the fetus; either way, he or she would be with the mother until age ten.

Private agreements were not the only way in which the categorical age determinations of author-jurists were ignored, sometimes with juristic justification and sometimes without. In some cases, the judge appointed a custodian – in the case of the death of the father, for instance, and the absence of agnatic male relatives. In one case, the judge appointed a mother as a custodian of her two minor sons, Muṣṭafā and Aḥmad, until they reached physical maturity. This appointment was done in the probate court of al-Qisma al-ʿArabiyya, using the same formulas used for the appointment of guardians.[14]

Maternal Nursing versus Wet-Nursing

Special attention was accorded unweaned children, whose best interests were often assumed to be fulfilled when they were nursed by their mothers, which was almost always the case. Based on the sample examined here, wet-nursing does not seem to have been a widespread practice as it was, say, among the middle classes in early modern England and France until the eighteenth century, or as was the case in Renaissance Italy. The preference in Islamic medical and juristic treatises was for maternal nursing, owing to an assumption about the mother's kindness toward her child, which made nonmaternal nursing less popular in early modern Egypt.[15] It was the norm in Ottoman-Egyptian society for mothers to nurse their children across different sectors of society, since our sample draws from courts such as al-Bāb al-ʿĀlī and Miṣr al-Qadīma, as the former often served the elite while the latter served people of lower socioeconomic status.[16] There were

[13] This woman clearly belonged to Cairo's upper classes, as evidenced by the many honorifics used in the case to refer to her, such as "protected" (*maṣūna*). "Court of Miṣr Al-Qadīma, Sijill 4 (955/1548), Archival Code 1006–000004," doc. 268, 36.

[14] This is a court concerned with the division of an estate after the death of a relative. "Court of Qisma ʿArabiyya, Sijill 3 (973/1566), Archival Code 1004–000003," Dār al-Wathāʾiq al-Qawmiyya, Cairo, doc. 151, 88.

[15] On the prevalence of wet-nursing in Medieval and early modern Europe, see further Christiane Klapisch-Zuber, *Women, Family, and Ritual in Renaissance Italy* (Chicago, IL: University of Chicago Press, 1985), 132–164; Stone, *Road to Divorce*, 170–172; Maidment, *Child Custody and Divorce*, 89–93; Flandrin, *Families in Former Times*, 203–206; Giladi, *Infants, Parents and Wet Nurses*, 31–35, 43–62, 106–114.

[16] These courts represented different socioeconomic backgrounds due to the different minimum transaction amounts required for notarization, with the al-Bāb al-ʿĀlī often serving

many cases in which the father gave up his right to demand custody of an infant, even if the mother remarried, to make sure that the child had enough time to be weaned by his mother, with fathers sometimes demanding to take the child after it is weaned in the event of remarriage. References to wet-nurses were rare and resorted to typically only when the mother's new husband did not allow her to nurse her child from a previous marriage, or when the mother died.[17]

The prevalence of maternal breastfeeding in Ottoman Egypt tallies fully with juristic discourse of the Mamluk period. According to Ibn Qayyim al-Jawziyya, the Prophet said that he was about to forbid men from having sex with their wives while they were breastfeeding (*ghayl*), but when he looked at the Byzantines and Persians, he realized that it did not harm their children. In another report, a man told the Prophet that the former did not have sex with his wife while she was breastfeeding out of concern for his children. The Prophet responded that if it were harmful, it would have hurt the Byzantines and Persians. In another contradictory report, the Prophet warns against having sex with nursing mothers for fear of causing the death of the children (recall that this was the common view in medieval and early modern Europe). While agreeing that having sex with a breastfeeding mother contaminates her milk, Ibn Qayyim reconciled the two reports by arguing that this only affects some children and that the Persians and Romans have not been negatively affected by it on a large scale. He did not encourage families to find wet-nurses unless the mother gets pregnant, because in this case, Ibn Qayyim reasoned, both the fetus and infant would share the mother's milk, which would not be enough for both of them.[18] The notion that sexual relations with a nursing woman spoils her milk goes back to Hellenistic medical theories. Although many Muslim doctors agreed with this theory, this popular notion did not influence juristic discourse, as no such ban exists in any of the legal schools, despite the contradictory Prophetic reports that could have given rise to dissenting juristic voices. Despite the views of Muslim doctors, jurists assumed that having sex with nursing women did not harm their nurslings.[19]

more elite members of society and Miṣr al-Qadīma serving lower socioeconomic groups. See further, Ibrahim, *Pragmatism in Islamic Law*, 2017, 137–139.

[17] For an example of wet-nursing when the mother had remarried, see "Court of Al-Bāb Al-ʿĀlī, Sijill 293 (1190/1776), Archival Code 1001–000656," doc. 55, 41.

[18] Al-Jawziyya, *Tuḥfat Al-Mawdūd Bi-Aḥkām Al-Mawlūd*, 338–356; Giladi, *Children of Islam*, 22–34; Giladi, *Infants, Parents and Wet Nurses*, 31–33.

[19] By the fifteenth century, jurists from the Maghrib, for instance, did not presume that having sexual relations with a nursing mother harmed the nursling. See al-Wansharīsī,

Breastfeeding was considered a right of both the mother and the child during the marriage and after separation. During the marriage, as for the conflict between the husband's right to have sexual access and the infant's right to be nursed as frequently as it needs, jurists such as the sixteenth-century Egyptian Shāfiʿī Ibn al-Haytamī (d. 973/1567) argued that the infant's right should be privileged.[20] After separation, when mothers could charge the father a fee for nursing, fathers could deny mothers such a right only when there was a cheaper option. If the mother volunteered to nurse the infant for free (as we saw in Chapter 2), the father had no way of taking away her nursling. In Giladi's estimation, while the pre-Islamic practice of wet-nursing was allowed by the new religion, it never developed into mercenary "professional" wet-nursing.[21] This was different from the situation in early modern France as we saw in Chapter 1, where sexual relations were assumed to spoil the milk of a nursing mother and where women were advised to privilege their husband's conjugal dues by putting their children out to nurse.[22] A very common type of agreement in Ottoman Egypt has the mother keeping custody of an unweaned child for two years, regardless of her marital status and place of residence.[23] The common occurrence of this agreement suggests that Ottoman-Egyptian society preferred that the child be nursed by her or his mother regardless of what they otherwise saw as less than ideal circumstances.

REMARRIAGE OF THE MOTHER

Ottoman judges and families dealt with the mother's remarriage in a nuanced way. Many different arrangements were made depending the circumstances of the children and their families. The welfare of the child was not assumed to reside in one particular arrangement, but rather in a contextual system of custody based on a mix of categorical juristic rules overlaid with private separation deeds. In times of conflict over custody, it was often the case that the mother's mother or sister would get custody

Al-Manhaj Al-Fāʾiq Wa'l-Manhal Al-Rāʾiq Wa'l-Maʿnā Al-Lāʾiq Bi-Ādāb Al-Muwaththiq Wa-Aḥkām Al-Wathāʾiq, 2:565–566; On wet-nursing in premodern Muslim societies, see further Giladi, *Infants, Parents and Wet Nurses.*

20 Al-Shirwānī, al-ʿIbādī, and al-Haytamī, *Ḥawāshī Tuḥfat Al-Muḥtāj Bi-Sharḥ Al-Minhāj*, 8:350; al-Shirbīnī, *Mughnī Al-Muḥtāj Ilā Maʿrifat Maʿānī Alfāẓ Al-Minhāj*, 3:589. Al-Haytamī's commentary is printed on the margin of al-Shirwānī and al-ʿIbādī's Ḥawāshī.

21 Giladi, *Infants, Parents and Wet Nurses*, 31–35, 43–62, 106–114.

22 Flandrin, *Families in Former Times*, 203–212; 235–238; Hunt, *Women in Eighteenth Century Europe*, 140–145.

23 doc. 367, p. 49; doc. 496, p. 52.

unless the parents reached an agreement, as the next in line, according to all Sunni schools, is the mother's mother. Many fathers, however, as already noted, entered into agreements giving mothers rights of custody regardless of their marital status. This must have been partly the result of a belief that a remarried mother was still a better caregiver than another female relative, as evidenced by the fact that many fathers signed such agreements without standing to make any financial gain, such as a relief from maintenance.

Women of different socioeconomic backgrounds were able to secure advantageous separation deeds. While elite women may have been partly responsible for the emergence of these private separation deeds, these transactions were not restricted to women of high status. Consider the following deed. In 991/1583, a woman by the name of Maʿshūq, whose father was not a man of high status (he was referred to simply as Ḥājj ʿAbd al-Karīm), and her husband Ḥājj ʿAlī, appeared before the Ḥanbalī judge, the choice of whom was motivated by the wish to not count the *khulʿ* as an instance of *ṭalāq* in line with Ḥanbalī law. The parents wanted to sign a *khulʿ* deed in which the father permitted the mother to remarry without losing custody. This was not done in exchange for relieving any of the father's financial obligations, yet the husband offered no such dispensation in the event that he or she moved out of Miṣr al-Qadīma.[24]

Even when mothers were unable to secure private separation deeds guaranteeing that they could keep custody despite remarriage, their children were often cared for by their own mothers or sisters. Some newlywed women preferred not to take care of children from a previous marriage in their new family, letting their own mothers assume that responsibility. In one case, the paternal aunt of two boys, Aḥmad and Muḥammad, was granted custody because, as the document explains, the mother had lost her right to custody by remarrying a person who was not a close relative of the child (he was *ajnabī*). The judge also determined the amount that the aunt would receive from the boys' inheritance for their maintenance.[25] Consider also the following case from the court of al-Bāb al-ʿĀlī in 1190/1776. Fāṭima told the judge that her daughter, Rābiya, who was not present at the court, was divorced from Aḥmad. Custody of their daughter, Zaynab, was transferred to the maternal grandmother (Fāṭima) upon Rābiya's remarriage. She complained to the judge that Āmna, Aḥmad's

[24] "Court of Miṣr Al-Qadīma, Sijill 13 (991/1583), Archival Code 1006–000151," doc. 81, 23.

[25] "Court of Qisma ʿArabiyya, Sijill 3 (973/1566), Archival Code 1004–000003," doc. 212, 125.

mother (the paternal grandmother), was trying to get custody of Zaynab "without legal grounds" (*bi-ghayri ṭarīqin sharʿī*). Fāṭima was fully aware that custody of the child was supposed to be transferred to her after the remarriage of her daughter and that the paternal grandmother's attempt to gain custody lacked legal justification. She was also aware that she had to emphasize her willingness to provide custody for free in order to preempt a potential request of the paternal grandmother to offer her own services for free, which would have earned her custody. The judge confirmed Fāṭima's custody rights.[26]

It was so common, however, that mothers wanted to retain custody of their children despite remarriage that many mothers made it a condition that the new husband be responsible for the financial support of her children from a previous marriage.[27] In 1091/1681, Muḥammad and Ward got married and registered their marriage contract at the court of Miṣr al-Qadīma. The couple agreed that Muḥammad would be responsible for the maintenance of Ward's two children from a previous marriage, Aḥmad and Ḥijāziyya. The new husband obligated himself to the upkeep of these two children without seeking any compensation from her or anyone else. According to the agreement, the two children would eat and drink with the new couple at the new husband's expense, as long as their mother, Ward, was still married to him.[28] Another father concluded a similar marriage agreement, but in which the future wife committed herself to providing housing for *him and his son* from a previous marriage for as long as they are married.[29] To get a sense of the frequency of these stipulations requiring husbands to support stepchildren in marriage contracts, consider the case of *sijill* 21 of the court of Miṣr al-Qadīma, which contained five such instances in the first 200 cases brought to the court.[30]

[26] "Court of Al-Bāb Al-ʿĀlī, Sijill 293 (1190/1776), Archival Code 1001–000656," doc. 108, 78.

[27] This condition was considered invalid by the Mālikī jurists. See, for instance, al-Zarqānī, *Sharḥ Al-Zarqānī ʿalā Mukhtaṣar Sayyidī Khalīl Wa-Maʿahu Al-Fatḥ Al-Rabbānī Fīmā Dhahala ʿanhu Al-Zarqānī*, 4:134.

[28] "Court of Miṣr Al-Qadīma, Sijill 22 (1092–1681), Archival Code 1006–000160," doc. 80, 29; "Court of Ṣāliḥiyya Al-Najmiyya, Sijill 3 (951/1544), Archival Code 1012–000003," doc. 125, 39; "Court of Miṣr Al-Qadīma, Sijill 21 (1081/1670), Archival Code 1006–000159," doc. 5, 3.

[29] In another case that did not involve children, the marriage stipulated that the husband would reside with the wife. "Court of Miṣr Al-Qadīma, Sijill 21 (1081/1670), Archival Code 1006–000159," doc. 150, 70; "Court of Al-Bāb Al-ʿĀlī, Sijill 3 (939/1533), Archival Code 1001–000003," doc. 73, 16.

[30] "Court of Miṣr Al-Qadīma, Sijill 21 (1081/1670), Archival Code 1006–000159," doc. 5, 3; doc. 40, 16; doc. 49, 16; doc. 107, 57; doc. 147, 70.

LIFESTYLE

There are no cases in the sample in which one party was denied custody due to lifestyle concerns, such as accusations of *fisq* (adultery), or lack of ritual practice such as fasting and praying. Acts of perceived immorality exist in all societies, which raises the question of why they were virtually absent in legal battles over custody, contrary to the situation in early modern England and the United States (see Chapter 1). This glaring absence is exceedingly powerful, since custody disputes included all sorts of maneuvers and creative legal and practical thinking. Despite juristic discourse, which emphasized uprightness as a precondition for assuming custody, it does not seem that the issue of its absence or questionable nature was frequently raised against potential custodians, suggesting perhaps that the practice of courts resembled Ibn Qayyim's pragmatic approach, which emphasized the child's interests over questions of uprightness that had no impact on these interests. This finding, however, is understandable in early modern Egyptian society, where family reputation and honor would be irreparably damaged due to accusations against the mother's behavior. People were perhaps more cautious about making these types of accusations in court, where they would be recorded and publicly accessible. One can also speculate that such facts may have played a role in private negotiations, but they never made it into the public arena of the courtroom.

There are no instances in our sample of early modern Egyptian women losing custody due to a challenge based on the mother's work outside of the home. We know from the records that women worked in the sixteenth through eighteenth centuries as bakers and as land laborers, for example. Members of the French Expedition even observed that many peasant women worked in the fields at the end of the eighteenth century.[31] This would change in the nineteenth century, when women's full-time employment outside of the home would constitute grounds for the loss of child custody, as we shall see in the next chapter.

RELIGION

The religion of the parents played a role in custody determinations. As we saw previously, Ḥanafī and Mālikī jurists allowed mothers to keep custody

[31] For a discussion of women's labor during the late eighteenth and early twentieth centuries, see further Judith E. Tucker, *Women in Nineteenth-Century Egypt* (Cambridge; New York, NY: Cambridge University Press, 1985), 40–42.

of their children with some restrictions. However, there was consensus that conversion from Islam forfeited a person's right to custody. Conversion to Islam, however, often helped non-Muslim mothers secure their claim to child custody. In 1190/1776, a woman by the name of Āmna came to the Ḥanafī judge in the court of al-Bāb al-ʿĀlī to ask him to confirm the custody of her two children. Āmna, the document tells us, had converted to Islam, which was why she was divorced from her Christian husband. After her waiting period had expired, she married a Muslim man and maintained custody of her two children, despite her remarriage. Āmna approached the judge out of concern for her child support payments and the retaining of her custody, because, according to her, the father had tried to take the children without legal justification. His lack of legal right to custody is due to his religious status; a non-Muslim father has no right of custody, according to the consensus of Sunni jurists. The judge ruled that she had the right of custody over the two children and that, despite the father's categorical disqualification from custody based on his religion, he was still required to pay child support and provide a clothing allowance.[32]

The mother might have converted from Christianity to Islam in order to get a divorce, since it was very difficult for Christian women to obtain a divorce in Egypt under the rules of the Coptic Church.[33] This remains to be the case in modern Egypt, where conversion is still a remedy in some cases where church rules do not allow for a divorce. Regardless of the motivation behind conversion, the legal status of the children is that they became Muslim, according to the rule that the child follows the "better" religion of either parent. As we see in this case, when there is a conflict between two undesirables with respect to custody – that is, the mother having remarried and the father being a non-Muslim – the religion of the father is placed at the highest level of priority in the list of influential factors. This approach was based on the patriarchal assumption that fathers have more power of indoctrination over their children than mothers do, with mothers being mostly associated with nurture, and fathers with moral and religious education (this assumption would change in the nineteenth century). While Ḥanafīs in particular allowed non-Muslim women to retain custody of the children (see Chapter 2), I have

32 "Court of Al-Bāb Al-ʿĀlī, Sijill 293 (1190/1776), Archival Code 1001–000656," doc. 4, 3.

33 On the stringent restrictions on divorce among Egyptian Copts, see Ibn al-ʿAssāl al-Ṣafī Abū al-Faḍāʾil, *Al-Majmūʿ Al-Ṣafawī*, ed. Girgis Fīlūthaws ʿAwaḍ (Cairo, n.d.), 2: 240–287.

found no agreements where party autonomy was granted to families over child custody and guardianship in which the father was a non-Muslim.

VISITATION RIGHTS AND JOINT CUSTODY

Early modern Egyptian jurists were not interested in regulating visitation, leaving this issue to customary practice. I have not encountered any case in which there were disputes over visitation rights. This issue must have been resolved through the mediation of relatives and negotiations between the parents. In the context of gender segregation, especially in wealthier households where it was strictly implemented, it would understandably be difficult for a mother to visit her ex-husband's house to see her children. It was more likely that the mother would see her children at her own house or at the house of a mother or a sister. Some women who may not have had such options or who belonged to households that strictly implemented gender segregation made sure to stipulate in their marriage contracts that their new husbands had no right to stop their children from visiting them.[34]

Forms of joint custody may be one of many stipulations worked into elaborate private separation deeds. In 955/1548, a woman appeared in the court of Miṣr al-Qadīma before the Ḥanafī judge to ask the agent (*wakīl*) of her husband to divorce her on the husband's behalf. Although the document is clear that the mother would be the custodian, the agreement adds a peculiar phrase: it says that their son, Sallām, would be "between the two parents" (*baynahumā*). Does this suggest that the son would spend the day with the father to be taught a trade, as well as basic education, but he would spend the night at the mother's residence? Children were expected to sleep at the custodian's home, even if they spent the day with the other parent.[35] As we have seen in juristic discourse, some jurists such as Ibn Qudāma contemplated the situation in which the father took care of a boy during the day, teaching him a trade and/or overseeing his education. By the end of the day, the child would return and sleep at his mother's house. There was an assumption that only boys needed this dispensation, as they were thought to be in need of the oversight of their father compared to girls. Since the father already had the right to spend time with his son during the day to oversee his education, there was no reason to

[34] For an example of such stipulations, see Hanna, "Marriage Among Merchant Families in Seventeenth-Century Cairo," 152.

[35] "Court of Miṣr Al-Qadīma, Sijill 4 (955/1548), Archival Code 1006–000004," doc. 27, 5.

specifically and unusually stipulate that the boy would be able to stay with both of them. Might it be that the father wanted to make sure that the boy would be sleeping some nights with the father and others with the mother? If that is the case, then this is an example of joint custody in which the mother is the primary caregiver. It is hard to assess the prevalence of this form of joint custody since this was the only case I was able to find in the sample. As we shall see in Chapter 6, the question of sleepovers is a thorny issue in modern Egyptian legislation, due to the assumption of the discourse of author-jurists that children must always sleep at the custodian's home.

RELOCATION WITH THE WARD

The law on relocating with the child (or traveling with the child more generally) was the result of the mix of formalist rules of jurists and the pragmatic adjudication of judges. As we saw in Chapter 3, the remarriage and travel separation deeds allowed mothers to maintain child custody regardless of their residence or that of the father. This was a way to enable women to move freely without being concerned about the inequities of the standard rules of the schools regarding relocation of the mother or the father. In juristic discourse, as we have seen previously, most jurists allowed the father to obtain custody as soon as he decided to relocate from the habitual place of residence, even when the child was of tender age. In an urban context like Ottoman Cairo, it was not likely that a six-month-old infant would be given over to his father simply because he wanted to leave the city. Social actors were aware of this possibility inherent in juristic discourse and found ways around it through private separation agreements. The disappearance of these agreements from our sample by the last quarter of the seventeenth century does not mean that parents stopped making agreements contradicting the categorical rules of jurists, but rather implies that such agreements were no longer binding, and so women had to rely on other means such as family mediations, financial incentives, and more importantly, the two families' own sense of what was best for the children.

To understand the expectations of many women who sought to relocate with their children without losing custody by signing private separation deeds, we must examine this issue in the larger context of women's control over their travel more broadly. Women's freedom of movement with their children was intimately linked to their control over their place of residence in the marriage itself. The court records are rife with cases of women refusing to move with their husbands outside of their hometown, leading to domestic disputes that were resolved in the courtroom. I have not found instances of judges forcing women to succumb to the husband's will with regard to their place of residence. When women refused to obey their husbands, they were considered disobedient (*nāshiz*), which would only lead to loss of maintenance rights, but there was no enforcement mechanism that judges used to require women to live with their husbands against their will. Certainly, the judge had the ability to subject these women to discretionary punishments, but I have never found any instances of enforcement of that nature. Judges simply asked woman to obey their husbands, warning them that the consequence of disobedience was the loss of maintenance.[36] This is strikingly different from the institution of the "house of obedience" introduced in modern Egypt.[37]

Some women tried to control their place of residence by writing a stipulation in the marriage contract – often using the Ḥanbalī school's more flexible approach to freedom of contract – stating that their husbands had no right to take them away from Cairo to its suburbs without their consent.[38] In 1092/1681, Qamar refused to move from the Ḥimdār quarter in Miṣr al-Qadīma to a village in Upper Egypt close to Malawī with her husband, Jād Allāh, who worked as a sailor. The document explained that they had agreed that he would not take her away from Cairo against her will. The domestic dispute was resolved with the husband agreeing not to ask her to move again and to provide maintenance in the event of his absence.[39] As I mentioned in Chapter 3, these stipulations must have served elite women (both in Mamluk and Ottoman Egypt) more than their poorer sisters, but women of all classes took advantage of this flexibility.

These common expectations of women's control over their place of residence whether during the marriage or after its dissolution could only be utilized when the woman was able to mobilize the necessary pressure on recalcitrant fathers. The different factors involved in the process of negotiations gave rise to many potential agreements, using a mix of pragmatic

36 See for example, "Court of Miṣr Al-Qadīma, Sijill 15 (1018/1609), Archival Code 1006–000153," doc. 121, 33.
37 For a good discussion of the institution, see Cuno, *Modernizing Marriage*.
38 "Court of Ṣāliḥiyya Al-Najmiyya, Sijill 3 (951/1544), Archival Code 1012–000003," doc. 125, 39.
39 "Court of Miṣr Al-Qadīma, Sijill 22 (1092–1681), Archival Code 1006–000160," doc. 107, 40.

and formalist solutions. We find instances in which the father agreed to give up his right to the mother to maintain custody despite remarriage to a "stranger" (*ajnabī*), but he was unwilling to allow her to move away with the child. In 991/1583, the father agreed not to challenge the mother over custody if she remarried, but no such license was made for her relocation with the child outside Miṣr al-Qadīma.[40] In 955/1548, a couple signed a separation agreement more in line with the predominant juristic discourse, stipulating that the mother would keep custody of the child as long as she remained unmarried and stayed in Miṣr al-Qadīma.[41] The frequency of men signing away such rights suggests that it was not taboo for many families that children, especially girls, be raised in the house of a stepfather. Other men were sure to emphasize that they would not give up this right, suggesting that they thought it was not in the interests of their children or that it was taboo for them. It was this tension that was eventually settled judicially in favor of the Ḥanafī position by the last quarter of the seventeenth century.

Absent an agreement with the mother giving her the right to take the child out of the place of habitual residence, Ottoman judges assumed that the father had absolute right of control over the child's travel. In 1057/1647, a divorced father brought a *habeas corpus* case before the Miṣr al-Qadīma Ḥanafī judge against his son's maternal grandfather, accusing him of unlawfully taking his son out of town. According to Maḥmūd, the father who lived in a village just outside of Cairo, the grandfather brought his son (as well as the boy's mother) into Cairo to work for someone from the Mutafarriqa military corps without the father's permission. The father asked the judge to force the grandfather to return his son. The grandfather acknowledged that he had brought the mother, his daughter, and her son from the village to Cairo, and further admitted that the boy had tragically drowned in the Nile. The son's body was found three days later in the Wāylī neighborhood of modern Cairo. The judge ruled that the grandfather was not guilty of negligent homicide, but he was still subjected to an unspecified discretionary punishment for taking the child away without the father's permission, indicating that the father had full control over the movement of the child as long as he had not given up such a right in an agreement with the mother.[42] Another ambiguity of this case is that we do

40 "Court of Miṣr Al-Qadīma, Sijill 13 (991/1583), Archival Code 1006–000151," doc. 81, 23.

41 "Court of Miṣr Al-Qadīma, Sijill 4 (955/1548), Archival Code 1006–000004," doc. 27, 5.

42 "Court of Miṣr Al-Qadīma, Sijill 18 (1057/1647), Archival Code 1006–000156," doc. 167, 61.

not know if the child was visiting his mother when the grandfather took them to Cairo or if he was in the mother's custody. Either way, the father's consent to travel should have been sought, according to the judge.

CHILD MAINTENANCE

Judges showed a concern for the welfare of the mother–child unit, as evidenced by their use of pragmatic eclecticism and pragmatic adjudication to ensure that women are able to get the maintenance they need for their children (*nafaqa*). Child maintenance and other costs associated with child care such as pregnancy maintenance (*nafaqat al-ḥaml*), nursing fees, and custody wages were essential elements of almost all separation agreements in Ottoman-Egyptian court records.[43] Many women used maintenance as a negotiating card, and received favorable custody arrangements in exchange for relieving the father of some of his financial obligations, relying on family support instead. In one case from 937/1530, a Cairene mother agreed with her former husband that she would be responsible for maintaining their daughter as long as the daughter lived with her. The father, according to the agreement, had no right to custody unless the mother willingly handed the daughter over to him.[44]

In addition to the cost of maintenance, which included food and water, a fee for nursing was often included in the custody arrangements found in Ottoman courts. For instance, a *khul*ʿ agreement brought to the court of Miṣr al-Qadīma in 1018/1609 established the duty of the father to pay two years of nursing fees.[45] The maintenance of the child also sometimes included explicit references to "custody wages" (*ujrat ḥaḍāna*). In 1057/1647, a woman brought a lawsuit against her ex-husband in the court of Miṣr al-Qadīma accusing him of not providing maintenance for their unweaned son. The husband not only agreed to pay for the child's nursing and custody wages, as well as food and other costs, but also signed an agreement that she would keep custody of the son regardless of her marital status or residence.[46]

The Ḥanafī school, the official school of the Ottoman Empire, had less than favorable rules of maintenance toward women, requiring that they

43 "Court of Miṣr Al-Qadīma, Sijill 15 (1018/1609), Archival Code 1006–000153," doc. 41, 14.
44 "Court of Al-Bāb Al-ʿĀlī, Sijill 1 (937/1530), Archival Code 1001–000001," doc. 69, 17.
45 "Court of Miṣr Al-Qadīma, Sijill 15 (1018/1609), Archival Code 1006–000153," doc. 21, 8.
46 "Court of Miṣr Al-Qadīma, Sijill 18 (1057/1647), Archival Code 1006–000156," doc. 7, 3–4.

have either an agreement or a court order stipulating the amount of maintenance if they wished to hold their husbands or ex-husbands liable for maintenance arrears. The other schools were less rigid, allowing maintenance arrears to be counted from the time of nonpayment, even without any agreements. As a precaution against women losing their past maintenance before Ḥanafī judges, separation agreements often contained a formula establishing the amount of maintenance to both children and divorcees and explicitly empowering women to borrow money if the fathers were late on their payments. Fathers were then required to repay such debts. Cuno observes similar strategies made by women in nineteenth-century Egypt, where Ḥanafism was the applicable law in family matters under the Khedives.[47] In one case from 991/1583, a Cairene father was absent for seven years without paying child maintenance. His unsubstantiated claim that his wife had previously voluntarily relieved him of his financial obligations during this time was rejected by the judge.[48] Failure to pay maintenance, whether for the wife or the child, like any debt, was punishable by imprisonment. One comes across many situations in which the judge imprisons the debtor at the request of the creditor. This imprisonment often ended when the family of the imprisoned person appeared before the court and paid the debt. This was the case for instance in 1018/1609, when a husband was put in jail until his debt was cleared.[49]

One case that illustrates the maneuvers that fathers made to be relieved of their financial obligations comes from eighteenth-century Cairo. In 1190/1776, a man by the name of ʿUthmān b. Ṣāliḥ al-Ḥalabī appeared before the Ḥanafī judge to sue his ex-wife's mother, Raḥma, for child custody. His divorcee, the defendant's daughter Āmina, had remarried, whereupon the grandmother assumed custody of Ḥusayn, their son who was at the time an unweaned infant. The wording of the document suggests that no judicial decision was made for the transfer of custody from the mother to the child's maternal grandmother and that it was common knowledge among the litigants that remarriage disqualified the mother from maintaining custody.[50] The father argued that his daughter, the child's sister, was willing to nurse the boy for free. According to most

47 Cuno, *Modernizing Marriage*, 143–157.
48 "Court of Miṣr Al-Qadīma, Sijill 13 (991/1583), Archival Code 1006–000151," doc. 87, 24.
49 "Court of Miṣr Al-Qadīma, Sijill 15 (1018/1609), Archival Code 1006–000153," doc. 29, 10; "Court of Miṣr Al-Qadīma, Sijill 21 (1081/1670), Archival Code 1006–000159," doc. 160, 74.
50 Ibrahim, *Pragmatism in Islamic Law.*

jurists as we saw in Chapter 1, if someone offers to nurse the child for free, the father is not obligated to pay the nursing fee to the mother or other female custodians. In other words, the grandmother would either hand over the child to be nursed or assume the nursing fee herself. The grandmother retorted that she volunteered to pay for the child's nursing herself. Accordingly, the judge ruled that the father was not responsible for the nursing fee and that the grandmother should retain custody until the child reaches the age of discernment, in accordance with Ḥanafī law.[51] The father must have wanted to free himself from this financial responsibility by convincing the sister to volunteer to nurse her brother. Had the grandmother, who was fully aware of the implications of the father's claim, agreed to let the sister nurse the baby either at the grandmother's house or at her own house,[52] she would be limiting the mother's access to the child. Instead, the grandmother was willing to commit herself financially to paying the nursing fee herself, which is the responsibility of the father according to Islamic law, in order to continue to provide the mother and herself with greater access to the child. It is also possible that the mother continued to nurse the child at her mother's house after her remarriage.

We also see that some Christians went to sharīʿa courts in order to adjudicate their custody disputes based on Islamic law. Take the example of Maryam, a Christian who in 1190/1776 brought a lawsuit against the maternal grandmother of her son's children. Maryam claimed that the mother of her son's two teenage daughters (*murāhiqatayn*), probably around 11 to 13 years,[53] had died and her mother had taken custody of the two girls. She said that she had priority of custody because she was willing to provide custody for the girls without charging a custody wage. She asked the Ḥanafī judge to force the maternal grandmother to give her the two girls since, according to Islamic law, she had the right to custody.

[51] "Court of Al-Bāb Al-ʿĀlī, Sijill 293 (1190/1776), Archival Code 1001–000656," doc. 55, 41.

[52] According to al-Kāsānī and Ibn ʿĀbidīn, the nursing should take place at the custodian's house. Yet some jurists allowed the non-maternal nurse to nurse the child at her own house. See Ibn ʿĀbidīn and al-Ḥaṣkafī, *Radd Al-Muḥtār ʿalā Al-Durr Al-Mukhtār Sharḥ Tanwīr Al-Abṣār*, 5:257; al-Miṣrī, al-Nasafī, and Ibn ʿĀbidīn, *Al-Baḥr Al-Rāʾiq Sharḥ Kanz Al-Daqāʾiq Wa-Maʿahu Al-Ḥawāshī Al-Musammāh Minḥat Al-Khāliq ʿalā Al-Baḥr Al-Rāʾiq*, 4: 343–346.

[53] It is hard to estimate the age associated with this term because it refers to a child who is close to maturity, which itself is not based on age but rather physical signs such as having wet dreams. "Court of Al-Bāb Al-ʿĀlī, Sijill 293 (1190/1776), Archival Code 1001–000656," doc. 131, 90.

The maternal grandmother acknowledged that she used to receive payments from the father for her custodianship (*ujrat haḍānatihimā*), adding that their father was well-off. However, she said she was willing to care for the children for free. In this case, she explained, she would have priority of custody. The judge told Maryam that since the father no longer paid the maternal grandmother for her care, the maternal grandmother had priority of custody over her.[54] Over a century after this case took place in Cairo, Ibn ʿĀbidīn said that this type of case still happened frequently (*wa-hādhihi taqaʿ kathīran*) in the nineteenth century.[55]

The judge then decided that the father must pay 120 silver pieces a month to the maternal grandmother for maintenance of the child, justifying his decision by saying that the father was well-off. While the document does not tell us how much the previous maintenance was prior to this lawsuit, it is clear that this amount was unusually high. The judge probably compensated the maternal grandmother for the loss of her custody fees with an increase in the *nafaqa*, which was within his power. Perhaps the judge also did not want the two children to suffer from the decrease in income resulting from this lawsuit. One cannot but think that this decision was motivated, though not explicitly, by a concern about the well-being of the children and their care provider whose suitability as a caregiver was never challenged by anyone involved in the case.[56]

Although child maintenance usually appears in court in the context of separation, there were situations in which a woman who was still married sued for child maintenance in the same way a wife would sue for her own maintenance when the husband did not provide for her or her children. In one case brought to the Ḥanbalī judge in the court of Miṣr al-Qadīma in 991/1583, Dīnār sued her husband, Muḥammad, for her maintenance and that of their daughter, Fāṭima. We know that Fāṭima was at least seven years old, as the mother mentioned that the father had left them with no support for seven years. The mother had to borrow money to pay for their expenses at the rate of one silver *niṣf* a day for the seven years he was absent. She asked to be reimbursed for the money she had borrowed. The husband claimed that she had absolved him of any maintenance in

54 "Court of Al-Bāb Al-ʿĀlī, Sijill 293 (1190/1776), Archival Code 1001–000656," doc. 131, 90.

55 Ibn ʿĀbidīn and al-Ḥaṣkafī, *Radd Al-Muḥtār ʿalā Al-Durr Al-Mukhtār Sharḥ Tanwīr Al-Abṣār*, 5:257.

56 "Court of Al-Bāb Al-ʿĀlī, Sijill 293 (1190/1776), Archival Code 1001–000656," doc. 131, 90.

return for divorce before he left, but being unable to provide documentation of such a separation deed, the husband lost the case.[57]

GUARDIANSHIP

Decisions about guardianship were made often amicably in the court. Unlike custodianship, I have not found any cases in which there were disagreements over guardianship between an agnatic male relative and a mother, for instance. While such disagreements must have taken place, they were not as frequent as custody disputes. As mentioned in Chapter 2, the natural guardian was the father and close agnatic relatives in the absence of a bequest made by the father. In the event of the father's passing, guardianship was often transferred to someone else through appointment either by the father in a bequest or by the judge. However, most guardianship responsibilities were taken over by the grandfather, uncle, or mother without notarization unless the child had assets. There are many examples in the court records of the father appointing a guardian over his children in a bequest.[58] As we saw in common law England, fathers had the power to guardianship "from the grave." Egyptian fathers had a similar power in Islamic juristic discourse and in Ottoman-Egyptian legal practice. In 970/1562, two men testified in court that a deceased father of a minor boy had appointed one Muḥammad al-Takrūrī as a guardian over his son.[59] By the end of the eighteenth century, no change in judicial practice of appointments of guardians can be detected from the sample.[60]

[57] There are several types of marriage dissolution in Islamic law, the most common of which are *ṭalāq* (repudiation), *khulʿ* (no-fault divorce), and *faskh* (annulment). *Ṭalāq* is a unilateral repudiation made by the husband against his wife, which is the prerogative of the husband. The second type is *khulʿ*, which is a no-fault, for-compensation divorce often initiated by the wife or her agent, but it can also be initiated by the husband. The third type is annulment (*faskh*), which sometimes takes the shape of a judicial divorce made by the judge and wife in limited circumstances such as the absence of the husband and his inability to provide maintenance or the impugnment of the probity of witnesses in limited circumstances. I shall use the word "divorce" to refer to all types of Islamic dissolutions of marriage when there is no need to specify the type of divorce being discussed. "Court of Miṣr Al-Qadīma, Sijill 13 (991/1583), Archival Code 1006–000151," doc. 87, 24.

[58] "Court of Qisma ʿArabiyya, Sijill 2 (970–971/1562–1563), Archival Code 1004–000002," doc. 38, 22; doc. 59, 36; doc. 103, 70.

[59] "Court of Qisma ʿArabiyya, Sijill 2 (970–971/1562–1563), Archival Code 1004–000002," doc. 38, 22.

[60] "Court of Qisma ʿArabiyya, Sijill 140 (1206/1792), Archival Code 1004–000703," Dār al-Wathāʾiq al-Qawmiyya, Cairo, doc. 3, 2; doc. 18, 17.

In the absence of a bequest, judges were in charge of making such appointments when the matter was brought to court, often to protect the ward's assets. The most common appointments were made to male agnatic relatives of the children,[61] but there are many examples of mothers being appointed as guardians by judges even when the child's paternal uncles and grandfathers were available.[62] The reason for such appointments was frequently mentioned as serving the interests of the ward.[63] Some guardians appointed agents to carry out the responsibilities of guardianship. In 1092/1681, Muḥammad al-Qahwajī, the guardian of a minor girl who was already married, came to the court of Miṣr al-Qadīma to designate his own cousin as his agent (*wakīl*) in matters relating to the minor.[64] These types of transactions were notarized in the court to avoid potential litigation or accusations of squandering the money of the ward. Guardians were sometimes not related to the child because the child has no relatives or due to their default or unwillingness. In these situations, judges often appointed religious figures who were considered both trustworthy and knowledgeable about the responsibilities of guardians.[65] Ottoman judges did not hesitate to fire guardians when they realized that it was in the best interests of the wards to remove them, explicitly stating that their decisions were motivated by the "welfare and good fortune" (*al-ḥaẓẓ wa-l-maṣlaḥa*) of the child.[66]

As we mentioned previously, there was a common type of agreement in which close members of the child's family, especially the mother, were asked to vet the appropriateness of appointing an agnatic relative as guardian. This was the judicial practice that was meant to guarantee that say the uncle's interest in guardianship was not motivated by a desire to embezzle the minor's assets. In two documents of *sijill* 1 of the Court of al-Qisma al-ʿArabiyya, for instance, the mother's consent to grant the uncle

[61] See, for instance, "Court of Qisma ʿAskariyya, Sijill 212 (1211/1796), Archival Code 1003–001009," Dār al-Wathāʾiq al-Qawmiyya, Cairo, doc. 152, 99.

[62] See, for instance, "Court of Qisma ʿArabiyya, Sijill 2 (970–971/1562–1563), Archival Code 1004–000002," doc. 95, 61. In this document, the mother was appointed by the Ḥanafī judge as both a custodian and guardian.

[63] "Court of Qisma ʿAskariyya, Sijill 1 (961/1554), Archival Code 1003–000001," Dār al-Wathāʾiq al-Qawmiyya, Cairo, doc. 192, 52.

[64] "Court of Miṣr Al-Qadīma, Sijill 22 (1092–1681), Archival Code 1006–000160," doc. 133, 48.

[65] "Court of Qisma ʿArabiyya, Sijill 2 (970–971/1562–1563), Archival Code 1004–000002," doc. 19, 13.

[66] "Court of Qisma ʿAskariyya, Sijill 26 (1019/1610), Archival Code 1003–000105," doc. 160, 77; "Court of Qisma ʿArabiyya, Sijill 3 (973/1566), Archival Code 1004–000003," doc. 176, 104.

the right of guardianship was highlighted by the scribe. In a third example from this sample, the judge sought the consent of both the mother and the paternal grandmother to the appointment of the uncle as guardian.[67] This was a way to verify both the good character and ability of either the agnatic male relatives or the mother to manage the child's financial assets. In one case, the guardian designated by the father in a bequest before his death gave up his right to guardianship over Maḥmūd, a minor boy. His resignation before the judge was attended by Maḥmūd's mother, who had been appointed as an overseer over her son and his guardian (more on this practice to come).[68] The scribe was sure to emphasize that she accepted his resignation, although her approval was irrelevant in juristic discourse. After the resignation of the guardian, the mother became the sole financial administrator of the child's estate. In fact, in the document following the guardian's resignation, the mother immediately notarized a financial transaction on behalf of her minor son.[69]

In another instance, the judge requested the consent of the uncle to the mother's appointment as guardian. In 970/1562, a woman came to the court having agreed with her deceased husband's adult son that she would be a guardian and custodian for her two sons, described as "minors" (*qāṣirān*). The scribe was sure to emphasize the fact that the children's brother consented to this arrangement. Having checked the consent of the brother who had the "natural" right to guardianship as an agnatic male relative of the children, the judge installed the mother as a guardian and custodian.[70] At other times, the judge did not seek the consent of any relatives in his appointment of guardians or custodians.[71]

Mothers in Ottoman Egypt were able to have guardians removed for untrustworthiness. In one case from 1115/1704, Dalāl, who had previously consented to the appointment of a guardian who does not seem to have been related to the child, went back to the judge to rescind her

[67] The first 200 cases were missing, and therefore I chose the following 200 as my sample. See "Court of Qisma ʿArabiyya, Sijill 1 (968–969/1561), Archival Code 1004–000001," doc. 201, 85; doc. 244, 114; doc. 344, 157.

[68] "Court of Qisma ʿArabiyya, Sijill 2 (970–971/1562–1563), Archival Code 1004–000002," doc. 60, 36.

[69] "Court of Qisma ʿArabiyya, Sijill 2 (970–971/1562–1563), Archival Code 1004–000002," doc. 60, 36.

[70] "Court of Qisma ʿArabiyya, Sijill 2 (970–971/1562–1563), Archival Code 1004–000002," doc. 95, 61.

[71] "Court of Qisma ʿArabiyya, Sijill 2 (970–971/1562–1563), Archival Code 1004–000002," doc. 173, 111.

consent after she discovered that the guardian was untrustworthy. The judge removed the guardian and appointed her in his stead.[72] Women guardians were also able to grant the power of attorney to others to manage the affairs of the children over whom they had guardianship, and remove agents at will.[73] It was common for fathers to designate mothers as guardians in their lives,[74] even though mothers were not necessarily expected to manage the affairs of children themselves. When ʿĪsā Aghā died in 1130/1718, his adult offspring, as well as his wife in her capacity as guardian, appointed his slave to represent all of them in court. The agent performed all types of transactions on behalf of both the adults and minors, all of whom were living with their mother.[75]

Women were often appointed as guardians, but the court vetted them through testimonies first. In 970/1562, a woman by the name of Khadīja requested that she be appointed as a guardian over her minor daughter after the death of the child's father. The judge asked her to prove to him that she was capable of performing the tasks associated with guardianship, including financial administration of the child's estate. The mother was able to bring two male witnesses to testify that she was capable of guardianship. Once the judge received these testimonies, he made the appointment.[76] Women's ability to act as guardians was also verified in another case, in which the judge granted guardianship to the mother after listening to testimonies supporting her guardianship.[77] Such testimonies were not required when it came to child custody.

In some cases, judges appointed more than one guardian as a way to ensure that the property of the child was secured, since the multiple guardians acted as checks against one another. In 968/1561, the judge in the Court of al-Qisma al-ʿArabiyya appointed two guardians over a minor boy whose parents had both passed away. The guardians were the boy's

72 "Court of Qisma ʿArabiyya, Sijill 80 (1115/1704), Archival Code 1004–000405," Dār al-Wathāʾiq al-Qawmiyya, Cairo, doc. 61, 40.

73 See, for instance, "Court of Qisma ʿArabiyya, Sijill 2 (970–971/1562–1563), Archival Code 1004–000002," doc. 56, 33. "Court of Qisma ʿArabiyya, Sijill 2 (970–971/1562–1563), Archival Code 1004–000002," doc. 48, 29.

74 "Court of Qisma ʿArabiyya, Sijill 2 (970–971/1562–1563), Archival Code 1004–000002," doc. 103, 70.

75 "Court of Būlāq, Sijill 64 (1130/1718), Archival Code 1005–000304," Dār al-Wathāʾiq al-Qawmiyya, Cairo, doc. 188, 71.

76 "Court of Qisma ʿArabiyya, Sijill 2 (970–971/1562–1563), Archival Code 1004–000002," doc. 37, 22.

77 "Court of Qisma ʿArabiyya, Sijill 2 (970–971/1562–1563), Archival Code 1004–000002," doc. 39, 23.

adult brother and their maternal grandfather.[78] The courts also had another function of guardianship, namely "overseer" (*nāẓir*), which was a position of oversight over the guardian, but sometimes assumed some of the functions of a guardian. The main objective behind the appointment of an overseer as the term indicates was to ensure that the ward's properties were doubly secure by adding another layer of oversight. Judges sometimes appointed more than one overseer over the ward and his or her guardian.[79] The documents of oversight (*niẓāra*) over the ward's property often stated that any decision made by the guardian had to be approved by the overseer. This was often done when the guardian was not a first-degree relative of the child. It was often the maternal side overseeing the agnatic guardian, which was a pragmatic way to ensure that corruption could be avoided since the judge and the overseer both have the power to supervise the financial transactions made by the guardian. In a case from 968–969/1561, the mother was appointed as an overseer over the guardian of her daughter.[80] In another instance, it was the maternal grandfather who was appointed as an overseer over the guardian because the mother had passed away.[81] There were other cases in which the guardian was the brother and the overseer was the paternal grandfather,[82] the sister was the guardian, and the overseer was a religious figure unrelated to the child,[83] or the mother was the guardian and the overseer was not related to the children. In one case, the overseer was in charge of collecting debts owed to their father. The overseer thus sometimes had functions that were similar to those of the guardian.[84]

It was clear that the guardian had more power in managing the financial affairs of children than overseers. In one telling case from 970/1562, a mother by the name of Badīʿa, who was already an overseer over her minor daughter, Mubāraka, came to the court to ask to be installed as

[78] "Court of Qisma ʿArabiyya, Sijill 1 (968–969/1561), Archival Code 1004–000001," doc. 222, 103.

[79] "Court of Qisma ʿArabiyya, Sijill 2 (970–971/1562–1563), Archival Code 1004–000002," doc. 78, 51.

[80] "Court of Qisma ʿArabiyya, Sijill 1 (968–969/1561), Archival Code 1004–000001," doc. 225, 103.

[81] "Court of Qisma ʿArabiyya, Sijill 1 (968–969/1561), Archival Code 1004–000001," doc. 283, 129.

[82] "Court of Qisma ʿArabiyya, Sijill 1 (968–969/1561), Archival Code 1004–000001," doc. 297, 135.

[83] "Court of Qisma ʿArabiyya, Sijill 1 (968–969/1561), Archival Code 1004–000001," doc. 339, 155.

[84] "Court of Qisma ʿArabiyya, Sijill 1 (968–969/1561), Archival Code 1004–000001," doc. 395, 181.

a guardian instead of an overseer. She said that two of the debtors refused to pay her the daughters' debts, insisting that they would pay their dues only to Mubāraka's legal guardian, who had been appointed by the judge (*min qibal al-shar' al-sharīf*). She explained that the guardian, al-Nūrī Nūr al-Dīn, had left Egypt (*al-diyār al-miṣriyya*) for a long time and requested that guardianship be transferred to her. The mother brought witnesses to testify that the guardian had been absent and that the ward's interests were harmed (*ḍā'a ḥāl al-qāṣira*) by his absence. The judge appointed the mother as guardian after removing her from the position as overseer. This was all done in the presence of the ward's two sisters, whose consent to the appointment was highlighted by the scribe. The judge then appointed the two sisters as overseers over their sister and the new guardian's administration of the ward's finances. In turn, the mother agreed to the appointment of the sisters. As such, the consent of the mother was sought when the judge appointed the overseers, and the consent of the sisters was sought when the judge appointed their mother as guardian.[85]

Another example shows that the guardian and overseer cooperated to achieve the best interests of the ward. In a series of notarized documents brought to the Ḥanafī judge in 970/1562, the judge first appointed Ma'shūq as a guardian over her minor son, Aḥmad.[86] In the following document, the same judge appointed al-Mu'allim Budayr as an overseer over the guardian and the child's properties, obligating her to seek the overseer's permission before performing any transactions on behalf of the ward.[87] In the following document, both the guardian and the overseer sued a third party for some debt on behalf of the child.[88] In another subsequent document in the register, the guardian gave the overseer the power of attorney to calculate and receive her son's inheritance in the Bāb al-Lūq market, which consisted mostly of debts that the deceased father was owed to other merchants.[89] Yet another document shows that the overseer had started collecting the debts on his own based on the agency granted to him by the guardian and that he sued another merchant for

85 "Court of Qisma 'Arabiyya, Sijill 2 (970–971/1562–1563), Archival Code 1004–000002," doc. 79, 51.

86 "Court of Qisma 'Arabiyya, Sijill 2 (970–971/1562–1563), Archival Code 1004–000002," doc. 183, 116.

87 "Court of Qisma 'Arabiyya, Sijill 2 (970–971/1562–1563), Archival Code 1004–000002," doc. 184, 116.

88 "Court of Qisma 'Arabiyya, Sijill 2 (970–971/1562–1563), Archival Code 1004–000002," doc. 185, 116.

89 "Court of Qisma 'Arabiyya, Sijill 2 (970–971/1562–1563), Archival Code 1004–000002," doc. 186, 116.

a debt owed to the deceased father,[90] as well as two other lawsuits against yet two more merchants.[91]

The situation in Ottoman Egypt was similar to eighteenth- and nineteenth-century Aleppo, where, according to Meriwether, the appointment of women as guardians was widespread.[92] To give the reader a sense of how widespread the practice was in early modern Egypt, consider that out of a total of 500 cases in three *sijills*, there were 70 appointments of guardians, 21 of which were made to women and the rest to men. To break down these 500 cases, consider that in *sijill* 2 of the Court of al-Qisma al-ʿArabiyya, out of a total of 200 cases, there were 27 appointments of guardians (*waṣī*) and overseers (*nāẓir*) made by the judge. Nine were made to women, usually mothers, and 18 to men, usually agnatic male relatives.[93] The situation was similar in *sijill* 3 of the same court, in which there were 24 appointments in the first 200 cases. Eighteen were made to men and six to women.[94] In the first hundred cases of *sijill* 212 of the Court of al-Qisma al-ʿAskariyya, there were 19 appointments, 13 of which were to men and six to women.[95]

CONCLUSION

As we have seen in Chapters 3 and 4, there were many ways in which the eight themes of age and gender, remarriage of the mother, lifestyle, religion, visitations, relocation with the ward, maintenance, and guardianship functioned in Egyptian society of the sixteenth through nineteenth centuries. A mix of formalist rules, pragmatic eclecticism, private separation deeds, and judicial discretion enabled judges and families to design various child custody and guardianship arrangements. This complex situation is strikingly different from the nineteenth- and twenty-first-century approach to child custody and guardianship (the subject of Chapters 5

90 "Court of Qisma ʿArabiyya, Sijill 2 (970–971/1562–1563), Archival Code 1004–000002," doc. 187, 117.

91 "Court of Qisma ʿArabiyya, Sijill 2 (970–971/1562–1563), Archival Code 1004–000002," doc. 188, 117; doc. 189, 117; For similar examples, see "Court of Qisma ʿArabiyya, Sijill 1 (968–969/1561), Archival Code 1004–000001," doc. 317, 145; doc. 339, 155.

92 Margaret L. Meriwether, "The Rights of Children and the Responsibilities of Women: Women as Wasis in Ottoman Aleppo, 1770–1840," in *Women, the Family, and Divorce Laws in Islamic History*, ed. Amira El Azhary Sonbol (Syracuse, NY: Syracuse University Press, 1996), 219–235.

93 "Court of Qisma ʿArabiyya, Sijill 2 (970–971/1562–1563), Archival Code 1004–000002."

94 "Court of Qisma ʿArabiyya, Sijill 3 (973/1566), Archival Code 1004–000003."

95 "Court of Qisma ʿAskariyya, Sijill 212 (1211/ 1796), Archival Code 1003–001009."

and 6). It was not clear, for instance, who would have custody of a given child simply based on age and gender, except that maternal nursing was valued to such an extent that most mothers were able to maintain custody of unweaned children regardless of their marital situation. Even if these women did not have custody, they were able to nurse their children at the house of their mothers or sisters after custody was transferred to these relatives. Judges exercised pragmatic adjudication to help children and enable their mothers to retrieve child maintenance arrears despite the Ḥanafī school's rigid rules. Even though religion played an important role in the theoretical rules of custody and guardianship, lifestyle and the mother's employment did not appear important in the courtroom.

What the Ottoman-Egyptian court records paint is a very complex picture that would change in the nineteenth century, when the diversity of Sunni legal pluralism would be narrowed and judges restricted to the Ḥanafī school. In Chapter 5, I show how child custody would become much more rigid, leaving families with fewer options since not only would their agreements cease to be binding, but they would also have no non-Ḥanafī options to which they could resort. This rigidity would become the subject of a debate that would eventually lead to the legal reforms of child custody and the Egyptian family more broadly beginning in 1929.

Part III

The Transition into Modernity

5

Child Custody in Egypt, 1801–1929

THE HISTORICAL CONTEXT: LAW AND SOCIETY

After Napoleon's Egyptian campaign in 1798, an Anglo-Ottoman offensive defeated the French in 1801, securing once again Ottoman control of Egypt. After a period of social upheaval, Mehmed Ali became Egypt's governor in 1805. As part of the assertion of his power – and, some may argue, in line with his secessionist ambitions – he created an army through drafting villagers. To serve the needs of his expanding army, Ali established many institutions such as modern hospitals, factories, and schools staffed with members of educational missions that he sent to Europe in the early years of his rule. The introduction of long-staple cotton to the agricultural sector in 1821 helped finance Ali's army and his modernizing project, which resulted in Egypt's greater integration into the world economy.[1]

Eighteenth-century Egyptian women of lower socioeconomic backgrounds worked in the markets as well as in manual jobs such as toiling the land to the extent that members of the French Expedition, as already noted, were surprised that peasant women worked in the fields, a fact that revealed French attitudes toward women's domesticity.[2] Women were

[1] Kenneth M. Cuno, "The Era of Muḥammad ʿAlī," in *The Islamic World in the Age of Western Dominance: The New Cambridge History of Islam*, ed. Francis Robinson, vol. 5 (Cambridge; New York, NY: Cambridge University Press, 2010), 79–106; Timothy Mitchell, *Colonising Egypt*, Cambridge Middle East Library (Cambridge; New York, NY: Cambridge University Press, 1988), 9–18, 34–36, 36–39; Fahmy, *All the Pasha's Men*, 9–12, 112–159; Roger Owen, *Cotton and the Egyptian Economy, 1820–1914: A Study in Trade and Development*, (Oxford: Clarendon Press, 1969), 3–160.

[2] For a discussion of women's labor during the late eighteenth and early twentieth centuries, see further Tucker, *Women in Nineteenth-Century Egypt*, 40–42.

joining the manual labor workforce in larger numbers under Mehmed Ali. After the men were rounded up to join the army, the women, in addition to spinning most of the yarn used by weavers in Egypt, also had to replace the labor that men had once provided.[3] Mehmed Ali's military conscription and the depletion of human resources in the countryside left many women no choice but to shoulder the responsibility of supporting their families without any help from their partners. Ali's short-lived attempt at modernizing Egypt ended with his loss to the European Powers. In 1840, he was forced to agree to the terms of the Convention of London, which included downsizing his navy and army.[4] These developments turned Egypt into a dependent economy that provided the raw materials for Europe's industries, destroying Mehmed Ali's project. By the 1870s, Egypt's debt crisis under Khedive Ismāʿīl further eroded state power. These rapid transformations had a huge impact on the Egyptian family and the law.[5]

In the first half of the nineteenth century, Mehmed Ali's educational missions that spanned from the 1810s to the 1840s addressed only men.[6] The missions consisted exclusively of men, and their objective was to return from Europe to educate the future men of the nation. It was not until the second half of the nineteenth century that women's education started to get the attention of modernists. During the 1860s and 1870s, the men of these educational missions such as Rifāʿa Rāfiʿ al-Ṭahṭāwī (1801–1873) and ʿAlī Mubārak (1823–1893) wrote about women's education. According to Kenneth Cuno, French laws such as the Guizot law of 1833, which made elementary school mandatory for boys, and the Faloux Law of 1850, which established a system of elementary education for girls, influenced the thought of al-Ṭahṭāwī and Mubārak.[7] Al-Ṭahṭāwī's views on women's education and his support for the new girls' schools that appeared in nineteenth-century Egypt represent one of the earliest examples of the valorization of a new family ideology among Egyptian

3 Tucker, *Women in Nineteenth-Century Egypt,* 81–85; On Mehmed Ali's rule, see further F. Robert Hunter, *Egypt under the Khedives, 1805–1879: From Household Government to Modern Bureaucracy* (Pittsburgh, PA: University of Pittsburgh Press, 1984), 3–32.

4 William M. Hale, *Turkish Foreign Policy Since 1774* (New York: Routledge, 2013), 18–19; Ehud R. Toledano, *State and Society in Mid-Nineteenth-Century Egypt* (Cambridge; New York, NY: Cambridge University Press, 1989), 1–6.

5 Toledano, *State and Society in Mid-Nineteenth-Century Egypt*; Hunter, *Egypt under the Khedives, 1805–1879*, 35–80.

6 On the educational missions, see further J. Heyworth-Dunne, *An Introduction to the History of Education in Modern Egypt*, 2nd edn. (London: Frank Cass and Company Limited, 1968), 157–181; 221–264; 288–301.

7 Cuno, *Modernizing Marriage*, 93–96.

modernists, an ideology inspired by a European family model developed throughout the course of the eighteenth and nineteenth centuries.[8]

According to al-Ṭahṭāwī, however, only elementary education for women was necessary since the main function of their education was to serve in domestic roles such as housekeeping and childrearing, rather than being full members of the public. This was consistent with the European domestic ideology of the time in which women were in charge of the private sphere, even though they were allowed to appear in public spaces. By contrast, Islamic law, despite a contrary minority position, generally does not obligate women to do housework or childcare, although it places more limits on their access to public spaces. In addition to domesticity or "true womanhood," an essential part of the new family ideology, there was emphasis on the love binding child and mother, and the importance of loving and nurturing children. Some historians have called this assumption of a unique bond between mother and child "the cult of motherhood," as we saw in Chapter 1. The new Egyptian family ideology was a hybrid of these European notions brought about by nineteenth-century educational missions and the maintenance–obedience relationship, which existed in premodern Islamic legal thought. Later modernists such as ʿĀʾisha Taymūr (1840–1902), Muḥammad ʿAbduh (1849–1905), Qāsim Amīn (1863–1908), Zaynab Fawwāz (1850–1914), and Malak Ḥifnī Nāṣif (1886–1918) helped further develop the new family ideology, making some modifications to the earlier modernist thought of al-Ṭahṭāwī.[9]

The new family ideology consisted of a number of interconnected ideas: (1) the stability of the family became a social good (e.g., divorce was considered a social ill); (2) the conjugal family was privileged over polygynous families; (3) companionate marriage was superior to "blind" marriage since it ensured the stability of the family; (4) mothers played a central role in childrearing and house-management; and (5) women's education was essential to guaranteeing a harmonious and companionate relationship with the husband, and to educating the children of the nation. The new family ideology was on full display in the highest household of Egypt. In 1873, Egypt's crown prince Tawfīq celebrated his marriage to Amīna Ilhāmī, the granddaughter of ʿAbbās Ḥilmī I (r. 1849–1854). In Cuno's estimation, the wedding celebrations displayed the new family

[8] On some of the changes that happened in the French family in the eighteenth and nineteenth centuries, see further Flandrin, *Families in Former Times*, 112–120; 135–136; 156–173; 177–212; Rifāʿa al-Ṭahṭāwī, *Al-Murshid Al-Amīn Li'l-Banāt Wa'l-Banīn* (Cairo: Dār al-Kitāb al-Miṣrī wa'l-Lubnānī, 2012), 6–7.

[9] Cuno, *Modernizing Marriage*, 81–97.

ideology, where the khedival family abandoned concubinage and polygyny. The new family image of the khedives was a monogamous, nuclear relationship based on marriage. When the crown prince became khedive, he was Egypt's first monogamous nineteenth-century ruler. Amīna had a prominent role as the khedive's only consort, giving women a new role in a new model family. By the 1870s, some Westerners had observed a decline in polygyny in the upper classes.[10] This ideology was promoted through the Arabic press, which flourished in the 1870s after the government relinquished its monopoly over publishing.[11]

Throughout the nineteenth and early twentieth centuries, joint-family households declined in both urban and rural areas. Egyptian nationalists and modernists emphasized women's education as the best way to ensure that they were able to raise children and to be their husbands' friends, equals, and companions. This "cult of motherhood" meant that maternal breastfeeding was assumed to be better for the child by the late nineteenth and early twentieth century. The mother also came to be responsible for the physical, moral and intellectual nurture of children, assuming some of the functions that, as we discussed earlier, were historically associated with the father. This was particularly clear in the court rulings of the early twentieth century. Aversion to prenuptial meetings between potential spouses declined in upper- and middle-class families. By the second quarter of the twentieth century, middle- and upper-class families had all but abandoned joint family households, opting instead for conjugal households where the mother was in charge of the domestic,[12] private sphere.[13] All of these radical changes in Egyptian society required further

[10] Cuno, *Modernizing Marriage*, 19–23.

[11] On the role of the press in promoting these ideas in late nineteenth-century Egypt, see Beth Baron, *The Women's Awakening in Egypt: Culture, Society, and the Press* (New Haven, CT: Yale University Press, 1994), 2; Hoda A. Yousef, *Composing Egypt: Reading, Writing, and the Emergence of a Modern Nation 1870–1930* (Stanford, CA: Stanford University Press, 2016).

[12] Cuno, *Modernizing Marriage*, 56–61. For an excellent discussion of the new discourse on motherhood and its role in the nationalist project of modernization, see further Omnia Shakry, "Schooled Mothers and Structured Play: Child Rearing in Turn-of-the-Century Egypt," in *Remaking Women: Feminism and Modernity in the Middle East*, ed. Lila Abu-Lughod (Princeton, NJ: Princeton University Press, 1998), 126–170; Hanan Kholoussy, *For Better, For Worse: The Marriage Crisis That Made Modern Egypt* (Stanford, CA: Stanford University Press, 2010), 100–122.

[13] Like their Ottoman-Egyptian predecessors, some women, especially of the upper and middle classes, were able to guarantee a commitment to monogamy on the part of the husband, ensure their freedom to visit relatives, and have a say over the place of the marital residence. On this phenomenon in nineteenth-century Egypt, see further Cuno, *Modernizing Marriage*, 58.

judicial discretion to determine what would be best for each child in a specific context, in line with Mamluk and Ottoman separation deeds, for instance. But instead of accommodating these social changes, the Egyptian legal system was made more rigid through a process of Ḥanafization that did not live up to the dynamism of Egyptian society of the nineteenth century and early twentieth century.

It is important to emphasize here that unlike Tucker, who assumes that the Egyptian family experienced radical changes owing to state centralization and economic policies, Cuno attributes the rise of the new family ideology developed in the upper and middle classes to khedival household politics and political marriage strategies, rather than to ideational or economic changes. This ideology, which was a hybrid of Western and precolonial Islamic ideas, moved ahead of social change and did not trickle down to the general population until the early twentieth century. This elite discourse was represented in the burgeoning periodical press of the era, but the rate of change in public opinion at the turn of the century cannot be gauged with any exactness.[14]

It is equally difficult to measure the nineteenth-century European missions and their impact on the Egyptian intelligentsia in gradually developing a new Egyptian family model (a process that had already been in motion before the British occupation of 1882). While the political marriage strategy was the catalyst for supporting the rise of the new family ideology, this ideology had ideational support in the writings of intellectuals before the British occupation. Yet these writings must have remained an elite discourse, unable to trickle down the social hierarchy until the proliferation of the printing press in the late decades of the nineteenth century. This hybrid gradually incorporated precolonial Islamic ideas such as the maintenance–obedience paradigm with new family ideology concepts, eventually leading to the wide social change that took place in the early twentieth century. In my view, the writings of al-Ṭahṭāwī, for instance, represent a moment of gradual transformation, as they departed in significant ways in their subject matter and social concerns from the writings of his teacher al-ʿAṭṭār as well as the writings of Fawwāz, Nāṣif, ʿAbduh, and Amīn. However, one should be cautious not to exaggerate the Ṭahṭāwī moment or the educational missions. Some scholars have, as Cuno rightly points out, treated Ṭahṭāwī's promise of monogamy to his wife as evidence of his "feminism." This approach ignores very similar contracts that predated the European missions,[15] thus magnifying the ideational role

[14] Cuno, *Modernizing Marriage*, 23. [15] Cuno, *Modernizing Marriage*, 80–122.

of the educational missions (in fact there are many examples in my sixteenth- to eighteenth-century sample of such contracts).

Nineteenth-Century Ḥanafization of Egypt's Laws

The changes in the structure of the nineteenth-century Egyptian family were met with increasing rigidity in the legal system due to the policy of Ḥanafization ushered in by the Ottomans after their reconquest of Egypt. In 1802, according to al-Jabartī, the Ottomans introduced innovations such as the abolition of deputy judges and the three judges of the non-Ḥanafī schools. All court transactions were supposed to be brought before the Ḥanafī judge or his Ḥanafī deputies.[16] This claim is confirmed by court evidence. Consider, for example, *sijill* 31, which covered cases from 1801 to 1810. In the beginning of the register, in 1801–1802, judicial affiliations were typically mentioned (most of whom were Ḥanafī), but by the end of the register, by around 1809, these affiliations were no longer mentioned in the *sijill,* as it had become common knowledge by that time that judges applied Ḥanafī law.[17]

The gradual but decisive Ḥanafization started as early as the reconquest of Egypt and the early years of Mehmed Ali's rule. Despite the clear shift, Mehmed Ali's 1835 decree prohibiting judges from issuing rulings based on non-Ḥanafī doctrine suggests that there were (unacceptable) lapses in observance of the general tendency.[18] Also in 1835, Mehmed Ali created the position of the grand mufti of Egypt. Prior to that, the Ḥanafī mufti affiliated with the Grand Sharīʿa Court in Cairo (Maḥkamat Miṣr al-Kubrā, or, al-Maḥkama al-Kubrā al-Sharʿiyya bi-Miṣr) was considered the highest-ranking mufti in Egypt. He gave legal counsel to the government and issued authoritative fatwas to resolve juristic disagreements. The chief mufti was on the Council of Scholars (al-Majlis al-ʿIlmī), which also included the chief muftis of the other three schools, the rector of al-Azhar, and the Head of the Descendants of the Prophet. On matters of public

16 Rudolph Peters, "What Does It Mean to Be an Official Madhhab?," in *The Islamic School of Law: Evolution, Devolution, and Progress*, eds. Peri Bearman, Rudolph Peters, and Frank E Vogel (Cambridge, MA: Harvard University Press, 2005), 157; ʿAbd al-Raḥmān b. Ḥasan al-Jabartī, *ʿAjāʾib Al-Āthār Fi'l-Tarājim Wa'l-Akhbār*, ed. ʿAbd al-Raḥīm ʿAbd al-Raḥmān ʿAbd al-Raḥīm (Cairo: Dār al-Kutub wa'l-Wathāʾiq al-Qawmiyya, 1998), 4:387–388.

17 "Court of Miṣr Al-Qadīma, Sijill 31 (1217–1802), Archival Code 1006–000169," Dār al-Wathāʾiq al-Qawmiyya, Cairo.

18 Baudouin Dupret, *Standing Trial: Law and the Person in the Modern Middle East* (London: I.B. Tauris, 2004), 269–270.

policy such as the printing of certain controversial books,[19] the government solicited the mufti's opinion. Meanwhile in the first half of the nineteenth century, Mehmed Ali founded secular courts in the fields of criminal, commercial, and administrative law, and later khedives expanded legislation in these fields throughout the nineteenth century.[20]

The process of Ḥanafization continued unabated throughout the remainder of the century. The Qadis' Ordinance (*Lā'iḥat al-Quḍāh*) of 1856 stipulated that judges should consult officially appointed Ḥanafī muftis in difficult cases, rather than forming opinions independently, to avoid making errors in interpreting the law. The ordinance stipulated that sharīʿa courts should follow the "sound opinions" (*al-aqwāl al-ṣaḥīḥa*) of the Ḥanafī school. Khedive Ismāʿīl promoted the Ḥanafī school, appointing a Ḥanafī Shaykh of al-Azhar against the historical record of Shāfiʿī and Mālikī appointments. The Sharīʿa Court Ordinance (*Lā'iḥat al-Maḥākim al-Sharʿiyya*) of 1880 continued this Ḥanafization drive by restricting judicial decisions to the "more preponderant opinion" (*arjaḥ al-aqwāl*) of the Ḥanafī school. The Sharīʿa Court Ordinance of 1897 assumed that the Ḥanafī school was the applicable law as per the practice of the nineteenth century.[21]

This process of Ḥanafization made the pluralistic legal system more rigid, not only because it restricted litigants to Ḥanafī law, but also owing to the increasing efficiency of the state and its ability to enforce Ḥanafī law more strictly. As we saw in Chapters 3 and 4, the Egyptian judicial authorities allowed private separation agreements that were at times in tension with juristic discourse. As an example of what Ḥanafization entailed, with respect to missing husbands, Cuno argues that Ḥanafī family law in Egypt was more rigid than the Ottoman Law of Family Rights promulgated in 1917.[22] The other three Sunni schools offered avenues for women of

[19] Rudolph Peters, "Muḥammad Al-ʿAbbāsī Al-Mahdī (D. 1897), Grand Muftī of Egypt, and His 'Al-Fatāwā Al-Mahdiyya,'" *Islamic Law and Society* 1:1 (1994): 81.

[20] Hunter, *Egypt under the Khedives, 1805–1879.*

[21] According to the Sharīʿa Court Ordinance of 1880, the Sharīʿa Court of Cairo served as another level of appeal from the decisions of Sharīʿa courts of first instance and appeal. The highest level of appeal could then be brought to the chief mufti against the decision of the Sharīʿa Court of Cairo. Judges were required, according to the ordinance, to refer difficult cases to the mufti affiliated to their court, but if he was unable to reach an answer, the issue should be referred to the chief mufti. The muftis' fatwas were no longer just "opinions." They were now binding according to these regulations of the Sharīʿa courts. Cuno, *Modernizing Marriage*, 137; Peters, "Muḥammad Al-ʿAbbāsī Al-Mahdī (D. 1897), Grand Muftī of Egypt, and His 'Al-Fatāwā Al-Mahdiyya,'" 74–78.

[22] Ḥanafī doctrine did not offer a reprieve to wives whose husbands had been absent for years. Under the regime of strict adherence to Ḥanafī law, women in nineteenth-century

missing husbands to get a judicial divorce on grounds of lack of maintenance or lack of sexual access (both of which were drawn upon in Mamluk and Ottoman Egypt), but the Ḥanafī *madhhab* did not offer these possibilities.[23] This rigidity of the legal system, coupled with Peters' judgment that the long-serving nineteenth-century chief mufti, al-Mahdī, was not an innovator but someone who made sure that Ḥanafī law reigned supreme in Egyptian courts, meant that custody and guardianship laws stood in tension with the new nineteenth-century family ideology.[24] Yet the impact of the new ideology on wide segments of Egyptian society would not be felt until the early twentieth century.

The rigidity of Islamic law as a consequence of the process of Ḥanafization, especially over the care of children, gave ammunition to the opponents of sharīʿa courts. By 1930, the debate over whether the sharīʿa courts should be integrated into a unified national judicial system gained renewed vigor. The proponents of unification, according to one sharīʿa judge, al-Zayn, were some of the judges of the National Courts (al-Maḥākim al-Ahliyya), whom he suspected of plotting to abolish Islamic law. In his view, they were the enemies of sharīʿa. Al-Zayn singles out ʿIzzat Efendi, a National Court judge, who wrote newspaper articles, as well as a report sent to the Ministry of Justice, criticizing sharīʿa court judges. In al-Zayn's view, the establishment of the National Courts was a death blow to sharīʿa that was launched by "Western crusaders" who conquered Muslims in the name of "civilization" (*madaniyya*). According to al-Zayn, the secular Probate Courts (al-Majālis al-Ḥisbiyya), established in the late nineteenth century, themselves were a blow to the sharīʿa. They were not designed out of concern for the "welfare of minors" (*maṣāliḥ al-quṣṣār*), but rather as an attempt to slowly abolish sharīʿa in different domains. He called for the reinstatement of Islamic law in all domains, a reference to the loss of Islamic law jurisdiction over criminal, commercial, and administrative matters to secular courts under Mehmed Ali and his successors. He added that the presence of sharīʿa judges on these courts was nothing more than

Egypt did not have access to the legal pluralism of the pre-nineteenth-century period, although there was a relaxation of the rules of evidence based on Ḥanafī practice that allowed women to rely on hearsay in establishing that their missing husbands were indeed dead. See Cuno, *Modernizing Marriage*, 146–147.

23 For examples from sixteenth-century Cairo where such judicial divorces were adjudicated by Ḥanbalī judges, see "Court of Ṣāliḥiyya Al-Najmiyya, Sijill 3 (951/1544), Archival Code 1012–000003," doc. 31, 11; doc. 41, 15.

24 Peters, "Muḥammad Al-ʿAbbāsī Al-Mahdī (D. 1897), Grand Muftī of Egypt, and His 'Al-Fatāwā Al-Mahdiyya,'" 81.

a façade, as they had little power.[25] A petition to the Minister of Justice was also published in the same volume in which ʿAbd al-Wahhāb Salīm recommended that these Probate Courts be abolished and reincorporated into sharīʿa courts.[26]

JURISTIC DISCOURSE ON CHILD CUSTODY IN THE NINETEENTH CENTURY

Judges in both nineteenth- and twentieth-century Egypt relied on a number of works, prominent among which are Ibn ʿĀbidīn's *Radd al-Muḥtār* and *al-ʿUqūd al-Durriyya fī Tanqīḥ al-Fatāwā al-Ḥāmidiyya*; Ibn Nujaym's *al-Baḥr al-Rāʾiq, al-Fatāwā al-Hindiyya, al-Fatāwā al-Mahdiyya*; and Qadrī Pāshā's compilation.[27] The work of Ibn ʿĀbidīn was one of the most cited in both nineteenth- and twentieth-century Egypt.[28] As we saw in Chapter 2, Ibn ʿĀbidīn offered a broad conception of the best interests of the child, more in line with Ibn Qayyim al-Jawziyya's thought, allowing the judge wide discretion in transcending some of the rules of author-jurists. In what follows, I briefly discuss some of the important issues debated in nineteenth- and twentieth-century Ḥanafī juristic discourse.

As already noted in Chapter 2, the nineteenth-century Ḥanafī jurist Ibn ʿĀbidīn's approach focused on broad, contextual conception of the best interests of the child. He allowed judges to determine, for instance, that a child was better off living with a remarried mother than with a remarried father by assessing who brought more benefit to the child or who was less harmful. The site in which he implemented the welfare-of-the-child concept was judicial discretion, rather than family autonomy. To him, the child's welfare was a matter of public policy in a narrow sense: that is, families' agreements on child custody arrangements contradicting juristic discourse were not binding. This position, as we saw in Chapter 3, is different from the Mālikī position, which considered such agreements to

25 Muḥammad al-Zayn, "Al-Majālis Al-Ḥasbiyya," *Al-Muḥāmā Al-Sharʿiyya: Majalla Qaḍāʾiyya Shahriyya Al-Sana Al-Ūlā* 2:1 (1930): 19–23.

26 ʿAbd al-Wahhāb Salīm, "Yajib Ilghāʾ Al-Majālis Al-Ḥasbiyya Wa-Ḍamm Ikhtiṣāṣihā Ilā Al-Maḥākim Al-Sharʿiyya: Iqtirāḥ ʿalā Maʿālī Wazīr Al-Ḥaqqāniyya," *Al-Muḥāmā Al-Sharʿiyya: Majalla Qaḍāʾiyya Shahriyya Al-Sana Al-Ūlā* 2:1 (1930): 225–226.

27 Niqābat al-Muḥāmiyyīn al-Sharʿiyyīn, "Case No. 283 of 1954 (Wāylī Court of Summary Justice)," *Al-Muḥāmā Al-Sharʿiyya: Majalla Qaḍāʾiyya Shahriyya Al-Sana Al-Khāmisa Wa'l-ʿIshrīn* 25:7 (1954): 453–459.

28 Shaham made a similar observation about the first half of the twentieth century; see Ron Shaham, *Family and the Courts in Modern Egypt: A Study Based on Decisions by the Sharīʿa Courts, 1900–1955* (Leiden; Boston, MA: Brill, 1997), 230.

be presumptively binding unless harm was proven. Thus, in accordance with Ḥanafī law, if a mother agreed to a *khul*ʿ arrangement on the condition that she would give up her right to custody, the condition would be invalid. Ibn ʿĀbidīn stated that he read a fatwa written by Abū-l-Suʿūd that a woman's agreement to give up her right to custody (during the tender years) in a separation deed was not binding if she changed her mind, since it is the child's right. He cited Abū-l-Suʿūd as saying that in questions of custody, the child's right is stronger than those of the parents.[29] To achieve his concern for the welfare of children, he eclectically selected Ḥanafī views that prioritized the interests of the female custodian and by extension those of the child. For instance, he opted for the approach that obligates the father to provide the mother with housing, adding that this is "more kind" (*huwa al-arfaq*).[30]

Another example shows that Ibn ʿĀbidīn had more concern for mothers and children. Relying on a statement in *al-Ḥāwī*, written by al-Kāsānī's student Jamāl al-Dīn al-Ghaznawī (d. 593/1196–97), in which al-Ghaznawī requires the father to bring the child to a place where the mother can see him every day, Ibn ʿĀbidīn argued that this statement applied to children who had passed the age of female custody. This is the age at which female relatives of the child, such as the mother, take care of the child, which varies from one school to another. According to this interpretation, there was no difference between mother and father in terms of the restriction on their movement unless the other parent consents. According to Ibn ʿĀbidīn, this interpretation was more kind to the mother (*al-arfaq bi-l-umm*).[31] This interpretation, which was never considered authoritative in any of the Sunni schools, would be taken up over a century later by Egypt's grand mufti ʿAbd al-Majīd Salīm. In 1942, Salīm issued a fatwa restricting a father's right to take his two boys, who were above the age of nine, from Cairo to Damietta, to protect the mother's right.[32] Other twentieth-century muftis, however, abided by the dominant position of the Ḥanafī school.[33] Surprisingly, however, the fatwas of the famous Egyptian reformer Muḥammad ʿAbduh with respect to child custody did not depart from dominant Ḥanafī positions, suggesting that he

[29] Muḥammad Amīn Ibn ʿĀbidīn, *Majmūʿat Rasāʾil Ibn ʿĀbidīn* (Beirut: Dār al-Kutub al-ʿIlmiyya, 2014), 1: 264–276.

[30] Ibn ʿĀbidīn, 1:268.

[31] Ibn ʿĀbidīn and al-Ḥaṣkafī, *Radd Al-Muḥtār ʿalā Al-Durr Al-Mukhtār Sharḥ Tanwīr Al-Abṣār*, 5:274–275.

[32] This case was brought to him in 1940. See Dār al-Iftāʾ al-Miṣriyya, *Al-Fatāwā Al-Islāmiyya Min Dār Al-Iftāʾ Al-Miṣriyya*, 13:194–197.

[33] Dār al-Iftāʾ al-Miṣriyya, 13:208–209.

was not concerned about this issue of reform, compared for instance with polygamy or other family law matters.[34]

Along with Ibn ʿĀbidīn, the long-serving chief mufti (1847–1897) Muḥammad al-ʿAbbāsī al-Mahdī (d. 1897) had a huge impact on the legal landscape of Egypt in the second half of the twentieth century. Mehmed Ali created the position of chief mufti in the 1830s, marginalizing the hitherto important role played by the chief judge sent by Istanbul.[35] The chief mufti functioned more like Shaykh al-Islām in Istanbul than the chief judge of Egypt prior to the nineteenth century. According to Peters, approximately 7 percent of the chief mufti's fatwas were issued for official institutions, especially the sharīʿa courts.[36] His fatwas show that he acted as a check over the practice of sharīʿa courts to make sure that judges abided by Ḥanafī law, and therefore he was not an agent of legal change in Peters' estimation.[37] This evaluation supports Judith Tucker's view that nineteenth-century judges often abided by laws underpinning traditional family structures and failed to accommodate the changing realities of the nineteenth century.[38]

Al-Mahdī dedicated a hefty 117 pages of his first volume of the *Fatāwā al-Mahdiyya* to child custody (compared with only ten pages on rituals).[39] His approach to the welfare of the child was more categorical in the sense that child's welfare was assumed to apply to whole categories of children based on their gender, their age, and the marital status of their mother, in accordance with the dominant approach in Ḥanafī law. He did not treat the interests of the child on a case-by-case basis as Ibn ʿĀbidīn did; al-Mahdī granted judges little discretion in determining, say, whether a child was better off living with his remarried mother in the tender years or with his father.[40] The dominant positions of the Ḥanafī school upon which

34 For a sample of his fatwas, see Dār al-Iftāʾ al-Miṣriyya, 13:246–258, 288–289, 299–300.

35 Cuno, *Modernizing Marriage*, 18.

36 Peters, "Muḥammad Al-ʿAbbāsī Al-Mahdī (D. 1897), Grand Muftī of Egypt, and His 'Al-Fatāwā Al-Mahdiyya,'" 66–82, at 69.

37 Peters, "Muḥammad Al-ʿAbbāsī Al-Mahdī (D. 1897), Grand Muftī of Egypt, and His 'Al-Fatāwā Al-Mahdiyya.'"

38 Tucker, *Women in Nineteenth-Century Egypt*, 60.

39 Peters observes that the paucity of material on ritual law suggests that despite the dominance of Ḥanafism in the nineteenth century, most of the population belonged to the Shāfiʿī and Mālikī schools. He supports his argument with reference to the fatwa collection of his Mālikī contemporary, Muḥammad ʿIllaysh, 26 percent of whose fatwa are of ritual law. Peters, "Muḥammad Al-ʿAbbāsī Al-Mahdī (D. 1897), Grand Muftī of Egypt, and His 'Al-Fatāwā Al-Mahdiyya,'" 70.

40 Muḥammad al-ʿAbbāsī al-Mahdī, *Al-Fatāwā Al-Mahdiyya Fi'l-Waqā'iʿ Al-Miṣriyya*, 1st edn. (Cairo: al-Maṭbaʿa al-Azhariyya al-Miṣriyya, 1883), 1:268.

al-Mahdī relied in the nineteenth century were later compiled and made more univocal by Qadrī Pāshā in what was practically an informal code.

QADRĪ PĀSHĀ'S COMPILATION OF 1875

In 1884, Philip Jallād (1857–1914), a Palestinian lawyer from Ḥaifa who moved to Alexandria during the reign of Ismāʿīl (r. 1863–1879) to work as a lawyer, started compiling his *magnus opus: Qāmūs al-Idāra wa'l-Qaḍā'*. This work contains legislation and treaties, as well as commentaries on the decisions of Egyptian courts.[41] *Qāmūs al-Idāra* lists the "personal status law" (*qānūn al-aḥwāl al-shakhṣiyya*) of Egypt, which was nothing other than Muḥammad Qadrī Pāshā's renowned compilation of Ḥanafī law known as *al-Aḥkām al-Sharʿiyya fī al-Aḥwāl al-Shakhṣiyya* (1875), which was reproduced verbatim in Jallād's *Qāmūs*. Qadrī's compilation was a response to the judicial need for a clear "code" of personal status in the Ḥanafī school as a consequence of the policy of Ḥanafization. This compilation was to be used both as a reference for judges and in training the judicial authorities. Although Qadrī's compilation was never promulgated as law, judges relied heavily on it in their legal rulings, as we shall see later.[42]

Qadrī Pāshā's compilation has been the de facto law of child custody in nineteenth-century Egypt since its publication.[43] Art. 391 of Qadrī Pāshā's compilation stipulates that the mother has the right to custody of a boy until he turns seven and until the girl reaches the age of nine,[44] which has been the practice of nineteenth-century courts since the beginning of the policy of Ḥanafization at the turn of the century, as we have already seen. This is borne out by the court rulings following the publication of Qadrī's compilation that we have examined. Qadrī Pāshā's prescription inscribed Egyptian judicial practice of the nineteenth-century age of Ḥanafization into one clear compilation. Thus, private separation agreements in which a mother gives up her right to custody were not binding, in accordance with Ḥanafī law and as explained by Ibn ʿĀbidīn.[45] Qadrī's

[41] See the introduction by Ṣābir ʿArab. Philip B. Yūsuf Jallād, *Qāmūs Al-Idāra Wa'l-Qaḍā'* (Maṭbaʿat Dār al-Kutub wa'l-Wathāʾiq al-Qawmiyya, 2003), 1:vi–vii.

[42] Jallād, 2:424–425; Muḥammad Zayn Ibyānī Bek, *Sharḥ Al-Aḥkām Al-Sharʿiyya Fi'l-Aḥwāl Al-Shakhṣiyya*, 1st edn. (Cairo: Maṭbaʿat al-Nahḍa, 1919), 318–351.

[43] Dupret, *Standing Trial*, 269–270.

[44] Jallād, *Qāmūs Al-Idāra Wa'l-Qaḍā'*, 2:424–425; Ibyānī Bek, *Sharḥ Al-Aḥkām Al-Sharʿiyya Fi'l-Aḥwāl Al-Shakhṣiyya*, 338–339.

[45] See Art. 288, Ibyānī Bek, *Sharḥ Al-Aḥkām Al-Sharʿiyya Fi'l-Aḥwāl Al-Shakhṣiyya*, 265.

compilation contained the dominant views of the Ḥanafī school, and rarely departed from them.[46] When he proposed an alternative, such as in Art. 407, which stipulates that the father is still responsible for child-support arrears even if the mother's acquisition of debts to support her children was done without the judge's permission, he did so as an attempt to bring the discourse in line with the practice of courts. As we saw in Chapter 4, judges made sure that child-support arrears are treated as debts of the father by including stipulations in separation deeds to this effect. According to the article, this was the practice of judges at the time, and was considered "more kind" (*arfaq*) than the alternative.[47] Despite Ibn ʿĀbidīn's broad definition of the child's welfare, Egyptian case law itself before and after Qadrī's compilation closely followed the dominant doctrines of the Ḥanafī school until the custody law reforms of 1929. In what follows, I illustrate with some examples from the courts and al-Mahdī's fatwa collection the new ways in which child welfare was envisioned by nineteenth-century jurists.

COURT PRACTICE

Although nineteenth-century jurists continued to assume that the welfare of the child was the ultimate goal of child custody, they did not have as many options to accommodate the individual needs of children. The child's welfare became defined narrowly according to the categorical rules of Ḥanafī jurists. In addition to the limitations of the Ḥanafī school, the discretionary power of the judiciary in assessing the parents' lifestyle choices disfavored working women, due to the influence of the domesticity ideology in vogue in the second half of the nineteenth century. In the nineteenth century, society and state seemed to be more interested in disciplining women than in achieving the best interests of the child, as evidenced by the increasing number of cases brought against women of bad morals, something that we did not find in the sample from the sixteenth to the eighteenth centuries. The welfare of children and their main care-givers, women, were *tout court* compromised by the legal and economic

[46] The father, for instance, could not relocate with the child within the age of female custodianship without the mother's consent. This view was unique to the Ḥanafīs, as we saw in Chapter 2. Another example is when a *maḥram* relative of the child volunteers to provide her custody for free, the mother is asked either to keep custody for free or hand over the child to the volunteer. See Arts. 37 and 392, Ibyānī Bek, *Sharḥ Al-Aḥkām Al-Sharʿiyya Fi'l-Aḥwāl Al-Shakhṣiyya*, 320, 339.

[47] Ibyānī Bek, *Sharḥ Al-Aḥkām Al-Sharʿiyya Fi'l-Aḥwāl Al-Shakhṣiyya*, 351.

changes that swept Egypt in the nineteenth century, in comparison to the more complex ways in which the interests of the child and the family were negotiated prior to the nineteenth century.

Age and Gender

The courts continued to issue separation deeds, but without allowing for stipulations contradicting Ḥanafī juristic discourse. In some of these examples, the custody of the children was mentioned but it was assumed that the state exclusively followed the Ḥanafī school. The judges' school affiliations were usually not mentioned, as had been the practice until the nineteenth century.[48] Both the discourse of jurists such as al-Mahdī and the court rulings of judges suggest that judges were not allowed to exercise much discretion in determining which parent better served the needs of the child in a broad sense. The discourse of al-Mahdī in this respect is strikingly different from that of the early nineteenth-century Ibn ʿĀbidīn, as the latter proposed certain discretions to allow judges to depart from the rigid rules of jurists for the accrual of benefit to the child, rather than only avoiding serious harm. Unlike Ibn ʿĀbidīn, in his fatwa collection, al-Mahdī consistently advised that custody should be transferred from mother to father when the boy turns seven and the girl nine, and when the mother remarries someone who is not a close relative of the child, giving the judge little discretion in treating each child individually. Perhaps part of the reason for al-Mahdī's rigidity compared to the flexibility of Ibn ʿĀbidīn's approach is their different functions in the legal landscape of nineteenth-century Egypt. Though they were both Ḥanafīs, al-Mahdī's task was to centralize and homogenize the administration of law. Such homogenization could best be achieved by granting judges less discretion in interpreting the Ḥanafī jurisprudential legacy.[49]

Before al-Mahdī's time, in 1835 in Ṭanṭā, a city in Lower Egypt, the judge determined what the unweaned child should receive in maintenance without discussing custody arrangements at all, suggesting that the age of

[48] By 1830s, for instance, the school affiliations of presiding judges are not mentioned. We are to assume that these judges are Ḥanafī. See "Court of Mudīriyyat Al-Gharbiyya (Ṭanṭā), Sijill 14 (1250/1835), Archival Code 1033–000014," Dār al-Wathāʾiq al-Qawmiyya, Cairo, docs 46, 9; doc. 101, 18; doc. 156, 29; doc. 169, 31.

[49] I owe the suggestion that al-Mahdī's role in legal centralization and homogenization may partly explain his child custody approach to one of the blind reviewers. See al-Mahdī, *Al-Fatāwā Al-Mahdiyya Fi'l-Waqāʾiʿ Al-Miṣriyya*, 1:261–266.

custody transfer was not subject to negotiation.[50] In 1837, Riḍwān petitioned the Cairo sharīʿa court to receive custody of his brother's ten-year-old niece, Sakīna, from her mother, Ṣafiyya. The document indicates that the judge had appointed the mother as Sakīna's guardian and not the paternal uncle. The uncle's petition stated that since the niece had reached the age of ten, the uncle had the right to have custody of her. The judge verified the child's age and once he ensured that she was indeed ten, he ordered that her custody be transferred to the uncle.[51] The appointment of the custodian as guardian as well suggests that there was convergence between custody and guardianship, a topic that we will return to later in our discussion of the twentieth century. In another instance in 1848, the parents did not negotiate custody or establish how long their son would be under the mother's custodianship since both parties knew that he would be transferred to the father as soon as he turned seven. They agreed that the mother would provide custody for the child as part of the compensation due to the husband as part of the *khulʿ* agreement, without further discussion of custody arrangements.[52]

In 1887, Farīḥa asked for a *khulʿ* from her husband, Muḥammad, in exchange for relieving her husband of her deferred dower, her maintenance, and her nursing fee of their one-year-old son, Sayyid. The document then adds that the mother would also pay for the maintenance of their son for the "remaining six years of his custody." In other words, both parties to this agreement, which was notarized before a judge following the Ḥanafī school, knew that the mother would retain custody of a boy until he turned seven.[53]

Nineteenth-century child custody jurisprudence was strictly and rigidly tied to the age and gender of the child, without allowing any family autonomy in departing from the Ḥanafī school's age determination in the court. Certainly, such arrangements in which one parent gave up his or her right to custody did occur, but without the force of the state behind them. In other words, nineteenth-century Egypt considered private

[50] "Court of Mudīriyyat Al-Gharbiyya (Ṭanṭā), Sijill 31 (1264/1848), Archival Code 1033–000031," Dār al-Wathāʾiq al-Qawmiyya, Cairo, 263, 27; see also doc. 293, 35; doc. 297, 35; "Court of Mudīriyyat Al-Gharbiyya (Ṭanṭā), Sijill 14 (1250/1835), Archival Code 1033–000014," doc. 46, 9; doc. 169, 31.

[51] "Court of Miṣr Al-Sharʿiyya, Sijill 1146 (1253/1837), Archival Code 1017–004051," Dār al-Wathāʾiq al-Qawmiyya, Cairo, doc. 63, 15.

[52] "Court of Mudīriyyat Al-Gharbiyya (Ṭanṭā), Sijill 31 (1264/1848), Archival Code 1033–000031," doc. 256. p. 24.

[53] "Court of Mudīriyyat Asyūṭ, Sijill 73 (1887), Archival Code 1139–000130," Dār al-Wathāʾiq al-Qawmiyya, Cairo, doc. 100, 13.

separation deeds departing from Ḥanafī doctrine to be null and void in a way similar to the landmark decision made in England in 1820 allowing the state to determine what was best for the children, which was always in line with the father's paternal right, regardless of what the parents or children wanted. In the absence of private separation deeds, some mothers resorted to desperate measures: one woman took her son right after he turned seven and left their place of habitual residence without informing the father of her whereabouts. Seven years later, when the child was fourteen, the father finally found her and asked the mufti whether he was entitled to custody of the fourteen-year-old. In line with Ḥanafī doctrine, the mufti granted him custody.[54]

The dominance of Ḥanafī doctrine and the judiciary's lack of accommodation of legal pluralism were clear in one question sent to al-Mahdī. A father asked whether he should give his seven-year-old son the choice between both parents. Al-Mahdī said that no choice is given to children according to Ḥanafī doctrine. It is most likely that the father was either a Shāfiʿī or had at least consulted a Shāfiʿī jurist, since relying on the child's wishes is based on Shāfiʿī or Ḥanbalī doctrine. The Shāfiʿī school is likely the source of this doctrine because most people in Lower Egypt had historically been Shāfiʿī, and many remained as such despite Ḥanafization, whereas the Ḥanbalī school did not have much of a following in Egypt in the nineteenth century.[55]

Remarriage of the Mother

Remarriage of the mother meant that she lost custody if the father petitioned for it. The state was not interested in enforcing this stipulation by, for example, inquiring at the instance of the registration of a marriage whether the mother has children from a previous marriage and establishing where these children would reside. Mothers remarried and continued to live with their children unless their custody was challenged by the father or his relatives. Consider the situation of a mother whose husband passed away while she was pregnant. She remarried when the infant was one year old. The mother and daughter lived with the new husband for two full years without being challenged by the relatives of the deceased father. After two years, the deceased father's male relatives, the guardians of the

[54] In another case, the father kidnapped a four-year-old boy. Al-Mahdī, *Al-Fatāwā Al-Mahdiyya Fi'l-Waqā'iʿ Al-Miṣriyya*, 1:274–275; 286.

[55] Ibid., 1:290.

three-year-old infant, petitioned for custody and received it. The mother, having to choose between regaining custody of her daughter and continuing her marriage, chose the former. She asked for a divorce, and upon getting divorced, she asked al-Mahdī for a fatwa to bring to the court that she was entitled to custody as soon as her waiting period from the divorce expired. The questioner's explanation for the mother's decision suggests the common ethos of maternal love dominating nineteenth-century Egypt, "God planted kindness in the heart of the mother" (*ja'ala Allāhu ta'ālā al-ra'fata fī qalbi al-umm*), such that she chose caring for her child over her marriage. Al-Mahdī's answer also assumes, in line with the blanket Ḥanafī position, that there was an inherent "harm" (*ḍarar*) to the child from being in the house of the stepfather. Unlike his predecessor, Ibn 'Ābidīn, al-Mahdī did not give judges any discretion in determining whether the stepfather was indeed harmful to the specific child at hand.[56] Treating the rules of jurists as mandatory rules continued into the late nineteenth and early twentieth centuries. A mufti in nineteenth-century Egypt argued that the father had absolute power over his minor child, such that he had the prerogative to marry her off without her consent and without the consent of her mother. The mother had no right to participate in major decisions affecting the child.[57]

Lifestyle

The two main areas of lifestyle concerns, namely women's work and uprightness, became increasingly subject to debate in this period. Jurists tended to choose less favorable approaches to women's lifestyle choices. The mother's bad morals (*fujūr*), which does not appear in our sixteenth- to nineteenth-century sample, became increasingly discussed in nineteenth-century fatwas. Asked a question about a boy who had not yet reached the age of seven and whose mother had bad manners, al-Mahdī confirmed that the child should be taken away from her once her bad manners were established. Al-Mahdī's fatwa does not mention the other position of some Ḥanafīs that allows such mothers to retain custody on the assumption that the child will not be influenced by the mother's behavior before the age of discernment, at which point his custody would be transferred to the father anyway. As we have also seen in Chapter 2, Ibn Qayyim al-Jawziyya did not consider such restrictions to be realistic since

[56] Ibid., 1:268. [57] Cuno, *Modernizing Marriage*, 130.

he assumed that most people indeed fall short of the juristic standards of uprightness.[58]

The appropriateness of women's work also came under scrutiny, and jurists reevaluated it in concert with the rising trends in popular philosophy of the nature of women and motherhood. According to Judith Tucker, women who worked to support their families in nineteenth-century Egypt were sometimes declared unfit to be custodians. Due to the erosion of traditional family structures brought about by the radical socioeconomic changes of the nineteenth century, including Mehmed Ali's aggressive military conscription of men for his army, corvée labor, and urbanization, many mothers had no option but to seek employment outside the home. Mehmed Ali's introduction of cotton and its large-scale cultivation as a cash crop led to the decline of cottage industries, forcing many women to work outside of the home and leading to the prevalence of wage labor. These economic changes also forced men to work outside of the home for longer hours, further bifurcating the private territory of women from that of men.[59] Certainly, Tucker's argument requires further evidence since we do not have good estimates of changes in economic activities during that period, and therefore Tucker's thesis deserves to be further explored.[60]

Women's work sometimes rendered them unfit to be mothers in the eyes of the law. Tucker speculates that members of the educational missions sent by Mehmed Ali to Europe internalized attitudes hostile to female labor and transferred them to Egypt.[61] While this may have been a convergence between the Egyptian upper-class concept of *mukhaddara* and European upper- and middle-class aversion to women's labor, women of lower classes never ceased to work, as evidenced by the court records of the period. This is likely the case, since the upper and middle classes in France condemned female labor, especially manual labor. There was a late eighteenth- and nineteenth-century French bourgeoisie trope against the "barbaric" practices of peasant French men who made their wives work in the fields. Members of Mehmed Ali's educational missions likely encountered

[58] Al-Mahdī, *Al-Fatāwā Al-Mahdiyya Fi'l-Waqā'iʿ Al-Miṣriyya*, 1:266; 291; 309.

[59] Further research needs to be conducted in order to fully understand these changes, since our current knowledge of women's employment and the effect of urbanization is still limited. On working women both in rural and urban settings in nineteenth-century Egypt, see further Tucker, *Women in Nineteenth-Century Egypt*, 40–101; Baron, *The Women's Awakening in Egypt*, 144–167. On the injustice of not accounting for such socioeconomic changes in lawmaking, see Amina Wadud, *Inside the Gender Jihad: Women's Reform in Islam* (Oxford: Oneworld, 2006), 137–145.

[60] On the creation of the Egyptian army, see further Fahmy, *All the Pasha's Men*.

[61] Tucker, *Women in Nineteenth-Century Egypt*, 88.

this urban attitude in Paris, which influenced their ideas about womanhood and its significance for the establishment of a modern Egyptian state.[62] The French upper class's aversion to women's manual labor was tied to their womanhood, whereas in Egypt, women of the upper and middle classes were often expected not to work at all – not on grounds of their womanhood but of their class. These two competing social mores fused together to create a new "enlightened" notion of womanhood and domesticity in Egypt in the nineteenth century.

By the end of the nineteenth century and into the early twentieth century, a debate about women's labor erupted in the media, exhibiting a hybrid ideology of women's domesticity inspired by the nineteenth-century Euro-American domesticity and the Islamic maintenance–obedience dynamic.[63] This new ideology represented a rupture with earlier pre-nineteenth-century social assumptions about women's and men's roles in the public and private spheres with respect to women's labor that were more informed, in my view, by class than by gender differentiation. Prior to the middle of the nineteenth century, slave women and women of lower socioeconomic backgrounds typically worked in public, whereas women of the middle and upper classes were often secluded, known as the *mukhaddarāt* in some of the sources of Ottoman Egypt. Certainly, there were also women of the upper and middle classes who ran their own businesses and trade as discussed in Chapter 3. The Euro-American domesticity doctrine (and the signing of the Anglo-Egyptian Convention of 1877 banning the slave trade) helped to further emphasize the role of gender over class in the separation between the two spheres, creating a new hybrid Egyptian female domesticity doctrine.

By the second half of the nineteenth century, women were fully associated with domestic duties, including educating children, a task that had heretofore been associated with fathers. Recall that in our large sample of sixteenth- to nineteenth-century Egypt we have not encountered cases in which women were denied custody due to the work of the mother, so one should assume that European notions of female domesticity were at least partly to blame for the judicial trend to treat women's work as contrary to their duties as mothers. Prior to the nineteenth century, family support structures meant that women were able to work and maintain custody within a community of shared responsibilities. In Islamic juristic discourse, a woman's work does not by itself disqualify her from custody as we saw in

[62] Flandrin, *Families in Former Times*, 112–118.
[63] Baron, *The Women's Awakening in Egypt*, 144–167.

Chapter 2; it only does so if the child is neglected. Women could entrust the care of their children to a relative while they worked. In fact, women were not expected to even spend the day with a boy who was old enough to go to school or learn a trade. The essential element in precolonial juristic discourse was that the child would sleep at the mother's place of residence, even if the father had him or her during the day. The Euro-American cult of motherhood, with its assumptions about the special nature of maternal love and her expanded role in molding the child's personality and acculturation, traversed the colonial world and found a home in Egypt, where judges assumed that the mother was better at caring for the child than a relative or a domestic servant.[64] Children were therefore expected to be with the mother all the time.

Muḥammad al-ʿAbbāsī al-Mahdī issued fatwas about whether or not the father had the right to take away his children from their working mothers. Consistent with juristic discourse, al-Mahdī did not consider the mother's work by itself to constitute grounds for her forfeiture of custody. The reason for the loss of custody was negligence of the child, but as this was a subjective process, it must have been influenced by the domestic ideology. In one case, the mother sold products at the market, and the father assumed that her work during the day harmed the child (*ḍayāʿ*). It became the judge's responsibility to determine whether the child was indeed harmed by the mother's work. This working woman clearly belonged to a lower socioeconomic class and may not necessarily have been influenced by the new family ideology, which did not have wide acceptance in larger segments of Egyptian society until the beginning of the twentieth century. One could assume that literacy and belonging to the upper echelons of Egyptian society were prerequisites for acceptance of the new family ideology in the last quarter of the nineteenth century. Thus, the frequency of questions in al-Mahdī's fatwa collection regarding women's work may suggest that some fathers were increasingly influenced by the cult of motherhood or simply that this issue was highly contested. Fathers sometimes did not even claim that the child was left unattended, but that the mother's work would presumptively lead to harm – literally "loss" (*ḍayāʿ*) – to the child.[65]

64 On the domesticity ideology that influenced nineteenth-century Egypt, see Glenna Matthews, *"Just a Housewife": The Rise and Fall of Domesticity in America* (New York, NY: Oxford University Press, 1987), 3–91.

65 I am indebted to one of the reviewers for suggesting that these frequent questions may have had to do more with the contestedness of the question than the frequency of actual cases. Other female occupations mentioned in al-Mahdī's fatwa collection include domestic

Fathers and judges, influenced by notions of maternal love, found alternative childcare options insufficient, as the mother was, by the second half of the nineteenth century, believed to be the best person to care for her children. In other instances, fathers clearly used the mother's work as a pretext to claim the right to custody. In one case, for instance, a father requested custody of his five-year-old daughter and two-year-old son on grounds of their mother's work, but he was willing not to petition for custody when the mother agreed not to ask him for maintenance of the two children if she could keep them with her. After their informal agreement, the mother petitioned the court for maintenance of the two children, saying that she stopped working and needed the father's support. The mufti supported her petition for maintenance.[66]

Religion

Nineteenth-century Egyptian courts closely followed the Ḥanafī doctrine allowing non-Muslim women custody until the age of discernment. This meant that the mother's religion would only affect her custody rights if her child was a girl; in this case, custody would be transferred two years earlier than if the mother had been a Muslim. According to Ḥanafī law, however, guardianship could not be given to non-Muslims. The situation of a non-Muslim man having children with a Muslim woman must have been rare, however, since Muslim women were not allowed to marry non-Muslim men. Yet Muslim men were allowed to marry non-Muslim, specifically Christian and Jewish, women, in which case the mother retained custody until the age of discernment (usually estimated at seven), as long as she did not teach the child her religion. The common case in which the father was a non-Muslim and the children were raised Muslim came about almost exclusively from cases of the wife's conversion. The court records from the Ottoman conquests until the contemporary period contain cases in which Egyptian Christians (especially women) converted to Islam, creating a situation in which the other party lost his right to custody.

In one Cairo court in 1837, there were six cases of conversion to Islam from Christianity and Judaism: four Christian women, a Christian man,

service, baking bread, and tailoring. Al-Mahdī, *Al-Fatāwā Al-Mahdiyya Fi'l-Waqā'i' Al-Miṣriyya*, 1:261–264; 275–277; 286; 290–291; 293; 295; 306; 313; 314; 318–319; 327; 330; 335; 338; 341; 348; 354; 359; 372–373.

66 Ibid., 348–349.

and a Jewish man.[67] One of the Christian female converts went to the court with her three children, an unweaned male infant and two girls whose ages were not mentioned. I would assume that the two girls had at least reached the age of discernment, since they were treated as having the agency to choose both their new religion and their new names. The mother and the two girls converted to Islam with their full volition and repeated the declaration of faith, while the unweaned infant, ʿAwaḍ, "followed his mother" (*tabiʿahā fī al-Islām*) in the conversion. His mother then chose the name Muḥammad as his Muslim name.[68] Regardless of the motivation behind the conversion, the whole family had now converted to Islam except for the father, whose only hope to have any custodial or guardianship rights would have been to convert as well. The mother had custody of the children, and there is no evidence that the father converted in order to challenge her custody rights. In another case, a Christian woman came with her "physically mature" (*bāligh*) daughter and her unweaned infant. Both the mother and her daughter converted and chose new Muslim names, while the infant followed his mother. Again, the mother had custody of these children regardless of their age since the father's religion disqualified him.[69]

Relocation with the Ward and Visitation Rights

As we saw in Chapter 2, mothers could not relocate with the ward without the permission of the father if the distance was long enough that the father could not visit his offspring and return to his home on the same day. This condition did not apply to the father when children were under his custodianship, that is, after the age of discernment. He was able to move freely without seeking the mother's consent. This situation happened frequently in the nineteenth century due to the expansion of the Egyptian bureaucracy, where many men moved across Egyptian towns with their government jobs.[70]

According to Ḥanafī doctrine, although the mother cannot move away from the habitual place of residence more than the distance at which

[67] "Court of Miṣr Al-Sharʿiyya, Sijill 1146 (1253/1837), Archival Code 1017–004051," doc. 12, 3; doc. 15, 4; doc. 27, 7; doc. 35, 8; doc. 42, 10; doc. 99, 24.
[68] "Court of Miṣr Al-Sharʿiyya, Sijill 1146 (1253/1837), Archival Code 1017–004051," doc. 42, 10.
[69] "Court of Miṣr Al-Sharʿiyya, Sijill 1146 (1253/1837), Archival Code 1017–004051," doc. 99, 24.
[70] Al-Mahdī, *Al-Fatāwā Al-Mahdiyya Fi'l-Waqā'iʿ Al-Miṣriyya*, 1:328.

prayers are legitimately shortened (or such that the father cannot visit the child and return on the same day), fathers were not subjected to the same restriction of their movement. Mothers were unable to require fathers to stay in the habitual place of residence with the children in their custody.[71] Yet the father could prevent the female custodian from traveling with the ward in excess of this distance, so long as her destination was not where the marriage contract was signed. Even if the mother did not observe this rule, the father was not allowed to withhold custody wages or maintenance, the justification being the welfare of the child.[72] In one question sent to al-Mahdī, the father left the habitual place of the residence of the custodial maternal grandmother and wished to deny the grandmother child support unless she brought the child to his new town of residence to see him. Al-Mahdī stated that the father had no right to withhold support or require the grandmother to bring the child to see him.[73] Fathers and mothers who were entitled to custody sometimes requested police intervention when a non-custodial parent relocated to another town with the ward.[74]

The frequency of visitations, according to the Ḥanafī school discussed previously, was a matter determined by custom. The assumption of the mother–child bond was so strong by the second half of the nineteenth century that one mufti departed significantly from established Ḥanafī doctrine out of consideration for the mother's bond with the child. The grand mufti, al-Mahdī, whose fatwa was binding on the judiciary due to the procedural reforms of the nineteenth century, received a request for a fatwa from Damietta in 1860. A father who had married a woman from Damietta wanted to take his ten-year-old son back to his hometown. The father had a fatwa from the mufti of Damietta stipulating, in line with established Ḥanafī doctrine, that the father had the right to relocate with the child without seeking the mother's consent. But the mother was able to secure a contradictory fatwa from one Shaykh ʿAlī Muḥammad al-Baqlī, permitting the judge to stop the father from taking the ward with him since it was far enough that she would not be able to see her son each day, out of kindness and concern for the mother (*rifqan bihā*). Confronted with two contradictory fatwas, the governor of Damietta sought the final judgment of al-Mahdī, who sided with the dominant position of the Ḥanafī school, which did not pay attention to the mother's

[71] Ibid., 1:295. [72] Ibid., 1:264. [73] Ibid., 1:262.

[74] In one case, the mother moved with her daughter from Cairo to Kurdufan in Sudan, prompting the father to sue for habeas corpus. Ibid., 1:362.

need to see her children but to the father's right to move freely with a child under his guardianship.[75]

In another case brought to al-Mahdī, the parents had a joint custody arrangement in which the father was to have their four-year-old girl during the day and the mother would take her at night, but it seemed that the father did not send the girl to her mother, prompting the latter to seek a fatwa. Al-Mahdī confirmed that the father had no right to refuse to give the daughter to her custodial mother.[76]

Out of hundreds of cases that I examined in the nineteenth-century court records, and hundreds of fatwas, I have not found a single case in which private separation deeds were drawn up to secure the mother's freedom of movement or her right to remarriage without losing custody rights. In 1887 Asyūṭ, for instance, out of 37 cases of separation – of which the court explicitly mentions that seven couples had children from the marriage in question – there were no private agreements of the type we saw in sixteenth- to eighteenth-century Ottoman Egypt.[77] In this sense, nineteenth-century practice on private separation deeds, which considered agreements allowing the mother to travel with the ward as nonbinding, was continuous with the last quarter of the seventeenth century and the eighteenth century. In fact, al-Mahdī cited the position of Shaykh al-Islām Abū-l-Su'ūd and Ibn 'Ābidīn that a custodian who drops her or his future right to custody can petition for it and recant their private agreement. Al-Mahdī added that the right to custody is only established for the present time and no future right can be given up.[78]

To sum up, relocation with the child was determined in accordance with the dominant position of the Ḥanafī school. When lower muftis departed from the dominant Ḥanafī position to accommodate evolving social views of the welfare of the mother and the child, their fatwas were overruled by the grand mufti. This confirms Peters' estimation that al-Mahdī, who served as a grand mufti for half of the nineteenth century, was conservative in his adherence to the letter of Ḥanafī law.

Child Maintenance

Judges continued to offer protections to mothers and children in accordance with Ḥanafī practice prior to the nineteenth century, as well as

[75] Ibid., 1:342–43. [76] Ibid., 1:300.

[77] "Court of Mudīriyyat Asyūṭ, Sijill 73 (1887), Archival Code 1139–000130," doc. 87, 11; doc. 88, 11; doc. 89, 11.

[78] Al-Mahdī, *Al-Fatāwā Al-Mahdiyya Fi'l-Waqā'i' Al-Miṣriyya*, 1:278–279.

Qadrī's compilation. Thus, unpaid child maintenance was treated as a debt that the father had to pay. In a case brought to the Court of Miṣr al-Sharʿiyya in 1837, the father had to pay 27 months of unpaid child maintenance to the mother of his daughter.[79] In some instances, one parent gave up her or his right to custody but without foreclosing a future change of mind.[80] Other separation deeds that did not modify the categorical juristic rules of the Ḥanafī school were binding. In one case, a couple signed an agreement determining how much the father would pay for their three-month-old baby until the end of the legal (*sharʿī*) age period of custody (*li-ghāyat muddat al-ḥaḍāna*).[81] In another agreement from 1887 in Miṣr al-Qadīma, a couple signed a separation deed in which they agreed that the father would pay one piaster a day in nursing fees for their infant.[82] As we saw in sixteenth- to nineteenth-century Egypt, fathers sometimes attempted to avoid paying child maintenance by finding a relative who was willing to provide child custody services free of charge, leaving the mother with two choices: she could either care for the child for free to maintain custody or hand over the child to the father's female relative, often his mother. This practice continued in nineteenth-century Egypt.[83]

Guardianship

In nineteenth-century Egypt, the system of guardianship continued to favor agnatic male relatives over mothers, unless there was a testamentary appointment. Yet many women were appointed by judges as guardians. In one case from 1828 in Ṭanṭā, the mother was the designated

[79] "Court of Miṣr Al-Sharʿiyya, Sijill 1146 (1253/1837), Archival Code 1017–004051," doc. 38, p. 9.

[80] In one case, the parents agreed (agreement type two) that the father would have custody of a three-year-old daughter and an eight-year-old son. The mother gave up her right to custody of the girl in this case since, according to Ḥanafī law, she was entitled to her custody at that age. "Court of Miṣr Al-Qadīma, Sijill 38 (1308–1887), Archival Code 1006–000176," Dār al-Wathāʾiq al-Qawmiyya, Cairo, doc. 45, 45.

[81] The formula "until the period of custody expires" (*ḥattā tantahī muddat al-ḥaḍāna*) was used extensively in the nineteenth century, which suggests that the Ḥanafī ages of custody were widely respected in case law. See, for instance, "Court of Miṣr Al-Qadīma, Sijill 38 (1308–1887), Archival Code 1006–000176," doc. 20, 20; doc. 43, 43.

[82] "Court of Miṣr Al-Qadīma, Sijill 38 (1308–1887), Archival Code 1006–000176," doc. 2, 2.

[83] Shaham, *Family and the Courts in Modern Egypt*, 181; al-Mahdī, *Al-Fatāwā Al-Mahdiyya Fi'l-Waqā'iʿ Al-Miṣriyya*, 1:263.

guardian (*waṣī*) over her minor son, even though the son had an adult half-brother.[84] The objective of protecting the child's assets led some fathers to appoint more than one guardian. In 1887 in Asyūṭ, a father appointed both his wife, Amīna, and his brother, Muḥammad Bek, as testamentary guardians over his four minor children. According to the will, neither guardian (*waṣī*) could execute the will or manage the minors' assets without consulting with the other party.[85] Absent family agreement, agnatic male relatives' rights remained superior to those of mothers with respect to guardianship arrangements in a fashion continuous with pre-nineteenth-century practice.[86]

Despite this continuity, the Egyptian judiciary introduced an innovation that we did not see in Ottoman court practice. While we saw that Ottoman judges sometimes appointed a guardian and an overseer to act as checks against the uprightness of one another or appointed two guardians to achieve the same purpose, the Egyptian judiciary in the nineteenth century under the "probate court" (*al-Majlis al-Ḥasbī*), established by Ismāʿīl in 1873 to protect the well-being of minors, introduced a new procedure whereby the *Majlis al-Ḥasbī* would appoint a guardian and then appoint a guarantor (*ḍāmin*) of any misappropriation of the children's assets. The *Majlis al-Ḥasbī* was part of the Egyptian state's effort to claim from the religious authorities the protection of children as its own responsibility. This effort was tied to the state's control over religious endowments during the reign of Mehmed Ali.[87] According to the court document, if the guardian misappropriated any of the children's money and could not repay it, the guarantors would be responsible for paying it back.[88] In another instance in the same register, a document explicitly states that

84 "Court of Mudīriyyat Al-Gharbiyya (Ṭanṭā), Sijill 11 (1244/1828), Archival Code 1033–000011," Dār al-Wathāʾiq al-Qawmiyya, Cairo, doc. 10, 2.

85 "Court of Mudīriyyat Asyūṭ, Sijill 73 (1887), Archival Code 1139–000130," doc. 93, 12.

86 Tucker, *Women in Nineteenth-Century Egypt*, 55–60.

87 On the Egyptian state's increasing nineteenth-century role as the protector of orphans, see further Beth Baron, "Orphans and Abandoned Children in Modern Egypt," in *Interpreting Welfare and Relief in the Middle East* (Leiden: Brill, 2008), 13–34; Mine Ener, *Managing Egypt's Poor and the Politics of Benevolence, 1800–1952* (Princeton, NJ: Princeton University Press, 2003); Jacqueline Gibbons, "Orphanages in Egypt," *Journal of Asian and African Studies* 40:4 (2005): 261–285. On the nineteenth-century probate court, see Shaham, *Family and the Courts in Modern Egypt*, 179; Jallād, *Qāmūs Al-Idāra Wa'l-Qaḍāʾ*, 4:24. On orphanages in early twentieth-century Egypt, see Beth Baron, "Islam, Philanthropy, and Political Culture in Interwar Egypt: The Activism of Labiba Ahmad," in *Poverty and Charity in Middle Eastern Contexts*, ed. Michael David Bonner, Mine Ener, and Amy Singer (Albany, NY: State University of New York Press, 2003).

88 "Court of Mudīriyyat Asyūṭ, Sijill 73 (1887), Archival Code 1139–000130," doc. 124, 16.

the *al-Majlis al-Ḥasbī* appointed a guardian and that a guarantor was not required since the guardian was known in the town.[89]

CONCLUSION

The nineteenth century witnessed rapid social and economic transformations that changed the very notion of "family." The new family ideology, which had emerged by the second half of the nineteenth century, came up against greater legal rigidity as a result of the process of Ḥanafization. This new family ideology, which according to Cuno was on full display in the 1870s, did not fit well with Ḥanafī law, whose approach to custody conflicted sharply with women's domesticity. Women were only allowed custody of boys until age seven and of girls until age nine, and private separation deeds in which a woman could theoretically have custody of children until emancipation were not allowed under Ḥanafī law. Ibn ʿĀbidīn's approach, which gave greater discretion to judges, was not operationalized in the courts, especially under al-Mahdī's rigid adherence to the categorical rules of pre-nineteenth-century Ḥanafī jurists.

Instead, the dominant Ḥanafī juristic position that made departures from juristic custody and guardianship rules conditional upon the context of potential gross harm to the child was implemented in court practice, whether the question was at what age should a child be transferred from the mother's to the father's custody, or whether the mother's remarriage should require her to forfeit her custody rights. The two most important jurists of the nineteenth century, Ibn ʿĀbidīn and al-Mahdī, had different visions of what constituted the child's welfare. In contrast with Ibn ʿĀbidīn's greater discretion for judges (albeit not to families, in accordance with Ḥanafī law), al-Mahdī followed the dominant Ḥanafī doctrine more closely, abiding by jurists' categorical rules more strictly. In the final tally, the child's welfare was defined much more narrowly in nineteenth-century practice than had been possible under the private separation deeds and legal pluralism of the sixteenth through nineteenth centuries. In what follows, we discuss legal reform through the introduction of non-Ḥanafī statutes in Egypt starting in 1929, when legislators would attempt to remove some of the rigidities of the Ḥanafī laws of custody over the remainder of the century.

89 "Court of Mudīriyyat Asyūṭ, Sijill 73 (1887), Archival Code 1139–000130," doc. 197, 24.

6

Twentieth- and Twenty-First-Century Child Custody, 1929–2014

In this chapter, I discuss child custody law in Egypt, focusing on the evolution of the concept of the best interests of the child in the age of de-Ḥanafization. The first section of this investigation starts with examining the earliest statutes on child custody, which heralded important departures from nineteenth-century Ḥanafization, and ends with a discussion of the abolition of sharīʿa courts in 1955. The second section deals with the period from the unification of the Egyptian legal system that joined sharīʿa and the hybrid of European and non-sharīʿa Egyptian jurisprudence under one national system, and it ends with the most recent reference to children in Egyptian legislation in 2014. Despite the introduction of European laws to Egypt's legal system in the nineteenth and twentieth centuries, family law remained intimately tied to premodern juristic discourses, albeit not to premodern court practices.

Cuno attributes the khedives' adoption of the conjugal family ideology to a host of internal khedival household politics, but in my opinion it goes back to Mehmed Ali's educational missions decades earlier. The views of people such as Rifāʿa al-Ṭahṭāwī and ʿAlī Mubārak about women's education and their role in society laid the foundations for the new family ideology, which was to become the new ideology in the palace's first family. By 1881, Khedive Tawfīq, the first monogamous khedive, emphasized the importance of monogamy and supported educating women so that they would educate the children of the nation and be their husbands' companions and equals rather than their slaves. By the end of the nineteenth century, the conjugal family and companionate marriage had become the ideals of modern life in the modernist imaginary. This family ideology, as Cuno rightly points out, predated the British invasion of Egypt in 1882.

The development of transport, education, and print culture in the last third of the nineteenth century contributed to the promotion of this ideology, with periodicals helping spread it beyond the upper and middle classes.[1]

The rise of the conjugal family and companionate marriage, as well as Egypt's signing of the Anglo-Egyptian Convention of 1877 forbidding the trade in slaves and giving an emancipatory route for those who were already enslaved in Egypt, tied female domesticity to a new vision for Egypt as a modern nation. The ideas of Islamic modernism and feminism, and Egyptian nationalism, had many overlaps when it came to the role of women and the family, yet there remained some tensions between the demands of feminist and nationalist leaders and those of some religious authorities. Consequently, the legislators' approach to accommodating the new family ideology was a tight balancing act in which reform could only be achieved piecemeal. Egypt's twentieth-century family law was, therefore, based on a series of legislative acts and a residual clause, often relegating issues not addressed by statutes to the Ḥanafī school of Islamic jurisprudence.[2] There was no attempt to recreate the legal landscape, but rather reformers accepted Ḥanafī rules by default as the law of the land, only targeting certain elements for legal change. These elements were modified, often through pragmatic eclecticism, to achieve the desired balance. Despite the rise of the conjugal family in the second half of the nineteenth century, Egyptian legislators did not start the process of legal reform of the rigid nineteenth-century Ḥanafized system until two decades into the twentieth century.

Prior to the child custody reforms inaugurated in 1929, several changes to nineteenth-century Egyptian family law were introduced throughout the 1920s. In Law No. 25 of 1920, some of the Ḥanafī rules of spousal maintenance were modified.[3] The minimum age of marriage was raised in Law No. 56 of 1923 to 16 for girls and 18 for boys.[4] Legislators also

[1] Cuno, *Modernizing Marriage*, 39–44; Baron, *The Women's Awakening in Egypt*; Yousef, *Composing Egypt: Reading, Writing, and the Emergence of a Modern Nation 1870–1930*.

[2] "Law No. 25 (1920) Concerning Maintenance and Certain Matters of Personal Status," *Al-Jarīda Al-Rasmiyya*, July 15, 1920.

[3] Fāṭima al-Zahrā' 'Abbās Aḥmad and Ḥilmī 'Abd al-'Aẓīm Ḥasan, *Qānūn Al-Aḥwāl Al-Shakhṣiyya Li'l-Muslimīn Wa'l-Qarārāt Al-Munaffidha Li-Aḥkāmih Wa-Ba'ḍ Aḥkām Al-Maḥkama Al-Dustūriyya Al-'Ulyā Al-Ṣādira Bi-Sha'nih* (Cairo: al-Maṭābi' al-Amīriyya, 2009), 1–3; "Law No. 25 (1920) Concerning Maintenance and Certain Matters of Personal Status," 52–55.

[4] Margot Badran, *Feminists, Islam, and Nation: Gender and the Making of Modern Egypt* (Princeton, NJ: Princeton University Press, 1995), 127–128; Kenneth M. Cuno, "African

narrowed the expansive male divorce rights in Art. 1 of Law 25 of 1929 in order to protect the conjugal family from what many enlightened Egyptians, influenced by the European discourse critical of Islamic law and society, perceived to be high rates of divorce among Muslims.[5] The remainder of the twentieth century witnessed a slow shift toward a broader best interests approach in which legislators granted judges more discretion in determining what would be best for each child depending on her or his particular circumstances. In what follows, I briefly discuss some of these legislative changes, as well as their implementation in Egyptian jurisprudence.

THE BEST INTERESTS OF THE CHILD, 1929–1955

Decree-Law No. 25 of 1929 regarding Certain Personal Status Provisions was the most important legislative act on child custody in the first half of the twentieth century. With the influence of the "tender years" doctrine, which, as we saw in Chapter 1, dominated European discourses of child custody infused with nineteenth-century patriarchal notions of female domesticity, Egyptian legislators of the early twentieth century expanded women's custody rights. The method adopted by legislators was to increase the age determined within Ḥanafī law for female custody transfer. Art. 7 of Law 25 of 1929 changed custody arrangements in such a way as to allow the judge to raise the age of custody transfer from seven to nine and from nine to eleven for boys and girls, respectively, so long as there is *maṣlaḥa* for the specific child from raising the age of custody transfer.[6] In the explanatory memorandum of Law No. 25 of 1929, the Ministry of Justice stated that the reason that they decided to raise the age of female custody is that the earlier age limits may not be sufficient for children to be independent of their mothers in some cases. Relying on juristic discourse, rather than referencing the practice of premodern Egyptian lawmaking under the Ottomans, twentieth-century jurists argued that the logic of custody transfer at seven and nine years was determined by the time at which boys do not need the care of their mothers and the time at which girls attain carnal awareness. Due to disagreements among jurists over the

Slaves in Nineteenth-Century Rural Egypt: A Preliminary Assessment," in *Race and Slavery in the Middle East: Histories of Trans-Saharan Africans in Nineteenth-Century Egypt, Sudan, and the Ottoman Mediterranean*, ed. Terence Walz and Kenneth M. Cuno (Cairo: American University in Cairo Press, 2010), 77–78.

5 "Law No. 25 (1929)," *Al-Jarīda Al-Rasmiyya* 27 (March 25, 1929): 203–219.

6 "Law No. 25 (1929)."

age at which these emotional developments transpire, the Ministry decided to allow judges the discretion to determine whether a given child needs his or her mother for two more years after reaching the age of custody transfer according to the Ḥanafī school.[7] The Ministry was concerned that the rigid Ḥanafī rules of custody were no longer suitable for Egyptian families.

Maḥmūd ʿArnūs, a sharīʿa judge, wrote an article published in *Majallat al-Muḥāmā al-Sharʿiyya* in 1930 and raised some problematic questions about custody over which courts have exhibited disagreements. These questions include when a female custodian moves with the child away from the habitual place of residence (usually where the divorce took place), does that disqualify her from custody? Does the child have to follow the father when he moves even if he is under the custody of women? According to ʿArnūs, these questions are subject to disagreement within the Ḥanafī school. He started his discussion by citing Ibn ʿĀbidīn as saying, in his commentary on *al-Durr*, that although there are three rights in child custody (child, father, mother), the strongest right belongs to the child. Giving priority to the child's right is the rationale behind allowing a woman to obtain custody after ceding it for the welfare of the child (treating private separation deeds as non-binding). The child's welfare (to protect the child from harm) is also the reason behind not allowing a woman to maintain custody in the case of remarriage, and therefore a mufti should make a decision after examining the situation of each particular child. He can decide whether or not custody should be transferred to the next in the line of custodians on a case-by-case basis.[8]

[7] "Law No. 25 (1929)," 217.

[8] This approach to custody would be adopted in different degrees by some Muslim majority nation states. To mention one example, this ethos of overlooking the mother's remarriage, which we observed in one strand of juristic discourse as well as wide practice in Ottoman courts and in the legal thought of Egyptian judges, was to become entrenched in law in Qatar. Art. 168 of Qatar's Family Law of 2006 reinforces the presumptions of premodern author-jurists regarding the remarriage of the mother, but after adding the important caveat that the judge may overlook this rule if the welfare of the child required that the mother be his or her custodian. The article suggests that welfare refers to a broad best interests approach. In addition, drawing on Mālikī law, albeit without acknowledging it, Art. 184 of the same law stipulates that if someone does not petition for custody within a year of learning of the remarriage of the mother (or female relative) to someone who is not a close relative of the child, he or she loses his or her claim to custody due to the lack of action for a year. The article, however, grants the judge the power to take away custody for remarriage if he determines that it is in the interests of the child (*maṣlaḥat al-maḥḍūn*). "Qatar Family Law No. 22 (2006)," *Official Gazette* 8 (August 28, 2006): 31–99.

As we saw previously, Ibn ʿĀbidīn's approach did not gain traction in nineteenth-century courts, but by the third decade of the twentieth century, a best interests approach was drawn from his work. Maḥmūd ʿArnūs cited Ibn ʿĀbidīn as saying that the child's interests can only be assessed based on the context of a particular child. The stepfather may have more mercy on the child than the stepmother. It is also possible that a relative who wants to take custody of the child intends to misappropriate his or her assets. A father may have a wife who hurts the child, or the custodian may have children who are not *maḥrams* of a female child. If the judge or mufti knows that the situation is as such, the child should not be taken away from a remarried mother because the ultimate goal of custody arrangements is the welfare of the child (*nafʿ al-walad*). This approach assumes that the judge should have full discretion in deciding who is better at taking care of the child, regardless of the rigid rules of jurists. It is a *best interests*, rather than *basic interests* approach, more similar to the recommendations of Ibn Qayyim al-Jawziyya. Having established the modus operandi in determining child custody arrangements based on Ibn ʿĀbidīn, Judge ʿArnūs begins to address the main questions,[9] cautioning that judges should see what serves the "welfare of the child" (*maṣlaḥat al-walad*) so long as it does not contradict the "clear textual sources" (*ṣarīḥ al-manqūl*). He did not mention juristic discourse but restricted himself to the textual sources that are clear in their meaning (recall Ibn Qayyim's approach). He added that courts of his day have kept abreast of changes in the times by allowing the husband, for instance, to move his wife to any place based on their assessment of the "welfare" (*maṣlaḥa*) of the couple. He reasoned that the same should be done with respect to allowing the father to move the custodian to a place outside of the habitual place of residence so long as it serves the welfare of the child without harming the parents.[10] This growing focus on children's specific needs and contexts must have been influential across the Muslim world, since lawyers and legal authorities from many Muslim countries subscribed to the *Muḥāmā al-Sharʿiyya* journal, including those in countries such as India, China, Yemen, the Hijaz, Syria, Palestine, Iraq, Turkey, Sudan, Tunisia, Algeria, and Morocco.[11]

[9] Maḥmūd ʿArnūs, "Baʿḍ Masāʾil Al-Ḥaḍāna," ed. Muḥarram Fahīm, *Al-Muḥāmā Al-Sharʿiyya: Majalla Qaḍāʾiyya Shahriyya Al-Sana Al-Ūlā* 2:1 (1930): 5–11.

[10] ʿIbid.

[11] Muḥarram Fahīm, ed., "Iftitāḥiyyat Al-ʿAdad Al-Awwal Min Al-Sana Al-Thāniya," *Al-Muḥāmā Al-Sharʿiyya: Majalla Qaḍāʾiyya Shahriyya Al-Sana Al-Ūlā* 2:1 (October 1930): 1–4.

The concept of *welfare of the child* was extensively invoked in the courts after the passing of Law 25 of 1929. In one case, judges assumed that the slow physical maturity of a boy was grounds for allowing the mother to keep the child for two more years after he reached the age of seven. Take, for example, the case of a maternal grandmother who had custody of her daughter's seven-year-old son until the father successfully petitioned for custody. In appealing the decision, the grandmother's lawyer made the argument that the child was too weak for the father to take care of him. The court decided to overturn the earlier ruling and allowed the grandmother to maintain custody of the child, citing the child's welfare (*maṣlaḥa*).[12] One court in 1930 used arguments (more on this case later) stating that the consideration of the "benefit" (*nafʿ*) of the child was the ultimate goal of child custody and that the judge's choice between a grandmother and a paternal uncle was driven by the child's welfare.[13] Another court invoked the welfare of the child to deny a father custody because he lived in Aswan, which has a hot climate that was thought to be dangerous to his son's health. The court based its decision on a medical report indicating that the child's liver problems would worsen if he moved to a hot climate.[14] In 1940, Egypt's grand mufti ʿAbd al-Majīd Salīm issued a fatwa that a girl whose age is estimated between 14 and 16 years and who had lost her virginity in a consensual relationship should not be given back to her parents for fear that they might hurt her in revenge for her loss of virginity.[15]

In actual practice, despite the discretion granted to the judge in assessing the welfare of the child for a two-year extension of custody, this welfare was often restricted to clear physical harm. Most judges did not otherwise depart widely from the Ḥanafī school. Some judges, however, implemented a broader concept of welfare that was not restricted to harm. For instance, using the welfare of the child discourse, *Al-Ahrām* newspaper reported, according to Hanan Kholoussy, that one mother argued in 1932 that her ex-husband's new wife would not care for the boy as well as she

[12] Niqābat al-Muḥāmiyyīn al-Sharʿiyīn, "Case No. 272 of 1929–1930 (Miṣr Sharia Court of First Instance)," ed. Muḥarram Fahīm, *Al-Muḥāmā Al-Sharʿiyya: Majalla Qaḍāʾiyya Shahriyya Al-Sana Al-Ūlā* 1:5 (1929): 417.

[13] Muḥarram Fahīm, ed., "Case No. 55 of 1929–1930, Al-Manṣūra Sharīʿa Court of First Instance," *Al-Muḥāmā Al-Sharʿiyya: Majalla Qaḍāʾiyya Shahriyya Al-Sana Al-Ūlā* 1:8 (1930): 644–738, at 698–701.

[14] Niqābat al-Muḥāmiyyīn al-Sharʿiyīn, "Case No. 1069 of 1934–1935 (Miṣr Sharia Court of First Instance)," *Al-Muḥāmā Al-Sharʿiyya: Majalla Qaḍāʾiyya Shahriyya Al-Sana Al-Khāmisa Wa'l-ʿIshrīn* 8:1 (37 1936): 195–198.

[15] Dār al-Iftāʾ al-Miṣriyya, *Al-Fatāwā Al-Islāmiyya Min Dār Al-Iftāʾ Al-Miṣriyya*, 13:129–131.

would care for her own offspring. The mother was granted an extension by the judge in accordance with Law 25 of 1929.[16] This decision was based on a broad best interests approach (rather than a basic interests approach). In some cases, judges asked children about the parent with whom they preferred to live.[17] As we saw previously, we did not find children's wishes being solicited in our sample prior to the twentieth century.

In accordance with Ḥanafī jurisprudence, private agreements in which a parent gives up her or his right to custody were not considered binding in twentieth-century Egyptian jurisprudence. This position was based on the child's right and welfare as we saw in Chapter 3. Courts considered agreements in which mothers dropped their custody right to be null and void. They argued, in accordance with pre-nineteenth-century Ḥanafī law, that since child custody was a right of the child, mothers had no right to concede their custody to the father.[18] The courts were less rigid when it came to mothers keeping custody of their children despite remarriage,[19] since by then the notion of maternal love more than offset the potential harm that could result from living with a stepfather. To illustrate, consider the following fatwa that was brought to Egypt's early twentieth-century grand mufti Muḥammad Bakhīt al-Muṭīʿī. A request for a fatwa was sent from the Ministry of Interior to al-Muṭīʿī about an agreement in which a mother gave up her right to custody of a boy below the age of seven but subsequently recanted her agreement: Is such an agreement binding? Citing the dominant view in the Ḥanafī school, including the fatwa of Abū-l-Suʿūd and the commentary of Ibn ʿĀbidīn, Egypt's mufti stated that such an agreement was not binding and that she had the right to regain custody.[20] Similarly, in 1944, ʿAbd al-Majīd Salīm considered a private separation deed in which the mother gave up her right to custody to be nonbinding.[21]

Age and Gender

The gradual shift from the basic interests approach, which was linked to gross harm, to a broader, more positive best interests approach continued

[16] See Kholoussy, *For Better, For Worse*, 120.

[17] Shaham, *Family and the Courts in Modern Egypt*, 190. [18] Ibid., 186; 192.

[19] Niqābat al-Muḥāmiyyīn al-Sharʿiyīn, "Case No. 3102 of 1951 (Sayyida Zaynab Sharia Court of Summary Justice)," *Al-Muḥāmā Al-Sharʿiyya: Majalla Qaḍāʾiyya Shahriyya Al-Sana Al-Khāmisa Wa'l-ʿIshrīn* 24:1 (1953): 106–109.

[20] Dār al-Iftāʾ al-Miṣriyya, *Al-Fatāwā Al-Islāmiyya Min Dār Al-Iftāʾ Al-Miṣriyya*, 13: 171–174.

[21] Ibid., 13:198–199.

to be uneven throughout the twentieth century, with some judges abiding by the pre-nineteenth-century Ḥanafī narrow definition of welfare and others relying on the marginal view that gave judges greater discretion. For example, premodern Sunni jurists considered a child's serious illness, especially mental illness, as grounds for maintaining her or his custody by women. The dominant position in the Ḥanafī school is that the mental illness of the child constitutes a weakness that requires the custody of women regardless of the child's age. However, there is a minority position that does not change the custody-transfer age due to such sickness. Egyptian lawyers of the early twentieth century, for instance, were aware of this minority position. One lawyer acting on behalf of the paternal uncle of a twelve-year-old mentally disabled child used it in his argument before the Manṣūra Sharīʿa Court of First Instance in 1930. The lawyer was appealing a decision by the Manṣūra Sharīʿa Summary Court that granted custody to the mother, his deceased brother's widow. The Manṣūra Sharīʿa Court of First Instance rejected the petition, confirming the lower court's ruling. It cited the child's mental illness as grounds for its decision, adding that according to *al-Fatḥ* (*Fatḥ al-Qadīr*) and *al-Jawhara* (*al-Jawhara al-Nayyira ʿalā Mukhtaṣar al-Qudūrī*), a child with a serious illness must stay with the mother regardless of age or gender.[22]

The uncle's lawyer appealed the decision by arguing first that the child was not mentally disabled and that even if she were, *al-Baḥr* and the commentary of *Radd al-Muḥtār* place her in the custody of men. The court interviewed the girl, Samīra, and determined that she was indeed mentally disabled and in a state in which she could not communicate (*tafāhum*). The court added that the child's mental incapacity was confirmed by a medical report presented to the summary court. Now the court was faced with the minority position presented by the plaintiff's lawyers and the majority position used by the first court to reject the petition. The court reasoned that the logic behind transferring custody from women to men was determined by the needs of the ward, which is why some jurists considered age as a sign of the lack of need on the part of the ward for the care of her or his mother. It concluded that keeping the child with the mother was more in line with the ultimate goal of child custody, that is, the welfare of the child (*nafʿ al-ṣaghīr*).[23]

[22] Niqābat al-Muḥāmiyyīn al-Sharʿiyīn, "Case No. 55 of 1929–1930 (Manṣūra Sharia Court of First Instance)," ed. Muḥarram Fahīm, *Al-Muḥāmā Al-Sharʿiyya: Majalla Qaḍāʾiyya Shahriyya Al-Sana Al-Ūlā* 1:8 (1929): 698–701.

[23] Ibid.

Another line of reasoning that the court adopted was based on a broad conception of the best interests of the child. This line of reasoning uses analogy to disallow custody to the natural custodian based on his hatred (*kurh*) of the child. According to the court, the interests of the child were the ultimate goal of child custody, which is why jurists stated that custody of children should be transferred from the mother to the next in the line of custodians if the mother married someone who was not a close relative of the child. Even though, the court reasoned, the mother is the best-suited person to look after the child, the benefit is diminished by the presence of a new husband, who would naturally hate (*yabghaḍu*) children from a previous marriage, so custody is taken away to protect the interests of the child. By the same token, if the agnatic relative hates the child, he should not be allowed to assume custody. The court then argued that they had evidence that the uncle hated the child since he had convinced his mother to remove Samīra from the list of beneficiaries of an endowment that the child's paternal grandmother had assigned to Samīra and the uncle's offspring. As a result, his own children received Samīra's share. Acting in this manner against the interests of Samīra, despite her mental illness, suggested that he hated her (*kurh shadīd lahā*). The court concluded that it is not in the interests (*maṣlaḥa*) of the girl to be under the custodianship of her paternal uncle. Based on this reasoning, the court decided to confirm the ruling of the first court and rejected the appeal petition.[24]

Although we have found instances of broad conceptions of the best interests of the child, there are other cases in which judges did not depart from Ḥanafī doctrine. For instance, some judges did not consider beating to represent harm to the child in line with Ḥanafī law, even though such behavior was not acceptable in Egyptian criminal law. In one case from the Damietta Sharʿiyya Summary Court, a father sued his daughter's maternal grandmother for custody transfer (*ḍamm*) since the daughter had already reached the age of 12. The grandmother refused to hand over the daughter, arguing that the father had beaten up his daughter six months earlier. The beating was so severe that the child had to be treated in hospital for almost 20 days. The father was found guilty of beating his daughter and had to pay a fine, yet the court decided that beating one's child is within the rights of the guardian and that there was a valid reason for the beating, namely that the child had stolen money from the father (recall the Case of the Abused Child). Had the court considered the welfare of the child broadly, they might have granted custody to the grandmother to avoid

[24] Ibid.

placing the child with a father who had beaten his daughter so severely, rather than relying on the Ḥanafī rule that justified beating as a form of discipline. The ruling was appealed by the maternal grandmother but was confirmed by the Court of Appeal.[25]

Remarriage of the Mother

Judges exercised more discretion in their interpretation of the welfare of the child vis-à-vis the categorical Ḥanafī rules of child custody with respect to granting custody to a remarried mother. Some twentieth-century judges (in line with Ibn ʿĀbidīn's thought) rejected fathers' petitions for child custody after the mother's remarriage on grounds of the father's own remarriage, based on a cultural assumption of hostility between children and their stepmothers. This was a clear rupture with premodern jurisprudence, which found that the child living with a stepmother was not considered grounds for denying custody. In fact, premodern jurists required the father to have a female relative or a wife living with him to take care of the child. Some judges, according to Shaham, invoked the child's welfare to argue that it was better for them to stay with their mothers despite remarriage rather than live with a hostile stepmother.[26] Other judges abided by Ḥanafī law, which does not presumptively consider a stepmother to be cause for disqualification.[27]

Other judges transferred custody to the father upon remarriage of the mother in accordance with the rules of Ḥanafī law. In line with the rules of Ḥanafī law, a woman by the name of Fāṭima had received custody of her grandson Yūsuf after her daughter, the child's mother, remarried. At some point the father stopped paying child maintenance, prompting Fāṭima to sue for support. The father's lawyer argued that the reason the father had refused to pay child support was due to the fact that the grandmother had forfeited her right to custody of Yūsuf because she lived in the house of her daughter's new husband. The judge decided that custody of Yūsuf, who was under the age of seven, should be transferred to the father. He explained that, according to *al-Qunya*, the custodian loses her right to custody if she stays in the house of those who dislike the child (*mubghiḍīn*), a reference to the assumed hostility between the new husband and the

[25] Niqābat al-Muḥāmiyyīn al-Sharʿiyīn, "Case No. 79 of 1929–1930 (Sharia Summary Court of Damietta)," ed. Muḥarram Fahīm, *Al-Muḥāmā Al-Sharʿiyya: Majalla Qaḍāʾiyya Shahriyya Al-Sana Al-Ūlā* 1:6 (1929): 537–538.

[26] Shaham, *Family and the Courts in Modern Egypt*, 187–188.

[27] Ibid., 192.

wife's children from prior marriages. The judge rejected the petition for maintenance, and the plaintiff did not appeal the ruling.[28]

Lifestyle

In the Ottoman period, it was rare for fathers to suggest that the mother's character was morally reproachable. In fact, we do not find any cases in our large 1517–1801 sample of fathers or mothers petitioning for custody on the grounds that the other parent was morally unfit. In the twentieth century, however, one finds cases in which certain character traits had an impact on the granting of custody. In some cases, men were able to wrest custody from mothers by bringing evidence to the court that the mother was sexually promiscuous or that she worked as a dancer or an actress.[29] One court considered the mother's adultery, for which there was police evidence, to be grounds for denying her custody of her two children aged eight and five. Abiding by Ibn ʿĀbidīn's work, which he cited, would have required the judge to grant custody of the five-year-old to the mother until he reached the age of discernment, at which some Ḥanafī jurists assumed that children could be influenced by the mother's behavior. The judge reasoned against this view by saying that children below the age of seven were still susceptible to being negatively impacted by the mother's behavior. Since child custody was designed for the "benefit of the ward" (*maṣlaḥat al-maḥḍūn*), he decided to deny the mother's petition for custody.[30] While one judge used the majority Ḥanafī position on immorality, which can often be evidenced by court convictions, some resorted to the minority position adopted by Ibn ʿĀbidīn, among others. One court considered the mother's immoral behavior (*fisq*), evidenced by her conviction of vandalism as well as testimonies attesting to her immorality, to be insufficient grounds to deny her custody as long as she did not neglect her four-year-old son. The judge also analogized her immorality to that of a non-Muslim who is permitted to have custody until the child reaches the age of discernment.[31]

28 Niqābat al-Muḥāmiyyīn al-Sharʿiyīn, "Case No. 391 of 1928–1929 (Sharia Court of Shabrakhīt)," ed. Muḥarram Fahīm, *Al-Muḥāmā Al-Sharʿiyya: Majalla Qaḍāʾiyya Shahriyya Al-Sana Al-Ūlā* 1:4 (1929): 325.

29 Shaham, *Family and the Courts in Modern Egypt*, 181–182.

30 Niqābat al-Muḥāmiyyīn al-Sharʿiyīn, "Case No. 1811 of 1952 (Mīt Ghamra Court of Summary Justice)," *Al-Muḥāmā Al-Sharʿiyya: Majalla Qaḍāʾiyya Shahriyya Al-Sana Al-Khāmisa Waʾl-ʿIshrīn* 25:1 (1954): 80–82.

31 Immorality was often equated with court convictions both in the premodern and modern periods, rendering serious violations of the law to be inherently immoral. Niqābat al-Muḥāmiyyīn al-Sharʿiyyīn, "Case No. 812 of 1943–1944 (The Aqṣur

Men's behavior was not subjected to the same level of scrutiny, although some fathers were also denied custody for immoral behavior.[32] Shaham found four cases in which fathers were disqualified from custodianship when they led an immoral life, and these include fathers who had been convicted of crimes. He also found two cases in which judges maintained the father's right despite his immoral behavior.[33] The best interests of the child discourse was prominent in these seemingly contradictory rulings, in which judges used the divergent views of the Ḥanafī school to make pragmatic child custody determinations based on their own sense of what was best for the child.

In one case brought to the Miṣr Sharīʿa Court of Summary Justice in 1922, Ibrāhīm Bek Mumtāz sued his sister, Fāṭima, for custody of his half siblings, Zaynab and Aḥmad. Both their parents had died prior to the lawsuit. The argument of Fāṭima's lawyer was that Ibrāhīm was irresponsible and untrustworthy (*ghayr amīn*). To support her argument, Fāṭima's lawyer claimed that Ibrāhīm had sold and spent all his inheritance of 41 acres of land to reclaim his mother's land and to treat her illness. Ibrāhīm Bek acknowledged that he had sold his inheritance for 800 pounds and that he had spent all of it. The judge reasoned that disposing of one's money irresponsibly, even if for charitable and commendable causes, is a sign of *fasād* (corruption), since it exceeded the level of moderation. Witnesses also testified that some of the land he had sold had not belonged to him, which indicates that he was not honest with the distribution of inheritance after his father's death. The court decided to reject the brother's petition, allowing the children to remain with their sister. It is not clear how old the two children were, but one can safely assume that they had reached the age of custody transfer from females to males, otherwise the defense would have brought up the age as well.[34]

As we saw in Chapter 5, women's work was sometimes used to deny them custody in the nineteenth century. By the twentieth century, as Shaham has rightly argued, many judges showed sympathy for women's need to work to support their families without being disqualified from

Court of Summary Justice)," *Al-Muḥāmā Al-Sharʿiyya: Majalla Qaḍāʾiyya Shahriyya Al-Sana Al-Khāmisa Wa'l-ʿIshrīn* 16:9–10 (1944): 250–251.

32 Niqābat al-Muḥāmiyyīn al-Sharʿiyyīn and ʿAbd al-Razzāq al-Qāḍī, "Case No. 2037 of 1937 (Miṣr Sharīʿa Court of First Instance)," *Al-Muḥāmā Al-Sharʿiyya: Majalla Qaḍāʾiyya Shahriyya Al-Sana Al-Khāmisa Wa'l-ʿIshrīn* 11:2 (1939): 67–68.

33 Shaham, *Family and the Courts in Modern Egypt*, 193.

34 Niqābat al-Muḥāmiyyīn al-Sharʿiyyīn, "Case No. 547 of 1922–1923 (Miṣr Sharīʿa Court of Summary Justice)," ed. Muḥarram Fahīm, *Al-Muḥāmā Al-Sharʿiyya: Majalla Qaḍāʾiyya Shahriyya Al-Sana Al-Ūlā* 1:5 (1929): 418–419.

custodianship.[35] A consensus emerged from Egyptian jurisprudence of the first half of the twentieth century wherein courts argued that what disqualifies a mother from custodianship is not the fact of her full-time work (*iḥtirāf*) but negligence of the child. Recall that Ibn Nujaym referred to a whole class of women who were working full-time in sixteenth-century Egypt, whom he called "professionals" (*muḥtarifāt*). These sixteenth-century Egyptian women could lose their spousal maintenance both because they did not dedicate their time to the spouse and because they did not need such maintenance on account of their full-time employment. However, they did not lose child custody as long as the child was not neglected. Using the same logic, many twentieth-century courts assumed that if a working mother makes child care arrangements, she is not disqualified from custody.

Accordingly, working mothers often kept custody of their young children even when challenged. In one case from 1948, the father sued for custody of his four-month-old son on the grounds that the mother worked full time as a schoolteacher. The mother countered that she worked from 8 a.m. to 3 p.m. and had two recesses at 9:25 a.m. and noon, during which she nursed the boy. She also had three sisters who lived with her and employed a domestic, suggesting that they helped her with the child's care. The mother also submitted a recent medical report showing that the infant was in good health. In its assessment of the child's welfare in this custody arrangement, the court cited a book on women's health, stating that a child needed to be nursed once every three hours. The judges reasoned that given the mother's work hours, including two recesses, she was fully capable of nursing the infant and providing childcare while she was working. Thus the court rejected the father's petition.[36] Similarly, a father failed to convince the court that his ex-wife's work as a headmistress disqualified her from being a custodian of their six-year-old boy.[37] Yet another man failed to convince another court that the mother's long hours of work in a coffeehouse disqualified her from custody of their son.[38]

35 Shaham, *Family and the Courts in Modern Egypt*, 195.

36 Niqābat al-Muḥāmiyyīn al-Shar'iyyīn, "Case No. 1182 of 1946–1947 (Asyūṭ Sharī'a Court of Summary Justice)," *Al-Muḥāmā Al-Shar'iyya: Majalla Qaḍā'iyya Shahriyya Al-Sana Al-Khāmisa Wa'l-'Ishrīn* 20:1 (49, 1948): 89–91.

37 Niqābat al-Muḥāmiyyīn al-Shar'iyyīn, "Case No. 288 of 1954 (Sayyida Zaynab Court of Summary Justice)," *Al-Muḥāmā Al-Shar'iyya: Majalla Qaḍā'iyya Shahriyya Al-Sana Al-Khāmisa Wa'l-'Ishrīn* 25:1 (1954): 111–112.

38 Kholoussy, *For Better, For Worse*, 109–110.

Religion

Religion in twentieth-century Egypt continued to play an important role in custody determinations, as it did in the Ottoman and khedival periods. This is an area of child custody law that underwent little change in the course of the nineteenth century and the first half of the twentieth century. In 1948, in the ʿAṭṭārīn Court of Summary Justice, ʿAlī Efendī sued both his father, Ḥasan, and his father's wife, Matilda, for custody of their two girls, Nina and Teresa. According to the petition, his father had converted to Maronite Christianity, the religion of his new wife, and was converting his two daughters. Their parents changed their names to Christian names and were taking them to church regularly. The adult brother added that their adult daughter had already converted and changed her name to Mary and that she was engaged to a Christian man. The brother was concerned that the two minor girls would end up like their adult sister. In reaching its decision, the court argued, in line with the discourse of Ibn ʿĀbidīn, that there were three rights (*ḥuqūq*) in child custody: the child's right, the mother's right, and the father's right. As much as possible, judges must reconcile the three sets of rights, but as soon as there is conflict, the child's right is given priority since the *ratio legis* behind child custody is the child's welfare (*nafʿ al-walad*). Since the child follows "the parent with the better religion" (*khayr al-abawayn dīnan*) and the father was born Muslim, then the children must follow the father's original religion. Before the prosecution, the father said that he had agreed with his Maronite wife that if they had boys, they would follow his religion and girls would follow hers. The court ruled that the father had indeed apostatized and called on the state (*walī al-amr*) to issue legislation to crack down on this rampant problem. The court transferred custody of Nina and Teresa from the parents and entrusted the brother with their care.[39]

Similarly, according to Kholoussy, an Egyptian father who could provide evidence that his Italian Christian ex-wife was raising their six-year-old son as a Christian was able to receive a custody order.[40] However, a Christian father who claimed to have converted to Islam and petitioned for custody of his children aged six and two, failed to convince the court that his conversion was genuine, given that he had previously converted to

[39] Niqābat al-Muḥāmiyyīn al-Sharʿiyyīn, "Case No. 295 of 1948 (ʿAṭṭārīn Court of Summary Justice)," *Al-Muḥāmā Al-Sharʿiyya: Majalla Qaḍāʾiyya Shahriyya Al-Sana Al-Khāmisa Wa'l-ʿIshrīn* 25:1 (1954): 99–105.

[40] Kholoussy, *For Better, For Worse*, 110–111.

Islam and then back to Christianity before converting again back to Islam.[41]

Visitation Rights

In the modern period, visitation was an area of the law that was under-regulated by statutes. For this reason, judges often had no choice but to resort to the jurisprudence of Ḥanafī jurists, especially the work of Ibn ʿĀbidīn, which was exceedingly influential in the first half of the twentieth century. Judges often granted visitation to one parent once a week.[42] In October 1929, a grandmother petitioned the Azbakiyya Court of Summary Justice to force the father of her deceased daughter's son to bring her grandson so that she could see him once a week. The judge cited the views of both *al-Durr al-Mukhtār* of al-Ḥaṣkafī and *Radd al-Muḥtār* of Ibn ʿĀbidīn, according to which the mother should not be prevented by the father from seeing her child, but the father is not required to bring the child to her. If she wishes to see the child, she must visit him or her at the father's place of residence. This is what the judge discovered after much research in Ḥanafī law, and he rejected the grandmother's petition.[43]

What the previous case shows is that although the grandmother had raised the child, acting as the sole caregiver for at least a part of the child's life until the age of custody transfer, she was not able to require the father to bring him to her for visitation. It is not clear why the maternal grandmother wanted the father to bring the child to her. One could speculate that she belonged to the upper classes, where women's seclusion was strictly applied.[44] Having established that the grandmother had to visit the father's residence if she were to see her grandson, the judges decided the frequency of such visits by analogy to nonparental visits to wives. In Ḥanafī doctrine, a wife is entitled to visits from relatives other than

[41] Niqābat al-Muḥāmiyyīn al-Sharʿiyyīn, "Case No. 1449 of 1949–1940 (Shubra Sharīʿa Court of Summary Justice)," ed. ʿAbd al-Razzāq al-Qāḍī, *Al-Muḥāmā Al-Sharʿiyya: Majalla Qaḍāʾiyya Shahriyya Al-Sana Al-Khāmisa Waʾl-ʿIshrīn* 11:1 (40, 1939): 128–129.

[42] Niqābat al-Muḥāmiyyīn al-Sharʿiyīn, "Case No. 220 of 1954 (Miṣr Al-Jadīda Court of Summary Justice)," *Al-Muḥāmā Al-Sharʿiyya: Majalla Qaḍāʾiyya Shahriyya Al-Sana Al-Khāmisa Waʾl-ʿIshrīn* 25:4 (1954): 304–305.

[43] Niqābat al-Muḥāmiyyīn al-Sharʿiyīn, "Case No. 2528 of 1928–1929 (The Azbakiyya Court of Summary Justice)," ed. Muḥarram Fahīm, *Al-Muḥāmā Al-Sharʿiyya: Majalla Qaḍāʾiyya Shahriyya Al-Sana Al-Ūlā* 1:6 (1929): 521–522.

[44] On the seclusion of upper-class women in the eighteenth and nineteenth centuries, see further Cuno, *Modernizing Marriage*, 91–93. Al-Jabartī spoke approvingly of the seclusion of upper-class women in the eighteenth century, see ibid., p. 91.

her parents at the frequency of one visit per year according to the dominant view in the Ḥanafī school, or once a month according to a minority position. By analogy, the grandmother's minimum visits to the father's residence would be once a year or once a month, with the judges not choosing one position of the two since this issue was not part of the grandmother's petition. One can only imagine the potential psychological damage and feeling of loss that the child must have felt upon suddenly not being able to see his main caregiver after the transfer of custody. The child was at that point seven years old and according to the Ḥanafī school, he did not know what is best for him; and, therefore, unlike in the Shāfiʿī and Ḥanbalī schools, he was not given a choice over his custody. In line with Ḥanafī doctrine, the court did not consult the child about whether or not he wished to see his grandmother: the best interests of this particular child, *tout court*, did not take precedence over Ḥanafī doctrine in this example of court adjudication.

In a similar case, the mother requested that the father bring her son to her residence because her husband forbade her from visiting her children. Although the judge cited the accepted legal principle that the welfare (*maṣlaḥa*) of the child should be given priority over that of his parents, he invoked Ḥanafī juristic discourse that all the father is required to do is allow the mother to see the children. There is nothing in Ḥanafī doctrine, the judge reasoned, that requires the father to bring the children to her residence. The mother's petition was rejected.[45] These instances of strict formalism on the part of some judges continued to exist in court adjudication, making the legal landscape ripe for legislative action to place the best interests of the child at the center of judicial lawmaking.

Relocation with the Ward

The Egyptian judge Maḥmūd ʿArnūs, whom we encountered in the section on remarriage of the mother, argued that if a mother violates the rules of travel from the custody town, this does not constitute grounds for taking away her custody rights. In order to support his position, he cited the views of Ibn ʿĀbidīn and Ibn Nujaym. According to the *Fatāwā* of Ibn Nujaym, even if a woman travels without the permission of the father, she is still entitled to child maintenance and custody wages for the period of her

[45] Niqābat al-Muḥāmiyyīn al-Sharʿiyyīn, "Case No. 1025 of 1928–1929 (Al-Labbān Court of Summary Justice)," ed. Muḥarram Fahīm, *Al-Muḥāmā Al-Sharʿiyya: Majalla Qaḍāʾiyya Shahriyya Al-Sana Al-Ūlā*, 1929, 714–715.

unpermitted travel. Citing *al-Fatāwā al-Mahdiyya*, ʿArnūs explained that a man from Rashīd married a woman from the same town, where the marriage was consummated. The couple subsequently divorced, and the mother took her daughter to Alexandria. Al-Mahdī's fatwa was that she was still entitled to child maintenance and custody wages. ʿArnūs added that it is not permissible to analogize this situation to that of a disobedient wife who would normally lose her maintenance for disobedience, due to the fact that in custody laws, the welfare of the child reigns supreme.[46]

On the question of travel with the ward, one also observes some trends brought about by modern technological advances in transportation, such as accounting for the transportation technology in the assessment of distance. Consider the case of ʿAlī Ḥusayn, who filed a lawsuit in 1929 against his ex-wife, Amīna Muḥammad ʿAlī. He claimed that his ex-wife had taken their daughter, Dawlat, who was under Amīna's custodianship, away from the father's town, Shibīn al-Kawm. According to the father, the mother had taken Dawlat to Cairo, which is farther than the permitted distance and asked the court to hand over the child to him. We know from the case that Dawlat was under the age of nine (*fī sinn al-ḥaḍāna*). Amīna's lawyer argued that the distance between Cairo and Shibīn al-Kawm was such that the father could go to see his daughter and return to his home on the same day. The claimant's lawyer argued that what is meant by being able to visit his child and return on the same day refers to the *sharʿī* day, that is, one of the three days that enable a person to shorten prayers (*masāfat al-qaṣr*), which he argued was 25 kilometers, and he explained that the distance between Shibīn al-Kawm and Cairo was 80 kilometers.[47]

The court's reasoning did not invoke the best interests of the child, and instead resorted to the juristic discourse of the Ḥanafī school. The court acknowledged that mothers are not permitted to move away with the child from the "custody location" (*makān al-ḥaḍāna*) to any town other than that in which the marriage contract was signed. The judge added that as long as the two places are close enough that the father could see his child and return on the same day, the mother could move with the child without any restrictions. The court's references were Ibn Nujaym's *al-Baḥr al-Rāʾiq*, and al-Astarūshinī's *Aḥkām al-Ṣighār*. According to the court, there were many faster means of transportation such as railways, cars, and buses, so the father could visit his daughter and return to Shibīn al-

[46] ʿArnūs, "Baʿḍ Masāʾil Al-Ḥaḍāna."

[47] Niqābat al-Muḥāmiyyīn al-Sharʿiyīn, "Case No. 1888 of 1928–1929 (The Azbakiyya Court of Summary Justice)," ed. Muḥarram Fahīm, *Al-Muḥāmā Al-Sharʿiyya: Majalla Qaḍāʾiyya Shahriyya Al-Sana Al-Ūlā* 1:4 (1929): 321–323.

Kawm on the same day. The court concluded that the mother should not be forced to give up custody due to her move, reasoning that premodern jurists established this rule even though they knew that the father's travel would entail certain costs, and, therefore, this cannot be an argument against allowing the mother to move away with her child from the custody location. The petition was rejected and the mother's custody was confirmed.[48] In this case, the court accepted the logic of premodern jurists who allowed the father to assume custody if the mother moved a long distance away from the father, but it defined this long distance in relation to advances in modern transportation.

Relying exclusively in their perception of the *ratio legis* of Ḥanafī jurisprudence on the distance at which custody is denied to women, one court argued in 1946 that the condition that the father should be able to see his child and return on the same day was not an absolute rule but rather a contingent instance of harm to the noncustodial relative when nighttime was dangerous for travelers. Now that streets are well-lit and transportation has become easier and faster, the noncustodial relative's inability to visit the child and return on the same day no longer represents harm. The court therefore rejected the petition of a paternal grandmother, arguing that the mother's relocation from the village of Musha in Asyūṭ to Alexandria (over 600 kilometers) did not forfeit the mother's right to custody.[49] This was a breakthrough decision that abandoned the Ḥanafī rules of either *masāfat al-qaṣr* or the father's ability to see the child and return on the same day in favor of the mother's care, which was by that time considered far superior to that of other relatives. This decision privileged a broad definition of the best interests of the child by which the judge determined what was best for a particular child, rather than relying only on a harm-avoidance approach.

Maintenance

As we saw in our discussion of pre-nineteenth-century Ottoman court practice, there were many binding agreements in which mothers received a divorce in exchange for relieving the father of child maintenance. A mother who failed to support her children after waiving her right to

48 Ibid.

49 Niqābat al-Muḥāmiyyīn al-Shar'iyīn, "Case No. 58 of 1946–47 (Asyūt Sharia Court of Summary Justice)," *Al-Muḥāmā Al-Shar'iyya: Majalla Qaḍā'iyya Shahriyya Al-Sana Al-Khāmisa Wa'l-'Ishrīn* 20:1 (49, 1948): 205–207.

maintenance was supported by her extended family, who as we saw previously, were present at the court and part of the separation deeds. As Judith Tucker observed, when traditional family structures eroded in the nineteenth century, judges continued to abide by juristic discourse, which allowed them to withhold spousal custody on grounds of the negligence stemming from mothers' full-time employment. This gap between evolving family structures and juristic discourse was lost on some of the judges of the nineteenth century. In the twentieth century, we find many judges bridging the gap by allowing women who had already given up maintenance in exchange for a divorce to have the father pay for maintenance due to the mother's indigence.[50] These judges relied on Ḥanafī juristic discourse, according to which the mother was entitled to child custody despite the agreement, in the event of indigence, as a way to protect the child from poverty.[51] With the exception of this circumstance, most judges accepted private agreements between the parents as long as they did not contradict Ḥanafī law.[52] Judges followed Ḥanafī doctrine with regard to allowing the father to bring a relative to take care of the child for free instead of the mother if the father was insolvent.[53] This was continuous with Ottoman-Egyptian and nineteenth-century practice. Some judges considered unpaid maintenance to be a debt on the father that does not expire, while others considered it to expire after one month.[54]

Guardianship

As we saw in the nineteenth century, the education of children became associated with mothers rather than fathers with the growth of the female

50 Niqābat al-Muḥāmiyyīn al-Sharʿiyīn, "Case No. 660 of 1945–1946 (Al-Minyā Sharia Court of Summary Justice)," *Al-Muḥāmā Al-Sharʿiyya: Majalla Qaḍāʾiyya Shahriyya Al-Sana Al-Khāmisa Wa'l-ʿIshrīn* 25:1 (1954): 76–78.

51 See al-Miṣrī, al-Nasafī, and Ibn ʿĀbidīn, *Al-Baḥr Al-Rāʾiq Sharḥ Kanz Al-Daqāʾiq Wa-Maʿahu Al-Ḥawāshī Al-Musammāh Minḥat Al-Khāliq ʿalā Al-Baḥr Al-Rāʾiq*, 4:134, 150–151.

52 There is a principle common to many Middle Eastern societies that "agreement is stronger than a judicial decision" (*al-tarāḍī yaghlib al-qāḍī*). Shaham, *Family and the Courts in Modern Egypt*, 231; Aharon Layish, *Divorce in the Libyan Family: A Study Based on the Sijills of the Sharīʿa Courts of Ajdābiyya and Kufra* (New York, NY; Jerusalem: New York University Press; Magnes Press, the Hebrew University, 1991), 188.

53 Niqābat al-Muḥāmiyyīn al-Sharʿiyīn, "Case No. 861 of 1954 (Sanballāwīn Court of Summary Justice)," *Al-Muḥāmā Al-Sharʿiyya: Majalla Qaḍāʾiyya Shahriyya Al-Sana Al-Khāmisa Wa'l-ʿIshrīn* 25:7 (1954): 448–450; Shaham, *Family and the Courts in Modern Egypt*, 188–189.

54 On maintenance in twentieth-century Egypt, see further Shaham, *Family and the Courts in Modern Egypt*, 166–168; 170–177.

domesticity doctrine. By 1929, one judge clearly assumed that the custodial mother was in fact in charge of managing the child's education and school fees. In order to force the father to pay the mother for the child's school fees, the judge reasoned that education is an essential part of the upbringing of a child, especially primary education.[55] Although premodern Islamic juristic discourse assumed that the father, or the male agnatic line in his absence, was responsible for the education and acculturation of children, especially boys, Egyptian nationalists by the end of the nineteenth century assigned such tasks to mothers. By the late nineteenth century and early twentieth century, the formal rules of guardianship remained constant while social values of the role of the mother in the private sphere changed so radically that legislative action was required to account for mothers' assumption of some of the responsibilities of guardians.

Although women were de facto responsible for the child's education, especially while she or he was under their custodianship, they had no power over schooling decisions. The successive guardianship legislation in the 1950s did not address this problem. For instance, after the 1952 Revolution, Law No. 118 of 1952 determined the situations in which custody over a person was forfeited, such as when the guardian was convicted of certain crimes.[56] Law No. 119 of 1952, Governing Guardianship over Property, set the age of majority at 21 and established the order of guardians, the prerogatives of different guardians, the types of transactions they were allowed to conduct, and their power vis-à-vis that of the judge.[57] The main objective of these laws was to establish clear rules for the powers of various types of guardians and to establish clearer checks and balances in order to guarantee the protection of the child's assets as well as her or his general welfare. These two laws, which were passed after the 1952 revolution, continued the state's homogenization of guardianship rules, making them more univocal and clear. Yet these guardianship laws ignored the tension inherent in the reality of mothers overseeing their children's education despite their lack of guardianship rights over schooling decisions.

55 Niqābat al-Muḥāmiyyīn al-Shar'iyīn, "Case No. 1239 of 1928–9 (The Jamāliyya Court of Summary Justice)," ed. Muḥarram Fahīm, *Al-Muḥāmā Al-Shar'iyya: Majalla Qaḍā'iyya Shahriyya Al-Sana Al-Ūlā* 1:2 (1929): 320–321.

56 Wizārat al-'Adl, "Law No. 118 (1952) on the Forfeiture of Guardianship over the Person," *Tashrī'āt*, 1953, 12–15.

57 "Law No. 119 (1952) Governing Guardianship over Property," *Al-Waqā'i' Al-Miṣriyya*, August 4, 1952.

The 1952 revolution would later change the legal landscape of Egypt more dramatically when it incorporated sharīʿa courts into a unified national legal system. On December 15, 1953, a constitutional subcommittee struck by Nasser gave its recommendation that sharīʿa courts be integrated into a unified judiciary. The decision sent shock waves through the ranks of sharīʿa judges. Two days later, the Syndicate of Sharīʿa Lawyers met in the Cairo Sharīʿa Court of First Instance to reject the recommendation.[58] In the end, the constitutional subcommittee's recommendation prevailed, leading to the abolition of sharīʿa courts in 1955. It is during the period of national courts that the best interests of the child took on a much broader meaning through explicit, incremental legislation that continued throughout the second half of the twentieth and early twenty-first century.

Shaham concludes that in the twentieth century, judges applying Islamic law to questions of custody and guardianship placed the "best interests of the child above any other interest, such as that of the custodial parent."[59] I would modify Shaham's conclusion to say that the march toward the best interests standard was very much like Euro-American jurisprudence in that it was uneven and nonlinear. In fact, while some judges as we saw previously, exhibited high levels of pragmatic adjudication, others were more formalistic in their approach. Some judges resisted the reforms of family law of the first half of the twentieth century, while others supported them. Shaham has observed that senior judges of the Court of First Instance picked and chose Ḥanafī positions that best served the interests of the child and her or his custodial mother, sometimes choosing nondominant views to achieve this end.[60] Others, as we have seen thus far, opted for a more formalist approach. The uneven jurisprudence of the first half of the twentieth century would later be reinforced with legislation pushing the best interests approach further into center stage in Egyptian lawmaking.

I agree with Shaham in his assessment of the faultiness of Anderson's assumption that the dominance of the welfare of the child in Egyptian courts of the twentieth century was due to the influence of British law.[61] As we saw previously, the welfare of the child discourse received a wider definition in the work of Ibn ʿĀbidīn (d. 1836), which predated the British

[58] Muḥarram Fahīm, "Qawānīn Wa-Qarārāt Wa-Awāmir Wa-Manshūrāt," *Al-Muḥāmā Al-Sharʿiyya: Majalla Qaḍāʾiyya Shahriyya Al-Sana Al-Khāmisa Wa'l-ʿIshrīn* 24:1 (1953): 126–127.

[59] Shaham, *Family and the Courts in Modern Egypt*, 194.

[60] Ibid., 174; 230–236.

[61] Ibid., 194.

Custody of Infants Act of 1839. It is unlikely that British influence was the primary catalyst for the focus on the welfare of the child in the late nineteenth and early twentieth centuries. To be sure, this situation would change by the second half of the twentieth century, when Egypt signed the Convention on the Rights of the Child (CRC) and consequently adjusted its child custody regime to the principles enshrined in this international convention.

THE BEST INTERESTS OF THE CHILD, 1955–2014

Due to the large number of successive legislations on child custody in the period from 1955 to 2014, I will organize the remainder of this chapter chronologically around statutes rather than the eight themes that we have discussed so far. Due to the overlap between the eight themes and the topics of the statutes discussed, I will still be able to cover most of our themes through these statutes, especially since the focus will remain on how this legislation relates to evolving conceptions of the child's welfare. In addition to these pieces of legislation, I will discuss some landmark decisions made by the Court of Cassation and the Supreme Constitutional Court in order to shed light on how some of these laws were understood and applied by Egypt's highest courts.

Law No. 44 of 1979 and Law No. 100 of 1985

Throughout the second half of the twentieth century, women's groups lobbied to allow mothers to have custody of children past the age of seven and nine, as stipulated by Law 25 of 1929, to accommodate the female domesticity assumption, which had become a widely accepted social good. It was not until 1979 that Sadat called parliament for an emergency session during its recess to issue Law No. 44 of 1979, only for it to be later deemed unconstitutional.[62] After the Supreme Constitutional Court's striking down of the law, the Mubarak regime ratified Law No. 100 of 1985, which was almost identical to the previous law. The list of female custodians was identical to the dominant order of the Ḥanafī school, in which the mother was followed by her mother, her mother's maternal female ascendants, the father's mother, his mother's maternal female ascendants, sisters of the

[62] Dawoud S. El Alami, "Law No. 100 of 1985 Amending Certain Provisions of Egypt's Personal Status Laws," *Islamic Law and Society* 1:1 (January 1994): 116–136.

child, the sisters' daughters, the child's aunts, and so on. All of these relatives had priority over the father and other male relatives during the tender years.[63] The concept of the welfare of the child would be invoked again in Law No. 100 of 1985, which extended maternal custody over sons to ten years of age and over daughters until 12.[64] After the attainment of ten for boys and 12 for girls, the court could extend the mother's custody to 15 years of age or until the daughter married, based on the welfare of the child (*maṣlaḥatihā*).

For the first time with this law, we see a concern for the psychological impact of the child's visitation environment, which stipulates that visitations should occur in a place that does not harm the child psychologically (*nafsiyyan*).[65] This allowed the judge to determine, on a case-by-case basis, what constitutes the child's welfare and what can cause her or him psychological harm. No legislation dealt directly with visitation, though, until Art. 20 of Law No. 100 of 1985, stipulating that both parents had the right to see the child, adding that the grandparents had the same right if the parents were not present.[66] Law No. 100 of 1985 left the matter of arranging visitation (*ruʾya*) to the parents, but if they failed to agree, the judge had the discretion to arrange it in a manner that would not harm the child psychologically. The law added that if the custodial parent refuses to grant visitation rights to the other parent, he or she would receive a warning from the judge. If he or she continued to deny the other parent visitation, the law granted the judge the power to transfer custody to the next person in the line of custodians for a period depending on the judge's discretion.[67]

Art. 20 of Law 100 of 1985 uses the same wording as its predecessor with respect to the issue of visitations.[68] The common form of access that we see in many Muslim jurisdictions involves "seeing" (*ruʾya*) the child. In Egypt, it is not a living arrangement in which the child sleeps at the

63 Ibid. 64 For a translation of the law, see Ibid.

65 "Law No. 100 (1985) Amending Certain Provisions of Egypt's Personal Status Laws," *Al-Jarīda Al-Rasmiyya* 27 (July 4, 1985): 4–11.

66 The twentieth-century American concept of grandparental visitation rights developed out of situations in which the nuclear family was dysfunctional, in which case grandparents replaced parents, but over time grandparental visitation rights developed as an independent right of the child, regardless of the health of the nuclear family or the wishes of the parents. See David M. Rosen, "American Families and American Law," in *Handbook of Marriage and the Family*, ed. Marvin B. Sussman, Suzanne K. Steinmetz, and Gary W. Peterson, 2nd ed. (New York, NY: Springer Science & Business Media, 2013), 1:563–568.

67 "Law No. 44 (1979) Amending Some of the Rules of Personal Status Law," *Al-Jarīda Al-Rasmiyya* 25:2 (June 21, 1979): 1–4.

68 "Law No. 100 (1985) Amending Certain Provisions of Egypt's Personal Status Laws."

noncustodial parent's house for some of the time, but rather short periods of visitation, usually not exceeding a few hours a week, often in a public park. This was the result of a narrow understanding of the premodern juristic tradition and a concern for standardization. In other words, although most Sunni jurists stated that custodial parents had no right to prevent the noncustodial parent from having access to the child as long as such access posed no danger to the child, modern Egyptian judges came up with visitation schedules that often did not exceed a play date of a few hours in a public park once a week, rather than building a visitation system based on the best interests of the child. As we have seen in Chapter 1, by the 1980s, the assumption of joint custody in different forms had become an important legal regime in child custody arrangements in England and the United States. Despite the gradual shift toward a more individual and positive approach to the best interests of the child, neither the primary caretaker nor joint custody found great support in Egypt.

Constitutional Challenge to Law No. 100 of 1985

The notion that the best interests standard is relative and that the absolute determinations of author-jurists are not binding for all generations was entrenched in a ruling issued by Egypt's Supreme Constitutional Court. In 1993, Case No. 7 of the eighth judicial year challenged the constitutionality of Law No. 100 of 1985 on the grounds that it violated Arts. II and IX of the Egyptian Constitution. Art. II states that the "principles of Islamic Shariʿa are the main source of legislation," whereas Art. IX states that "the family is the basis of society founded on religion, morality, and patriotism. The State strives to preserve the genuine character of the Egyptian family." The case stipulated that raising the age of custody transfer and granting the judge further discretion in such transfers violated Arts. II and IX of the constitution.[69]

In response, the court argued that based on the explanatory memorandum of the law, the objective of the legislator of Law No. 100 of 1985 was to insure the stability of the children in order for them to feel secure in the home environment. This stability was achieved by ensuring the continuity of custodianship by raising the age both in legislation and in allowing the judge further discretion to raise the age until 15 for boys and until marriage for girls. According to the court, the law, which was

[69] Case No. 7 of 8th Judicial Year (Supreme Constitutional Court May 15, 1993).

based on the Mālikī school, would guarantee the psychological stability (*al-istiqrār al-nafsī*) necessary for the child's good upbringing. As we saw earlier, while the Mālikī school allows for the age to be puberty for boys and marriage for girls, it does not allow the judge – though it empowered families – the type of discretion enshrined in Law No. 25 of 1985. The court reasoned that based on the previous jurisprudence of the Supreme Constitutional Court, no legislation shall contradict the principles of Islamic law which are apodictic with respect to their authenticity and meaning. Beyond these apodictic rules, *ijtihād* (independent legal reasoning) is permitted. This *ijtihād* guarantees that the laws keep abreast of changing times and places in order to ensure the welfare of society, which is based on the general purposes of sharīʿa.[70]

According to the court, after conducting an inductive survey of the views of jurists, it became clear that the main *ratio legis* for their rules was the welfare of the child (*nafʿ al-maḥḍūn*). Children should be under the custodianship of their mothers when they are young since mothers are better at caring for young children. Further, Islamic law does not make the age determinations absolute as is suggested by the many disagreements among jurists over the appropriate age at which a child should be transferred from the custody of women to men. The court then established the *parens patriae* right of the state (*walī al-amr*) to change the requirements of the welfare (*maṣlaḥa*) of the child as it sees fit. According to the court, the child's mental and psychological wellness must be born in mind while determining the ages at which children should be transferred from the custody of women to that of men. The court added that ensuring the continuity of custody, that is, keeping the child with the mother, serves the interests of the child. In any event, the court added that raising the age of custody is in conformity with the Mālikī school.[71] This ruling, which was issued in 1993, three years after Egypt's ratification of the CRC in 1990, further solidified the prerogative of the state to grant judges greater discretion in determining what is best for children. Following the ratification of the CRC, laws using language emphasizing the child's interests were successively enacted, using language similar to the CRC.

Law No. 12 of 1996

The concept of the best interests of the child was adopted in 1996 in Egypt's first Child Law (Law No. 12 of 1996), which was motivated by

[70] Ibid. [71] Ibid.

Egypt's ratification of the CRC in 1990. In Art. 3 of this law, legislators stated that "all decisions and procedures relating to children, by whomever initiated and enforced, must give priority to the protection of the child and to the child's interests." This wording resembles the wording of Art. 3 of the CRC: "In all actions concerning children, whether undertaken by public or private social welfare institutions, courts of law, administrative authorities or legislative bodies, the best interests of the child shall be a primary consideration."

Law No. 1 of 2000

The best interests standard was reinforced in Egypt's custody statutes in Art. 70 of Law No. 1 of 2000, which said that in the event of a dispute over custody, the public prosecutor may carry out an investigation to determine the child's welfare (*maṣlaḥatuh*) and grant custody on that basis until a court ruling is issued.[72] The law also empowered the judge to make a decision regarding disputes over travel. The rector of al-Azhar starting in 2010, Aḥmad al-Ṭayyib, understood this to give the judge full discretion in whether to allow the travel or not based on the welfare of the child (*maṣlaḥat al-ṣaghīr*), rather than privileging the father in the case of travel.[73] Art. 20 of the law rejected private separation deeds in which the mother gives up her right to custody or the maintenance of the children.[74]

Law No. 10 of 2004

Law No. 10 of 2004 goes the furthest in accommodating the CRC and modern social science research. It established family courts with the objective of speeding up litigation. Art. 2 of the law stipulated that a family court would be made up of three judges, as well as one social worker and a psychiatrist to help the judge. At least one of these specialists must be a female. According to Arts. 5 and 6, each family court must have at least one mediation office affiliated to the Ministry of Justice whose services are accessible free of charge. Each office must consist of a sufficient number of legal, social, and psychiatric specialists. The new law made mediation

72 "Law No. 1 (2000)," *Al-Jarīda Al-Rasmiyya* 4:2 (January 29, 2000): 2–30.
73 Aḥmad al-Ṭayyib, *Al-Fatāwā Al-Islāmiyya Min Dār Al-Iftā' Al-Miṣriyya* (Cairo: Maṭba'at Dār al-Kutub wa'l-Wathā'iq al-Qawmiyya, 2011), 27:73–74.
74 "Law No. 1 (2000)."

obligatory before resorting to litigation. Art. 10 stipulates that family courts shall not be housed in the same spaces as other courts and that they must be equipped to deal with the attendance of children to express their views. In addition to the legislator seeking to protect children from the stressful setting of regular courts, Art. 10 adds that the court shall base its decisions on the best interests of the child (*maṣāliḥ al-ṭifl al-fuḍlā*). This is the first time the word "best" (*fuḍlā*) was used in the long history of Egyptian legislation, reflecting the by-now ubiquitous "best interests of the child" wording. It is not clear why legislators felt the need to move beyond the standard "welfare" (*maṣlaḥa*), which, as we have seen thus far, has been used in premodern juristic discourse for many centuries. Does this terminological shift suggest an underlying shift in approach? No explanation was given by legislators as to why they chose this term.[75]

The centrality of social scientists in the new law was designed so that they could give judges advice on what is best for a particular child in a given situation as is common in contemporary Euro-American jurisdictions. According to Art. 11, these social scientists must attend all the court proceedings relating to divorce, annulment, custody, the child's residence, visitations, travel with the ward, and paternity disputes. The court can also solicit their help with other matters related to family law.

Art. 4 establishes a prosecution department dedicated to family law matters, which must be involved in all petitions and appeals. Art. 1 establishes one level of appeal, whereas Art. 14 states that decisions of the Family Court of Appeal cannot be brought before the Court of Cassation.[76] However, the Public Prosecutor, according to Art. 250 of Law No. 13 of 1968 (Law of Civil and Commercial Procedure), may appeal cases in which litigants were not allowed to appeal before the Court of Cassation.[77]

Law No. 4 of 2005

In 2003, al-Azhar's Islamic Research Academy (IRA) issued a fatwa stating that ending the age of female custody at 15 for both boys and girls does not violate Islamic law. This fatwa was a prelude to a new amendment to Decree-Law (*marsūm*) No. 25 of 1929, raising the age of female custody

75 "Law No. 10 (2004) Promulgating the Law on the Establishment of the Family Courts," *Al-Jarīda Al-Rasmiyya* 12:2 (March 18, 2004): 3–9.

76 "Law No. 10 (2004) Promulgating the Law on the Establishment of the Family Courts."

77 "Law No. 13 (1968) of Civil and Commercial Procedure," *Al-Jarīda Al-Rasmiyya*, n.d.

to 15 for both boys and girls.[78] Law No. 4 of 2005 extended the age of female custody for boys from 10 and 12 for boys and girls, respectively, to 15 for both, ending the different treatments of boys and girls based on the Ḥanafī school. Upon attaining the age of 15, the judge asks the child if he or she wishes to continue living with the mother or be transferred to the custody of the father.[79] This is the first time since 1517, according to our sample, that children's wishes were supposed to be solicited. The Ḥanafī view that children's views are not to be solicited dominated court practice from the Ottoman conquests in 1517 to Law No. 4 of 2005, despite the Shāfiʿī and Ḥanbalī positions that we discussed in Chapter 2.

The constitutionality of the law was challenged in 2008 – similar to the challenge leveled to Law 100 of 1985 – on the grounds that it contravened constitutional Art. II, relating to the principles of Islamic law being the main source of legislation, and Art. IX, stipulating that the family is the basis of society. The claimant argued that raising the age to 15 would lead to the disintegration of the family and was in violation of Islamic law. The court repeated its previous jurisprudence, arguing that Art. II refers to the principles of Islamic law that are certain with respect to their authenticity and meaning. The court added that with non-apodictic rules, the state (*walī al-amr*) has the prerogative to exercise *ijtihād* in a way that ensures the welfare (*maṣlaḥa*) of the child.[80]

Using a child welfare strategy, rather than a women's rights strategy, many women's groups have been pushing for further modifications of custody laws. In 2007, the National Council for Women (NCW) requested a fatwa from the IRA regarding its proposed amendments to Egyptian custody law, which included moving the father in priority on the list of tender-age custodians to the position right after the maternal grandmother; in the 1985 law, the father was preceded by the mother and a long list of female antecedents. They also wanted to grant grandparents independent visitation rights, since in Law 100 of 1985, they only have visitation if the parents are present. The proposed amendments included punishing a noncustodial parent who fails to conduct his or her visitation three times in a row by depriving them of their visitation rights. One final amendment would allow the noncustodial parent to have sleepovers during weekends and holidays. The IRA agreed with all the amendments but

[78] "Law No. 4 (2005) Amending Art. 20 of Decree-Law No. 25 of 1920," *Al-Jarīda Al-Rasmiyya* 9:2 (March 8, 2005): 3.

[79] "Law No. 4 (2005) Amending Art. 20 of Decree-Law No. 25 of 1920."

[80] "Supreme Constitutional Court Case No. 125 of 27th Judicial Year 2008," *Al-Jarīda Al-Rasmiyya* 20:2 (May 19, 2008): 84–90.

made a reservation that noncustodial parents may have the child stay over during weekends and holidays if the custodial parent consents to this arrangement.[81]

It is striking that despite al-Azhar's emphasis on the welfare of the child, a reservation was made about the custodial parent's consent, rather than focusing on what the judge determined to be in the child's best interests. Be that as it may, no reform to visitation and access, or the provision of a form of joint custody akin to what was seen, albeit rarely, in Ottoman courts and premodern juristic discourse, has yet become law despite the attempts of feminist groups. One would expect that the modern social sciences, which Egypt's judiciary has incorporated into the very functioning of Family Courts (as per Law No. 10 of 2004) would contribute to a legislative change.[82] In particular, one would expect that social science research on childhood, father studies, and mother studies would eventually lead to visitation laws that take into account the child's need to have a close relationship with both parents.[83]

The gradual shift from the basic to best interests approach reached its pinnacle in a fatwa issued in 2006 by Egypt's former grand mufti ʿAlī Jumʿa, who argued that jurists assigned custody to women during the tender age as a means to protect the ward rather than as a goal in itself. Thus, a mother should be denied custody if her custody did not lead to achieving its objectives or if her custody harmed the child.[84] In other words, departures from the doctrines of the school were not restricted to the harm test, but they were expanded to include accrued welfare. In another fatwa, he stated that the decision of the judge must bear in mind the welfare of the specific child.[85] After the January 2011 Egyptian Revolution, there has been much pressure on the IRA to reconsider the issue of child custody, and fathers even organized sit-ins to pressure al-Azhar to review the law. Under pressure and reports about the Salafi Nour party supporting the fathers, the IRA reviewed the child law of 2005 and

81 "Ḥaḍānat Al-Aṭfāl" (Cairo: National Council for Women, n.d.), www.conference.ncwegypt.com/index.php/docsara/140-custody; Marwā al-Bashīr, "Majmaʿ Al-Buḥūth Yaḥsim Al-Jadal: Qānūn Al-Ḥaḍāna Muṭābiq Li'l-Sharīʿa," *Al-Ahrām Newspaper*, May 25, 2012, www.masress.com/ahram/151360.

82 "Law No. 126 (2008)," *Al-Jarīda Al-Rasmiyya* 24:2 (June 15, 2008): 2–27.

83 Marsha Kleine Pruett and Carrie Barker, *The Scientific Basis of Child Custody Decisions*, ed. Robert M Galatzer-Levy, Louis Kraus, and Jeanne Galatzer-Levy (Hoboken, NJ: Wiley, 2009), 417–430.

84 ʿAlī Jumʿa, *Al-Fatāwā Al-Islāmiyya Min Dār Al-Iftāʾ Al-Miṣriyya* (Cairo: Maṭbaʿat Dār al-Kutub wa'l-Wathāʾiq al-Qawmiyya, 2010), 30:147–149.

85 Jumʿa, 30:155.

came to the same conclusions it had reached in 2003 and 2007. Throughout all of these deliberations, what is striking is that the best interests of the child doctrine was used by al-Azhar scholars to accept some feminist demands, yet the IRA rejected other demands that they deemed completely contradictory to premodern juristic discourse.[86]

The Case of the Converted Father

A case that illustrates the importance of the interests discourse in Egyptian law comes from the early twenty-first century. In 2000, a Christian father of twin sons converted to Islam when his two children were five years old. In 2004, he sued his wife for custody of their then nine-year-old twins, arguing that since he had become Muslim, the religion of the children belonged to the "better" religion, Islam. He added that he was concerned that the children's Christian mother would teach his children hatred of Islam. In 2006, the newly established ʿAṭṭārīn Family Court granted the father custody, ordering the mother to hand over the children. The mother's appeal was rejected in 2008. Since Law No. 10 (2004) Promulgating the Law on the Establishment of the Family Courts did not allow litigants to challenge the lower court's interpretation of the law at the Court of Cassation, the public prosecutor, by virtue of the power granted by Art. 250 of the Civil and Commercial Procedure Law of 1968, appealed the ruling before the Court of Cassation.[87]

The public prosecutor's petition used a mix of reasoning based on Egyptian legislation and the jurisprudence of the Ḥanafī school, which is the law on issues not addressed by statutes. He argued that the Ḥanafī school did not deny a non-Muslim mother (*kitābiyya*) the right of custody unless she did things that could harm the child's religion, such as feeding the children pork or allowing them to consume alcohol. The court agreed with the public prosecutor's reasoning, adding that the mother's kindness (*shafaqa*) toward her child does not change with the change of religion and explaining that *dhimmī*s (non-Muslims) under the protection of a Muslim polity, have the same rules of custody as Muslims. The court added that in order for the children to be taken away, the court should have ensured that

86 "Ḥaḍānat Al-Aṭfāl"; al-Bashīr, "Majmaʿ Al-Buḥūth Yaḥsim Al-Jadal: Qānūn Al-Ḥaḍāna Muṭābiq Li'l-Sharīʿa."

87 "Law No. 13 (1968) of Civil and Commercial Procedure"; "Case No. 15277 of 78th Judicial Year (Court of Cassation)," *Maḥkamat Al-Naqd: Majmūʿat Al-Aḥkām Al-Ṣādira Min Al-Hayʾa Al-ʿĀma Lil-Mawād Al-Madaniyya Wa-Min Al-Dawāʾir Al-Madaniyya*, 2009.

the mother had influenced the children to have non-Muslim beliefs. According to the court, the sharīʿa does not hastily deny a non-Muslim woman custody unless there is cause. While the court confirmed that the children's religion belonged to the better religion of the two parents, it did not accept the custody transfer from the mother to the father since the children were under the mother's custodianship, according to Law No. 25 of 1929, as amended by Law No. 100 of 1985 and Law No. 4 of 2005, all of which placed the age of transfer at 15. The court decided that the ruling of the lower courts had made a mistake in the application of the law.[88]

Interestingly, the court did not mention anything about the majoritarian Ḥanafī position that the children should still be handed over to the Muslim father once they reached the age of discernment, not the age of 15. In other words, what the court did is a *talfīq* of sorts, that is to say, since the Ḥanafī school imposes the rule of transfer at the age of discernment for boys, which is seven years, the Egyptian state's modified age of 15 (based on the Mālikī school) was then fused with the Ḥanafī position, the applicable law on family matters. In fact, the court's decision is similar to the Mālikī position, which allows mothers to retain custody until their normal custody right expires, so long as they do not give the child alcohol or pork.[89] The court must have resorted to *talfīq* instead of citing Mālikī law, since it is not the applicable law on issues not covered by statutes in Egypt. This jurisprudence could have a tremendous impact on one of the long-held views of premodern Ḥanafī jurists, namely that a non-Muslim mother could not maintain custody of a child beyond the age of discernment. As we saw in Chapter 2, the Ḥanbalī and Shāfiʿī schools did not even grant the non-Muslim mother this right. It is very surprising that the court invoked not new legal interpretation through *ijtihād* by arguing for instance, that the legal opinions behind the Ḥanafī juristic position were premised on what constituted the best interests of the child and therefore the judge should have assessed the mother's behavior on a case-by-case basis. Instead, they invoked premodern Ḥanafī law as it existed without claiming to try to change it.[90]

To conclude, what is clear from the Supreme Constitutional Court's reasoning as well as legislation of child custody law in Egypt is that legislators and justices see the designation of these years not as

88 "Case No. 15277 of 78th Judicial Year (Court of Cassation)."

89 *Talfīq* means combining two legal opinions in the same transaction. On *talfīq*, see further Ibrahim, *Pragmatism in Islamic Law*, 2015, 105–125; al-Dasūqī, *Ḥāshiyat Al-Dasūqī ʿalā Al-Sharḥ Al-Kabīr*, 2:529.

90 "Case No. 15277 of 78th Judicial Year (Court of Cassation)."

a women's-rights approach to custody as much as they see it as representing the new knowledge about the needs of children. There is no assumption that raising the age of custody over the second half of the twentieth century was designed to serve women's interests. Certainly, these two objectives are not mutually exclusive. The women activists who pushed for the new laws may have been motivated by some notion of women's rights, but it would have been hard to convince the male-dominated legislature that raising the age of child custody for women all the way up to 15 serves the cause of gender equality. In fact, this is a case in which men's access to child custody was curbed on the grounds of the interests of children. It is important to emphasize once more that the blanket age-based approach was not satisfactory to the CRC, since it made custody arrangements contingent on abstract conceptions of the needs of all children as opposed to treating them as individuals.[91]

Law No. 126 of 2008

We encounter the "best interests" terminology again in Law No. 126 of 2008, which amended some of the rules of the 1996 child law, where Art. 3 stipulates that the protection of the child and his or her best interests (*maṣāliḥi al-fuḍlā*) should take priority in all decisions and procedures relating to childhood.[92] The Child Law 126 of 2008 also grants custodians (usually women) greater guardianship rights in the domain of education, entrenching in statute a trend that we have observed throughout the late nineteenth and early twentieth centuries, when mothers rather than fathers became associated with the education of their children.[93] This process of the feminization of children's education was the product of European conceptions of female domesticity in the nuclear family as well as the greater access to education that women had in the late nineteenth and early twentieth centuries. Custodial mothers were empowered to participate in guardianship over the child's education along with the father (recall the case of Hayfā from Chapter 3). The same "best interests" wording would appear again following the overthrow of Mohamed Morsi, Egypt's first freely elected president. Egypt's post-Morsi

[91] For a general discussion of child custody in a number of modern Arab states, see Lynn Welchman, *Women and Muslim Family Laws in Arab States: A Comparative Overview of Textual Development and Advocacy* (Amsterdam: Amsterdam University Press, 2007), 133–149.

[92] "Law No. 126 (2008)." [93] Ibid.

constitution of 2014 stipulates that "the State shall endeavor to achieve the best interests (*al-maṣlaḥa al-fuḍlā*) of children in all matters taken against them."[94]

Committee on the Rights of the Child

Despite Egypt's legislative efforts since its ratification of the CRC in 1990, these statutes did not satisfy the requirements of the Committee on the Rights of the Child, which was established to monitor compliance with the CRC. In 2013, for instance, the committee criticized Egypt for making custody decisions contingent on the child's age rather than the best interests of a given child. In paragraph 11 of its 2013 report, the committee expressed its concern that some of the "provisions of domestic law, including family law, are still not in full conformity with the provisions of the Convention," and that the committee "notes with concern the limited use of the Convention in national courts, despite Art. 151 of the Constitution pursuant to which the Convention has the force of domestic law." In paragraph 36, the committee welcomed the use of the principle of the best interests of the child in Art. 3 of the Child Law of 2008, giving the principle "paramount priority in all decisions and measures taken or implemented concerning children." Despite the encouraging stipulation, the committee was concerned that the best interests principle "was not well understood and known among State authorities and civil servants and remains insufficiently integrated in policies, programs and decision-making processes." Finally, the committee criticized the categorical determinations of the dominant strand of premodern juristic discourse by saying that "when, in matters relating to custody of the child, the starting point for consideration is age, there is a risk that each child is not treated individually."[95]

The 2016 Child Custody Bill

The issue of child custody has once more become a subject of public debate after a bill was presented to Egypt's parliament in December 2016. If passed,

94 "Constitution of the Arab Republic of Egypt 2014" (www.sis.gov.eg), accessed July 7, 2016, www.sis.gov.eg/Newvr/Dustor-en001.pdf.

95 Committee on the Rights of the Child, "Concluding Observations of the Committee on the Rights of the Child: Egypt," *United Nations Convention on the Rights of the Child*, July 15, 2011, www.ohchr.org/EN/countries/MENARegion/Pages/EGIndex.aspx.

the new law would enable the noncustodial parent (usually fathers since mothers have custody until the child turns at least 15) to have the child sleep over at his or her home once or twice a week. In addition to the weekly sleepovers, the noncustodial parent would be entitled to having the child stay with them for a month during the summer break, a week during the midterm break, and half the feast (*ʿĪd*) vacations. The law would also criminalize refusal to hand over the child to the custodial parent by a jail term of three to twelve months. One of the most controversial stipulations of the law is that it changes the premodern Islamic order of priority of custodianship, moving the father up the line right behind the mother and above the maternal mother or aunt. Upon the mother's disqualification from custody by remarriage, the father would have custody rather than the mother's female relatives. No such stipulation exists for remarriage of the father in accordance with the dominant view of premodern jurists (although, as already noted, there was a minority position that assigned custody on a case-by-case basis). In line with the ubiquitous domesticity doctrine, the law requires the father in this event to have a female relative to take care of the child who would still be in the tender years. The law assumes that men are by nature incapable of taking care of children themselves and that women are inherently superior caretakers. These changes were rejected by many women, including a mother who told the BBC that sleepovers would be harmful to her and to the child because the father may take the child out of the country. Others argued that this piecemeal approach to child custody legislation is futile. Hiba Hajras, a member of the National Council for Women and a member of parliament, argued, "We need a completely new law based on a clear philosophy that privileges the best interests of the child (*al-Maṣlaḥa al-Fuḍlā li-ṭifl*)." She reasoned that the 1929 law is old and no amount of modification would fix its many problems.[96]

One guest on a popular Egyptian talk show argued that the disintegration of the family is the main cause of terrorism, citing two terrorists as children of divorced couples, including the terrorist behind the bombing of a church on December 11, 2016, which claimed the lives of 25 people. Without paying attention to the best interests of the child in our legislative

[96] Sally Nabil, "Ḥaḍānat Al-Aṭfāl Tuthīru Jadalan Fī Miṣr" (London: BBC, December 22, 2016), www.bbc.com/arabic/media-38404013; Aḥmad Salīm, "Limādhā Athāra Iqtirāḥ Taʿdīl Qānūn Al-Ḥaḍāna Fī Miṣr Kull Hādhā Al-Jadal?," *Raṣīf*, December 12, 2016, http://raseef22.com/life/2016/12/09/%D9%84%D9%85%D8%A7%D8%B0%D8%A7-%D8%A3%D8%AB%D8%A7%D8%B1-%D8%A7%D9%82%D8%AA%D8%B1%D8%A7%D8%AD-%D8%AA%D8%B9%D8%AF%D9%8A%D9%84-%D9%82%D8%A7%D9%86%D9%88%D9%86-%D8%A7%D9%84%D8%AD%D8%B6%D8%A7%D9%86%D8%A9/.

action, he argued, we would be creating terrorists and drug addicts, adding that 80 percent of drug addicts come from divorced families. Another argument he presented is that Egypt is bound by treaties such as the CRC, which it must respect, hence the need for new legislation on child custody. On the other side of the table of this loud argument, an opponent of the new bill objected to the stipulation that allows the father to host children for "sleepovers" (*istiḍāfa*) as opposed to mere "visits" (*ru'ya*) in public parks. He argued that sleepovers are not consistent with Islamic law. "Show me the word "*istiḍāfa*" in Sharīʿa!", he yelled.[97] He may be right that the word does not exist in the juristic discourse of Sharīʿa, but as already noted, some jurists did not oppose different forms of joint custody, arguably including sleepovers.

CONCLUSION

Child custody statutes in the twentieth century were drawn in two directions. The first was a certain notion of domesticity and the conjugal family that developed in the late nineteenth and early twentieth centuries, partly due to the influence of Euro-American discourses. The second was an emerging world order where a broad conception of the best interests of the child was entrenched in international conventions, which most Muslim states have ratified. Egypt has demonstrated a disorderly approach to dealing with the tension between the dominant premodern juristic discourse which has a narrow, negative approach to child welfare and the international standard of the best interests of the child (to say nothing of Egypt's praxeological legal history). Egyptian legislators have slowly broadened the boundaries of juristic discourse through statutes, the introduction of the social sciences into the courtroom, and the jurisprudence of higher courts, such as the Court of Cassation and the Supreme Constitutional Court. These combined forces have slowly chipped away at the categorical designations of child welfare among premodern Sunni jurists.

However, these efforts have not yet provided the type of judicial discretion expected by the CRC, as evidenced by the critiques of the

[97] Salīm, "Limādhā Athāra Iqtirāḥ Taʿdīl Qānūn Al-Ḥaḍāna Fī Miṣr Kull Hādhā Al-Jadal?"; Aḥmad Mūsā, "Khināqa ʿalā Al-Hawā' Bayna Ḍuyūf Aḥmad Mūsā Bi-Sabab Qānūn Ḥaḍānat Al-Aṭfāl" (Cairo, December 21, 2016), www.youtube.com/watch?v=IbJAh6E9R6Y; Aḥmad Farīd Mūsā, "Ḥalaqa Nāriyya ʿan Qānūn Al-Usra" (Cairo: al-Balad, December 20, 2016), www.youtube.com/watch?v=8IA5P6DNDao.

committee charged with observance. The hybridization of Islamic law and the Euro-American conjugal family ideal led to a child custody regime in twentieth-century Egypt that has become hard to challenge in a way similar to the hybridization of the "house of obedience" (*bayt al-ṭāʿa*), a hybrid of French and Islamic jurisprudence imported into Egypt via Algeria. Despite its partly French provenance, this institution was not abolished until much later than its abolition in France, as it had a life of its own in Egypt.[98] The hybridization of the conjugal family with Islamic juristic discourse in Egypt led to a strong regime of child custody based on strict female domesticity and a strong presumed bond between mother and child. This regime was organically hybridized with Islamic law through the work of early modernists such as Rifāʿa al-Ṭahṭāwī, Muḥammad ʿAbduh, Qāsim Amīn, ʿĀʾisha Taymūr, Zaynab Fawwāz, and Malak Hifnī Nāṣif, among others. The naturalization of the female domesticity discourse in Egyptian nationalist and Islamic modernist discourse enabled this ideology to have a lasting impact on modern Egyptian law. Despite the immense resources that can be found in premodern Islamic juristic discourse and practice, which could be mobilized to bring Islamic custody laws in full conformity with the CRC, Egypt's efforts have not yet been fully successful, due in my view to the absence of a process of naturalization similar to the one initiated by nationalists in the nineteenth century with respect to the domesticity ideology.

Egyptian social values about the domesticity of women and the centrality of their role to childrearing have themselves become the biggest obstacle to changing Egyptian legislation fully in order for it to conform with the CRC convention. But of course, reconciling Egyptian law with the CRC as part of Egypt's treaty obligations is not the objective of all those involved in the debate, as evidenced by the recent 2016 Child Custody Bill. Many voices claim that the dominant Islamic legal approach is superior to the CRC, hence the resistance to some of the reforms of child custody law. The new Euro-American discourses of gender equality and the removal of presumptions such as the tender years doctrine from state legislations in Euro-America have not succeeded in uprooting nineteenth-century and early twentieth-century Egyptian ideas about motherhood. This situation has left Egyptian legislators torn between the social ideology of female domesticity, which is still dominant in contemporary Egypt, and the legislative drive for a case-by-case best interests discourse that in theory flattens the gender bias in custody arrangements. The result has been piecemeal

[98] Cuno, *Modernizing Marriage*, 185–204.

legislation that has not fully satisfied the requirements of the CRC, but has maintained a link to social values of the cult of motherhood. This explains the tension that Egypt has experienced where legislators have granted judges increasing discretion in determining the child's welfare, while maintaining a presumptive categorical system of age determinations that are not tailored to individual children. This tension was best illustrated when Egyptian legislators started using the "best" (*fuḍlā*) interests of the child rather than continuing to use the "welfare of the child" (*maṣlaḥat al-walad*) as it had been used in Islamic juristic discourse for over a millennium to pay lip service to the CRC, while maintaining an age presumption.

Conclusion

In the first chapter, I discussed Euro-American approaches to child custody and guardianship to show the ways in which jurists from these legal traditions dealt with the main eight themes of this book (age and gender, the mother's marital status, lifestyle, religion, visitations, relocation with the ward, maintenance, and guardianship) as they relate to the child's welfare. Despite the multifarious nature of the Euro-American legal traditions' approach to child custody and guardianship, there were important parallels, especially with respect to their similar domesticity doctrine and their focus on treating the welfare of children on a case-by-case basis. The new family ideology, which traversed the entire colonial world, had a significant impact on modern Egypt. Equally influential was Euro-America's jurisprudence, which helped develop and support the concept of the best interests of the child and its entrenchment in international conventions, which Egypt signed and sought to accommodate in its national laws.

In order to address the eight themes in the Islamic legal tradition, I have relied on juristic discourse in the premodern period to find explicit discussions of whether custody is a right of the custodian or the child, as well as exploring the rationalizations advanced by jurists to justify their rules, especially as they relate to the child's welfare. I then compared the letter of the law with the actual practice of both Ottoman (1517–1801) and nineteenth- to twenty-first-century Egypt (1801–2014), addressing the main eight themes of this book as they relate to the welfare of the child through jurisprudence and statutes.

I have found that most reasons and justifications given by jurists for the choice of child custody rules were based on the child's welfare, in a narrow, negative sense, often associated both with gross abuse and considered to apply to all children as a category. The reason for the gross abuse choice of jurists, rather than a broader, positive best interests approach is that they wanted to balance the interests of the child against those of the custodian. Due to their interest in standardizing the rules of child custody and guardianship, these rules, albeit based on the child's welfare, were treated as categorical rules that applied to all children at all times, leaving little discretion to judges in assessing the individual needs of each child. This is particularly the case in the Ḥanafī and Mālikī schools in which child custody is transferred from mother to father at a certain age without soliciting the child's wishes. However, there were some rules that retained a focus on children as individuals – this is clear in the Shāfiʿī and Ḥanbalī schools' reliance on children's wishes in the determination of custody arrangements.

Both the child's choice of custodian at the age of seven in the Shāfiʿī school and the transfer of child custody from mother to father at the same age in the Ḥanafī school were justified in terms of the child's welfare. The first example, however, where the best interests of the child are determined by the child herself, corresponds to our modern values of the case-by-case approach of best interests, whereas the automatic transfer from mother to father in the Ḥanafī school does not. Despite the existence of some best interests rules in the age of *taqlīd*, that is, rules treating children on a case-by-case basis, the welfare of the child in mainstream juristic discourse was (1) defined negatively in the sense of avoidance of harm, rather than accruing benefit, and (2) based on categorical rules rather than treating children on a case-by-case basis.

Against this dominant discourse and the majority of custody and guardianship rules, another discourse coexisted with the mainstream view. Some elements of this discourse can be seen in the work of some early scholars such as Ibn ʿAbd al-Barr, but it was best articulated by Ibn Taymiyya and his student Ibn Qayyim al-Jawziyya, with the latter showing a deep concern for both social realities and the welfare of children and by extension their mothers. These maverick jurists challenged the two main assumptions of juristic discourse in the age of *taqlīd* by expanding the welfare discourse beyond harm to include the accrual of benefit and by treating children as individuals with varying needs. This approach naturally assumes that judges and perhaps families would have to fill in the space of discretion that would be taken over from the categorical rules of jurists.

What motivated these two scholars to devise such an approach? The answer to this question lies in their contextual and methodological approaches. Methodologically, this approach was the natural result of an anti-clerical attitude that often challenged the accretions of juristic discourses. It was also a pragmatic and realistic solution to observed social problems. A similar anti-clericalism and pragmatic jurisprudence led Ibn Taymiyya and Ibn Qayyim – notwithstanding important differences between them – to call for greater discretionary power for judges in matters of child custody and guardianship. This approach would later be adopted by some Ḥanafīs such as Ibn ʿĀbidīn, albeit without citing the views of Ibn Taymiyya and Ibn Qayyim. The two traditions of pursuing the categorical welfare of all children versus championing the individual welfare of a given child coexisted in juristic discourse well into the modern period.

Were the Mamluks and Ottomans influenced by the challenge leveled by Ibn Taymiyya and Ibn Qayyim to the rigid rules of child custody? Despite the dominance of the categorical, basic interests approach to child custody and guardianship in juristic discourse, the reality of court practice both in the Mamluk and Ottoman periods accommodated a different view of what constituted the welfare of the child, which was based not on the child's wishes but on a holistic view of what families thought was best for children and families together. As already noted in Chapter 1, the child's wishes (in many US jurisdictions for instance) and the parents' agreements (in the case of French law and in some US jurisdictions) have been both considered elements of what constitutes the child's best interests in the twentieth- and twenty-first centuries. In Ottoman-Egyptian society, the child's wishes were not considered representative of her or his best interests (more in line with Ḥanafī doctrine), but family agreements were considered in full conformity with the interests of children and parents. The judiciary did not give children any voice in their custody arrangements according to our sample, but it gave full discretion in managing the child's affairs to both families and judges, with the latter exercising oversight over such private agreements. When children were abused, judges annulled such agreements. Absent such abuse, these agreements were considered binding until the last quarter of the seventeenth century.

The pragmatic jurisprudence of Ibn Taymiyya and Ibn Qayyim and the pragmatic adjudication of the Mamluk and Ottoman judiciaries were meant to solve social problems and bring the law in conformity with dominant social values, or perhaps more precisely the values of the juristic class. In this monograph, I have shown another element of pragmatic adjudication, which went beyond pragmatic eclecticism by designing elements of lawmaking that were in reality not fully conceptualized by any school,[1] despite some overlaps with Mālikī jurisprudence. In a society where the child's wishes were generally not considered a reflection of her or his welfare and in which the child's welfare was tied more closely with private family agreements, private separation deeds were permitted by the judiciary as a way to achieve the child's interests. These agreements were widely practiced in Mamluk Egypt, with even jurists as far away from Egypt as al-Wansharīsī being fully aware of the prevalence of these types of agreements, which continued unhindered in the first one and a half centuries of Ottoman rule in Egypt.

These types of agreements were possible because many Mamluk and Ottoman-Egyptian women had waged jobs, as Rapoport rightly argued in the case of Mamluk women, enabling them a level of independence that both made divorce more frequent and allowed them to at once have custody and be free to move and remarry. Women who did not have the financial independence to finance their own freedom relied on their extended families to maneuver the legal system to gain custody and access to their children while remaining free to remarry and move; certainly, family power and influence in the residential quarter must have played a role in countering the power of patriarchy. Men who asserted their rights based on juristic discourse by refusing to enter into such agreements were able to gain custody of children once women moved away or remarried, yet in asserting their privileged status in these situations of remarriage and relocation, they had to grapple with power relations in their own quarters and pressure from the extended families, as well as conceptions of child welfare, wherein women were considered superior caregivers, especially in the first years of the child's life. Many members of Ottoman-Egyptian families were present at the proceedings of these agreements and acted as guarantors. Women sometimes gave up child maintenance payments in exchange for full custody and even guardianship rights, with their families being present and willing to support the children in the event of the mother's insolvency. Other women planned their marriages in such a way as to require future husbands to support their children and to obligate the new spouse to commit to having the children live with the

[1] I have shown elsewhere a way in which both the judiciary and author-jurists operating outside of the court context managed to accommodate social needs in the face of some of the more austere rules of author-jurists through allowing a flexible system of forum and doctrinal selection, what I have called elsewhere *pragmatic eclecticism*. Ibrahim, *Pragmatism in Islamic Law*, 2017; Ibrahim, "Al-Shaʿrānī's Response to Legal Purism."

new couple. Despite these avenues of flexibility and accommodation of the expectations of Egyptian, especially urban, women, author-juristic discourses were the last resort when the families were unable to reach such agreements, or were drawn upon when the welfare of the child was at risk.

It is not surprising that there was no judicial discussions of these agreements in Ottoman court records simply because it was a continuous practice with the Mamluk period, with scribes continuing business as usual when the Ottomans arrived. No disruption was made to the practice despite the brief Ottoman experiment with Ḥanafization. These agreements were notarized by Ḥanafī judges even though they were rejected by the sweeping majority of Ḥanafī jurists. Despite the Mālikī provenance of most of the rules associated with this type of agreement, there was no attempt to justify such practice in the court records along specifically Mālikī lines.

There was always strong Ḥanafī juristic opposition to the agreement type in which fathers gave up their future right to custody in the event that the mother remarried or moved away, on the grounds that these agreements were both based on a future right that could not be dropped and that the binding nature of these agreements contradicts the fact that child custody is a right of the child rather than the parents. This tension extended even in the Mālikī school where jurists were unable to reconcile their own law of obligations, which assumed that one cannot give up a right they do not have with these private separation deeds. Despite their awareness of the weakness and contradiction of their position, Mālikī jurists did not abolish this practice, nor did they manage to valorize it in juristic discourse; and the practice was allowed to stand in tension with both other areas of the Mālikī law of obligations and the majority of Sunni jurists.

While this practice was taking place in the courts, one could observe a strand of social practice that clearly rejected such agreements by insisting that children could stay with their mothers so long as they do not remarry, or so long as they do not move away. In fact, we even find some guardians trying to offer the female custodian some incentives to remain unmarried. This suggests that there was a growing social rejection of children living with their stepfathers and an assumption that mothers were better caregivers for children of a tender age. By the last quarter of seventeenth-century Egypt, private separation deeds which were not in line with Ḥanafī doctrine were no longer considered binding, and the stipulations suggesting their binding nature disappeared. The remarriage and travel type of agreements disappeared suddenly from our sample, and never again appeared in Egyptian courts. The judiciary had assumed that the child's interests enshrined in premodern juristic discourse could not be violated through private agreements. In fact, Art. 20 of Law No. 1 of 2000 clearly stipulates that any giving up of the right to custody or maintenance in a private separation agreement is null and void. An analogy to England can be illustrative. Private separation deeds, an important aspect of child custody law in early modern England, were considered not worth the ink with which they were written by 1820, since they challenged the father's absolute right.

No judicial decree dealt with this issue, although I found many other decrees dealing with other important public policy issues, such as the alienation of religious endowments, sentencing in absentia, and the division of estates. By not treating such agreements as binding, in line with Ḥanafī jurisprudence, the Ottoman judiciary effectively treated child custody as an issue of public policy, over which families had no discretion and in which author-juristic rules dominated. This strand of social practice coexisted with the Mamluk, Mālikī ethos of family autonomy, perhaps partly due to the influence of Turkish-speaking members of the new Ottoman-Egyptian elite that slowly dominated Egyptian society and politics throughout the sixteenth and seventeenth centuries. The hybridization of the Mamluk and Ottoman elites into one semi-coherent elite group must have slowly shifted the view among the middle and upper classes of Ottoman-Egyptian society in favor of the view more hostile to giving women such wide rights in separation deeds. This shift might have also been driven by the purist Kadizadelis, who were influential in Egypt in the seventeenth century, but in the absence of any central decree issued by the judiciary to ban these agreements, this issue remains puzzling.

Mamluk and Ottoman judges did not abide by narrow formalistic rules, but rather pragmatically navigated juristic discourse in such a way as to permit families, rather than children, to design agreements that in some cases were unthinkable even to the most permissive Mālikīs, where for instance a father lost both his custody and guardianship rights. Were some elements of Islamic substantive law an ideal doctrine for a not-so-ideal society, as Schacht has argued? Most scholars of Islamic law have rightly rejected this notion on the grounds that it implied legal rigidity and the lack of what one may call a jurisprudence of accommodation in Islamic law. One of the findings of this study is that accommodation of juristic discourse was not the only way that jurists envisioned the link between juristic discourse and practice. Some jurists in some historical contexts accepted varying levels of tensions between theory and practice. There was no attempt to offer justifications of both the notion of giving up a future right and of making such forfeiture binding in any of the Sunni schools, including the Mālikī school, despite the wide practice of these separation deeds. Such tensions and perhaps inconsistencies occurred in some parts of the vast literature of substantive law, especially in the realm of transactions (*muʿāmalāt*). In the realm of rituals, there were higher standards for the strict correlation between the theory and practice of the law, such as in the case of the permission of *talfīq* in order to accommodate ritualistic practices contradicting strict adherence to one school.[2]

However, there remained always unjustified, unaddressed areas of tension or outright incompatibility between juristic discourse and practice. Behnam Sadeghi has shown, for instance, that Ḥanafī jurists sometimes ignored inconsistencies in their school and at times it took them centuries to address them.[3] The tension between the dominant Ḥanafī perception of law and the counter practices, some of which were based on the Mālikī school, must have contributed to the silent demise of the most problematic of private separation deeds of the remarriage and travel type once the social forces that animated private separation deeds in the Mamluk period had been realigned.

ISLAMIC LAW AND THE STATE

Was the pragmatic adjudication of the Mamluk and Ottoman judiciaries part of the state's legal-social engineering? In order to answer this question, one has to think of the ways in which the Mamluk and Ottoman authorities through their *siyāsa* prerogative intervened in the legal process and the operation of the law. The secular authorities utilized two areas of *siyāsa*, namely (1) establishing legal procedure and (2) removing disagreement among the schools by choosing one opinion to be used in practice (*ḥukm al-ḥākim* [understood as both judge and ruler] *yarfaʿ al-khilāf*). These two approaches were utilized extensively both by Mamluk and Ottoman authorities, such as the Mamluk authorities' appointment of four chief judges and the restriction of judgment to the preponderant view of the school, as well as the Ottomans' jurisdictional restrictions, whether thematic (passing a judgment on someone in absentia) or relating to court hierarchy such as restricting certain cases to Cairo's court of al-Bāb al-ʿĀlī, al-Qisma al-ʿAskariyya, or al-Qisma al-ʿArabiyya in Ottoman Egypt. In addition to these largely procedural interventions, the Mamluk

[2] Ibrahim, *Pragmatism in Islamic Law*, 2017.
[3] Behnam Sadeghi, *The Logic of Law Making in Islam: Women and Prayer in the Legal Tradition* (Cambridge: Cambridge University Press, 2013), 80–124.

authorities established *siyāsa* courts with jurisdictions exceeding public policy-related issues. Rapoport has argued convincingly that these *siyāsa* courts were designed to bring into focus legal equity at the expense of the formalism of the Sharīʿa.[4]

These *siyāsa* courts were arguably similar to the equity courts of early modern England whose objective was to counter the rigidity and formalism of the Common Law. In addition to these Mamluk *siyāsa* courts, the Sharīʿa courts of both Mamluk and Ottoman Egypt, which were overseen by chief judges appointed by secular authorities, played a role in evading the formalism of juristic discourse in favor of more flexible arrangements that better suited Mamluk and later Ottoman-Egyptians. This was clear in the judicial practice of pragmatic eclecticism and the permission of private separation deeds under both polities. All these procedural, jurisdictional, and substantive interventions on the part of state authorities helped temper the formalism of the Sharīʿa. One cannot emphasize enough the importance of the state through its judiciary in legal engineering. Jurists may influence social customs (which often but not always overlap with their own values) by valorizing one social vision and rejecting another, pronouncing one as law and rejecting another as otherwise, as we saw with respect to the change in the status of private separation deeds. Despite the important role of jurists, it was the Mamluk and Ottoman states that decided through their judiciaries which social custom and which juristic opinion to be privileged in lawmaking.

MODERNITY

In nineteenth-century Egypt, the Ḥanafization policies of Mehmed Ali and his successors meant that the more flexible early modern system of child custody in Egypt was rendered more rigid. Judges had to follow the dominant doctrines of the Ḥanafī school. A grand mufti like al-Maḥdī, whose fatwas were binding on the judiciary, insured that the doctrines of the Ḥanafī school were closely followed by Egyptian judges. The rigidities of the Ḥanafī school conflicted with the emerging discourse of the conjugal family, where women were in charge of the rearing and

4 Rapoport, "Royal Justice and Religious Law: *Siyāsah* and Shariʿah under the Mamluks". On the role of the state in Islamic law, see further Stilt, *Islamic Law in Action*; Burak, *The Second Formation of Islamic Law*; Knut S. Vikør, *Between God and the Sultan: A History of Islamic Law* (Oxford: Oxford University Press, 2005); Sherman Jackson, *Islamic Law and the State: The Constitutional Jurisprudence of Shihāb Al-Dīn Al-Qarāfī* (Leiden; Boston, MA: Brill, 1996).

education of children. The limit of the age of seven for boys and nine for girls as practiced in nineteenth-century Egypt fell short of the needs of the new ideology of female domesticity, which was gaining ground in Egypt in the second half of the nineteenth century. More pragmatic judges, whose fatwas departed from the Ḥanafī school to accommodate some of the transformations of the nineteenth century, were put in check by al-Mahdī's fatwas. It was not until 1929 that legislative action was taken to increase the age at which children no longer need their mother by two years if the judge deemed it necessary. This change of law was based on a more individual approach to the welfare of the child. Successive statutes, the last of which was Law No. 4 of 2005, raised the age all the way to 15 for both boys and girls and allowed them to choose a custodial parent after that age. Interestingly, this was the first time in Egyptian law since 1517 that children's voices carried weight in Egyptian legislation, a sign of the influence of the best interests of the child as understood in international law following Egypt's ratification of the CRC, rather than a rediscovery of the Shāfiʿī or Ḥanbalī approaches to child custody.

In the same way Euro-American laws of child custody and guardianship evolved from a gross abuse, basic interests approach to granting the judge wide discretionary powers in assessing the best interests of each child on a case-by-case basis, Egyptian law in the twentieth century likewise developed through many statutes and Court of Cassation decisions. Egyptian legislators have been torn between categorical age determinations, which support the still dominant cult of motherhood (or the domestic ideology), and the best interests of the child discourse, which by definition rejects such categorical determinations. As a result, Egypt's many legislative actions in the past fifteen years have been a tight balancing act between the CRC, with its inherent international pressures, and the local assumptions about the centrality of mothers to child custody, the result of the nineteenth-century hybrid of female domesticity and Islamic conceptions of womanhood. While Egyptian legislators have maintained the categorical age system, they have given judges, children, and the public prosecutor greater discretionary power, as did the jurisprudence of the Court of Cassation and the Constitutional Court, paving the way for further decentering of premodern juristic discourses. Other statutes incorporated the social sciences into the courtroom, signaling an important shift to specialized expertise to influence the outcome of adjudication on child custody and guardianship on a case-by-case basis.

DOES THE ISLAMIC DISCURSIVE TRADITION INCLUDE COURT PRACTICES?

If we view Islamic law as a discursive tradition that contains both praxial and doctrinal elements as I suggested in the Introduction, we can argue that many of the pragmatic adjudicative solutions of Ottoman judges are part of the legacy of Islamic law, even if not fully valorized by author-jurists. The consistent utilization of private separation deeds for centuries, for instance, as well as the scribal practices and formularies associated with these agreements represent acts of valorization. The discretion granted to children, judges, and families in the discourses of author-jurists and the practices of Ottoman judges and scribes could be mobilized to create custody agreements tailored to each specific child. This could be achieved through a mix of mediation in which social workers and psychiatrists (as outlined by Law No. 10 of 2004), families, and judges oversee private separation deeds.[5] The reason that many Mālikīs accepted these practices even though they constituted tension or contradiction with their law of obligations was due to their utility and utilization in the courts. It is these court practices, which constitute judicial custom, upon which modern reformers can rely to reform modern child custody law to respond, for instance, to the opponent of the 2016 child custody bill who yelled on Egyptian TV, "Show me the word "*istiḍāfa*" in Sharīʿa!" It is often the case that cultural purists, such as this talk show guest, exaggerate cultural difference due in part to a lack of understanding of the complexity of the legacy of Islamic law both as juristic discourses and pragmatic court practices.

[5] Ibrahim, "Islamic Law as a Discursive Tradition"; Asad, *The Idea of an Anthropology of Islam*; Ahmed, *What Is Islam?*, 1–175.

Bibliography

Abramowicz, Sarah. "English Child Custody Law, 1660–1839: The Origins of Judicial Intervention in Paternal Custody." *Columbia Law Review* 99:5 (1999): 1344–1391.

Abū al-Faḍā'il, Ibn al-ʿAssāl al-Ṣafī. *Al-Majmūʿ Al-Ṣafawī*. Edited by Girgis Fīlūthaws ʿAwaḍ. 2 vols. Cairo, n.d.

Agmon, Iris. *Family & Court: Legal Culture and Modernity in Late Ottoman Palestine*. Syracuse, NY: Syracuse University Press, 2006.

Agrama, Hussein Ali. *Questioning Secularism: Islam, Sovereignty, and the Rule of Law in Modern Egypt*. Chicago, IL: University of Chicago Press, 2012.

Aḥmad, Fāṭima al-Zahrā' ʿAbbās, and Ḥilmī ʿAbd al-ʿAẓīm Ḥasan. *Qānūn Al-Aḥwāl Al-Shakhṣiyya Li'l-Muslimīn Wa'l-Qarārāt Al-Munaffidha Li-Aḥkāmih Wa-Baʿḍ Aḥkām Al-Maḥkama Al-Dustūriyya Al-ʿUlyā Al-Ṣādira Bi-Sha'nih*. Cairo: al-Maṭābiʿal-Amīriyya, 2009.

Ahmed, Shahab. *What Is Islam? The Importance of Being Islamic*. Princeton, NJ: Princeton University Press, 2015.

Akkach, Samer. *ʿAbd Al-Ghani Al-Nabulusi: Islam and the Enlightenment*. Oxford: Oneworld Publications, 2014.

Al-Ḥaṭṭāb al-Ruʿaynī, Abū ʿAbd Allāh Muḥammad al-Maghribī. *Mawāhib Al-Jalīl Li-Sharḥ Mukhtaṣar Khalīl*. Edited by Zakariyyā ʿUmayrāt. 8 vols. Beirut: Dār al-Kutub al-ʿIlmiyya, 1995.

Ali, Kecia. *Marriage and Slavery in Early Islam*. Cambridge, MA: Harvard University Press, 2010.

Alston, Philip. "The Best Interests Principle: Towards a Reconciliation of Culture and Human Rights." *International Journal of Law, Policy and the Family* 8:1 (1994): 1–25.

Alston, Philip, and UNICEF, and International Child Development Centre. *The Best Interests of the Child: Reconciling Culture and Human Rights*. Oxford; New York, NY: Clarendon Press; Oxford University Press, 1994.

Anjum, Ovamir. *Politics, Law and Community in Islamic Thought: The Taymiyyan Moment*. New York, NY: Cambridge University Press, 2012.

An-Na'im, Abdullahi. "Cultural Transformation and Normative Consensus on the Best Interests of the Child." *International Journal of Law, Policy and the Family* 8:1 (1994): 62–81.

ʿArnūs, Maḥmūd. "Baʿḍ Masāʾil Al-Ḥaḍāna." Edited by Muḥarram Fahīm. *Al-Muḥāmā Al-Sharʿiyya: Majalla Qaḍāʾiyya Shahriyya Al-Sana Al-Ūlā* 2:1 (1930): 5–11.

Asad, Talal. *The Idea of an Anthropology of Islam*. Washington, DC: Center for Contemporary Arab Studies, Georgetown University, 1986.

Astarūshinī, Muḥammad b. Maḥmūd b. al-Ḥusayn. *Aḥkām Al-Ṣighār*. Edited by Muṣṭafā Ṣumayda. Beirut: Dār al-Kutub al-ʿIlmiyya, 1997.

Asyūṭī, Shams al-Dīn Muḥammad b. Aḥmad al-Minhājī al-. *Jawāhir Al-ʿUqūd Wa-Muʿīn Al-Quḍāh Wa'l-Muwaqqiʿīna Wa'l-Shuhūd*. Edited by Musʿad ʿAbd al-Ḥamīd Muḥammad Saʿdanī. 2 vols. Beirut: Dār al-Kutub al-ʿIlmiyya, 1996.

Atçıl, Abdurrahman. *Scholars and Sultans in the Early Modern Ottoman Empire*. Cambridge: Cambridge University Press, 2016.

Bacon, Michael. *Pragmatism: An Introduction*. Cambridge; Malden, MA: Polity, 2012.

Badran, Margot. *Feminists, Islam, and Nation: Gender and the Making of Modern Egypt*. Princeton, NJ: Princeton University Press, 1995.

Baldwin, James. "Islamic Law in an Ottoman Context: Resolving Disputes in Late 17th/Early 18th-Century Cairo." PhD Dissertation, New York University, 2010.

Baldwin, James E. *Islamic Law and Empire in Ottoman Cairo*. Edinburgh: Edinburgh University Press, 2017.

Balkhī, Niẓām al-Dīn. *Al-Fatāwā Al-Hindiyya*. 2nd edn. Cairo: Al-Maṭbaʿa al-Kubrā al-Amīriyya, 1893.

Baron, Beth. "Islam, Philanthropy, and Political Culture in Interwar Egypt: The Activism of Labiba Ahmad." In *Poverty and Charity in Middle Eastern Contexts*. Edited by Michael David Bonner, Mine Ener, and Amy Singer. Albany, NY: State University of New York Press, 2003, 239–254.

——. "Orphans and Abandoned Children in Modern Egypt." In *Interpreting Welfare and Relief in the Middle East*. Leiden: Brill, 2008, 13–34.

——. *The Women's Awakening in Egypt: Culture, Society, and the Press*. New Haven, CT: Yale University Press, 1994.

Barrow, John Henry. *The Mirror of Parliament*. Longman, Brown, Green & Longmans, 1838.

Bashīr, Marwā al-. "Majmaʿ Al-Buḥūth Yaḥsim Al-Jadal: Qanūn Al-Ḥaḍāna Muṭābiq Li'l-Sharīʿa." *Al-Ahram Newspaper*. May 25, 2012. www.masress.com/ahram/151360.

Bayhaqī, Abū Bakr Aḥmad b. al-Ḥusayn b. ʿAlī. *Al-Sunan Al-Kubrā*. Edited by Muḥammad ʿAbd al-Qādir ʿAtā. 3rd edn. 11 vols. Dār al-Kutub al-ʿIlmiyya, 2003.

Bearman, P., T. Bianquis, C.E. Bosworth, E. van Donzel, and W.P. Heinrichs, eds. "Bāligh." *Encyclopaedia of Islam*. Leiden: Brill, 2013.

Bidelman, Patrick Kay. *Pariahs Stand Up!: The Founding of the Liberal Feminist Movement in France, 1858–1889*. Westport, CT: Greenwood Press, 1982.

Blakesley, Christopher. "Child Custody and Parental Authority in France, Louisiana and Other States of the United States: A Comparative Analysis." *Boston College International and Comparative Law Review* 4:2 (1981), 283–359. http://lawdigitalcommons.bc.edu/iclr/vol4/iss2/3.

Buhūtī, Manṣūr b. Yūnus b. Idrīs al-. *Sharḥ Muntahā Al-Irādāt Daqā'iq Ūlā Al-Nahy Li-Sharḥ Al-Muntahā*. Edited by ʿAbd Allāh b. ʿAbd al-Muḥsin al-Turkī. 7 vols. Beirut: Mu'assasat al-Risāla, 2000.

Burak, Guy. "Evidentiary Truth Claims, Imperial Registers, and the Ottoman Archive: Contending Legal Views of Archival and Record-Keeping Practices in Ottoman Greater Syria (Seventeenth-Nineteenth Centuries)." *Bulletin of the School of Oriental and African Studies* 79:2 (2016), 1–22.

——. *The Second Formation of Islamic Law: The Hanafi School in the Early Modern Ottoman Empire*. New York: Cambridge University Press, 2015.

Cardozo, Benjamin N. *The Nature of the Judicial Process*. New Haven, CT: Yale University Press, 1991.

Case No. 7 of 8th Judicial Year (Supreme Constitutional Court May 15, 1993).

"Case No. 15277 of 78th Judicial Year (Court of Cassation)." *Maḥkamat Al-Naqd: Majmūʿat Al-Aḥkām Al-Ṣādira Min Al-Hay'a Al-ʿĀmma Lil-Mawād Al-Madaniyya Wa-Min Al-Dawāir Al-Madaniyya*, 2009.

Committee on the Rights of the Child. "Concluding Observations of the Committee on the Rights of the Child: Egypt." *United Nations Convention on the Rights of the Child*, July 15, 2011. www.ohchr.org/EN/countries/MENARegion/Pages/EGIndex.aspx.

"Constitution of the Arab Republic of Egypt 2014." www.sis.gov.eg. Accessed July 7, 2016. www.sis.gov.eg/Newvr/Dustor-en001.pdf.

Coons, John E., and Robert H. Mnookin. "Toward a Theory of Children's Rights." In *The Child and the Courts*. Edited by Ian F.G Baxter and Mary A. Eberts. Toronto: Carswell Co., 1978.

Cooper, John M. *Reason and Human Good in Aristotle*. Cambridge, MA: Harvard University Press, 1975.

Cott, Nancy F. *The Bonds of Womanhood: "Woman's Sphere" in New England, 1780–1835*. New Haven, CT: Yale University Press, 1997.

Cotter, Thomas F. "Legal Pragmatism and Intellectual Property Law." In *Intellectual Property and the Common Law*. Edited by Shyamkrishna Balganesh. Cambridge: Cambridge University Press, 2013, 211–229.

——. "Legal Pragmatism and the Law and Economics Movement." *Georgetown Law Journal* 84:6 (1996): 2071–2142.

Coulson, Noel James. *A History of Islamic Law*. Edinburgh: Edinburgh University Press, 1962.

"Court of Al-Bāb Al-ʿĀlī, Sijill 1 (937/1530), Archival Code 1001–000001," Dār al-Wathā'iq al-Qawmiyya, Cairo.

"Court of Al-Bāb Al-ʿĀlī, Sijill 3 (939/1533), Archival Code 1001–000003," Dār al-Wathā'iq al-Qawmiyya, Cairo.

"Court of Al-Bāb Al-ʿĀlī, Sijill 55 (1000/1592), Archival Code 1001–000104," Dār al-Wathā'iq al-Qawmiyya, Cairo.

"Court of Al-Bāb Al-ʿĀlī, Sijill 293 (1190/1776), Archival Code 1001–000656," Dār al-Wathā'iq al-Qawmiyya, Cairo.

"Court of Al-Bāb Al-ʿĀlī, Sijill 311 (1202/1787–8), Archival Code 1001–000702," Dār al-Wathāʾiq al-Qawmiyya, Cairo.
"Court of Babay Al-Saʿāda Wa'l-Kharq, Sijill 1 (1050/1640), Archival Code 1011–000101," Dār al-Wathāʾiq al-Qawmiyya, Cairo.
"Court of Būlāq, Sijill 26 (1016/1607), Archival Code 1005–000101," Dār al-Wathāʾiq al-Qawmiyya, Cairo.
"Court of Būlāq, Sijill 64 (1130/1718), Archival Code 1005–000304," Dār al-Wathāʾiq al-Qawmiyya, Cairo.
"Court of Miṣr Al-Qadīma, Sijill 1 (934/1528), Archival Code 1006–000001," Dār al-Wathāʾiq al-Qawmiyya, Cairo.
"Court of Miṣr Al-Qadīma, Sijill 3 (950/1544), Archival Code 1006–000003," Dār al-Wathāʾiq al-Qawmiyya, Cairo.
"Court of Miṣr Al-Qadīma, Sijill 4 (955/1548), Archival Code 1006–000004," Dār al-Wathāʾiq al-Qawmiyya, Cairo.
"Court of Miṣr Al-Qadīma, Sijill 8 (971/1564), Archival Code 1006–000008," Dār al-Wathāʾiq al-Qawmiyya, Cairo.
"Court of Miṣr Al-Qadīma, Sijill 10 (978/1570), Archival Code 1006–000010," Dār al-Wathāʾiq al-Qawmiyya, Cairo.
"Court of Miṣr Al-Qadīma, Sijill 13 (991/1583), Archival Code 1006–000151," Dār al-Wathāʾiq al-Qawmiyya, Cairo.
"Court of Miṣr Al-Qadīma, Sijill 15 (1018/1609), Archival Code 1006–000153," Dār al-Wathāʾiq al-Qawmiyya, Cairo.
"Court of Miṣr Al-Qadīma, Sijill 16 (1025/1616), Archival Code 1006–000154," Dār al-Wathāʾiq al-Qawmiyya, Cairo.
"Court of Miṣr Al-Qadīma, Sijill 17 (1053/1643), Archival Code 1006–000155," Dār al-Wathāʾiq al-Qawmiyya, Cairo.
"Court of Miṣr Al-Qadīma, Sijill 18 (1057/1647), Archival Code 1006–000156," Dār al-Wathāʾiq al-Qawmiyya, Cairo.
"Court of Miṣr Al-Qadīma, Sijill 20 (1076/1665–6), Archival Code 1006–000158," Dār al-Wathāʾiq al-Qawmiyya, Cairo.
"Court of Miṣr Al-Qadīma, Sijill 21 (1081/1670), Archival Code 1006–000159," Dār al-Wathāʾiq al-Qawmiyya, Cairo.
"Court of Miṣr Al-Qadīma, Sijill 22 (1092–1681), Archival Code 1006–000160," Dār al-Wathāʾiq al-Qawmiyya, Cairo.
"Court of Miṣr Al-Qadīma, Sijill 31 (1217–1802), Archival Code 1006–000169," Dār al-Wathāʾiq al-Qawmiyya, Cairo.
"Court of Miṣr Al-Qadīma, Sijill 38 (1308–1887), Archival Code 1006–000176," Dār al-Wathāʾiq al-Qawmiyya, Cairo.
"Court of Miṣr Al-Sharʿiyya, Sijill 61 (1306/1895), Archival Code 1017–000160," Dār al-Wathāʾiq al-Qawmiyya, Cairo.
"Court of Miṣr Al-Sharʿiyya, Sijill 1146 (1253/1837), Archival Code 1017–004051," Dār al-Wathāʾiq al-Qawmiyya, Cairo.
"Court of Mudīriyyat Al-Gharbiyya (Ṭanṭā), Sijill 11 (1244/1828), Archival Code 1033–000011," Dār al-Wathāʾiq al-Qawmiyya, Cairo.
"Court of Mudīriyyat Al-Gharbiyya (Ṭanṭā), Sijill 14 (1250/1835), Archival Code 1033–000014," Dār al-Wathāʾiq al-Qawmiyya, Cairo.

"Court of Mudīriyyat Al-Gharbiyya (Ṭanṭā), Sijill 31 (1264/1848), Archival Code 1033–000031," Dār al-Wathā'iq al-Qawmiyya, Cairo.
"Court of Mudīriyyat Asyūṭ, Sijill 73 (1887), Archival Code 1139–000130," Dār al-Wathā'iq al-Qawmiyya, Cairo.
"Court of Qanāṭir Al-Sibā', Sijill 3 (961/1554), Archival Code 1007–000003," Dār al-Wathā'iq al-Qawmiyya, Cairo.
"Court of Qisma 'Arabiyya, Sijill 1 (968–9/1561), Archival Code 1004–000001," Dār al-Wathā'iq al-Qawmiyya, Cairo.
"Court of Qisma 'Arabiyya, Sijill 2 (970–1/1562–3), Archival Code 1004–000002," Dār al-Wathā'iq al-Qawmiyya, Cairo.
"Court of Qisma 'Arabiyya, Sijill 3 (973/1566), Archival Code 1004–000003," Dār al-Wathā'iq al-Qawmiyya, Cairo.
"Court of Qisma 'Arabiyya, Sijill 80 (1115/1704), Archival Code 1004–000405," Dār al-Wathā'iq al-Qawmiyya, Cairo.
"Court of Qisma 'Arabiyya, Sijill 140 (1206/1792), Archival Code 1004–000703," Dār al-Wathā'iq al-Qawmiyya, Cairo.
"Court of Qisma 'Askariyya, Sijill 1 (961/1554), Archival Code 1003–000001," Dār al-Wathā'iq al-Qawmiyya, Cairo.
"Court of Qisma 'Askariyya, Sijill 26 (1019/1610), Archival Code 1003–000105," Dār al-Wathā'iq al-Qawmiyya, Cairo.
"Court of Qisma 'Askariyya, Sijill 212 (1211/ 1796), Archival Code 1003–001009," Dār al-Wathā'iq al-Qawmiyya, Cairo.
"Court of Ṣāliḥiyya Al-Najmiyya, Sijill 3 (951/1544), Archival Code 1012–000003," Dār al-Wathā'iq al-Qawmiyya, Cairo.
Crecelius, Daniel. "Incidences of *Waqf* Cases in Three Cairo Courts: 1640–1802." *Journal of the Economic and Social History of the Orient* 29:2 (1986): 176–189.
Cuno, Kenneth M. "African Slaves in Nineteenth-Century Rural Egypt: A Preliminary Assessment." In *Race and Slavery in the Middle East: Histories of Trans-Saharan Africans in Nineteenth-Century Egypt, Sudan, and the Ottoman Mediterranean*. Edited by Terence Walz and Kenneth M. Cuno. Cairo: American University in Cairo Press, 2010, 77–98. http://search.ebscohost.com/login.aspx?direct=true&scope=site&db=nlebk&db=nlabk&AN=891298.
——. *Modernizing Marriage: Family, Ideology, and Law in Nineteenth and Early Twentieth Century Egypt*. Syracuse: Syracuse University Press, 2015.
——. "The Era of Muḥammad 'Alī." In *The Islamic World in the Age of Western Dominance: The New Cambridge History of Islam*. Edited by Francis Robinson. Cambridge; New York, NY: Cambridge University Press, 2010, 5:79–106.
Currie, James Muhammad Dawud. "Kadizadeli Ottoman Scholarship, Muḥammad Ibn 'abd Al-Wahhāb, and the Rise of the Saudi State." *Journal of Islamic Studies* 26: 3 (2015): 265–288.
Damīrī, Bahrām al-. *Al-Shāmil Fī Fiqh Al-Imām Mālik*. Edited by Aḥmad b. 'Abd al-Karīm Najīb. 2 vols. Cairo: Markaz Najībwayh li'l-Makhṭūṭāt wa-Khidmat al-Turāth, 2008.

Dār al-Iftā' al-Miṣriyya. *Al-Fatāwā Al-Islāmiyya Min Dār Al-Iftā' Al-Miṣriyya.* Cairo: Maṭba'at Dār al-Kutub wa'l-Wathā'iq al-Qawmiyya, 2012.

Dardīr, Abū al-Barakāt Aḥmad b. al-, and Aḥmad b. Muḥammad al-Ṣāwī. *Al-Sharḥ Al-Saghīr 'alā Aqrab Al-Masālik Ilā Madhhab Al-Imām Mālik.* Edited by Muṣṭafā Kamāl Waṣfī. Cairo: Muṣṭafā Kamāl, 1986.

Dasūqī, Shams al-Dīn Muḥammad b. 'Arafa al-. *Ḥāshiyat Al-Dasūqī 'alā Al-Sharḥ Al-Kabīr.* 4 vols. Cairo: Dār Iḥyā' al-Kutub al-'Arabiyya, 1984.

Dedek, Helge. "The Splendour of Form: Scholastic Jurisprudence and 'Irrational Formality'." *Law and Humanities* 5:2 (2011): 349–383.

Dewey, John. "Logical Method and Law." *Philosophical Review* 33: 6 (1924): 560–572.

Dupret, Baudouin. *Standing Trial: Law and the Person in the Modern Middle East.* London: I.B. Tauris, 2004.

Dworkin, Ronald. *Law's Empire.* Cambridge, MA: Belknap Press, 1986.

Eagleton, Terry. *Literary Theory: An Introduction.* Minneapolis, MN: University of Minnesota Press, 1983.

Eekelaar, John. "The Interests of the Child and the Child's Wishes: The Role of Dynamic Self-Determinism." *International Journal of Law, Policy and the Family* 8:1 (1994): 42–61.

El Alami, Dawoud S. "Law No. 100 of 1985 Amending Certain Provisions of Egypt's Personal Status Laws." *Islamic Law and Society* 1:1 (January 1994): 116–136.

Emery, Robert E. *Renegotiating Family Relationships: Divorce, Child Custody, and Mediation.* New York, NY: Guilford Press, 2012.

Ener, Mine. *Managing Egypt's Poor and the Politics of Benevolence, 1800–1952.* Princeton, NJ: Princeton University Press, 2003.

Engel, Barbara Alpern. *Breaking the Ties That Bound: The Politics of Marital Strife in Late Imperial Russia.* Ithaca: Cornell University Press, 2011.

Ergene, Boğaç A. *Local Court, Provincial Society, and Justice in the Ottoman Empire Legal Practice and Dispute Resolution in Çankırı and Kastamonu (1652–1744).* Leiden; Boston, MA: Brill, 2003.

Evans, Hugh Davey. *Maryland Common Law Practice: A Treatise on the Course of Proceeding in the Common Law Courts of the State of Maryland.* Baltimore, MD: J. Robinson, 1839.

Fadel, Mohammad. "The Social Logic of *Taqlīd* and the Rise of the *Mukhtaṣar.*" *Islamic Law and Society* 3:2 (1996): 193–233.

Fahīm, Muḥarram, ed. "Case No. 55 of 1929–30, Al-Manṣūra Sharia Court of First Instance." *Al-Muḥāmā Al-Shar'iyya: Majalla Qaḍā'iyya Shahriyya Al-Sana Al-Ūlā* 1:8 (1930): 644–738.

——. ed. "Iftitāḥiyyat Al-'Adad Al-Awwal Min Al-Sana Al-Thāniya." *Al-Muḥāmā Al-Shar'iyya: Majalla Qaḍā'iyya Shahriyya Al-Sana Al-Ūlā* 2:1 (October 1930): 1–4.

——. "Qawānīn Wa-Qarārāt Wa-Awāmir Wa-Manshūrāt." *Al-Muḥāmā Al-Shar'iyya: Majalla Qaḍā'iyya Shahriyya Al-Sana Al-Khāmisa Wa'l-'Ishrīn* 24:1 (1953), 126–127.

Fahmy, Khaled. *All the Pasha's Men: Mehmed Ali, His Army, and the Making of Modern Egypt.* Cairo; New York, NY American University in Cairo Press, 2002.

Farber, Daniel A. "Legal Pragmatism and the Constitution." *Minnesota Law Review* 72 (1987–1988): 1331–1387.

——. "The Inevitability of Practical Reason: Statutes, Formalism, and the Rule of Law." *Vanderbilt Law Review* 45 (1992): 533–559.

Faron, Olivier. "Father Child Relations in France: Changes in Paternal Authority in the Nineteenth and Twentieth Centuries." *The History of the Family* 6:3 (2001): 365–375.

Fish, Stanley. "Almost Pragmatism: Richard Posner's Jurisprudence." *The University of Chicago Law Review* 57:4 (1990): 1447–1475.

Flandrin, Jean-Louis. *Families in Former Times: Kinship, Household, and Sexuality in Early Modern France*. Cambridge; New York, NY: Cambridge University Press, 1979.

Fulchiron, Hugues. *Autorité parentale et parents désunis*. Paris: Editions du Centre national de la recherche scientifique, 1985.

——. "Custody and Separated Families: The Example of French Law." *Family Law Quarterly* 39:2 (2005): 301–313.

Gibbons, Jacqueline. "Orphanages in Egypt." *Journal of Asian and African Studies* 40:4 (2005): 261–285.

Giladi, A. "*Ṣaghīr.*" In *Encyclopaedia of Islam*. P. Bearman, T. Bianquis, C.E. Bosworth, E. van Donzel, and W.P. Heinrichs, eds. Leiden: Brill, 2013.

Giladi, Avner. *Children of Islam: Concepts of Childhood in Medieval Muslim Society*. New York, NY: St. Martin's Press, 1992.

——. *Infants, Parents and Wet Nurses: Medieval Islamic Views on Breastfeeding and Their Social Implications*. Leiden; Boston, MA: Brill, 1999.

Goldstein, Mark L. *Handbook of Child Custody*. Cham: Springer, 2015.

Gordon, Michael. *The American Family in Social-Historical Perspective*. New York, NY: St. Martin's Press, 1973.

Grossberg, Michael. *Governing the Hearth: Law and the Family in Nineteenth-Century America*. Chapel Hill, NC: University of North Carolina Press, 1985.

Gutas, Dimitri. *Greek Thought, Arabic Culture the Graeco-Arabic Translation Movement in Baghdad and Early 'Abbāsid Society (2nd–4th/8th–10th Centuries)*. London; New York, NY: Routledge, 1998.

"Ḥaḍānat Al-Aṭfāl." Cairo: National Council for Women, n.d. www.conference.ncwegypt.com/index.php/docsara/140-custody.

Ḥajjāwī, Sharaf al-Dīn Mūsā b. Sālim Abū al-Najā al-. *Al-Iqnā' Li-Ṭālib Al-Intifā'*. Edited by 'Abd Allāh b. 'Abd al-Muḥsin al-Turk. 3rd edn. Riyadh: Darat al-Malik 'Abd al-'Azīz, 2002.

Ḥalabī, Ibrāhīm b. Muḥammad b. Ibrāhīm al-, 'Abd al-Raḥmān b. Muḥammad b. Sulaymān al-Kalībūlī Dāmād Afandī, and Muḥammad b. 'Alī b. Muḥammad al-Ḥiṣnī al-Ḥaṣkafī. *Multaqā Al-Abḥur; Majma' Al-Anhur: Al-Durr Al-Muntaqā Fī Sharḥ Al-Multaqā*. 4 vols. Beirut: Dār al-Kutub al-'Ilmiyya, 1998.

Hale, William M. *Turkish Foreign Policy since 1774*. New York: Routledge, 2013.

Hallaq, Wael B. *Sharī'a: Theory, Practice, Transformations*. Cambridge, UK; New York, NY: Cambridge University Press, 2009.

——. "The *Qāḍī*'s *Dīwān* (*Sijill*) before the Ottomans." *Bulletin of the School of Oriental and African Studies* 61:3 (1998): 415–436.

Hanna, Nelly. "Marriage among Merchant Families in Seventeenth-Century Cairo." In *Women, the Family, and Divorce Laws in Islamic History*. Edited by Amira El Azhary Sonbol. Syracuse, NY: Syracuse University Press, 1996, 143–145.

Hart, H. L. A. *The Concept of Law*. Oxford: Clarendon Press, 1961.

Ḥaṣkafī, Muḥammad b. ʿAlī b. Muḥammad al-Ḥiṣnī al-, and Muḥammad b. ʿAbd Allāh b. Aḥmad al-Ghazzī al-Timurtāshī. *Al-Durr Al-Mukhtār Sharḥ Tanwīr Al-Abṣār Wa-Jāmiʿ Al-Biḥār*. Edited by ʿAbd al-Munʿim Khalīl Ibrāhīm. Beirut: Dār al-Kutub, 2002.

Hathaway, Jane. *The Arab Lands under Ottoman Rule, 1516–1800*. Harlow; New York, NY: Pearson Longman, 2008.

——. *The Politics of Households in Ottoman Egypt: The Rise of the Qazdağlis*. New York, NY: Cambridge University Press, 1997.

Haytamī, Ibn Ḥajar al-. *Al-Fatāwā Al-Kubrā Al-Fiqhiyya*. 4 vols. Cairo: ʿAbd al-Ḥamīd Aḥmad Ḥanafī, n.d.

Heyworth-Dunne, J. *An Introduction to the History of Education in Modern Egypt*. 2nd edn. London: Frank Cass and Company Limited, 1968.

Ḥillī, Abū al-Qāsim Najm al-Dīn Jaʿfar b. al-Ḥusayn al-Muḥaqqiq al-. *Sharāʾiʿ Al-Islām Fī Masāʾil Al-Ḥalāl Wa'l-Ḥarām*. Edited by Āyat Allāh al-Sayyid Ṣādiq al-Shīrāzī. 10th edn. Beirut: Markaz al-Rasūl al-Aʿẓam li'l-Taḥqīq wa'l-Nashr, 1998.

Hirschler, Konrad. "From Archive to Archival Practices: Rethinking the Preservation of Mamluk Administrative Documents." *Journal of the American Oriental Society* 136:1 (2016): 1–28.

Hoexter, Miriam. "*Qāḍī, Muftī* and Ruler: Their Roles in the Development of Islamic Law." In *Law, Custom, and Statute in the Muslim World*. Edited by Ron Shaham. Leiden: Brill, 2006, 67–85.

Holmes, Oliver Wendell. *The Common Law*. Boston, MA: Little, Brown, and Co., 1881.

Hookway, Christopher. *The Pragmatic Maxim: Essays on Peirce and Pragmatism*. Oxford: Oxford University Press, 2012.

Hunt, Margaret. *Women in Eighteenth Century Europe*. Abingdon: Routledge, 2014.

Hunter, F. Robert. *Egypt under the Khedives, 1805–1879: From Household Government to Modern Bureaucracy*. Pittsburgh, PA: University of Pittsburgh Press, 1984.

Ibn al-Ḥājib, Jamāl al-Dīn b. ʿUmar. *Jāmiʿ Al-Ummahāt*. Edited by Abū ʿAbd al-Raḥmān al-Akhḍar al-Akhḍarī. Damascus: Al-Yamāma, 1998.

Ibn Mufliḥ al-Maqdisī, Shams al-Dīn Muḥammad. *Kitāb Al-Furūʿ*. Edited by ʿAbd Allāh b. ʿAbd al-Muḥsin Turkī. 1st edn. Riyadh: Muʾassassat al-Risāla, 2003.

Ibn Qudāma al-Maqdisī, Muwaffaq al-Dīn. *Al-Mughnī*. Edited by Rāʾid b. Ṣabrī b. Abī ʿAlafa. Beirut: Bayt al-Afkār al-Dawliyya, 2004.

——. *ʿUmdat Al-Fiqh Fi'l-Madhhab Al-Ḥanbalī*. Edited by Aḥmad Muḥammad ʿAzzūz. Beirut: Al-Maktaba al-ʿAṣriyya, 2003.

Ibn Taymiyya, Taqī al-Dīn. *Majmū ʿ Fatāwā Shaykh Al-Islām Aḥmad Ibn Taymiyya*. Edited by ʿAbd al-Raḥmān b. Muḥammad Ibn Qāsim and Muḥammad b. ʿAbd al-Raḥmān b. Muḥammad Ibn Qāsim. 37 vols. Riyadh: Wizārat al-Shuʾūn al-Islāmiyya wa'l-Awqāf wa'l-Daʿwa wa'l-Irshād, 2004.

——. *Risāla Fī Taslīm Al-Bint Ilā Al-Abb Aw Al-Umm*. Edited by Saʿd al-Dīn b. Muḥammad al-Kibbī. Riyadh: Maktabat al-Maʿārif li'l-Nashr wa'l-Tawzīʿ, 2010.

Ibn ʿAbd al-Barr, Abū ʿUmar Yūsuf. *Al-Kāfī Fī Fiqh Ahl Al-Madīna Al-Mālikī*. 2nd edn. 1 vol. Beirut: Dār al-Kutub al-ʿIlmiyya, 1992.

Ibn ʿĀbidīn, Muḥammad Amīn. *Majmūʿat Rasāʾil Ibn ʿĀbidīn*. 2 vols. Beirut: Dār al-Kutub al-ʿIlmiyya, 2014.

Ibn ʿĀbidīn, Muḥammad Amīr b. ʿUmar, and Muḥammad b. ʿAlī b. Muḥammad al-Ḥiṣnī al-Ḥaṣkafī. *Radd Al-Muḥtār ʿalā Al-Durr Al-Mukhtār Sharḥ Tanwīr Al-Abṣār*. Edited by ʿĀdil Aḥmad ʿAbd al-Mawjūd, ʿAlī Muḥammad Muʿawwaḍ, and Muḥammad Bakr Ismāʿīl. 14 vols. Riyadh, Saudi Arabia: Dār ʿĀlam al-Kutub, 2003.

Ibrahim, Ahmed Fekry. "Al-Shaʿrānī's Response to Legal Purism: A Theory of Legal Pluralism." *Islamic Law and Society* 20:1–2 (2013): 110–140.

——. "Islamic Law as a Discursive Tradition." In *Sustainable Diversity in Law: Essays in Memory of H. Patrick Glenn*. Edited by Helge Dedek. Oxford: Oxford University Press, forthcoming.

——. *Pragmatism in Islamic Law: A Social and Intellectual History*. Syracuse: Syracuse University Press, 2015.

——. *Pragmatism in Islamic Law: A Social and Intellectual History*. 2nd edn. Syracuse: Syracuse University Press, 2017.

——. "Rethinking the *Taqlīd* Hegemony: An Institutional, *Longue-Durée* Approach." *Journal of the American Oriental Society* 136:4 (2016): 801–816.

——. "Rethinking the *Taqlīd-Ijtihād* Dichotomy: A Conceptual-Historical Approach." *Journal of the American Oriental Society* 136:2 (2016): 285–303.

——. "The Codification Episteme in Islamic Juristic Discourse between Inertia and Change." *Islamic Law and Society* 22:3 (2015): 157–220.

Ibyānī Bek, Muḥammad Zayn. *Sharḥ Al-Aḥkām Al-Sharʿīyya Fi'l-Aḥwāl Al-Shakhṣiyya*. 1st edn. Cairo: Maṭbaʿat al-Nahḍa, 1919.

İnalcık, Halil, and Donald Quataert. *An Economic and Social History of the Ottoman Empire, 1300–1914*. 2 vols. Cambridge: Cambridge University Press, 1994.

ʿĪsā, ʿAbd al-Rāziq. *Al-Marʾa Al-Miṣriyya Qabl Al-Ḥadātha Mukhtārāt Min Wathāʾiq Al-ʿAṣr Al-ʿUthmānī*. Cairo: Dār al-Kutub wa'l-Wathāʾiq al-Qawmiyya, 2012.

Ivanyi, Katharina Anna. "Virtue, Piety and the Law: A Study of Birgivi Mehmed Efendi's Al-Tariqa Al-Muhammadiyya," 2012. http://dataspace.princeton.edu/jspui/handle/88435/dsp015d86p0259.

Jabartī, ʿAbd al-Raḥmān b. Ḥasan al-. *ʿAjāʾib Al-Āthār Fi'l-Tarājim Wa'l-Akhbār*. Edited by ʿAbd al-Raḥīm ʿAbd al-Raḥmān ʿAbd al-Raḥīm. Cairo: Dār al-Kutub wa'l-Wathāʾiq al-Qawmiyya, 1998.

Jackson, Sherman. *Islamic Law and the State: The Constitutional Jurisprudence of Shihāb Al-Dīn Al-Qarāfī*. Leiden; Boston, MA: Brill, 1996.

——. "Kramer versus Kramer in a Tenth/Sixteenth Century Egyptian Court: Post-Formative Jurisprudence between Exigency and Law." *Islamic Law and Society* 8:1 (2001): 27–51.

——. "*Taqlīd*, Legal Scaffolding and the Scope of Legal Injunctions in Post-Formative Theory: *Muṭlaq* and *ʿĀmm* in the Jurisprudence of Shihāb Al-Dīn Al-Qarāfī." *Islamic Law and Society* 3:2 (1996): 165–192.

Jallād, Philip B. Yūsuf. *Qāmūs Al-Idāra Wa'l-Qaḍā'*. 3 vols. Cairo: Maṭbaʿat Dār al-Kutub wa'l-Wathā'iq al-Qawmiyya, 2003.

Jawziyya, Ibn Qayyim al-. *Iʿlām Al-Muwaqqiʿīn ʿan Rabb Al-ʿĀlamīn*. Edited by Abū ʿUbayda Mashhūr b. Ḥasan Āl Salmān and Abū ʿUmar Aḥmad ʿAbd Allāh Aḥmad. 7 vols. Riyadh: Dār Ibn al-Jawzī, 2002.

——. *Tuḥfat Al-Mawdūd Bi-Aḥkām Al-Mawlūd*. Edited by ʿUthmān b. Jumʿa Ḍumayriyya. Jedda: Dār ʿĀlam al-Fawā'id, 2010.

——. *Zād Al-Maʿād Fī Hudā Khayr Al-ʿIbād*. Edited by Shuʿayb al-Arna'ūṭ and ʿAbd al-Qādir al-Arna'ūṭ. 3rd edn. 6 vols. Beirut: Mu'assasat al-Risāla, 1998.

Johansen, Baber. "Formes de Langage et Fonctions Publiques: Stéréotypes, Témoins et Offices Dans La Preuve Par l'écrit En Droit Musulman." *Arabica* 44:3 (1997): 333–376.

——. "Signs as Evidence: The Doctrine of Ibn Taymiyya (1263–1328) and Ibn Qayyim Al-Jawziyya (d. 1351) on Proof." *Islamic Law and Society* 9:2 (2002): 168–193.

Jumʿa, ʿAlī. *Al-Fatāwā Al-Islāmiyya Min Dār Al-Iftā' Al-Miṣriyya*. Cairo: Maṭbaʿat Dār al-Kutub wa'l-Wathā'iq al-Qawmiyya, 2010.

Kaplan, Y.S. "Child Custody in Jewish Law: From Authority of the Father to the Best Interest of the Child." *Journal of Law and Religion* 24:1 (2009): 89–122.

Kāsānī, Alā' al-Dīn al-. *Badā'iʿ Al-Ṣanā'iʿ Fī Tartīb Al-Sharā'iʿ*. Edited by ʿAlī Muḥammad Muʿawwaḍ and ʿĀdil Aḥmad ʿAbd al-Mawjūd. 2nd edn. 10 vols. Beirut: Dār al-Kutub al-ʿIlmiyya, 2003.

Kennedy, Duncan. "Form and Substance in Private Law Adjudication." *Harvard Law Review* 89:8 (1976): 1685–1778.

Kholoussy, Hanan. *For Better, For Worse: The Marriage Crisis That Made Modern Egypt*. Stanford, CA: Stanford University Press, 2010.

Klapisch-Zuber, Christiane. *Women, Family, and Ritual in Renaissance Italy*. Chicago, IL: University of Chicago Press, 1985.

Klinck, Dennis R. *Conscience, Equity and the Court of Chancery in Early Modern England*. Surrey: Ashgate, 2010.

Kramer, Matthew H. "The Philosopher-Judge: Some Friendly Criticisms of Richard Posner's Jurisprudence." *The Modern Law Review* 59:3 (1996): 465–478.

"Law No. 1 (2000)." *Al-Jarīda Al-Rasmiyya* 4:2 (January 29, 2000): 2–30.

"Law No. 4 (2005) Amending Art. 20 of Decree-Law No. 25 of 1920." *Al-Jarīda Al-Rasmiyya* 9:2 (March 8, 2005): 3.

"Law No. 10 (2004) Promulgating the Law on the Establishment of the Family Courts." *Al-Jarīda Al-Rasmiyya* 12:2 (March 18, 2004): 3–9.

"Law No. 13 (1968) of Civil and Commercial Procedure." *Al-Jarīda Al-Rasmiyya*, n.d.
"Law No. 25 (1920) Concerning Maintenance and Certain Matters of Personal Status." *Al-Jarīda Al-Rasmiyya*, July 15, 1920.
"Law No. 25 (1929)." *Al-Jarīda Al-Rasmiyya* 27 (March 25, 1929): 203–219.
"Law No. 44 (1979) Amending Some of the Rules of Personal Status Law." *Al-Jarīda Al-Rasmiyya* 25:2 (June 21, 1979): 1–4.
"Law No. 100 (1985) Amending Certain Provisions of Egypt's Personal Status Laws." *Al-Jarīda Al-Rasmiyya* 27 (July 4, 1985), 4–11.
"Law No. 119 (1952) Governing Guardianship over Property." *Al-Waqā'i' Al-Miṣriyya*, August 4, 1952, 12–15.
"Law No. 126 (2008)." *Al-Jarīda Al-Rasmiyya* 24:2 (June 15, 2008): 2–27.
Layish, Aharon. *Divorce in the Libyan Family: A Study Based on the Sijills of the Sharīʿa Courts of Ajdābiyya and Kufra*. New York, NY; Jerusalem: New York University Press; Magnes Press, the Hebrew University, 1991.
Levit, Nancy. "Practically Unreasonable – A Critique of Practical Reason: A Review of the Problems of Jurisprudence by Richard A. Posner." *Northwestern University Law Review* 85:2 (1991): 494–518.
Libson, Gideon. *Jewish and Islamic Law: A Comparative Study of Custom during the Geonic Period*. Cambridge, MA; London: Harvard University Press, 2003.
Lieberman, Victor B. *Strange Parallels: Southeast Asia in Global Context, c 800–1830: Volume 2 Mainland Mirrors: Europe, Japan, China, South Asia, and the Islands*. New York, NY: Cambridge University Press, 2013.
Linant De Bellefonds, Yvon. "Ḥaḍāna." In Encyclopaedia of Islam. Edited by P. Bearman, Th. Bianquis, C.E. Bosworth, E. van Donzel, and W.P. Heinrichs. Leiden: Brill, 2005.
——. *Traité de Droit Musulman Comparé*. Paris, LaHaye: Mouton et Cie, 1965.
Mahdī, Muḥammad al-ʿAbbāsī al-. *Al-Fatāwā Al-Mahdiyya Fi'l-Waqā'iʿ Al-Miṣriyya*. 1st edn. Cairo: al-Maṭbaʿa al-Azharīyya al-Miṣriyya, 1883.
Mahmood, Saba. *Religious Difference in a Secular Age: A Minority Report*. Princeton, NJ: Princeton University Press, 2015.
Maidment, Susan. *Child Custody and Divorce: The Law in Social Context*. Croom: Helm, 1985.
Mainardi, Patricia. *Husbands, Wives, and Lovers: Marriage and Its Discontents in Nineteenth-Century France*. New Haven, CT: Yale University Press, 2003.
Mardāwī, ʿAlāʾ al-Dīn Abū al-Ḥasan ʿAlī b. Sulaymān al-. *Al-Inṣāf Fī Maʿrifat Al-Rājiḥ Min Al-Khilāf*. Edited by Rāʾid b. Ṣabrī Ibn Abī ʿAlfa. 2 vols. Beirut: Bayt al-Afkār al-Dawliyya, 2004.
Margolis, Maxine L. *Mothers and Such: Views of American Women and Why They Changed*. Berkeley, CA: University of California Press, 1984.
Mason, Mary Ann. *From Father's Property to Children's Rights: The History of Child Custody in the United States*. New York, NY: Columbia University Press, 1994.
Massad, Joseph A. *Desiring Arabs*. Chicago, IL: University of Chicago Press, 2008.
Matthews, Glenna. *"Just a Housewife": The Rise and Fall of Domesticity in America*. New York, NY: Oxford University Press, 1987.

Māwardī, Abū Ḥasan ʿAlī al-.*Al-Ḥāwī Al-Kabīr*. Edited by Maḥmūd Maṭrajī, Yāsīn Nāṣir Maḥmūd al-Khaṭīb, ʿAbd al-Raḥmān Shumayla al-Ahdal, Ḥasan ʿAlī Kūrkūlū, and Aḥmad Ḥājj Muḥammad Shaykh Māḥī. 22 vols. Beirut: Dār al-Fikr, 1994.

Meriwether, Margaret L. "The Rights of Children and the Responsibilities of Women: Women as Wasis in Ottoman Aleppo, 1770–1840." In *Women, the Family, and Divorce Laws in Islamic History*. Edited by Amira El Azhary Sonbol. Syracuse, NY: Syracuse University Press, 1996, 219–235.

Miṣrī, Ibn Nujaym Zayn al-Dīn al-, Abū al-Barakāt ʿAbd Allāh Ḥāfiẓ al-Dīn al-Nasafī, and Muḥammad Amīn Ibn ʿĀbidīn. *Al-Baḥr Al-Rāʾiq Sharḥ Kanz Al-Daqāʾiq Wa-Maʿahu Al-Ḥawāshī Al-Musammāh Minḥat Al-Khāliq ʿalā Al-Baḥr Al-Rāʾiq*. Edited by Zakariyyā ʿUmayrāt. 9 vols. Beirut: Dār al-Kutub al-ʿIlmiyya, 1997.

Mitchell, Timothy. *Colonising Egypt*. Cambridge; New York, NY: Cambridge University Press, 1988.

Morris, Rosalind C, and Gayatri Chakravorty Spivak. *Can the Subaltern Speak? Reflections on the History of an Idea*. New York, NY: Columbia University Press, 2010.

Murphy, John P. *Pragmatism: From Peirce to Davidson*. Boulder, CO: Westview Press, 1990.

Mūsā, Aḥmad. "Khināqa ʿalā Al-Hawāʾ Bayna Ḍuyūf Aḥmad Mūsā Bi-Sabab Qānūn Ḥaḍānit Al-Aṭfāl." Cairo, December 21, 2016. www.youtube.com/watch?v=IbJAh6E9R6Y.

Mūsā, Aḥmad Farīd. "Ḥalaqa Nāriyya ʿan Qānūn Al-Usra." Cairo: al-Balad, December 20, 2016. www.youtube.com/watch?v=8IA5P6DNDao.

Nabil, Sally. "Ḥaḍānat Al-Aṭfāl Tuthīru Jadalan Fī Miṣr." London: BBC, December 22, 2016. www.bbc.com/arabic/media-38404013.

Nawawī, Muḥyī al-Dīn Abū Zakariyyā al-. *Rawḍat Al-Ṭālibīn*. Edited by Zuhayr al-Shāwīsh. 12 vols. Beirut: Maktab al-Islāmī, 1991.

Niqābat al-Muḥāmiyyīn al-Sharʿiyīn. "Case No. 55 of 1929–1930 (Manṣūra Sharia Court of First Instance)." Edited by Muḥarram Fahīm. *Al-Muḥāmā Al-Sharʿiyya: Majalla Qaḍāʾiyya Shahriyya Al-Sana Al-Ūlā* 1:8 (1929): 698–701.

——. "Case No. 58 of 1946–47 (Asyūt Sharia Court of Summary Justice)." *Al-Muḥāmā Al-Sharʿiyya: Majalla Qaḍāʾiyya Shahriyya Al-Sana Al-Khāmisa Wa'l-ʿIshrīn* 20:1 (1948–1949): 205–207.

——. "Case No. 79 of 1929–1930 (Sharia Summary Court of Damietta)." Edited by Muḥarram Fahīm. *Al-Muḥāmā Al-Sharʿiyya: Majalla Qaḍāʾiyya Shahriyya Al-Sana Al-Ūlā* 1:6 (1929): 537–538.

——. "Case No. 220 of 1954 (Miṣr Al-Jadīda Court of Summary Justice)." *Al-Muḥāmā Al-Sharʿiyya: Majalla Qaḍāʾiyya Shahriyya Al-Sana Al-Khāmisa Wa'l-ʿIshrīn* 25:4 (1954): 304–305.

——. "Case No. 272 of 1929–1930 (Miṣr Sharia Court of First Instance)." Edited by Muḥarram Fahīm. *Al-Muḥāmā Al-Sharʿiyya: Majalla Qaḍāʾiyya Shahriyya Al-Sana Al-Ūlā* 1:5 (1929): 417.

——. "Case No. 283 of 1954 (Wāylī Court of Summary Justice)." *Al-Muḥāmā Al-Shar'iyya: Majalla Qaḍā'iyya Shahriyya Al-Sana Al-Khāmisa Wa'l-'Ishrīn* 25:7 (1954): 453–459.

——. "Case No. 288 of 1954 (Sayyida Zaynab Court of Summary Justice)." *Al-Muḥāmā Al-Shar'iyya: Majalla Qaḍā'iyya Shahriyya Al-Sana Al-Khāmisa Wa'l-'Ishrīn* 25:1 (1954): 111–112.

——. "Case No. 295 of 1948 ('Aṭṭārīn Court of Summary Justice)." *Al-Muḥāmā Al-Shar'iyya: Majalla Qaḍā'iyya Shahriyya Al-Sana Al-Khāmisa Wa'l-'Ishrīn* 25:1 (1954): 99–105.

——. "Case No. 391 of 1928–1929 (Sharia Court of Shabrakhīt)." Edited by Muḥarram Fahīm. *Al-Muḥāmā Al-Shar'iyya: Majalla Qaḍā'iyya Shahriyya Al-Sana Al-Ūlā* 1:4 (1929): 325.

——. "Case No. 547 of 1922–1923 (Miṣr Sharia Court of Summary Justice)." Edited by Muḥarram Fahīm. *Al-Muḥāmā Al-Shar'iyya: Majalla Qaḍā'iyya Shahriyya Al-Sana Al-Ūlā* 1:5 (1929):418–419.

——. "Case No. 660 of 1945–1946 (Al-Minyā Sharia Court of Summary Justice)." *Al-Muḥāmā Al-Shar'iyya: Majalla Qaḍā'iyya Shahriyya Al-Sana Al-Khāmisa Wa'l-'Ishrīn* 25:1 (1954): 76–78.

——. "Case No. 812 of 1943–44 (The Aqṣur Court of Summary Justice)." *Al-Muḥāmā Al-Shar'iyya: Majalla Qaḍā'iyya Shahriyya Al-Sana Al-Khāmisa Wa'l-'Ishrīn* 16:9–10 (1944): 250–251.

——. "Case No. 861 of 1954 (Sanballāwīn Court of Summary Justice)." *Al-Muḥāmā Al-Shar'iyya: Majalla Qaḍā'iyya Shahriyya Al-Sana Al-Khāmisa Wa'l-'Ishrīn* 25:7 (1954): 448–450.

——. "Case No. 1025 of 1928–9 (Al-Labbān Court of Summary Justice)." Edited by Muḥarram Fahīm. *Al-Muḥāmā Al-Shar'iyya: Majalla Qaḍā'iyya Shahriyya Al-Sana Al-Ūlā*, 1929, 714–715.

——. "Case No. 1069 of 1934–35 (Miṣr Sharia Court of First Instance)." *Al-Muḥāmā Al-Shar'iyya: Majalla Qaḍā'iyya Shahriyya Al-Sana Al-Khāmisa Wa'l-'Ishrīn* 8:1 (1936–1937): 195–198.

——. "Case No. 1182 of 1946–47 (Asyūt Sharia Court of Summary Justice)." *Al-Muḥāmā Al-Shar'iyya: Majalla Qaḍā'iyya Shahriyya Al-Sana Al-Khāmisa Wa'l-'Ishrīn* 20:1 (1948–1949): 89–91.

——. "Case No. 1239 of 1928–9 (The Jamāliyya Court of Summary Justice)." Edited by Muḥarram Fahīm. *Al-Muḥāmā Al-Shar'iyya: Majalla Qaḍā'iyya Shahriyya Al-Sana Al-Ūlā* 1:2 (1929): 320–321.

——. "Case No. 1449 of 1949–40 (Shubra Sharia Court of Summary Justice)." Edited by 'Abd al-Razzāq al-Qāḍī. *Al-Muḥāmā Al-Shar'iyya: Majalla Qaḍā'iyya Shahriyya Al-Sana Al-Khāmisa Wa'l-'Ishrīn* 11:1 (1939–1940): 128–129.

——. "Case No. 1811 of 1952 (Mīt Ghamra Court of Summary Justice)." *Al-Muḥāmā Al-Shar'iyya: Majalla Qaḍā'iyya Shahriyya Al-Sana Al-Khāmisa Wa'l-'Ishrīn* 25:1 (1954): 80–82.

——. "Case No. 1888 of 1928–1929 (The Azbakiyya Court of Summary Justice)." Edited by Muḥarram Fahīm. *Al-Muḥāmā Al-Shar'iyya: Majalla Qaḍā'iyya Shahriyya Al-Sana Al-Ūlā* 1:4 (1929): 321–323.

——. "Case No. 2528 of 1928–9 (The Azbakiyya Court of Summary Justice)." Edited by Muḥarram Fahīm. *Al-Muḥāmā Al-Shar'iyya: Majalla Qaḍā'iyya Shahriyya Al-Sana Al-Ūlā* 1:6 (1929): 521–522.

——. "Case No. 3102 of 1951 (Sayyida Zaynab Sharia Court of Summary Justice)." *Al-Muḥāmā Al-Shar'iyya: Majalla Qaḍā'iyya Shahriyya Al-Sana Al-Khāmisa Wa'l-'Ishrīn* 24:1 (1953): 106–109.

Niqābat al-Muḥāmiyyīn al-Shar'iyīn, and 'Abd al-Razzāq al-Qāḍī. "Case No. 2037 of 1937 (Miṣr Sharia Court of First Instance)." *Al-Muḥāmā Al-Shar'iyya: Majalla Qaḍā'iyya Shahriyya Al-Sana Al-Khāmisa Wa'l-'Ishrīn* 11:2 (1939): 67–68.

Oliphant, Robert E., and Nancy Ver Steegh. *Family Law.* New York: Aspen Publishers Online, 2007.

Sheikh, Mustapha. *Ottoman Puritanism and Its Discontents: Ahmad Al-Aqhisari and the Qadizadelis.* Oxford, New York, NY: Oxford University Press, 2017.

Owen, Roger. *Cotton and the Egyptian Economy, 1820–1914: A Study in Trade and Development.* Oxford: Clarendon Press, 1969.

Parker, Stephen. "The Best Interests of the Child – Principles and Problems." *International Journal of Law, Policy and the Family* 8:1 (1994): 26–41.

Peirce, Leslie P. *Morality Tales Law and Gender in the Ottoman Court of Aintab.* Berkeley, CA: University of California Press, 2003.

Peters, Rudolph. "Muḥammad Al-'Abbāsī Al-Mahdī (D. 1897), Grand Muftī of Egypt, and His 'Al-Fatāwā Al-Mahdiyya.'" *Islamic Law and Society* 1:1 (1994): 66–82.

——. "The Battered Dervishes of Bab Zuwayla: A Religious Riot in Eighteenth-Century Cairo." In *Eighteenth Century Renewal and Reform in Islam.* Edited by Nehemia Levtzion and John Voll. Syracuse, NY: Syracuse University Press, 1987, 66–82.

——. "What Does It Mean to Be an Official Madhhab?" In *The Islamic School of Law: Evolution, Devolution, and Progress.* Edited by Peri Bearman, Rudolph Peters, and Frank E Vogel. Cambridge, MA: Harvard University Press, 2005, 149–152.

Posner, Richard A. *Overcoming Law.* Cambridge, MA: Harvard University Press, 1995.

——. "Pragmatic Adjudication." *Cardozo Law Review* 18 (1996–1997): 1–20.

——. *The Problematics of Moral and Legal Theory.* Cambridge, MA: Belknap Press of Harvard University Press, 1999.

——. *The Problems of Jurisprudence.* Cambridge, MA: Harvard University Press, 1990.

Pruett, Marsha Kleine, and Carrie Barker. *The Scientific Basis of Child Custody Decisions.* Edited by Robert M Galatzer-Levy, Louis Kraus, and Jeanne Galatzer-Levy. Hoboken, NJ: Wiley, 2009.

Putnam, Ruth Anna. "Justice in Context." *Southern California Law Review* 63 (1990 1989): 1797–1810.

——. "Taking Pragmatism Seriously." In *Hilary Putnam: Pragmatism and Realism.* Edited by James Contant and Urszula M. Żegleń. London; New York, NY: Routledge, 2002, 7–11.

Qādirī, Muḥammad b. Ḥussain b. ʿAlī al-Ṭūrī al-. *Takmilat Al-Baḥr Al-Rāʾiq Sharḥ Kanz Al-Daqāʾiq*. Edited by Zakariyyā ʿUmayrāt. Beirut: Dār al-Kutub al-ʿIlmiyya, 1997.

Qarāfī, Badr al-Dīn Muḥammad b. Yaḥyā al-. "*Taḥqīq Al-Ibāna Fī Ṣiḥḥat Isqāṭ Mā Lam Yajib Min Al-Ḥaḍāna*." In *Min Khizānat Al-Madhhab Al-Mālikī*. Edited by Jalāl ʿAlī al-Qadhdhāfī. Beirut: Dār Ibn Ḥazm, 2006, 349–428.

——. "Qatar Family Law No. 22 (2006)." *Official Gazette* 8 (August 28, 2006): 31–99.

Rapoport, Yossef. *Marriage, Money and Divorce in Medieval Islamic Society*. Cambridge: Cambridge University Press, 2005.

——. "Royal Justice and Religious Law: *Siyāsah* and Shariʿah under the Mamluks." *Mamluk Studies Review* 16 (2012): 71–102.

Rescher, Nicholas. *Realistic Pragmatism: An Introduction to Pragmatic Philosophy*. Albany, NY: State University of New York Press, 2000.

Rorty, Richard. *Consequences of Pragmatism: Essays, 1972–1980*. Minneapolis, MN: University of Minnesota Press, 1982.

——. "The Banality of Pragmatism and the Poetry of Justice." *Southern California Law Review* 63 (1989–1990): 1811–1819.

Rosen, David M. "American Families and American Law." In *Handbook of Marriage and the Family*. Edited by Marvin B. Sussman, Suzanne K. Steinmetz, and Gary W. Peterson, 2nd edn. New York, NY: Springer Science & Business Media, 2013, 553–570.

Rubellin-Devichi, Jacqueline. "The Best Interests Principle in French Law and Practice." *International Journal of Law, Policy and the Family* 8:2 (August 1, 1994): 259–280.

Sadeghi, Behnam. *The Logic of Law Making in Islam: Women and Prayer in the Legal Tradition*. Cambridge: Cambridge University Press, 2013.

Saḥnūn b. Saʿīd al-Tanūkhī. *Al-Mudawwana Al-Kubrā*. 4 vols. Beirut: Dār al-Kutub al-ʿIlmiyya, 1994.

Salīm, Aḥmad. "Limādhā Athāra Iqtirāḥ Taʿdīl Qānūn Al-Ḥaḍāna Fī Miṣr Kull Hādhā Al-Jadal?" *Raṣīf*. December 12, 2016. http://raseef22.com/life/2016/12/09/%D9%84%D9%85%D8%A7%D8%B0%D8%A7-%D8%A3%D8%AB%D8%A7%D8%B1-%D8%A7%D9%82%D8%AA%D8%B1%D8%A7%D8%AD-%D8%AA%D8%B9%D8%AF%D9%8A%D9%84-%D9%82%D8%A7%D9%86%D9%88%D9%86-%D8%A7%D9%84%D8%AD%D8%B6%D8%A7%D9%86%D8%A9/.

Salīm, ʿAbd al-Wahhāb. "Yajib Ilghāʾ Al-Majālis Al-Ḥasbiyya Wa-Ḍamm Ikhtiṣāṣihā Ilā Al-Maḥākim Al-Sharʿiyya: Iqtirāḥ ʿalā Maʿālī Wazīr Al-Ḥaqqāniyya." *Al-Muḥāmā Al-Sharʿiyya: Majalla Qaḍāʾiyya Shahriyya Al-Sana Al-Ūlā* 2:1 (1930): 225–226.

Sarakhsī, Shams al-Dīn al-. *Al-Mabsūṭ*. 30 vols. Beirut: Dār al-Maʿrifa, 1993.

Sayyid-Marsot, Afaf Lutfi. *Women and Men in Late Eighteenth-Century Egypt*. Austin, TX: University of Texas Press, 1995.

Schacht, Joseph. *An Introduction to Islamic Law*. Oxford [Oxfordshire]; New York, NY: Clarendon Press, 1964.

Shāfiʿī, Muḥammad b. Idrīs al-. *Al-Umm*. Edited by Rifʿat Fawzī ʿAbd al-Muṭṭalib. 11 vols. Manṣūra: Dār al-Wafāʾ, 2001.

Shaham, Ron. *Family and the Courts in Modern Egypt: A Study Based on Decisions by the Sharīʿa Courts, 1900–1955*. Leiden; Boston, MA: Brill, 1997.

Shakry, Omnia. "Schooled Mothers and Structured Play: Child Rearing in Turn-of-the-Century Egypt." In *Remaking Women: Feminism and Modernity in the Middle East*. Edited by Lila Abu-Lughod. Princeton, NJ: Princeton University Press, 1998, 126–170.

Shirwānī, ʿAbd al-Ḥamīd al-, Aḥmad b. Qāsim al-ʿIbādī, and Ibn Ḥajar al-Haytamī. *Ḥawāshī Tuḥfat Al-Muḥtāj Bi-Sharḥ Al-Minhāj*. Beirut: Dār Ṣadir, 1972.

Shaw, Stanford J. *The Financial and Administrative Organization and Development of Ottoman Egypt, 1517–1798*. Princeton, NJ: Princeton University Press, 1962.

——. "The Land Law of Ottoman Egypt (960/1553): A Contribution to the Study of Landholding in the Early Years of Ottoman Rule in Egypt." *Der Islam* 38:1 (1963): 106–137.

Shaybānī, Muḥammad b. al-Ḥasan al-. *Al-Aṣl*. Edited by Mehmet Boynukalın. 12 vols. Beirut: Dār Ibn Ḥazm, 2012.

Shestack, Jerome J. "The Philosophic Foundations of Human Rights." *Human Rights Quarterly* 20:2 (1998): 201–234.

Shīrāzī, Abū Isḥāq al-. *Al-Muhadhdhab Fī Fiqh Al-Imām Al-Shāfiʿī*. Edited by Muḥammad al-Zuḥaylī. Damascus: Dār al-Qalam, 1996.

Shirbīnī, Shams al-Dīn Muḥammad b. al-Khaṭīb al-. *Mughnī Al-Muḥtāj Ilā Maʿrifat Maʿānī Alfāẓ Al-Minhāj*. Edited by Muḥammad Khalīl ʿAytānī. 1st edn. Beirut: Dār al-Maʿārif, 1997.

Shook, John R., and Joseph Margolis. *A Companion to Pragmatism*. Malden, MA; Oxford: Blackwell Pub., 2006.

Sijistānī, Abū Dawūd Sulaymān b. al-Ashʿath al-. *Sunan Abī Dawūd*. Edited by Shuʿayb al-Arnaʾūṭ and Muḥammad Kāmil Qurabellī. Damascus: Dār al-Risāla al-ʿĀlamiyya, 2009.

Sinai, Yuval, and Benjamin Shmueli. "Calabresi's and Maimonides's Tort Law Theories-A Comparative Analysis and a Preliminary Sketch of a Modern Model of Differential Pluralistic Tort Liability Based on the Two Theories." *Yale Journal of Law & the Humanities* 26:1 (2015): 59–133.

Singer, Joseph. "Legal Realism Now." *California Law Review* 76:2, no. 2 (1988): 465–544.

Singer, Joseph William. "Property and Coercion in Federal Indian Law: The Conflict between Critical and Complacent Pragmatism." *Southern California Law Review* 63 (1989–1990): 1821–1841.

Stein, Peter. "Interpretation and Legal Reasoning in Roman Law." *Chicago-Kent Law Review* 70:4 (June 1, 1995): 1539–1556.

Stilt, Kristen. *Islamic Law in Action: Authority, Discretion, and Everyday Experiences in Mamluk Egypt*. Oxford: Oxford University Press, 2011.

Stone, Lawrence. *Broken Lives: Separation and Divorce in England, 1660–1857*. Oxford; New York, NY: Oxford University Press, 1993.

——. *Road to Divorce: England 1530–1987*. Oxford; New York, NY: Oxford University Press, 1990.

Subkī, Tāj al-Dīn al-. *Mu'īd Al-Ni'am Wa-Mubīd Al-Niqam*. Edited by Muḥammad 'Alī al-Najjār, Abū Zayd Shalabī, and Muḥammad Abū al-'Uyūn. 1st edn. Cairo: Maktabat al-Khānjī, 1948.

——. "Supreme Constitutional Court Case No. 125 of 27th Judicial Year 2008." *Al-Jarīda Al-Rasmiyya* 20:2 (May 19, 2008): 84–90.

Ṭahṭāwī, Rifā'a al-. *Al-Murshid Al-Amīn Li'l-Banāt Wa'l-Banīn*. Cairo: Dār al-Kitāb al-Miṣrī wa'l-Lubnānī, 2012.

Tamanaha, B.Z. "Pragmatism in U.S. Legal Theory: Its Application to Normative Jurisprudence, Sociolegal Studies, and the Fact-Value Distinction." *American Journal of Jurisprudence* 41:1 (1996): 315–355.

Ṭayyib, Aḥmad al-. *Al-Fatāwā Al-Islāmiyya Min Dār Al-Iftā' Al-Miṣriyya*. Cairo: Maṭba'at Dār al-Kutub wa'l-Wathā'iq al-Qawmiyya, 2011.

Terman, Rochelle. "Islamophobia, Feminism and the Politics of Critique." *Theory, Culture & Society Theory, Culture & Society*, 33:2 (2015): 77–102.

Thelen, Tatjana, and Haldis Haukanes. *Parenting after the Century of the Child: Travelling Ideals, Institutional Negotiations and Individual Responses*. Farnham, Surrey; Burlington, VT: Ashgate, 2010.

Toledano, Ehud R. "Review Article: Mehmet Ali Paşa or Muhammad Ali Basha? An Historiographic Appraisal in the Wake of a Recent Book." *Middle Eastern Studies* 21:4 (1985): 141–159.

——. *State and Society in Mid-Nineteenth-Century Egypt*. Cambridge; New York, NY: Cambridge University Press, 1989.

Trans-Atlantic Divorce Mediation Conference, Vermont Law School, and Dispute Resolution Project, eds. *The Role of Mediation in Divorce Proceedings: A Comparative Perspective (United States, Canada and Great Britain)*. South Royalton, VT: Vermont Law School, 1987.

Tucker, Judith E. *Women, Family, and Gender in Islamic Law*. Cambridge, UK; New York, NY: Cambridge University Press, 2008.

Tucker, Judith E. *Women in Nineteenth-Century Egypt*. Cambridge; New York, NY: Cambridge University Press, 1985.

Uniform Law Commission. "Marriage and Divorce Act, Model Summary." Accessed February 9, 2015. www.uniformlaws.org/ActSummary.aspx?title=Marriage%20and%20Divorce%20Act,%20Model.

Vikør, Knut S. *Between God and the Sultan: A History of Islamic Law*. Oxford: Oxford University Press, 2005.

Wadud, Amina. *Inside the Gender Jihad: Women's Reform in Islam*. Oxford: Oneworld, 2006.

Wakako, Kumakura. "Who Handed over Mamluk Land Registers to the Ottomans? A Study on the Administrators of Land Records in the Late Mamluk Period." *Mamluk Studies Review* XVIII (2014–2015): 279–298.

Wansharīsī, Abū al-'Abbās Aḥmad b. Yaḥyā al-. *Al-Manhaj Al-Fā'iq Wa'l-Manhal Al-Rā'iq Wa'l-Ma'nā Al-Lā'iq Bi-Ādāb Al-Muwaththiq Wa-Aḥkām Al-Wathā'iq*. Edited by 'Abd al-Raḥmān b. Ḥammūd b. 'Abd al-Raḥmān al-Aṭram. 2 vols. Dubai: Dār al-Buḥūth li'l-Dirāsāt al-Islāmiyya, 2005.

Warner, Richard. "Pragmatism and Legal Reasoning." In *Hilary Putnam: Pragmatism and Realism*. Edited by James Contant and Urszula M. Żegleń. London; New York, NY: Routledge, 2002, 25–37.

Wizārat al-ʿAdl. "Law No. 118 (1952) on the Forfeiture of Guardianship over the Person." *Tashrīʿāt*, 1953, 12–15.

Weitzman, Lenore J. *The Divorce Revolution: The Unexpected Social and Economic Consequences for Women and Children in America*. New York; London: Free Press; Collier Macmillan, 1985.

Welchman, Lynn. *Women and Muslim Family Laws in Arab States: A Comparative Overview of Textual Development and Advocacy*. Amsterdam: Amsterdam University Press, 2007.

West, Cornel. *The American Evasion of Philosophy a Genealogy of Pragmatism*. Madison, WI: University of Wisconsin Press, 1989.

Wilson, Steven Harmon. *The U.S. Justice System: Law and Constitution in Early America*. Santa Barbara, CA: ABC-CLIO, 2012.

Wroath, John. *Until They Are Seven: The Origins of Women's Legal Rights*. Winchester: Waterside Press, 2006.

Yousef, Hoda A. *Composing Egypt: Reading, Writing, and the Emergence of a Modern Nation 1870–1930*. Stanford, CA: Stanford University Press, 2016.

Zahraa, Mahdi, and Normi A. Malek. "The Concept Of Custody In Islamic Law." *Arab Law Quarterly* 13:2 (1998): 55–177.

Zarqānī, ʿAbd al-Bāqī b. Yūsuf al-. *Sharḥ Al-Zarqānī ʿalā Mukhtaṣar Sayyidī Khalīl Wa-Maʿahu Al-Fatḥ Al-Rabbānī Fīmā Dhahala ʿanhu Al-Zarqānī*. Edited by ʿAbd al-Salām Muḥammad Amīn. 8 vols. Beirut; Dār al-Kutub al-ʿIlmiyya, 2002.

Zayn, Muḥammad al-. "Al-Majālis Al-Ḥasbiyya." *Al-Muḥāmā Al-Sharʿiyya: Majalla Qaḍāʾiyya Shahriyya Al-Sana Al-Ūlā* 2:1 (1930): 19–23.

Ze'evi, Dror. "The Use of Ottoman Sharīʿa Court Records As a Source for Middle Eastern Social History: A Reappraisal." *ILS Islamic Law and Society* 5: 1 (1998): 35–56.

Zilfi, Madeline C. *The Politics of Piety: The Ottoman Ulema in the Postclassical Age (1600–1800)*. Minneapolis, MN: Bibliotheca Islamica, 1988.

Zuḥaylī, Wahba al-. *Al-Fiqh Al-Islāmī Wa-Adillatuhu*. 2nd edn. Damascus: Dār al-Fikr, 1985.

Index

Other titles in the series

Agricultural Innovation in the Early Islamic World: The Diffusion of Crops and Farming Techniques, 700–1100, Andrew M. Watson
Muslim Tradition: Studies in Chronology, Provenance and Authorship of Early Hadith, G. H. A. Juynboll
Social History of Timbuktu: The Role of Muslim Scholars and Notables 1400–1900, Elias N. Saad Sex and Society in Islam: Birth Control before the Nineteenth Century, B.F. Musallam
Towns and Townsmen of Ottoman Anatolia: Trade, Crafts and Food Production in an Urban Setting 1520–1650, Suraiya Faroqhi
Unlawful Gain and Legitimate Profit in Islamic Law: Riba, Gharar and Islamic Banking, Nabil A. Saleh
Men of Modest Substance: House Owners and House Property in Seventeenth-Century Ankara and Kayseri, Suraiya Faroqhi
Roman, Provincial and Islamic Law: The Origins of the Islamic Patronate, Patricia Crone
Economic Life in Ottoman Jerusalem, Amnon Cohen
Mannerism in Arabic Poetry: A Structural Analysis of Selected Texts (3rd Century AH/9th Century AD–5th Century AH/11th Century AD), Stefan Sperl
The Rise and Rule of Tamerlane, Beatrice Forbes Manz
Popular Culture in Medieval Cairo, Boaz Shoshan
Early Philosophical Shiism: The Ismaili Neoplatonism of Abu Ya'qub Al-Sijistani, Paul E. Walker
Indian Merchants and Eurasian Trade, 1600–1750, Stephen Frederic Dale
Palestinian Peasants and Ottoman Officials: Rural Administration around Sixteenth-Century Jerusalem, Amy Singer
Arabic Historical Thought in the Classical Period, Tarif Khalidi
Mongols and Mamluks: The Mamluk-Ilkhanid War, 1260–1281, Reuven Amitai-Preiss
Knowledge and Social Practice in Medieval Damascus, 1190–1350, Michael Chamberlain
The Politics of Households in Ottoman Egypt: The Rise of the Qazdağlis, Jane Hathaway
Hierarchy and Egalitarianism in Islamic Thought, Louise Marlow
Commodity and Exchange in the Mongol Empire: A Cultural History of Islamic Textiles, Thomas T. Allsen
State and Provincial Society in the Ottoman Empire: Mosul, 1540–1834, Dina Rizk Khoury
The Mamluks in Egyptian Politics and Society, Thomas Philipp and Ulrich Haarmann (eds.)
The Delhi Sultanate: A Political and Military History, Peter Jackson
European and Islamic Trade in the Early Ottoman State: The Merchants of Genoa and Turkey, Kate Fleet
The Ottoman City between East and West: Aleppo, Izmir, and Istanbul, Edhem Eldem, Daniel Goffman, and Bruce Masters

The Politics of Trade in Safavid Iran: Silk for Silver, 1600–1730, Rudolph P. Matthee
The Idea of Idolatry and the Emergence of Islam: From Polemic to History, G. R. Hawting
A Monetary History of the Ottoman Empire, Şevket Pamuk
Classical Arabic Biography: The Heirs of the Prophets in the Age of Al-Ma'mun, Michael Cooperson
Empire and Elites after the Muslim Conquest: The Transformation of Northern Mesopotamia, Chase F. Robinson
Poverty and Charity in Medieval Islam: Mamluk Egypt, 1250–1517, Adam Sabra
Culture and Conquest in Mongol Eurasia, Thomas T. Allsen
Christians and Jews in the Ottoman Arab World: The Roots of Sectarianism, Bruce Masters
Arabic Administration in Norman Sicily: The Royal Diwan, Jeremy Johns
Law, Society and Culture in the Maghrib, 1300–1500, David S. Powers
Revival and Reform in Islam: The Legacy of Muhammad al-Shawkani, Bernard Haykel
Tolerance and Coercion in Islam: Interfaith Relations in the Muslim Tradition, Yohanan Friedmann
Guns for the Sultan: Military Power and the Weapons Industry in the Ottoman Empire, Gábor Ágoston
Marriage, Money and Divorce in Medieval Islamic Society, Yossef Rapoport
The Empire of the Qara Khitai in Eurasian History: Between China and the Islamic World, Michal Biran
Domesticity and Power in the Early Mughal World, Ruby Lal
Power, Politics and Religion in Timurid Iran, Beatrice Forbes Manz
Postal Systems in the Pre-Modern Islamic World, Adam J. Silverstein
Kingship and Ideology in the Islamic and Mongol Worlds, Anne F. Broadbridge
Justice, Punishment and the Medieval Muslim Imagination, Christian Lange
The Shiites of Lebanon under Ottoman Rule, 1516–1788, Stefan Winter
Women and Slavery in the Late Ottoman Empire, Madeline Zilfi
The Second Ottoman Empire: Political and Social Transformation in the Early Modern World, Baki Tezcan
The Legendary Biographies of Tamerlane: Islam and Heroic Apocrypha in Central Asia, Ron Sela
Non-Muslims in the Early Islamic Empire: From Surrender to Coexistence, Milka Levy-Rubin
The Origins of the Shiʿa: Identity, Ritual, and Sacred Space in Eighth-Century Kufa, Najam Haider
Politics, Law, and Community in Islamic Thought: The Taymiyyan Moment, Ovamir Anjum
The Power of Oratory in the Medieval Muslim World, Linda G. Jones
Animals in the Qurʿan, Sarra Tlili
The Logic of Law Making in Islam: Women and Prayer in the Legal Tradition, Behnam Sadeghi
Empire and Power in the Reign of Süleyman: Narrating the Sixteenth-Century Ottoman World, Kaya Şahin
Law and Piety in Medieval Islam, Megan H. Reid

Women and the Transmission of Religious Knowledge in Islam, Asma Sayeed
The New Muslims of Post-Conquest Iran: Tradition, Memory, and Conversion, Sarah Bowen Savant
The Mamluk City in the Middle East: History, Culture, and the Urban Landscape, Nimrod Luz
Disability in the Ottoman Arab World, 1500–1800, Sara Scalenghe
The Holy City of Medina: Sacred Space in Early Islamic Arabia, Harry Munt
Muslim Midwives: The Craft of Birthing in the Premodern Middle East, Avner Giladi
Doubt in Islamic Law: A History of Legal Maxims, Interpretation, and Islamic Criminal Law, Intisar A. Rabb
The Second Formation of Islamic Law: The Hanafi School in the Early Modern Ottoman Empire, Guy Burak
Sexual Violation in Islamic Law: Substance, Evidence, and Procedure, Hina Azam
Gender Hierarchy in the Qur'an: Medieval Interpretations, Modern Responses, Karen Bauer
Intellectual Networks in Timurid Iran: Sharaf al-Din 'Ali Yazdi and the Islamicate Republic of Letters, Ilker Evrim Binbaş
Authority and Identity in Medieval Islamic Historiography: Persian Histories from the Peripheries, Mimi Hanaoka
The Economics of Ottoman Justice: Settlement and Trial in the Sharia Courts, Top of Form Metin Coşgel and Boğaç Ergene
The Mystics of al-Andalus: Ibn Barrajan and Islamic Thought in the Twelfth Century, Yousef Casewit
Muhammad's Heirs: The Rise of Muslim Scholarly Communities, 622–950, Jonathan E. Brockopp
The First of the Modern Ottomans: The Intellectual History of Ahmed Vasif, Ethan Menchinger
Non-Muslim Provinces under Early Islam: Islamic Rule and Iranian Legitimacy in Armenia and Caucasian Albania, Alison Vacca
Women and the Making of the Mongol Empire, Anne F. Broadbridge
Slavery and Empire in Central Asia, Jeff Eden
Christianity in Fifteenth-Century Iraq, Thomas A. Carlson
Child Custody in Islamic Law: Theory and Practice in Egypt since the Sixteenth Century, Ahmed Fekry Ibrahim

